THE IMPERIAL PRESIDENCY AND THE CONSEQUENCES OF 9/11

Praeger Security International Advisory Board

Board Cochairs

Loch K. Johnson, Regents Professor of Public and International Affairs, School of Public and International Affairs, University of Georgia (U.S.A.)

Paul Wilkinson, Professor of International Relations and Chairman of the Advisory Board, Centre for the Study of Terrorism and Political Violence, University of St. Andrews (U.K.)

Members

Eliot A. Cohen, Robert E. Osgood Professor of Strategic Studies and Director, Philip Merrill Center for Strategic Studies, Paul H. Nitze School of Advanced International Studies, The Johns Hopkins University (U.S.A.)

Anthony H. Cordesman, Arleigh A. Burke Chair in Strategy, Center for Strategic and International Studies (U.S.A.)

Thérèse Delpech, Director of Strategic Affairs, Atomic Energy Commission, and Senior Research Fellow, CERI (Fondation Nationale des Sciences Politiques), Paris (France)

Sir Michael Howard, former Chichele Professor of the History of War, and Regis Professor of Modern History, Oxford University, and Robert A. Lovett Professor of Military and Naval History, Yale University (U.K.)

Lieutenant General Claudia J. Kennedy, USA (Ret.), former Deputy Chief of Staff for Intelligence, Department of the Army (U.S.A.)

Paul M. Kennedy, J. Richardson Dilworth Professor of History and Director, International Security Studies, Yale University (U.S.A.)

Robert J. O'Neill, former Chichele Professor of the History of War, All Souls College, Oxford University (Australia)

Shibley Telhami, Anwar Sadat Chair for Peace and Development, Department of Government and Politics, University of Maryland (U.S.A.)

Jusuf Wanandi, co-founder and member, Board of Trustees, Centre for Strategic and International Studies (Indonesia)

Fareed Zakaria, Editor, Newsweek International (U.S.A.)

THE IMPERIAL PRESIDENCY AND THE CONSEQUENCES OF 9/11

Lawyers React to the Global War on Terrorism

VOLUME 1

Edited by James R. Silkenat and Mark R. Shulman

Foreword by Barry Kamins, Bettina B. Plevan,
E. Leo Milonas, and Evan A. Davis

PRAEGER SECURITY INTERNATIONAL
Westport, Connecticut · London

Library of Congress Cataloging-in-Publication Data

The imperial presidency and the consequences of 9/11 : lawyers react to the global war on terrorism / edited by James R. Silkenat and Mark R. Shulman.
   v. cm.
   Includes bibliographical references and index.
   ISBN 0–275–99440–6 (set : alk. paper) — ISBN 0–275–99441–4 (vol 1 : alk. paper) — ISBN 0–275–99442–2 (vol 2 : alk. paper)
1. War and emergency powers—United States. 2. Terrorists—Legal status, laws, etc.—United States. 3. Prisoners of war—Legal status, laws, etc.—United States. 4. Detention of persons—Cuba—Guantánamo Bay Naval Base. 5. Trials (Genocide)—Iraq. 6. War on Terrorism, 2001– 7. Executive power—United States I. Silkenat, James R. II. Shulman, Mark R.
   KF5060.I47 2007
   342.73'062—dc22   2006100488

British Library Cataloguing in Publication Data is available.

Library of Congress Catalog Card Number: 2006100488
ISBN-10: 0–275–99440–6 (set code)   ISBN-13: 978–0–275–99440-2 (set code)
        0–275–99441–4 (Vol. 1)   978–0–275–99441-9 (Vol. 1)
        0–275–99442–2 (Vol. 2)   978–0–275–99442-6 (Vol. 2)

First published in 2007

Praeger Security International, 88 Post Road West, Westport, CT 06881
An imprint of Greenwood Publishing Group, Inc.
www.praeger.com

Printed in the United States of America

The paper used in this book complies with the
Permanent Paper Standard issued by the National
Information Standards Organization (Z39.48–1984).

10 9 8 7 6 5 4 3 2 1

Contents

About the Editors and Contributors

EDITORS

JAMES R. SILKENAT is a partner in the firm of Arent Fox PLLC in New York City. He is a former Chair of the 16,000-member ABA Section of International Law and helps coordinate Arent Fox's international practice in New York, where he specializes in international finance, securities, and corporate law. He is also a former Chair of the ABA's Section Officers Conference and a member of the Executive Committee of the ABA Board of Governors. He has served for 15 years as a member of the American Bar Association House of Delegate and Chairs New York's Delegation in the ABA House of Delegates.

From 1980 to 1986, Mr. Silkenat was Legal Counsel for the International Finance Corporation, the private-sector-oriented affiliate of the World Bank in Washington, D.C., where he concentrated on privatization issues (including projects in China, Pakistan, Indonesia, Zimbabwe, and other countries). He has also handled significant privatization efforts in Australia, Peru, and Turkey. He is also the founder and former Chair of the ABA's Privatization Committee.

Mr. Silkenat received his J.D. from the University of Chicago Law School, where he was Editor of the *University of Chicago Law Review*. He also received an L.L.M. in International Law from New York University School of Law.

Mr. Silkenat was formerly Chair of the ABA Committee on the People's Republic of China and was the founder of the *China Law Reporter*. He has led Delegations to China for both the ABA and the Association of the Bar of the City of New York, and to the Common Market and Mexico for the ABA. He has also served as a Fellow of the National Endowment for the Humanities and as a Fellow in the U.S. State Department Scholar/Diplomat Program.

Mr. Silkenat is the Editor of *The Moscow Conference on Law and Bilateral Economic Relations, The Law of International Insolvencies and Debt Restructurings, The ABA Guide to Foreign Law Firms* (1988, 1993, 1999, and 2004 Editions), and *The ABA Guide to International Business Negotiations* (1994 and 2002 Editions). He is also the author of more than 100 articles on international law, finance, and public policy, and he has published articles in the *Harvard Law Review, Business Week,* the *New York Times,* and the *Stanford Law Review,* among other publications. He also served as Adjunct Professor of Law at Georgetown University Law Center, where he taught a graduate seminar on international project financing.

Mr. Silkenat also previously served as Chair of both The Lawyers Committee for Human Rights (now, Human Rights First) and The Council of New York Law Associates (now, The Lawyers Alliance for New York). He is a Life Fellow for the American Bar Foundation, has served as Chair of the Fellows of the American Bar Foundation, and is a member of the Council on Foreign Relations. Mr. Silkenat is also a former Chair of the International Human Rights Committee of the Association of the Bar of the City of New York, the City Bar's Task Force on International Legal Services, and the City Bar's Council on International Affairs.

Mr. Silkenat has particular expertise in the negotiation and drafting of international investment funds and international joint-venture agreements, Eurodollar and other international loan agreements, and related documentation, and he has worked on international mergers and acquisitions (including privatizations and restructurings) in both developing and developed countries.

MARK R. SHULMAN is Assistant Dean for Graduate Programs and International Affiliations and an Adjunct Professor of Law at Pace Law School. Until 2003, he practiced corporate law at the international firm of Debevoise & Plimpton.

Immediately prior to joining Pace, Mr. Shulman directed the Worldwide Security Program at the EastWest Institute. He has previously taught in the History Department at Yale University, at Columbia University's School of International and Public Affairs and at Columbia Law School, as well as the U.S. Air War College.

Mr. Shulman has published widely in the fields of history, law, and international affairs. Along with Sir Michael Howard and Professor George Andreopoulos, he edited *The Laws of War: Constraints on Warfare in the Western World.* He wrote *Navalism and the Emergence of American Sea Power, 1882–1893,* as well as numerous articles and book chapters. Mr. Shulman received his B.A. from Yale, a Masters degree from Oxford, and a Ph.D. in history from the University of California at Berkeley. He received his J.D. from Columbia where he served as Editor-in-Chief of the *Journal of Transnational Law,* on the board of which he continues to sit. He has also enjoyed Postdoctoral Fellowships at Yale and Georgetown and is a Visiting Scholar at Yale's International Security Program. He has also been a Visiting Research Scholar at the Naval War College.

He is currently Chair of the New York City Bar's International Human Rights Committee and a member of the City Bar's Council on International Affairs.

CONTRIBUTORS

JAMES J. BENJAMIN, JR. is a partner at Akin Gump Strauss Hauer & Feld LLP. Before joining Akin Gump, he served for more than five years as a federal prosecutor in the U.S. Attorney's Office for the Southern District of New York and he also served as a law clerk at the U.S. Supreme Court for Justices Lewis F. Powell Jr. and John Paul Stevens. He has published articles extensively in the *New York Law Journal,* his most recent article being titled "Rule 10b5-1 and Criminal Insider Trading Cases" (New York Law Journal, July 2004).

JOSEPH G. DAVIS is a partner in the Litigation Department of Willkie Farr & Gallagher LLP in Washington, D.C. Mr. Davis specializes in complex litigation and corporate compliance matters. Mr. Davis represents corporations and individuals in proceedings before federal and state courts and other tribunals. He is a graduate of Amherst College and the University of California at Berkeley School of Law (Boalt Hall).

NICOLE DELLER is a senior program officer at the World Federalist Movement-Institute for Global Policy and the Chair of the International Security Affairs Committee of the New York City Bar Association. Before joining WFM, Ms. Deller was a research associate and consultant for the Lawyers' Committee on Nuclear Policy and the Institute for Energy and Environmental Research.

MILES P. FISCHER is a lawyer in private practice in New York City. He is currently on the Board of Director-Advisors at the National Institute of Military Justice. He has also served as Chair on the Military Affairs and Justice Committee of the New York City Bar.

MARTIN S. FLAHERTY is Leitner Family Chair in International Human Rights and Professor of Law and Co-Director of the Joseph P. Crowley Program in International Human Rights at Fordham Law School in New York. He is a former Chair of the Committee on International Human Rights of the New York City Bar. He has published widely on constitutional law, foreign affairs, and international human rights in such journals as the *Columbia Law Review,* the *Yale Law Journal,* and the *University of Chicago Law Review*.

THOMAS H. MORELAND is a partner at Kramer Levin Naftalis and & Franklin LLP. He handles a wide variety of complex civil litigation matters in international and domestic arbitration. He has served as Vice President and Chair of the Executive Committee of the New York City Bar. He was also a founding member and currently serves as the Chairman of the Board of Volunteers of Legal Service, Inc., which facilitates pro bono service by lawyers in New York City.

ALAN R. ROTHSTEIN serves as General Counsel of the New York City Bar, where he coordinates the extensive law reform and public policy work of this 22,000-member Association. Prior to his 20 years with the Association, Rothstein was the Associate Director of Citizens Union and also practiced with the firm of Weil, Gotshal & Manges. Prior to earning his J.D. from New York University, Mr. Rothstein worked as an Economist in the environmental consulting field and for the New York City Economic Development Administration. Mr. Rothstein currently serves on the Board of Directors for Volunteers of Legal Service, Inc.

MARGARET L. SATTERTHWAITE is an Assistant Professor of Clinical Law and Faculty Director of the Center for Human Rights and Global Justice at New York University School of Law. She has written extensively in the field of international human rights law, and her most recent publications include "Fate and Whereabouts Unknown: Detainees in the 'War on Terror'" (*Center for Human Rights and Global Justice,* 2005) and "Crossing Borders, Claiming Rights: Using Human Rights Law to Empower Women Migrant Workers" (*Yale Human Rights & Development Law Journal,* 2005).

STEPHEN J. SHAPIRO is a lawyer in private practice in New York City. He is a past Chair of the Committee on Military Affairs and Justice of the New York City Bar.

DANIEL SILVERMAN serves as counsel for the Labor and Employment Group at Skadden Arps, Slate, Meagher & Flom LLP. Prior to joining Skadden, he had a distinguished career at the National Labor Relations Board where he acted in various capacities from trial attorney to the Regional Director at the New York City office. He is the Chairman of the Committee on Labor and Employment Law of the New York City Bar. Mr. Silverman also is as an Adjunct Professor at Cardozo Law School.

CLAUDIA SLOVINSKY has been an immigration and nationality attorney for over 20 years and heads her own law firm in New York City. She serves as the Chair of the Immigration and Nationality Committee of the New York City Bar and is a frequent lecturer on immigration issues both to the immigration bar and lay audiences. She also serves on the Board of the American Friends Service Committee Immigrant Rights Program, and is a member of the American Immigration Lawyers Association and the National Immigration Project of the National Lawyers Guild.

MARIANN SULLIVAN is the Deputy Chief Court Attorney for the New York State Appellate Division, First Department. She is the former Chair of the Committee on Legal Issues Pertaining to Animals of the New York City Bar and a current member of that Committee, as well as of the Special Committee on Animals and the Law of the New York State Bar Association. She co-authored "Foxes in the Henhouse: Animals, Agribusiness and the Law" (*Animal Rights: Current Debates and New Directions,* 2004).

Foreword

BARRY KAMINS, BETTINA B. PLEVAN, E. LEO MILONAS, AND EVAN A. DAVIS

The September 11 attacks profoundly affected the Association of the Bar of the City of New York. We watched the towers burn and then collapse. We lost friends and colleagues. As we dealt with our shock and loss, we immediately began to receive calls from lawyers in New York and around the country asking: how can we help? We coordinated an enormous volunteer effort so that the New York legal community could help families who lost loved ones deal with their loss, and persons who were injured or displaced to rebuild their lives. Every victim's family who wanted a lawyer received free assistance, as thousands of lawyers pitched in with great dedication.

While our attention, and indeed that of the City and nation, was focused on helping individuals and families, we also observed the beginning of the government's response to the attacks. We were alert as to what to anticipate: a strong, rapid reaction by the government, through administrative and legislative actions, to attempt to deal with the terrorist threat. We were aware that the scope of the threat was not clear and that a climate of fear was pervasive. We also were mindful that it is in just those times that individual rights—basic constitutional protections—would be most in jeopardy. Since the founding of the Association in 1870, we had seen it before. We spoke out during the "Red Scare" of 1919 and during the McCarthy period in the early 1950s, and we were often only one of the few establishment organizations to do so.

Of our 160 committees, at least a dozen addressed subject matter that would be implicated by government policy. The first impact of governmental action was felt by immigrants from nations with a substantial Muslim population. Extensive roundups and detention of male immigrants from these countries, and the draconian policies imposed, signaled that there would be a need for a strong response from the legal community. What made our work more difficult is the secrecy with which the government attempted to act, preventing contact between detainees and the outside world (including their attorneys) and barring access to immigration proceedings.

In short order, there followed the USA PATRIOT Act and the President's Military Commission Order. It then became clear that the Executive Branch had embarked upon a strategy of enhancing its power. We were told the purpose was to more effectively engage the terrorist threat. However, as we and the world have since learned, the effort was part of a broader plan to generally empower the Executive Branch to what many felt was an unprecedented level. It further became clear that the exercise of this Presidential power was to be at the expense of individual rights, and of the authority of the Congress and, to a greater extent, the Judiciary.

At times of constitutional crisis, it is particularly essential that the legal community mobilize and make itself heard. Lawyers are the guardians of the Constitution and have the unique perspective to understand how changes in law and government policy will affect constitutional rights and values. We are also equipped to provide direct assistance to those whose rights are deprived, and indeed many Association members have undertaken the direct representation of detainees and others who have legitimate claims that their rights have been abrogated. Lawyers must also serve as strong advocates for the independence of the Judicial Branch. By its very nature, the federal bench cannot defend itself from criticism, however unwarranted, and from attempts to limit the courts' jurisdiction.

This Association zealously undertook these solemn responsibilities. The resulting body of careful analysis, legal exposition and, when appropriate, strong advocacy is on display in these volumes. Each of the materials presented is introduced by a preface that provides the context. You will see that these efforts—all by the dedicated volunteers who staff our committees—were all focused on preserving the rule of law, and our fundamental Constitutional principles and liberties.

Throughout the post-9/11 period, one question continued to be asked: should not the preservation of individual rights and the rule of law be secondary to the cause of national security? National security is a primary concern, but our Constitution was born in a time of great uncertainty and was designed by leaders who had experienced one war and clearly anticipated more. The Constitution and the Bill of Rights were clearly meant to remain in effect through wars and other crises. War-related powers were meticulously meted out between the legislative and executive branches, and there is nothing in Article III to suggest that judges should have different powers during times of crisis.

We have seen too many examples over the years of how the exercise of power in the name of national security—both in the United States and in other nations—has caused the loss of a moral and legal compass. The "war on terrorism" may be uncharted territory, but it is certain to be of long duration, and may well affect the rights of law-abiding Americans in ways that our previous crises have not. Throughout this struggle, it is essential to have an independent bar serving as the protectors of our laws. This Association will continue to serve that function, and to work with others to make sure that the basic character of our free nation is preserved.

The Association will always be indebted to the men and women who volunteered their time and energy to assist those who suffered from the 9/11 attacks. We are also very grateful to the committee members who advocated and continue to advocate for the rule of law.

Barry Kamins, President 2006–2008
The Association of the Bar of the City of New York

Bettina B. Plevan, President 2004–2006
The Association of the Bar of the City of New York

E. Leo Milonas, President 2002–2004
The Association of the Bar of the City of New York

Evan A. Davis, President 2000–2002
The Association of the Bar of the City of New York

Acknowledgments

This massive book owes its existence to the voluntary labors of dozens of talented but busy people. Each chapter is the product of a Committee of the City Bar of New York—a marvelous organization that provides an outlet for the civic-minded members of the nation's most diverse bar. In inviting various attorneys to contribute introductory remarks for these chapters, we tried to reach out to the principal author of the specific report or letter underlying the chapter. When that proved futile for one reason or another, we relied on the Association's general counsel and jack of all trades, Alan R. Rothstein, to provide the appropriate perspective. Alan's resourcefulness and erudition frequently made the difference between a compilation of reports and a book that would remain useful as a guide and resource for years to come.

A debt of gratitude is also owed to the outstanding members of the American Bar Association whose leadership on human rights and Constitutional issues have helped shape the work evidenced in this book. In particular, Michael S. Greco, Jerome J. Shestack, Neal R. Sonnett, Mark D. Agrast, Steven D. Walther, Robert A. Stein, and Robert F. Drinan have each provided the moral, intellectual, and personal standards that have guided this effort.

Likewise, this book could not have been published without the careful assistance of future lawyers Edward Quilice and Galit Waysglas. For over a year, these fine young people managed the complex tasks of identifying and locating reports and letters, overseeing the preface-writing process, and ensuring timely submission to the publisher. Likewise, Mark's assistant, Deborah Zipf, did much of the heavy lifting for this project.

To Alan, Edward, Galit, and Deborah, thank you. To the many lawyers who participated in the writing of the reports and letters that follow, thanks would be inappropriate: you were serving your profession with great energy, probity, and intelligence. This book is evidence of your dedication.

Introduction

MARK R. SHULMAN AND JAMES R. SILKENAT

Over the past five years, members of the Association of the Bar of the City of New York have produced an impressive variety of hard-hitting reports, letters, and briefs addressing issues arising out of the so-called "global war on terror." For the most part, these publications have taken positions critical of the U.S. government's conduct and of the legal justifications offered by the Administration of President George W. Bush. These critiques are nonpartisan. Lawyers from many political orientations—members of both major parties—have drafted and signed them. Rather, the authors of these materials represent the independent voice of the nation's largest and most influential municipal bar.

Lawyers are frequently maligned as being amoral guns-for-hire, willing to take any position that pays. And with America's adversarial legal system, we are thankful to have lawyers willing to take unpopular cases. Without them, freedom of expression and freedom of choice would be far narrower. Without them, many more innocent people would be imprisoned or even executed. Someone must defend unpopular or marginalized people or rights are diminished for each of us. Many lawyers represent the unpopular at their standard billing rates. Many defend those who cannot pay on a *pro bono* basis. Even beyond that, lawyers frequently dedicate their time to protecting the legal system as the embodiment of our republic's values. What lawyer jokes invariably ignore is the tremendous amount of work lawyers do on principle.

Bar associations around the country (indeed around the world) perform critical roles in channeling the creative and honorable impulses of lawyers. The City Bar is one of the largest and oldest in the nation, established in 1870. For a century and a quarter, its members have worked to channel the efforts of a diverse group of individuals into improving the law and its implementation. For much of its history, however, the City Bar worked without much recognition outside the somewhat rarified circles of its membership. As with many venerable and important institutions, that low profile was raised considerably during the tumultuous events of the late 1960s and early 1970s when its President, the distinguished corporate lawyer Francis T.P. Plimpton, asked, "Are our unobtrusive, calmly analytical committee reports adequate for our stormy present?"[1] Plimpton was wondering if the stately organization was effective at promoting the role of law in ways that would help the United States address the day's raging debates.

Plimpton answered his own question with a charge. "I submit that our expert committees should continue their hard working expert ways, but that they should be infused and all our membership infused, with a new sense of urgent and deeply felt concern at the crisis that confronts our legal institutions and law itself, and a new determination, in the long and high tradition of this Association, to seek out and steadfastly fight for the changes that can and should be made to meet the just demands of today and tomorrow. Let us be militant activists, militant activists for the constructive reform of the law we were founded to promote."[2] And this new activism did infuse the City Bar with a spirit of reform and justice. A few short months later, that spirit was put to the test.

In the spring of 1970 President Richard M. Nixon ordered U.S. troops to move from Vietnam into Cambodia to attack Communist sanctuaries. "The invasion of Cambodia set up a galvanic shock in the New York legal community," wrote Mr. Plimpton in a City Bar report. "Does the President of the United States have the right to start a new war? There had been no consultation with Congress," he noted.[3] Standing up for the rule of law and, in particular, the separation of powers that protects this Republic from descending into autocracy, Plimpton told lawyers gathered in the Association's Great Hall that when "the President ordered American troops to invade Cambodia, he was acting on his own, in blithe and unilateral disregard of the Congress, which under the Constitution has the sole right to declare war."[4]

Plimpton decried this act as a threat to the Constitutional order. The "fact remains that the result of the President's action was a new war, war in another country, war by unilateral Presidential fiat, war without Congressional consultation, without Congressional authorization and without Congressional support."[5]

And with that conclusion, Plimpton (a Republican who embodied the legal establishment) led a "march on Washington," but not just any march on Washington. On May 20, 1970, some 1,200 lawyers from leading New York firms—many on chartered cars on the 6:30 train— invaded the nation's capital. Dividing into some 150 teams of six or seven people dressed in their corporate finest, the lawyers met with lawmakers and other high-ranking officials. Plimpton's first appointment, Senator Sam J. Ervin, Jr. (D–NC), stood him up. But after meeting with a full house of Washington lawyers, Plimpton called on the U.S. Solicitor General, his old friend Erwin Griswold. Griswold in turn arranged for Plimpton to discuss the legality of the war with U.S. Attorney General John M. Mitchell and then with Under Secretary of State Elliott Richardson.[6] With this sort of lobbying, the leading members of the preeminent bar were deploying their reputations, their time, and their wits in order to promote greater adherence to the spirit and the letter of the law.

Over the quarter of a century that followed, hundreds of lawyers have worked to live up to Francis Plimpton's spirit of reform and justice. When planes crashed into the Twin Towers of New York's World Trade Center on September 11, 2001, members of the Association sprang into action—not chasing ambulances as the cynic might suggest but running in advance of them to rescue the wounded and distraught. In the months that followed, the Association also served as a clearinghouse for assistance both to lawyers and to those who needed lawyers.

Equally as important, members of the Association have continued to devote countless hours to research and write the kind of "expert reports" that Plimpton spoke of two decades before. Such work has been done both by the City Bar on its own and in cooperation with the American Bar Association House of Delegates, particularly through the ABA Sections of Criminal Law, International Law, and Individual Rights and Responsibilities. The Association's Committee on Military Affairs issued the first of these reports within a few months after 9/11. This report decried the impact of President George W. Bush's Military Order of November 13, 2001, regarding "Detention, Treatment, and Trial of Certain Non-Citizens in the War Against

Terrorism." This report contained a timely and prescient analysis of an issue that continues to plague us years later. The Association's interest in ensuring that the Administration (the United States) not carve out areas beyond the law has subsequently resulted in several other significant publications by the Association, including two amicus briefs to the U.S. Supreme Court, letters to the General Counsel and the Inspector General of the Department of Defense, and three important committee reports. The most recent of these reports broke the story nationally about how the U.S. is engaged in "Torture by Proxy" by removing detainees to other jurisdictions in order to facilitate inhumane interrogations. International media picked up and ran with this information, but the practice may still continue, despite the remarkable work of the Association and a strongly worded letter from the President of the Association to Congress seeking to end U.S. involvement in these abhorrent practices.

By the summer of 2002, the Association's Committee on International Security Affairs found itself facing another of Plimpton's issues: whether the President has the authority to order the invasion of a sovereign state without an act of Congress? Just as the Association had concluded in 1970, the Committee argued persuasively that he has not.

More recently the Association has also been working to ensure that lawyers who have counseled the government poorly be held accountable for their advice. These efforts are reflected in the letter to the leaders of the Senate Judiciary Committee in connection with the nomination of the General Counsel of the Defense Department for a seat on a U.S. Court of Appeals.

The Association's vigilance on rule of law issues after 9/11 has drawn its members into some unpredictable areas. One traditional role for the Association is to comment on legislation proposed either by the U.S. Congress or by the state legislatures. One recent bill proposed using antiterrorism laws to deter (or punish) protestors against the inhumane treatment of animals in a slaughterhouse. This may sound far-fetched, but similar laws have actually been enacted in California and Oklahoma.

The important work of the Association continues on terrorism and rule of law issues, but after five years, it seems like an appropriate time to collect its contributions to this important work into one book. If the reports were an early draft of history, this work may be considered a second draft and useful resource for the history of the years following 9/11. Over the course of American history, wartime administrations have frequently overstepped the legal boundaries. During the Quasi War with France, President John Adams sponsored the notorious Alien and Sedition Acts. Facing all out Civil War, Abraham Lincoln suspended the writ of *habeas corpus*. Managing the United States' efforts during the catastrophic First World War, Woodrow Wilson jailed dissenters for speaking out, including one man who had received nearly a million votes in the 1912 Presidential election. In the panic of the Second World War, Franklin Roosevelt's Administration was responsible for the odious internment of tens of thousands of Americans of Japanese descent. And Vietnam era Presidents had their intelligence agencies collect information on U.S. citizens who were opposing the wars in Southeast Asia.

And yet, from each of these missteps, the nation's legal system rebounded after the war ended. By the time of the Presidential campaign of 1800, boisterous dissent had returned to American politics. Immediately after the Civil War, the Supreme Court ruled that Lincoln was wrong to suspend the most essential writ. President Warren G. Harding had ordered Eugene V. Debs released from prison early. The United States apologized to its *Issei* and *Nisei* brethren and offered reparations. And the intelligence community was ordered not to conduct surveillance of U.S. persons. Unlike previous wars, however, the struggle to defeat global terrorism is one that may not end soon or neatly. Therefore, our legal system cannot wait until the danger has completely passed before righting some of its wrongs. And these historical lessons seem oddly relevant as dissent is squashed, ethnic minorities interned, and domestic surveillance once is again in the government's toolkit.

The pendulum may already have swung back. Two weeks after the Association's Committee on International Security Affairs released its war powers report, President Bush did an about-face and sought Congressional authorization to invade Iraq. In 2004 the Supreme Court found, with the Association's *amici* brief, that the detainees at Guantanamo Bay were not beyond the reach of the law. Two years later, the Court found the President's military tribunal to be unconstitutional. And New York will not use a "terrorism statute" to jail animal rights protestors for photographing poultry factories.

We hope that this book proves useful in explaining how the rule of law fosters the national interest in stability and security, while helping to maintain a sphere of individual liberty. We also hope that this book illustrates the constructive role that civilian lawyers can play in the political process, helping to explicate the law—its objectives and its implications. And in the end, we hope that this book will encourage young lawyers to follow in Francis Plimpton's footsteps, using their skills to serve their neighbors, their country, and their world, as well as their paying clients.

NOTES

1. Francis T.P. Plimpton, "Centennial Convocation of the Association of the Bar of the City of New York" (February 17, 1970) reprinted in Pauline Ames Plimpton ed., The Plimpton Papers: Law and Diplomacy (1985) 75 at 77.

2. *Id.*

3. Report cited in Pauline Ames Plimpton ed., The Plimpton Papers: Law and Diplomacy (1985) 85.

4. "Meeting on Military Action in Southeast Asia at the House of the Association—May 19, 1970" quoted at length in Pauline Ames Plimpton ed., The Plimpton Papers: Law and Diplomacy (1985) 85 at 86.

5. *Id.* at 86–87.

6. *Id.* at 88–89. The fact that he was a registered Republican opposing the actions of a President from the same party gave ome considerable credibility to Plimpton. To many, Plimpton embodied the Establishment. Born to a wealthy publisher who had descended from very early English settlers in Massachusetts, Plimpton had been educated at Exeter, Amherst and Harvard Law School. Along with Eli Whitney Debevoise and William E. Stevenson, in 1933 he founded the firm that eventually became Debevoise & Plimpton LLP. Over the decades, he built and maintained an extensive network of leaders. His old friend Solicitor General Griswold had been Dean at Harvard Law School, and Under Secretary (later Attorney General) Richardson served with Plimpton on Harvard's governing Board of Overseers.

CHAPTER 1

Inter Arma Silent Leges: *In Times of Armed Conflict,* Should *the Laws be Silent? A Report on the President's Military Order of November 13, 2001, Regarding "Detention, Treatment, and Trial of Certain Non-Citizens in the War Against Terrorism"*

PREFACE BY MILES P. FISCHER AND STEPHEN J. SHAPIRO

Since 1946 the Association's Committee on Military Affairs and Justice has reported on the intersection of the law and the military. Our report, *Inter Arma Silent Leges,* was a timely continuation of that tradition, being the first response of its kind to the President's Military Order of November 13, 2001. The first internal draft of the Report was dated November 15, 2001; the Report came out just one month later.

Between the date the Military Order was issued and the date our Report was released, the three principal authors[1] of the Report attended the annual program of the American Bar Association's Standing Committee on Law and National Security on November 29–30, 2001, in Washington, D.C. There, we had an opportunity to interact directly with the senior Administration lawyers responsible for the production and ultimate implementation of the Military Order.[2] Their answers heightened our concern about the procedures authorized by the Military Order and significantly influenced the Report, as did views expressed by other attendees (many in uniform) who were strongly supportive of national security interests but stunned by the Military Order.

The Military Order raised profound questions of constitutional law, statutory law, international law, and national policy. Our early analysis of these issues proved to be a seminal one when the American Bar Association (ABA) adopted a Resolution[3] along the lines of the recommendations in our Report over those appearing in the ABA's own report, and it was even the subject of other legal commentary.

The implementing orders for U.S. military commissions, issued over the course of several years, responded to many of the criticisms we raised in our Report, as well as in follow-on documents, including the Committee's letter dated March 21, 2003 (published herein), but nonetheless so far leaving the Military Order on the books with a legacy of controversy over the precepts of constitutional, statutory, and international law on which we reported in 2001. It is striking that the

Administration immediately drew back from its effort to block *habeas corpus* proceedings through the text of the Military Order, which we had so strongly criticized. It sought instead to avoid prisoner recourse to the courts through *habeas corpus* by locating both the prisoners and the military commissions outside the continental United States at Guantanamo Bay—a gambit blocked by the United States Supreme Court in its *Rasul* decision.

The most dramatic subsequent development is the decision of the Supreme Court in *Hamdan v. Rumsfeld*[4] on June 29, 2006, holding that the military commissions created under the Military Order lack the power to proceed because their structure and procedures violate both the Uniform Code of Military Justice (UCMJ) and Common Article 3 of the four Geneva Conventions. The plurality opinion reflects as to the Military Order, as implemented by subsequent regulations, many of the concerns we expressed as to the Military Order itself. However, that decision is not the end of the story. The Court's interpretation of treaty and statutory law is subject to Congressional action. In October 2006, as this publication was going to press, Congress passed the Military Commissions Act of 2006 which sought to undo the impact of the Hamdan decision by eliminating detainees' right to *habeas corpus* proceedings and recourse to claims arising under the Geneva Conventions.[5]

Throughout, we have regretted that policy makers did not use established procedures for courts martial under the UCMJ, to the extent constitutionally applicable to *enemy combatants* charged with *offenses against the law of war,* and the body of military law established by the well-respected Court of Appeals for the Armed Forces. We continue to urge consideration of that alternative in a manner consistent with international law and, more broadly, the rule of law in the tradition of our nation and its Armed Forces.

INTRODUCTION[6]

On November 13, 2001, President Bush issued a "Military Order" (the "Order") regarding "Detention, Treatment, and Trial of Certain Non-Citizens in the War Against Terrorism."[7] The Order would apply to all non-citizens determined by the President (1) to be members of the international organization known as al Qaeda,[8] or (2) to have engaged in, aided or abetted or conspired to commit, acts of international terrorism or acts in preparation therefore that have caused, threaten to cause or have as their aim to cause injury or adverse affects on the United States, its citizens, national security, foreign policy or economy; or (3) to have intentionally harbored such persons.[9] Such individuals are to be "detained at an appropriate location designated by the Secretary of Defense outside or within the United States."[10] There is no time period set forth with respect to such detention; nor is there any sunset provision, for that matter, for the Order itself.

The Order authorizes the creation of military commissions to try such persons, when and if they are to be subject to prosecution.[11] Further, such individuals, whether detained or tried under the Order, are not permitted under its terms to seek "any remedy" or "maintain any proceeding" in any U.S. federal or state court, any foreign court or any international tribunal.[12] Presumably, this very broad prohibition on *any* proceeding or remedy is an attempt, when read with the detention provisions of the order, to deny the detainees the privilege of the writ of habeas corpus and thereby prolong their detention as a matter of public safety when necessary, as determined by the President. Further still, although military commissions bear certain similarities to courts martial under the Uniform Code of Military Justice[13] (including, for example, by providing trial by appointed judges—rather than a jury—of both fact and law), the similarity is misleading. Courts martial follow procedural rules closely parallel to those of the federal criminal courts, while the commissions to be established under the Order are very different and may function *without regard to "principles of law and the rules of evidence generally recognized in the trial of criminal cases."*[14] Further, they are not subject even to the *procedural* rules governing courts martial, which include the right of appeal to a higher court and, ultimately, to the Supreme Court of the United States.

The "privilege of habeas corpus" is a fundamental Constitutional right. The Order's literal terms suspend it by preventing subject persons from pursuing *any judicial remedy in any court* whatsoever. When combined with the provisions for unlimited detention (including the recent rule-making announced by the Attorney General providing for virtually unlimited detention of certain aliens before INS [Immigration and Naturalization Service] courts), it seems plain that this is a use to which the Order may be put, despite only recent public statements by the Administration to the contrary.[15] If so, such use would be an extreme measure, not used since the time of the Civil War rebellion. Moreover, suspension of the privilege of habeas corpus is permitted only in the two crisis circumstances of rebellion or invasion. Even then, the power to suspend habeas corpus is vested by Constitution only with the Congress and not to the President.[16]

In both the area of the President's authority to create military commissions for the trial of the persons subject to the Order and his authority to detain persons without charge and to suspend habeas corpus, the issuance of the Order raises serious questions of both constitutional law and statutory interpretation, in addition to important international and domestic policy considerations.

This report considers, therefore, whether (1) if the Order were employed for detention or trial of alleged al Qaeda members or supporters, whether in the U.S. or abroad, it would be found to be constitutional; (2) if so, whether it complies with statute; (3) whether its use would be effective as a matter of policy and, (4) if not, what alternatives exist.

Based on the legal and policy analysis and conclusions below, we urge that with respect to this or any similar military order that is issued, Congress and the President should assure that the order will:

1. Not be applicable to persons lawfully present in the United States, including United States citizens and lawful resident aliens;

2. Not be applicable to persons apprehended or to be tried in the United States, except for persons subject to the settled and traditional law of war who engage in conduct alleged to be in violation of such law of war;

3. Not be applicable to cases in which violations of Federal or state criminal laws, as opposed to violations of such law of war, are alleged;

4. Not permit indefinite detention of persons subject to the order;

5. Require that its proceedings be governed by the Uniform Code of Military Justice and provide the rights afforded in courts-martial thereunder, including but not limited to the right of appellate review by the judicial branch and the privilege of the writ of habeas corpus.

The American Bar Association should address these issues promptly. As the voice of the nation's organized bar, it must speak out to protect the rights afforded in the Constitution and the delicate balance of power the Constitution provides among the branches of our government during times when it may seem popular or expedient to flaunt basic constitutional values. The Military Order should not be allowed to encroach on these values, which underlie the country's power, its role in the world scheme, and its democratic way of life.

THE CONTEXT OF THE ORDER

The Order was issued two months after the September 11, 2001 terrorist attacks against the World Trade Center and the Pentagon ("9/11 attacks") by 18 foreign nationals believed by the U.S. Government to have been associated with the al Qaeda organization based primarily in Afghanistan.[17] Al Qaeda has been accused of providing the inspiration, training, financing and control of the 9/11 attacks, as well as assaults on two U.S. embassies in Africa, and on the *U. S.S. Cole* in Yemeni waters. In response to the 9/11 attacks, the Congress on September 18 authorized military action[18] but did not declare war. The United States' decision to use force was supported generally by resolutions of the United Nations Security Council[19] and specifically by the North Atlantic Treaty Organization, as well as by many national governments. On September 21, the President declared that a National Emergency had been in existence since September 11.[20] After the Islamic fundamentalist Taliban "government" of Afghanistan refused to surrender the al Qaeda leaders, U.S. and U.K. armed forces launched a military campaign against Taliban forces in Afghanistan.

Almost simultaneously with issuance of the Military Order on November 13, Afghan units opposing the Taliban and assisted by U.S. air support expelled the Taliban from the country's major cities, including from its capital Kabul. Although the course of the conflict remains uncertain due to its ongoing nature, it is, as this is written, within the realm of possibility that some al Qaeda leaders (as opposed to soldiers or leaders from the Taliban's armed forces) may be captured and come within the control of U.S. armed forces, at which time it would have to be determined when, where and how they might be tried.

These acts occurred against the domestic backdrop of the discovery of a number of intentionally-inflicted cases of anthrax infection in Florida, Washington, D.C., New York City and Connecticut. Some anthrax-tainted letters were discovered in the mail, including ones delivered to government officers. As of this writing there have been 5 deaths from 18 confirmed cases of anthrax infection.[21] No evidence has been disclosed as of now to indicate that these incidents are related in any way to the 9/11 attacks or even to al Qaeda, but their occurrence —and their undiscovered source—nonetheless informs the public debate about terrorist activities at this time.

Moreover, a large number of foreign nationals have been detained within the U.S.—according to Justice Department officials exceeding 1,000 in number but whose actual number remains undisclosed—many of whom are still in custody. It appears that some if not all of these detainees may be transferred from the control and custody of the Department of Justice (*i.e.,* Immigration and Naturalization Service) to the control and custody of the Department of Defense, as such transfer is directed by the Order.

It should be noted that events with respect to the Order—including its interpretation and possible application—are fast-moving and may be evolving even as this Report is being prepared.[22] In view of the importance of the matter, the Committee has opted to work primarily from the text of the Order and the powers asserted by the President therein, giving consideration to the discussions and interviews referred to and the material published in the press by members of the Administration, but with the awareness that such views are not only not binding on the President but could again be revised at any time. Indeed, if the powers asserted by the President in the Order were upheld, this President or a future President could use the Order as precedent to exercise those powers in a different context and without the gloss now presented by his representatives.

THE PRESIDENT'S AUTHORITY TO ORDER TRIAL BY MILITARY COMMISSION AND TO ESTABLISH AD HOC RULES FOR THEIR USE

Authority Cited by the Order.

The Order states that it is issued under three sources of authority:

1. The President's authority as Commander-in-chief of the Armed Forces[23];
2. The Authorization for Use of Military Force Joint Resolution (Public Law 107-40, 115 Stat. 224); and
3. Sections 821 and 836 of Title 10, United States Code (the Uniform Code of Military Justice).

Although civilian lawyers are unfamiliar with military commissions, they are nevertheless not unknown in American history. Such commissions have been upheld by the U.S. Supreme Court, and, despite disuse for nearly one-half century during which time the U.S. has participated in several major armed conflicts, they are in fact contemplated by existing law.[24] U.S. military commissions convicted British Major Andre of espionage in the Revolutionary War, tried those accused of the assassination of President Lincoln, imposed the death penalty on German saboteurs who landed on Long Island during World War II (including one who claimed U.S. citizenship), and tried some 1,200 German war crimes defendants (more than eight times the number tried by the international Nuremberg tribunal) and many Japanese defendants.

Judicial Authority—The *Quirin* Case

U.S. Supreme Court cases have clearly established the constitutionality of military commissions within at least the prototypical declared war between nations involving members of the armed forces of an enemy state. Less clear is the support for military commissions in the context of an act of mass murder by 18 individuals neither members of the armed forces of any nation state nor, even, organized in a conventional military or even para-military formation.

In *Ex parte Quirin,*[25] impliedly relied upon by President Bush (and explicitly by officials in his Administration) as a precedent for the Order,[26] the Supreme Court upheld during a declared war a military commission's jurisdiction over German military saboteurs who had landed in the U.S. from a German submarine and then operated in civilian clothing and, therefore, in violation of the laws of war. The prosecution, in opposing the defendants' application for a writ of habeas corpus in *Quirin,* asserted that no federal court had jurisdiction to hear the case because the military commission's authority was exempt from habeas corpus under the terms of its constitutive order.[27] The Court rejected that contention, holding that even alien members of enemy armed forces were entitled to the writ when found within the U.S. Having found jurisdiction, the Court went on to consider the merits of the military commission's authority notwithstanding the absence of Fifth and Sixth Amendment protections in the conduct of the trial before the commission, such as the right to trial by jury and other procedural rights that are normal in criminal cases. The Court upheld the authority of the commission, grounded on the time-honored practice of trying unlawful, enemy-state combatants in a declared war by military commission, which the Court found to be exempt from the constitutional right to trial by jury. That exemption exists, the Court said, because the practice of such military proceedings was recognized by the law of war prior to the adoption of the Constitution and was consistently followed in subsequent wars between the U.S. and other countries, as well as during the Civil War.[28]

The *Quirin* decision addressed a case arising within the territory of the U.S. during declared war, and, accordingly in view of other cases addressing the distinctive rights of citizens and aliens, its constitutional holding must be limited to that situation. With respect to aliens outside the

U.S., the authority to convene military commissions to try law of war violations is subject only to statutory and international law limitations.[29]

Legislative Authority—the UCMJ

Although the *Quirin* Court did not find it necessary to determine whether the President had independent authority as Commander-in-Chief to create such commissions,[30] we believe that although the President may have implied authority to do so absent Congressional action, when Congress acts, Congress has the exclusive authority to define the use of military commissions by exercise of its powers "to constitute tribunals inferior to the Supreme Court,"[31] "to define offenses against the law of nations,"[32] and "to make rules for the government and regulation of the land and naval forces."[33] In a manner that appears to be consistent with the constitutionally permitted exclusion from the domestic right to trial by jury of proceedings before traditional military commissions, Congress has specifically authorized military commissions to act under the laws of war.[34] As will be discussed, however, use of such commissions—as *Quirin* found—requires a war, at the least *de facto,* if not declared.

Substantively, Article 21 of the UCMJ,[35] among the statutory provisions cited in the Order as authority for its issuance,[36] provides that the UCMJ does not deprive military commissions "of concurrent jurisdiction with respect to *offenders* or *offenses* that by statute or by the law of war may be tried by military commissions, provost courts or other military tribunals."[37] The classic case where both the *offender* and the *offense* are covered is when Japanese General Yamashita was tried for war crimes committed against U.S. personnel during the then recently ended World War II. Either the defendant's whereabouts (Yamashita was in custody, taken during battle) or the predicate offense (traditional war crimes) could serve as a basis for jurisdiction in that case. As an example of jurisdiction over the offender, the U.S., as an occupying power, could use military commissions to try persons within occupied territory pending establishment of civil government, as it did extensively in the post-war occupation of Germany and Japan. This was so whether or not the offense related to the war, generally applying local law then in effect.[38] Article 21, and therefore, statutory support for military commissions (and constitutional authority within the U.S. under *Quirin*), reaches its limits as to persons who are neither offenders, nor charged with offenses, traditionally tried under the law of war by such military commissions.

Offenses—The Law of War

With respect to the offense, it is not at all clear that at the time of the 9/11 attack the U.S. was engaged in a war or even armed conflict to which the law of war[39] could be applied. International treaty law has black letter rules defining when the law of war (or as now often termed, the law of armed conflict) applies. Common Article 2 of the Geneva Conventions[40] provides that "the present Convention shall apply to all cases of declared war or of any other armed conflict which may arise between two or more of the High Contracting Parties, even if the state of war is not recognized by one of them."

Thus, for a state of war to exist under the classic definition of war, the conflict must be between states. "The law of war has been conceived primarily for armed conflicts between States or groups of States, that is, for international armed conflicts."[41] This international law requirement is unfulfilled with respect to the persons covered by the Order. It is fulfilled for international law purposes with respect to Afghanistan, with whose *de facto* Taliban government the United States is engaged in armed conflict (albeit an undeclared war under US domestic laws).

Conflicts *not* between states are covered by the laws of war to a lesser degree, as made more precise in the 1977 Protocols. Protocol II for "non-international conflicts", that is, non-state conflicts, applies to those conflicts which "take place in the territory of a High Contracting Party between its armed forces and dissident armed forces or other organized armed groups which, under responsible command, exercise such control over a part of its territory as to enable them to carry out sustained and concerted military operations and to implement this Protocol."[42] Clearly this definition—also—does not apply to al Qaeda, as it does not exercise control over any part of U.S. territory.[43]

Illustrative of the need for a predicate war is the 1865 opinion of Attorney General James Speed issued with respect to whether military tribunals (by which he meant the courts for military justice generally) could be used to try the civilian assassins of President Lincoln, whom he found to be serving the war aims of the enemy. He found that such persons were subject to the laws of war and trial by military tribunal because—*in times of war:*

A bushwacker, a jayhawker, a bandit, a war rebel, an assassin, being public enemies, may be tried, condemned and executed as offenders against the laws of war. . . . The civil courts have no more right to prevent the military, *in time of war,* from trying an offender against the laws of war than they have a right to interfere with and prevent a battle.[44]

Some have argued, including officials in the Bush Administration, that this is a "new kind of war," one in which state participants are not required for a determination of war because of the amorphous nature of international terrorism. Others have argued that while a "war" is required for the Order to be lawful, the armed conflict of the United States with Afghanistan's Taliban puts the country at war for some if not all domestic law purposes, the existence of the conflict would, thus, allow the Order's actions toward the non-citizen residents to whom it is directed by virtue of their nexus with international terrorism generally, even if they have no relationship to Afghanistan or the Taliban. Still others have refined this latter argument by "imputing" the al Qaeda to the Taliban, or, even, vice-versa, noting that recent evidence indicates that al Qaeda may have in fact been controlling the Taliban.[45]

Although the United States has not declared war and the President, in fact, said that he was not seeking a declaration of war, it is not difficult to find that for *international* law purposes the United States is at war in Afghanistan.[46] However, in this regard, it is important to note that the Order is not limited to the "enemy aliens" with whom we are at war, i.e., all Afghans, much less to the Taliban and not even to al Qaeda. It goes to all non-citizens, U.S. resident or not, alleged to commit the acts set forth in it. In contrast, had the Order been limited to enemy aliens, members of an armed body, they would be classic "offenders" subject to the law of war, including the Geneva Protocols. Had the Order been directed to the al Qaeda and the Taliban as a *combined entity,* it might arguably be easier to characterize that joint force as an enemy subject to the laws of war during a time of war with them. Separating al Qaeda from the state elements of territory, governance and organized troops makes it that much more difficult to view as a military, as distinguished from a criminal (though terrorist) organization.

The 1942 Order, which served as the basis for the military commission in *Quirin,* stated the specific, objective and wholly traditional standard. It applied to:

all persons who are subjects, citizens or residents of any nation at war with the United States or who give obedience to or act under the direction of any such nation. . . .

It is doubtful whether the constitutional logic behind the Court's opinion in *Quirin* upholding that order could be stretched to apply instead to the current Order's novel application to "any individual who is not a United States citizen with respect to whom I determine . . . there is reason to believe that such individual . . . has engaged in, aided or abetted, or conspired to commit, acts of international terrorism, or acts in preparation therefore, that have caused, threaten to cause, or have as their aim to cause, injury to or adverse effects on the United States, its citizens, national security, foreign policy, or economy…"[47]

This point, it should be emphasized, does not diminish the right of the US armed forces fighting in Afghanistan to both capture and try by military commission abroad members of either the Taliban or al Qaeda who are participating in the combat. Abroad, many of the constitutional guarantees under the Fourth, Fifth and Sixth Amendments do not apply to non-citizens,[48] and certainly not to persons captured during hostilities conducted by the US armed forces.[49]

Offenders—In the U.S. and Abroad

With respect to determining the offender status of persons subject to the Order, civilians residing in the U.S. and not in or near a theater of military operations or engaged as combatants are examples of offenders who have never been subject to the jurisdiction of military commissions under our laws. For example in the Civil War *Ex parte Milligan*[50] case, "Milligan, a citizen twenty years resident in Indiana, who had never been a resident of any of the states in rebellion, was found not to be subject to trial by a military commission because he was not an enemy belligerent either entitled to the status of a prisoner of war or subject to the penalties imposed upon unlawful belligerents." *Quirin, supra,* at 45. Yet, non-citizen, U.S. residents accused of the crimes set forth in the Order relating to 9/11, such as aiding, abetting and harboring al Qaeda, but who may fall far short of violating the laws of war applicable to saboteurs and the like, are among the direct targets of the Order (compare this to Mr. Milligan, who was accused of rebellion).

The application for domestic statutory and constitutional purposes of the laws of war should be distinguished from the international law regarding the existence of a state of war or the right of the U.S. to take military action in self-defense against an attack or against a country that harbors the attackers. As indicated above, the latter action has been affirmed internationally by the Security Council of the United Nations and by the North Atlantic Treaty Organization and domestically by Congress. Moreover, as also indicated above, there is no substantive issue as to the statutory or constitutional authority of a military commission to try aliens outside the U.S.

The issue of greatest importance is whether the present circumstances permit the application of the laws of war under domestic law to deny the application of constitutional rights otherwise available to persons within the U.S. That question is most acute as to a circumstance in which armed members of the Taliban, with whom we are engaged in an undeclared war, say, or of al Qaeda, the specific subjects of the Order and whose personal status is less clear, are found entering or already in the United States to commit hostile acts.

For these persons (at least unlawful, Taliban combatants), the subject matter authority for the President to utilize a military commission to try such persons based on their acts seems clear under the Constitution as interpreted by *Quirin*. With respect to the individual status of such captured "combatants," the Taliban members would almost certainly qualify as combatants under the law of armed conflict (although potentially unlawful, depending on such factors as their uniforms and behavior) whose prosecution is subject to the provisions of the international law of armed conflict.[51] The al Qaeda members are more difficult to characterize, depending on the evidence linking them to being controlled by, or controlling, the Taliban, a state-like entity, leaving some doubt as to the legality of the use of a commission to try them in the United States without a jury trial.

On the other hand, the persons charged only with "aiding", "abetting", "conspiracy" or simply "harboring" the other persons subject to the Order, that is, people who have committed traditionally civilian criminal acts rather than the "commission" of military-like terrorist acts themselves may not be tried in a military commission as the Order contemplates. Such persons are guaranteed by the Bill of Rights, as interpreted by the Supreme Court in *Milligan* and *Quirin,* a trial by jury. The aliens detained by the U.S. and charged with crimes were accused of subsidiary offenses, such as immigration violations, money laundering, credit card fraud or other money-raising crimes. Persons charged with civil crimes are exceedingly unlikely to come within the class of persons traditionally tried by the law of war, and, to such extent, the Order must be facially invalid.

SUBSTANTIVE OVERREACH—PERVASIVE DEATH PENALTY AND UNRELATED TERRORISM

A corollary of the jurisdictional application of the laws of war is the resulting substantive penalty. The traditional laws of war are draconian in applying the death penalty to irregular combatants out of uniform and not carrying arms openly. Mere presence in the enemy force constitutes the offense without more. Thus, if the laws of war apply to such irregulars, the death penalty follows. If the laws of war do not apply, a military commission has no jurisdiction. This extreme black and white result should require the greatest caution in extending the laws of war to situations not traditionally contemplated.

Moreover, the Order by its terms may be applied to the commission of acts of international terrorism whether or not related to al Qaeda or the 9/11 attacks. It could, for example, be applied to prosecute aliens in the U.S. supporting terrorism in Northern Ireland having "adverse effects on . . . [U.S.] foreign policy", a legitimate government measure but far removed from a U.S. war. This broad jurisdictional reach is consistent with the concept of a "war on terrorism" but inconsistent with any definable "war" in the sense known to U.S. jurisprudence.[52]

As these principles are therefore applied to the Order, the Order does not confine its scope to either offenders or offenses traditionally tried by the law of war, as provided by law, implied in the Constitution and required by the *Quirin* Court. Absent Congressional action, we cannot see how the President in the current situation has authority permitting him to convene military commissions to proceed inside the U.S. without providing grand jury indictment, jury trials or the right to confront witnesses, among other exceptions from constitutionally guaranteed rights.[53]

We must, therefore, conclude that the Order substantively violates both Article 21 of the UCMJ and, as to persons within the U.S., the Constitution, as well, to the extent that it covers offenses and offenders not covered by the law of war as historically described in *Quirin.* That possible legal infirmity and, at the very least, uncertainty, severely undercuts the policy objectives of the Order as more fully discussed below.

PROCEDURAL CONCERNS UNDER THE UCMJ

In addition to the substantive issue, there is a procedural concern. The Order cited as additional authority Section 36 of the UCMJ,[54] which provides that in cases under the UCMJ the President may prescribe by regulation the procedures for military commissions subject to two qualifications. First, the procedures "shall, so far as he considers practicable, apply the principles of law and the rules of evidence generally recognized in the trial of criminal cases in the United States district courts." In the Order, President Bush declares *in haec verba* that such principles and rules are not practicable to apply under the order. That extraordinary finding is presumably his prerogative, whether or not it is a wise exercise thereof.

Secondly, and more importantly for present purposes, Article 36 specifies that the procedures "may not be contrary to or inconsistent with this chapter [the UCMJ]." The Order only outlines the parameters for procedures to be implemented by orders and regulations of the Secretary of Defense.[55] However, the framework of the Order is already inconsistent with the essential elements of due process provided for in the UCMJ in numerous respects.[56] Accordingly, if Section 36 is indeed necessary authority for the Order, then the Order appears to be procedurally defective.

Exclusive Jurisdiction to Military Commissions

Finally, the Order states that "with respect to any individual subject to this order...military tribunals shall have exclusive jurisdiction with respect to offenses by the individual...."[57] This grant of exclusive jurisdiction to military commissions appears to conflict with the Congressional intent set forth in Article 18 of the UCMJ, which provides that for purposes of prosecutions for violations of the law of war, general courts martial shall have jurisdiction concurrent with military tribunals:

General courts-martial also have jurisdiction to try any person who by the law of war is subject to trial by a military tribunal and may adjudge any punishment permitted by the law of war.

Inasmuch as the UCMJ by its terms applies to prisoners of war,[58] we conclude that Order conflicts with Congress' determination that courts martial and military tribunals (commissions) should have concurrent jurisdiction with respect to prosecution of POWs for violations of the laws of war.

PREVENTIVE ARREST, INDEFINITE DETENTION AND THE SUSPENSION OF HABEAS CORPUS

The provisions of the Order regarding detention of persons subject to it permit seemingly indefinite detention without charges, trial,[59] or the right to seek a remedy in federal or state courts. Thus, they provide for 'preventive arrests,' unlimited detention and literally suspends the privilege of the writ of habeas corpus, notwithstanding statements by Administration officials to the contrary. These provisions are clearly unconstitutional as to the writ of habeas corpus and extremely controversial as to detention.

Preventive arrests are anathema to American values. It is bedrock in American constitutional law that the deprivation of liberty may only occur pursuant to the principles and mechanisms of due process enshrined in the Bill of Rights. To determine whether liberty has, in fact, been properly deprived, the Framers maintained the privilege of the writ of habeas corpus.

Habeas Corpus

The privilege of the writ of habeas corpus is considered a "*magna carta* of the kingdom."[60] Justice Story said of it:

It is...justly esteemed the great bulwark of personal liberty; since it is the appropriate remedy to ascertain, whether any person is rightfully in confinement or not, and the cause of his confinement; and if no sufficient ground of detention appears, the party is entitled to his immediate discharge. This writ is most beneficially construed; and is applied to every case of illegal restraint, whatever it may; for every restraint upon a man's liberty is, in the eye of the law, an imprisonment, wherever may be the place, or whatever may be the manner, in which the restraint is effected.[61]

Chief Justice Rehnquist has praised the privilege: "It has been rightly regarded as a safeguard against executive tyranny, and an essential safeguard to individual liberty."[62]

Beginning in the nineteenth century and continuing without exception through to the present day, the Supreme Court has consistently held that non-citizens within the jurisdiction of the United States are "persons" within the meaning of the Fifth Amendment and are thus entitled to the protections of the due process clause.[63] In fact, it was recognized by the Supreme Court in the wartime cases *Quirin* and *Yamashita* as available even to members of the German military and to the Japanese command within the U.S. (or in Yamashita's case, in the Philippines, under U.S. rule) to test the authority of a military commission to detain and try them.[64] It is also available to persons charged under the UCMJ and held for court martial under that statute.[65]

As noted, the President's Order states that the authority for its issuance is (1) the President's authority as Commander-in-chief of the Armed Forces, (2) the Authorization for Use of Military Force Joint Resolution (Public Law 107-40, 115 Stat. 224) and (3) Sections 821 and 836 of the UCMJ.

The Constitution states in Article I (the enumeration of Congress' powers), Section 9 (a list of limitations on those Congressional powers):

Clause 2: The Privilege of the Writ of Habeas Corpus shall not be suspended, unless when in Cases of Rebellion or Invasion the public Safety may require it.

It seems plain from the text of the Constitution that only the Congress, not the President— whether as Commander-in-chief or otherwise—has the authority to suspend habeas corpus, and then only in the two circumstances mentioned. The Supreme Court has upheld that principle and the most prominent of commentators on the Constitution have agreed.[66]

The other bases cited in the Order for the President's authority to detain the subject persons indefinitely without recourse offer no support either. The text of Congress' Resolution Authorizing Use of Military Force—the second cited basis—does nothing to alter habeas corpus whatsoever, much less authorize the President to do so. In fact, it plainly refers specifically and solely to the use of *military force,* hence its title. Section 2, the substantive section of the Resolution, is titled "Authorization For Use Of United States Armed Forces" and provides simply: "That the President is authorized to use all necessary and appropriate force....,"[67] with nothing said about arrests, detentions, habeas corpus or the like. It therefore appears clear that the Use of Force Resolution cited by the President as a basis for his authority in issuing the Order also does not, in fact, provide such authority.

Finally, the Order refers for authority to Sections 821 and 836 of the UCMJ, both of which go to the issue of military commissions, as discussed, *supra.* Neither provide Congressional suspension of the privilege of habeas corpus or have anything to do with that subject but are cited, apparently, for authority regarding the Order's establishment of military commissions, discussed *supra,* and, thus, too, offer no authority for the detention provisions of the Order.

It appears clear, therefore, that the three bases cited in the Order by the President do not in fact provide the legal authority necessary to validate these provisions of the Order effectively suspending habeas corpus. The conclusion is that the power to suspend the privilege of the writ of habeas corpus is given to the Congress and that the President may not exercise it.

Congress, in fact, *has* acted with respect to the events of September 11, 2001 specifically in connection with habeas corpus. On October 26, 2001, it adopted legislation sought by the Administration; the USA Patriot Act of 2001,[68] whose full name is "Uniting and Strengthening America by Providing Appropriate Tools Required to Intercept and Obstruct Terrorism (USA Patriot Act) Act [sic] of 2001." The Act was intended, as its name indicates, to provide a comprehensive set of "tools" to the federal government in the service of law enforcement and intelligence gathering.

The USA Patriot Act specifically addresses habeas corpus in Section 412 (Mandatory Detention Of Suspected Terrorists; Habeas Corpus; Judicial Review).[69] That Section amends Section 236 of the Immigration and Nationality Act to provide that aliens subject to the Act who are detained must be criminally charged or placed in removal proceedings within seven days following commencement of detention unless release of the alien will result in activity that endangers the national security of the United States. In that case, the Attorney General must so certify and recertify every 6 months thereafter, if the alien is to continue in detention. Importantly, habeas corpus proceedings to review decisions made under the Section are available to the suspect alien on application to the Supreme Court, any Justice of the Supreme Court, any circuit judge of the D.C. Circuit Court of Appeals, or any district court with jurisdiction. Further still, determinations by district courts or circuit court judges are subject to appeal to the D.C. Circuit Court of Appeals.[70]

This provision of the Congressional act differs profoundly from the President's Order with respect to the application of habeas corpus to aliens arrested within the United States and suspected of connection to terrorism, which provides no release process, no certification process, no right to a petition of habeas corpus and no right to appeal adverse decisions. The analogy to the Steel Seizure Case is apparent. There, the President—by seizing strike-bound steel mills in order to continue production of steel to supply the armed forces then engaged in Korea— acted contrary to the will of Congress expressed through various statutory schemes in an area the power over which belonged to Congress. Of such extreme and far reaching Presidential behavior contrary to the expressed will of Congress, Justice Jackson wrote in his concurring opinion:

When the President takes measures incompatible with the expressed or implied will of Congress, his power is at its lowest ebb, for then he can rely only upon his own constitutional powers minus any constitutional powers of Congress over the matter. Courts can sustain exclusive presidential control in such a case only by disabling the Congress from acting upon the subject. Presidential claim to a power at once so conclusive and preclusive must be scrutinized with caution, for what is at stake is the equilibrium established by our constitutional system....In short, we can sustain the President only by holding that seizure of such strike-bound industries is within his domain and beyond control by Congress. Thus, this Court's first review of such seizures occurs under circumstances which leave presidential power most vulnerable to attack and in the least favorable of possible constitutional postures.

Id., at 637–638. Justice Jackson continued his analysis by finding that neither the President's Constitutional 'Executive' powers, nor his Commander-in-Chief authority (whether in time of war *de facto* or war *de jure*), nor his obligation to faithfully execute the laws could trump the Constitutions' plain grant of authority to Congress to raise and support armies and to provide and maintain a navy.[71]

Here, as noted, the power to suspend habeas corpus is granted to the Congress by Article I of the Constitution, and the USA Patriot Act—which fails to suspend the privilege—is the act of Congress on the subject. It is, therefore, our conclusion that the Order, which effectively seeks to suspend the privilege of habeas corpus for those aliens subject to it and detained under it, impermissibly seeks to exercise a power not only reserved to the Congress but one already exercised by the Congress in this specific area in a contrary manner. As such, determinations under the Order will likely be subject to successful Constitutional attack on this ground, leading to a significant amount of litigation at a time when efficiency and speed of process is the desired result. The Order in this regard, therefore, not only appears to be illegal, but unwise.

In response to questioning from various sources, including members of this Committee, Administration officers stated that the Administration had no intention of opposing the right of detained persons to seek the writ of habeas corpus, and that the Order was not intended to do so despite the language of Section 7. They acknowledged that the *nearly identical* provisions of the 1942 Order in question in *Quirin* did seek to suspend habeas corpus and had been ruled unconstitutional.[72] Such informal statements about the true meaning of the Order or the President's intent in issuing it, without amendment of the Order or Congressional legislation, are less than satisfactory.[73]

SEVERABILITY

If a provision of the Order, such as suspending habeas corpus, were to be found unconstitutional, it is unclear what effect that finding would have on the remainder of the Order, since the Order lacks a severability provision. In *Quirin, supra,* the 1942 Order lacked a severability provision and its attempt to suspend habeas corpus was found to be invalid without affecting the substance of the military commission's authority set forth in the remaining portion of that order. The Court in *Quirin* did not discuss severability.

Although it used virtually the same language for the suspension of habeas corpus which appears in the Order (and which was found invalid), the 1942 order expressly provided for the possibility of correction by the regulations to follow:

[S]uch persons shall not be privileged to seek any remedy or maintain any proceeding directly or indirectly, or to have any such remedy or proceeding sought on their behalf, in the courts of the United States, or of its States, territories, and possessions, *except under such regulations as the Attorney General, with the approval of the Secretary of War, may from time to time prescribe.*[74]

The Order provides no such opportunity for subsequent correction and, thus, the courts may take a different view of the absence of a severability provision than did the *Quirin* court.

DETENTION OF ENEMY ALIENS

Congress has also acted, albeit not recently, in the form of the Alien Enemies Act, 50 U.S.C. 21, permitting the detention or expulsion of aliens over age 14 within the US who are citizens of a foreign government or state with which the US is in a declared war or subject to "any invasion or predatory incursion...perpetrated, attempted or threatened against the territory of the United States."[75] While the 9/11 attacks may have constituted a "predatory incursion against the territory of the United States", they were not perpetrated by a "foreign nation or government" as required by Section 21 and, thus, the Alien Enemies Act does not apply to the 9/11 attacks.

These provisions—including this statute, its predecessors and those like it (*e.g.,* those establishing military areas within the United States during World War II, serving as the basis for Executive Order 9066 in 1942), were classically applied, if at all, in declared war against the entire class of enemy aliens, all citizens of the enemy state, along with the expropriation of enemy property.[76] In World War II, they were also put into effect ruthlessly against Japanese nationals found in the United States, in an operation now viewed as a national disgrace. Similar steps were taken against U.S. citizens of Japanese descent.[77] It is noted that the Commission on Wartime Relocation and Internment of Civilians, established in 1980 by Congress to review the 1942 Executive Order providing for the internment found there was "no justification in military necessity for the exclusion,...there was no basis for the detention."[78]

Broad, class-based detention or expulsion, when confined to enemy aliens, may have made sense in the context of traditional war between national states against persons owing allegiance to the enemy and reasonably be expected to act on its behalf, but such actions have little relevance to the contemporary crisis involving a cross-border, multinational extremist *culture* and not an enemy state or states. Such a culture has no "citizens," and, thus, determining who to detain or expel as the Order aggressively does—other than based on their individual *actions*—is nearly impossible without casting a net so broad as to be pernicious. Consequently it is not surprising that the Order failed to cite 50 U.S.C. 21 or indeed any statutory authority for its unlimited detention provisions.

The Administration has sought to portray the Order as applying only to enemy combatants. The White House Counsel said recently that "The order covers only foreign enemy war criminals"[79]—and even then only for "violations of the laws of war."[80] The Order itself, however, does *not* in fact specify either the claimed limitation on the class of subject persons or the claimed limitation on the activities by which they become subject to the Order.

The detention provisions of the Order are, therefore, surprising, both in view of the U.S. acknowledgment of its egregious error in World War II—oft cited as precedent—and of the present acquiescence by Congress (through the USA Patriot Act) in expanding the detention powers over aliens suspected of terrorist connections and the specific provision of the right of habeas corpus with appeals from decisions when doing so.

No act of Congress has been found that provides for either the detention provisions referred to in the Order or for authority for the President to act in the area. Simply, the Order purports to give the President this power by fiat. That claim will most certainly be tested by habeas corpus proceedings within the U.S. to determine whether the Order trumps the Constitution's award of authority in this area to Congress, which has acted through Section 412 of the USA Patriot Act.

With respect to indefinite detention without remedy, on the one hand, we have no doubt that regarding aliens in the United States during time of declared war, the federal government could create a scheme substantially restricting the rights they were previously provided that would be upheld by the courts. Much, however, would depend on the factual circumstances. In World War II, the internment of Japanese nationals (as distinct from the internment of U.S. citizens of Japanese descent) occurred at a time of very substantial and genuine threats to the security of the nation as a whole. In fact, Chief Justice Rehnquist, in perhaps a prescient speech reviewing this history in May of 2000 provided this conclusion: "The authority of the government to deal with enemy aliens in time of war, according to established case law from our Court, is virtually plenary."[81] In the present circumstances, however, absent any enemy nation, it is impossible to identify the nationals or citizens of the "enemy." Consequently, the term "enemy alien" has no determinable meaning.

We conclude that the Order's provision of indefinite detention of aliens suspected of terrorist connections or harboring those who have them—particularly given the denial of *all remedy*—is improper since the President does not have the Constitutional authority to issue an order applicable to aliens in the U.S., and Congress has already provided a different scheme with respect to such persons.[82] As a practical matter, we believe that these provisions of the Order, if utilized, will not only lead to widespread litigation testing both the President's authority to issue it and as it may be applied to the individual detainee, which litigation is likely to be successful at least with respect to the question of the Order's suspension of habeas corpus.[83]

Even if the President has the authority to detain persons within the classes targeted by the Order, it would remain to be determined whether a particular detainee within the U.S. is within one of those classes. Therefore, such habeas corpus proceedings might extend not only to determination of a commission's substantive and procedural authority, but also to whether as a matter of fact the detainee came within the jurisdictional predicate of the Order, namely, membership in al Qaeda or commission or certain kinds of involvement in acts of international terrorism or harboring of persons under the prior categories. While the Order purports to give the President authority to define such persons, the corresponding findings may themselves be subject to finding in habeas corpus proceedings, equivalent to challenging probable cause for arrest.[84] This would have the result of placing before the federal District Courts the very issues—whether an individual is an al Qaeda member—the Administration is seeking to keep from those courts.

INTERNATIONAL LAW

International law may also have a bearing on the Order. Common Article 3 of the four Geneva Conventions of 1949, which establishes minimal standards even in armed conflicts not of an international nature, and *a fortiori* in international conflicts, in paragraph 1(d) prohibits persons who have laid down their arms from being subjected to "the passing of sentences and the carrying out of executions without previous judgment pronounced by a regularly constituted court, affording all of the judicial guarantees which are recognized as indispensable by civilized peoples."

The U.S. is a party to, and has ratified, the Geneva Conventions and in 1997, violations of Common Article 3 were added to the definition of "war crimes" for the purposes of the War Crimes Act of 1996.[85] Compliance with such international laws of armed conflict is specifically required of the U.S. Armed Forces pursuant to Department of Defense's Law of War Program.[86]

It follows that the international standard has become binding U.S. law. It would be unlawful for the President to authorize a procedure that resulted in the passing of sentences or carrying out executions without such a regularly constituted court affording the judicial guarantees required by the Common Article 3.[87]

Pending issuance of the regulations for commissions, it would be premature to speculate whether they would violate the applicable international standards, which it should be noted do not require trial by jury, U.S. rules of evidence or habeas corpus. In fact, it is has been reported that a Swiss military court has tried at least one war crime defendant from the former Yugoslavia and one from Rwanda, although on request a case was remanded to the International Court for the Former Yugoslavia.[88] It would, however, be highly questionable if the regulations did not require proof beyond a reasonable doubt (or an internationally acceptable alternative standard), public trials, defense right to choice of counsel or independent judges.

Moreover, the United States certainly desires to avoid adverse effects on its international prestige and foreign policy effectiveness which would potentially result from any erroneous convictions or, worse, executions in haste of persons possibly misidentified or otherwise misjudged. Thus, in addition to legal and ethical concerns, this practical factor should urge upon the United States a scrupulous regard for the rule of law, including by establishing fair procedures as the Order promises to do.

Should the definitive procedures for such a fair trial as issued by the Secretary of Defense fall short of accepted international standards, and, until they are defined, it can be expected that many countries will decline to permit extradition of defendants for trial by military tribunals. This issue is separate from the death penalty issue, which already blocks or conditions extradition to the regular U.S. courts. Military commissions would, however, aggravate that issue to the extent that every irregular combatant becomes vulnerable to the death penalty by participation in a non-uniformed force.

The U.S. has vigorously objected to incidents in which it believes that U.S. citizens have not been accorded minimal judicial rights. Recent examples include a secret trial for espionage in Russia, an execution by order of a special military court in Nigeria and a terrorism conviction by a hooded military court in Peru. Obviously, it would not be productive in future incidents for the U.S. to be tarnished with a repudiation of the very civil rights for foreign nationals it seeks to affirm for its own nationals abroad.

U.S. POLICY SHOULD BE TO PROMOTE RESPECT FOR THE RULE OF LAW, EVEN WHEN PROSECUTING THOSE WHO LACK SUCH RESPECT

The principal justification of the Order is the paramount national security interest in public safety and national security. In pursuit of that, it relies on mechanisms such as indefinite detention and secrecy (intended, it is said, to permit removal from the public realm persons suspected of terrorist connections) and potentially secret trials (designed, it is said, to protect classified, or even classifiable, information).

To the extent, however, that the Order seeks to 'stack the deck' against defendants, it betrays uncertainty about the ability to obtain a conviction even in a secret, non-jury trial under existing civilian or military law,[89] and, we believe, does a disservice to the entire process. It would permit indefinite detention without charges, much less trial, a tack likely to be used when is there is insufficient evidence to convict even by loose standards; and all without the possibility of judicial review. We do not believe that the full range of such procedures contemplated by the Order are necessary and, as a result, hope that the procedural regulations now being crafted do not take full advantage of the overbroad provisions of the Order.

Further, as a practical matter, such overbroad provisions may well hamper the very swiftness with which the government understandably seeks to act in this crisis. Given the constitutional and statutory questions about the validity of the Order with respect to persons placed in custody within the United States, the availability to them of habeas corpus proceedings (including the likelihood that the courts hearing the petitions will go on to determine the validity of the substantive characterization of defendants by the President as members of al Qaeda or another class of persons covered by the Order), and the likely appeals therefrom (notwithstanding the Order's attempt to close them off), it is probable that the Administration will not achieve the quick and final resolution of cases against alleged terrorists that it seeks. Indeed, the defects in the Order—unless they are corrected by the procedures to come or otherwise—make it particularly vulnerable to attack.[90]

Further still, the Order suffers from a lack of a sunset mechanism. Examples of presidential use of military commissions—such as for the Lincoln assassins and the Quirin saboteurs—were pursuant to either one-time operations, as with the Lincoln assassination, or were issued with respect to a declared war that had a visible victory marker, *i.e.,* the defeat of the enemy nation, and thus a clear end date.[91] Here, in an undeclared war with the allies professing that the 'new war on terrorism' could last 50 years against an undefined enemy beyond al Qaeda,[92] the almost total curtailment of liberties previously available to foreign nationals living in or visiting this country has no natural end in sight.[93]

It is of utmost regret that the 9/11 crisis has led the executive branch to give the impression that it would deny as to any class of persons almost the entirety of the procedural rights that have characterized this Republic since 1789, apparently without any effort to find a workable alternative. Even if the Order is never used in practice, or if wiser heads prevail and it is used in a more reasonable manner than its language permits, the Order stands as an historic repudiation of the legal ideals on which the Nation was founded, potentially permitting a reversion to the worst practices of the Star Chamber, Inquisition and other notorious tribunals that put the interests of State or Church ahead of individual rights. Protestations that the Order is but "one tool available, and hasn't been used yet"[94] ring hollow when matched with the Order's stunning scope, exclusive jurisdiction and total absence of review.

These national domestic ideals should be reason enough either to temper the Order in order to avoid a court finding it (or portions of it) unconstitutional, unlawful or unsupportable. Such tempering might be accomplished by its amendment, by Congressional action or, at the least and as has now apparently been promised,[95] by issuing balanced procedures to put it into effect. After reaching out to the entire world to embrace the American cause against terrorism as a fight for civilization on behalf of all nations, including such former adversaries as Iran and Syria in need of rule-of-law models, the Order effectively declares the second class status of foreign nationals under our laws by asserting our right to make preventive arrests of such persons on the determination of one person, detain them indefinitely without charge, prosecute them in secret and based on *ad hoc* rules, and then apply the death penalty when even less than all judges find them guilty of crimes not yet specified. After the nation's demonstration of strength, resolve and resilience in the face of the unprecedented attack of 9/11, the Order threatens to becomes a confession of weakness, of the inability of the United States to utilize established means of prosecution and to marshal sufficient evidence to prove the complicity of al Qaeda in the attacks of 9/11.

We believe that national security must be preserved, and that it must be done while giving as much respect as possible in a time of national emergency to the great American values—embodied in our laws of due process—which make this nation both a target and worth defending. Justice Rehnquist has acknowledged that in times of great national security, the laws, while "muted," are not, in fact, silent—even during war.[96] We acknowledge that the balance is difficult, but also that the national will to seek such balance—not a clear tip of the scale—is not only essential but is the greatest show of strength the United States can offer.

RECOMMENDATIONS AND ALTERNATIVES

Validating the Order

With respect to validating the Order, a Congressional declaration of war would most certainly put the full powers of the national government at work in the anti-terrorism war. Justice Jackson said famously in the *Steel Seizure Case* that when the President acts "pursuant to an express or implied authorization of Congress, his authority is at its maximum, for it includes all that he possess in his own right plus all that Congress can delegate...[and acts so taken] would be supported by the strongest of presumptions and the widest latitude of judicial interpretation..."[97]

Directed certainly against the Taliban government of Afghanistan, conceivably the declaration of war could also include (but should not be limited to) those named international terrorist *organizations,* notably al Qaeda, to whom that enemy state gave aid and comfort and even vice-versa. President Jefferson, for example, was authorized by Congress in 1802 (following skirmishes with the Barbary pirates in the Mediterranean) "to cause to be done all such other acts of precaution or hostility as the state of war will justify, and, may, in his opinion require," finding, in fact, that a "state of war now exists."[98] Al Qaeda may be analogous to pirates of old.[99] Such a Congressional declaration would lay to rest legal concerns with respect to both the President's authority to establish military commissions in a time of undeclared war, since it would now be declared, and also to the status of those persons related to such enemy organizations, since an enemy will have been defined.

However, a declaration of war carries with it enormous implications for the conduct of daily life in the United States. To declare war solely, or even primarily, to rectify the legal problems with the underpinnings of the President's desire to utilize military commissions to try without traditional due process alien civilians arrested in the United States seems to us too radical a solution. Nor would a declaration of war resolve the constitutional issues relating to *domestic* use of commissions in a war for crimes not uniquely violative of the law of war, issues that arose in the Civil War in the context of the *Milligan* case.

Alternatives to Military Commissions for Prosecution

The analysis above demonstrates that the Constitution requires that due process—including jury trials—be given to defendants arrested or tried in the United States for civilian-style crimes that are not violations of the laws of war. Thus, for these defendants, whether they be al Qaeda conspirators or merely harborers, Article 3 federal District Courts must be the forum for their prosecution.

However, with respect to those persons captured abroad in combat or for otherwise violating the traditional laws of war, the Order's proposition of military commissions is not preferred choice. The better approach is to use an alternative means of prosecution.

A menu of alternatives is available to the national government to permit effective prosecution of alleged terrorists and their supporters found in the United States, and thereby avoid the substantive and procedural defects in the Order. The choices include trials in federal district courts, international tribunals, or even UCMJ courts martial. Each has its advantages and its disadvantages with respect to the goal of swift and fair prosecution within the rule of law.

Other goals which some commentators now suggest are paramount and thus argue for the practical use of commissions—e.g., the need to avoid the requirement that US troops in combat give Miranda warnings to captured al Qaeda or Taliban,[100] courthouse, judge and juror protection, revelations of intelligence through open trials, the slow pace of trials, and the ability to admit into evidence under loose rules material that otherwise could not be admitted in federal District Court or even courts martial trials, such as hearsay—seem to us important but far less so (particularly since to a large extent they can be addressed) than the larger goal referred to above. One need only consider the impact on the development of international humanitarian law that the conduct and decisions of the Nuremberg Tribunal had—laying the ground work for the principle of individual responsibility for wrongful state acts—through its process of open trials, uniform procedures modeled primarily on the British and American systems and careful, written decisions to understand that while obtaining a guilty verdict is important, it is not all-important.

International Tribunals

The use of international tribunals, perhaps one created for the purpose of this prosecution, is possible. Nuremberg was certainly a precedent. Such a tribunal, however, presents problems of international representation on the bench, not least because of the divergence of views with our allies over the death penalty, and would, in all likelihood, be the only courts to which certain countries would transfer defendants within their custody given the political and cultural realities.[101]

Further, to avoid the spectacle of Judeo-Christian civilization sitting combined in judgment on the Muslim civilization—an image some say Bin Laden seeks to foster—participation by Islamic judges would be necessary. At that point, developing rules of procedure gets complicated. Further still, experience with recent international tribunals shows these entities to be truly slow in action, as well as expensive. In such tribunals, juries would not be a concern, but, even given the good faith of most judges, the protection of classified information would have to be assumed to be impossible.

The International Criminal Court ("ICC"), were it in effect, would be a likely tribunal for cases involving foreign defendants accused of violating either the international law of armed conflict or crimes against humanity.[102]

Significantly, crimes against humanity under Article 7 of the Rome Statute are not premised upon the existence of an "armed conflict" within the meaning of the Geneva Conventions and

Protocols but instead is premised on the occurrence of any of the listed acts directed toward a civilian population provided they are "widespread and systematic." Thus, this section would include within its subject matter jurisdiction the terrorist acts of 9/11 and others being discovered in the course of the anti-terror campaign. The ICC would be especially useful to try defendants in the custody of countries that might refuse to extradite defendants to the United States, whether for their own domestic political reasons or based on objections to capital punishment or to the procedures of military commissions. The ICC is not an option at this time because the Court is not yet established, due in large part to opposition to the statute by the United States.

Federal District Courts

Time-honored criminal proceedings in the Federal District Courts would be the tried and true solution, not least because it has been proven to work with respect to prosecuting terrorists, including members of al Qaeda. In fact, the federal government has already determined to take the first steps toward prosecuting Bin Laden in Federal District Court by seeking—and obtaining—his indictment in the Southern District of New York. It also will be prosecuting Zacarias Moussaoui, the so-called "20th hijacker", in Federal District Court in Virginia. However, the Federal District Courts may be less adapted to trying enemy combatants (lawful or unlawful) detained in armed conflict.

The idea that such trials are slow, that jurors would refuse to serve or that there would be so many defendants that the work would never be done does not strike us as persuasive. These courts are, in fact, contemplated for use in these circumstances. They have not only convicted al Qaeda members but also have successfully tried and convicted a plethora of serious spies in the service of foreign powers at both the CIA and FBI in recent years.

It should be recalled that the Constitution itself was conceived and drafted in a time of great concern regarding national security, and these issues were never far from the minds of the Framers. "American courts have tried international criminals who have violated the law of nations—including pirates and slave traders—since the beginning of the nation. We have convicted hijackers, terrorists and drug smugglers (including Panama's Manuel Noriega, who surrendered to American soldiers after extended military operations)."[103]

However, the circumstances of the 9/11 attacks would admittedly present exceptional difficulties in administering a fair jury trial where hardly any American citizen has not been touched by the events in controversy. Further, despite established procedures to control confidential information,[104] such procedures relate primarily to pre-trial procedures and are not impenetrable for determined wrongdoers. Nonetheless, while we believe these impediments could be overcome for the purposes of providing the required civilian trials in U.S. District Courts, they are more difficult to overcome for purposes of providing a law of war trial of a foreign combatant.

Courts Martial Under the UCMJ

For use abroad, the alternative we find most acceptable to the commissions proposed by the Order combines most of the benefits sought with fewest of the potential risks: court martial under the UCMJ. White House Counsel Alberto Gonzales described the long, successful and professional history of the American military justice this way: "The American military justice system is the finest in the world, with longstanding traditions of forbidding command influence on proceedings, of providing zealous advocacy by competent defense counsel, and of procedural fairness,"[105] (unfortunately, Judge Gonzales improperly ascribed these attributes to *military commissions* when they apply instead to *military courts martial,* a very different kind of tribunal).

Military courts martial, as described above, combine an essentially non-jury trial in a secure environment—a naval vessel or military base—pursuant to established rules of procedure, evidence and appeal based on written records. The due process provided in these courts is genuine, despite the old adage about military justice and military music, even while the trial process is made more efficient than in civilian courts. A criminal trial in a court martial setting is far quicker than a comparable one in a federal District Court, and not only are there provisions for presenting secret material in camera, the setting on a protected military installation would make such information all the more secure.[106] In any case, a public trial—as was given even to the worst members of the Third Reich—is desirable to demonstrate both the fairness of our system and our confidence that using it is not a sign of weakness but of strength.

A general court martial of persons arrested in the United States would, however, require statutory amendment to confer upon such a court clear jurisdiction to try cases not only under the present UCMJ, but also—to the extent that there is any doubt—under the international law of armed conflict, as well as such other laws as Congress may determine to apply. Absent Congressional action, such a court could be assured of constitutional validity for trials of alien defendants only outside the U.S. or of offenders within the United States for offenses within the traditional law of war.

Military Commissions

For the reasons explained in this Report, we do not recommend the use of military commissions, particularly as described in the Order, to prosecute persons arrested in the United States for acts not traditional violations of the laws of war. They are, however, a potential means of dealing with aliens arrested and tried abroad, but only, in our view, with procedures consistent with the rule of law.

One possible variation on the commissions contemplated by the Order would be military commissions under U.S. law and administration but including foreign jurists on the model of the post World War II war crimes commissions, using procedures consistent with international standards (though not necessarily the same as UCMJ courts martial). This would make them somewhat akin to purely international tribunals but under greater U.S. control as they would still be U.S. military commissions. However, lack of the right to a jury trial alone would prevent such hybrid commissions from adjudicating cases involving (i) aliens in the U.S. or (ii) U.S. citizens anywhere not tried for law of war offenses.

It is recommended in any case that at the appropriate time—which we note is not during a period of national emergency and armed conflict—the Congress examine the use of military commissions for the purpose of clarifying statutory authority therefore. The various Articles of the UCMJ that contemplate commissions could be supplemented by one which provides clear authority for their use and the circumstances in which the President may so establish them. Importantly, Congress could at that time provide the guidelines and framework for the ultimate procedures—e.g., standards of proof, nature of evidence—the President would issue as Commander-in-Chief for trials under such commissions.

IN SUMMATION

Viewing these alternatives on a spectrum of their qualities would show the military commission at the top with respect to U.S. control of confidential information and correspondingly at the bottom with respect to international credibility and procedural fairness, while an international tribunal would be at the reverse end of that spectrum, at least with respect to international credibility. Federal District Courts and UCMJ courts martial would be somewhere in the middle, with the District Courts having relatively higher credibility, lower control of confidential information, a slow pace and a high level of due process, and UCMJ courts martial in a somewhat reverse position.

Given the most likely circumstances here—prosecuting members and supporters of international terrorist organizations found and arrested *outside* the United States for offenses against the laws of war—we believe the choice of courts martial under the Uniform Code of Military Justice is a reasonable one and certainly preferable to military commissions where national security considerations truly require extraordinary measures while basic rights of due process still demand respect. With respect to persons arrested within the United States, Article III courts *must* constitutionally be used for offenders and offenses not involving the laws of war.

Moreover, UCMJ courts martial substantially meet the security needs that are most acute for the type of defendants likely to be apprehended abroad in a shooting war, including the foreign based command and control of al Qaeda. The domestic courts are, or can be made, sufficiently secure for the civilian type of defendants likely to be apprehended in the U.S. whether for committing acts of violence or for various supporting activities (*e.g.,* "harboring" or even stealing in order to raise cash) which are only questionably subject to the laws of war and in any case pose less severe security issues. In order to avoid the uncertainty inherent in applying the traditional definitions of the laws of war to contemporary circumstances, Congress should consider enacting a statutory definition appropriate to these circumstances.

In the last analysis, it is the behavior of a nation in a time of crisis that determines its greatness. Utilizing the historically fair, widely admired military justice system to prosecute abroad law of war offenses at this point in time where and when it is most appropriate—complete as this system is with rights and remedies available to defendants—while using Article III courts domestically, reflects a confidence in this nation's unique ability to balance the necessary expediency required at this moment with the deliberate fairness expected of it always.

APPENDIX A
NOVEMBER 13, 2001 MILITARY ORDER ISSUED BY PRESIDENT GEORGE W. BUSH

Detention, Treatment, and Trial of Certain Non-Citizens in the War Against Terrorism

By the authority vested in me as President and as Commander in Chief of the Armed Forces of the United States by the Constitution and the laws of the United States of America, including the Authorization for Use of Military Force Joint Resolution (Public Law 107-40, 115 Stat. 224) and sections 821 and 836 of title 10, United States Code, it is hereby ordered as follows.

Section 1. Findings.

(a) International terrorists, including members of al Qaida, have carried out attacks on United States diplomatic and military personnel and facilities abroad and on citizens and property within the United States on a scale that has created a state of armed conflict that requires the use of the United States Armed Forces.

(b) In light of grave acts of terrorism and threats of terrorism, including the terrorist attacks on September 11, 2001, on the headquarters of the United States Department of Defense in the national capital region, on the World Trade Center in New York, and on civilian aircraft such as in Pennsylvania, I proclaimed a national emergency on September 14, 2001 (Proc. 7463, Declaration of National Emergency by Reason of Certain Terrorist Attacks).

(c) Individuals acting alone and in concert involved in international terrorism possess both the capability and the intention to undertake further terrorist attacks against the United States that, if not detected and prevented, will cause mass deaths, mass injuries, and massive destruction of property, and may place at risk the continuity of the operations of the United States Government.

(d) The ability of the United States to protect the United States and its citizens, and to help its allies and other cooperating nations protect their nations and their citizens, from such further terrorist attacks depends in significant part upon using the United States Armed Forces to identify terrorists and those who support them, to disrupt their activities, and to eliminate their ability to conduct or support such attacks.

(e) To protect the United States and its citizens, and for the effective conduct of military operations and prevention of terrorist attacks, it is necessary for individuals subject to this order pursuant to section 2 hereof to be detained, and, when tried, to be tried for violations of the laws of war and other applicable laws by military tribunals.

(f) Given the danger to the safety of the United States and the nature of international terrorism, and to the extent provided by and under this order, I find consistent with section 836 of title 10, United States Code, that it is not practicable to apply in military commissions under this order the principles of law and the rules of evidence generally recognized in the trial of criminal cases in the United States district courts.

(g) Having fully considered the magnitude of the potential deaths, injuries, and property destruction that would result from potential acts of terrorism against the United States, and the probability that such acts will occur, I have determined that an extraordinary emergency exists for national defense purposes, that this emergency constitutes an urgent and compelling government interest, and that issuance of this order is necessary to meet the emergency.

Sec. 2. Definition and Policy.

(a) The term "individual subject to this order" shall mean any individual who is not a United States citizen with respect to whom I determine from time to time in writing that:

(1) there is reason to believe that such individual, at the relevant times,

(i) is or was a member of the organization known as al Qaida;

(ii) has engaged in, aided or abetted, or conspired to commit, acts of international terrorism, or acts in preparation therefor, that have caused, threaten to cause, or have as their aim to cause, injury to or adverse effects on the United States, its citizens, national security, foreign policy, or economy; or

(iii) has knowingly harbored one or more individuals described in subparagraphs (i) or (ii) of subsection 2(a)(1) of this order; and

(2) it is in the interest of the United States that such individual be subject to this order.

(b) It is the policy of the United States that the Secretary of Defense shall take all necessary measures to ensure that any individual subject to this order is detained in accordance with section 3, and, if the individual is to be tried, that such individual is tried only in accordance with section 4.

(c) It is further the policy of the United States that any individual subject to this order who is not already under the control of the Secretary of Defense but who is under the control of any other officer or agent of the United States or any State shall, upon delivery of a copy of such written determination to such officer or agent, forthwith be placed under the control of the Secretary of Defense.

Sec. 3. Detention Authority of the Secretary of Defense.

Any individual subject to this order shall be—
(a) detained at an appropriate location designated by the Secretary of Defense outside or within the United States;
(b) treated humanely, without any adverse distinction based on race, color, religion, gender, birth, wealth, or any similar criteria;
(c) afforded adequate food, drinking water, shelter, clothing, and medical treatment;
(d) allowed the free exercise of religion consistent with the requirements of such detention; and
(e) detained in accordance with such other conditions as the Secretary of Defense may prescribe.

Sec. 4. Authority of the Secretary of Defense Regarding Trials of Individuals Subject to this Order.

(a) Any individual subject to this order shall, when tried, be tried by military commission for any and all offenses triable by military commission that such individual is alleged to have committed, and may be punished in accordance with the penalties provided under applicable law, including life imprisonment or death.
(b) As a military function and in light of the findings in section 1, including subsection (f) thereof, the Secretary of Defense shall issue such orders and regulations, including orders for the appointment of one or more military commissions, as may be necessary to carry out subsection (a) of this section.
(c) Orders and regulations issued under subsection (b) of this section shall include, but not be limited to, rules for the conduct of the proceedings of military commissions, including pretrial, trial, and post-trial procedures, modes of proof, issuance of process, and qualifications of attorneys, which shall at a minimum provide for—
(1) military commissions to sit at any time and any place, consistent with such guidance regarding time and place as the Secretary of Defense may provide;
(2) a full and fair trial, with the military commission sitting as the triers of both fact and law;
(3) admission of such evidence as would, in the opinion of the presiding officer of the military commission (or instead, if any other member of the commission so requests at the time the presiding officer renders that opinion, the opinion of the commission rendered at that time by a majority of the commission), have probative value to a reasonable person;
(4) in a manner consistent with the protection of information classified or classifiable under Executive Order 12958 of April 17, 1995, as amended, or any successor Executive Order, protected by statute or rule from unauthorized disclosure, or otherwise protected by law,
   (A) the handling of, admission into evidence of, and access to materials and information, and
   (B) the conduct, closure of, and access to proceedings;
(5) conduct of the prosecution by one or more attorneys designated by the Secretary of Defense and conduct of the defense by attorneys for the individual subject to this order;
(6) conviction only upon the concurrence of two-thirds of the members of the commission present at the time of the vote, a majority being present;
(7) sentencing only upon the concurrence of two-thirds of the members of the commission present at the time of the vote, a majority being present; and

(8) submission of the record of the trial, including any conviction or sentence, for review and final decision by me or by the Secretary of Defense if so designated by me for that purpose.

Sec. 5. Obligation of Other Agencies to Assist the Secretary of Defense.

Departments, agencies, entities, and officers of the United States shall, to the maximum extent permitted by law, provide to the Secretary of Defense such assistance as he may request to implement this order.

Sec. 6. Additional Authorities of the Secretary of Defense.

(a) As a military function and in light of the findings in section 1, the Secretary of Defense shall issue such orders and regulations as may be necessary to carry out any of the provisions of this order.

(b) The Secretary of Defense may perform any of his functions or duties, and may exercise any of the powers provided to him under this order (other than under section 4(c)(8) hereof) in accordance with section 113(d) of title 10, United States Code.

Sec. 7. Relationship to Other Law and Forums.

(a) Nothing in this order shall be construed to—
(1) authorize the disclosure of state secrets to any person not otherwise authorized to have access to them;
(2) limit the authority of the President as Commander in Chief of the Armed Forces or the power of the President to grant reprieves and pardons; or
(3) limit the lawful authority of the Secretary of Defense, any military commander, or any other officer or agent of the United States or of any State to detain or try any person who is not an individual subject to this order.
(b) With respect to any individual subject to this order-
(1) military tribunals shall have exclusive jurisdiction with respect to offenses by the individual; and
(2) the individual shall not be privileged to seek any remedy or maintain any proceeding, directly or indirectly, or to have any such remedy or proceeding sought on the individual's behalf, in (i) any court of the United States, or any State thereof, (ii) any court of any foreign nation, or (iii) any international tribunal.
(c) This order is not intended to and does not create any right, benefit, or privilege, substantive or procedural, enforceable at law or equity by any party, against the United States, its departments, agencies, or other entities, its officers or employees, or any other person.
(d) For purposes of this order, the term "State" includes any State, district, territory, or possession of the United States.
(e) I reserve the authority to direct the Secretary of Defense, at any time hereafter, to transfer to a governmental authority control of any individual subject to this order. Nothing in this order shall be construed to limit the authority of any such governmental authority to prosecute any individual for whom control is transferred.

Sec. 8. Publication.

This order shall be published in the Federal Register.
GEORGE W. BUSH
THE WHITE HOUSE,
November 13, 2001

APPENDIX B
1942 ROOSEVELT ORDER

Proc. No. 2561, July 2, 1942, 7 F.R. 5101, 56 Stat. 1964

WHEREAS the safety of the United States demands that all enemies who have entered upon the territory of the United States as part of an invasion or predatory incursion, or who have entered in order to commit sabotage, espionage or other hostile or warlike acts, should be promptly tried in accordance with the law of war;

NOW, THEREFORE, I, Franklin D. Roosevelt, President of the United States of America and Commander in Chief of the Army and Navy of the United States, by virtue of the authority vested in me by the Constitution and the statutes of the United States, do hereby proclaim that all persons who are subjects, citizens or residents of any nation at war with the United States or who give obedience to or act under the direction of any such nation, and who during time of war enter or attempt to enter the United States or any territory or possession thereof, through coastal or boundary defenses, and are charged with committing or attempting or preparing to commit sabotage, espionage, hostile or warlike acts, or violations of the law of war, shall be subject to the law of war and to the jurisdiction of military tribunals; and that such persons shall not be privileged to seek any remedy or maintain any proceeding directly or indirectly, or to have any such remedy or proceeding sought on their behalf, in the courts of the United States, or of its States, territories, and possessions, except under such regulations as the Attorney General, with the approval of the Secretary of War, may from time to time prescribe.

APPENDIX C
CONGRESSIONAL RESOLUTION AUTHORIZATION FOR USE OF MILITARY FORCE

One Hundred Seventh Congress
of the United States of America
AT THE FIRST SESSION
Begun and held at the City of Washington on Wednesday,
the third day of January, two thousand and one
Joint Resolution
To authorize the use of United States Armed Forces against those responsible for the recent attacks launched against the United States.
Whereas, on September 11, 2001, acts of treacherous violence were committed against the United States and its citizens; and
Whereas, such acts render it both necessary and appropriate that the United States exercise its rights to self-defense and to protect United States citizens both at home and abroad; and
Whereas, in light of the threat to the national security and foreign policy of the United States posed by these grave acts of violence; and
Whereas, such acts continue to pose an unusual and extraordinary threat to the national security and foreign policy of the United States; and
Whereas, the President has authority under the Constitution to take action to deter and prevent acts of international terrorism against the United States: Now, therefore, be it
    Resolved by the Senate and House of Representatives of the United States of
    America in Congress assembled,

Section 1. Short Title

This joint resolution may be cited as the 'Authorization for Use of Military Force'.

Sec. 2. Authorization for Use of United States Armed Forces.

(a) IN GENERAL— That the President is authorized to use all necessary and appropriate force against those nations, organizations, or persons he determines planned, authorized, committed, or aided the terrorist attacks that occurred on September 11, 2001, or harbored such organizations or persons, in order to prevent any future acts of international terrorism against the United States by such nations, organizations or persons.

(b) War Powers Resolution Requirements—

(1) SPECIFIC STATUTORY AUTHORIZATION— Consistent with section 8(a)(1) of the War Powers Resolution, the Congress declares that this section is intended to constitute specific statutory authorization within the meaning of section 5(b) of the War Powers Resolution.

(2) APPLICABILITY OF OTHER REQUIREMENTS— Nothing in this resolution supercedes any requirement of the War Powers Resolution.

Speaker of the House of Representatives.

Vice President of the United States and
President of the Senate.

APPENDIX D
USA PATRIOT ACT OF 2001 (IN PART)

Public Law No: 107-56, October 26, 2001.

SEC. 412. MANDATORY DETENTION OF SUSPECTED TERRORISTS; HABEAS CORPUS; JUDICIAL REVIEW.

(a) IN GENERAL— The Immigration and Nationality Act (8 U.S.C. 1101 et seq.) is amended by inserting after section 236 the following:

"SEC. 236A. (a) DETENTION OF TERRORIST ALIENS—

'(1) CUSTODY— The Attorney General shall take into custody any alien who is certified under paragraph (3).

'(2) RELEASE— Except as provided in paragraphs (5) and (6), the Attorney General shall maintain custody of such an alien until the alien is removed from the United States. Except as provided in paragraph (6), such custody shall be maintained irrespective of any relief from removal for which the alien may be eligible, or any relief from removal granted the alien, until the Attorney General determines that the alien is no longer an alien who may be certified under paragraph (3). If the alien is finally determined not to be removable, detention pursuant to this subsection shall terminate.

'(3) CERTIFICATION— The Attorney General may certify an alien under this paragraph if the Attorney General has reasonable grounds to believe that the alien—

'(A) is described in section 212(a)(3)(A)(i), 212(a)(3)(A)(iii), 212(a)(3)(B), 237(a)(4)(A)(i), 237(a)(4)(A)(iii), or 237(a)(4)(B); or

'(B) is engaged in any other activity that endangers the national security of the United States.

'(4) NONDELEGATION— The Attorney General may delegate the authority provided under paragraph (3) only to the Deputy Attorney General. The Deputy Attorney General may not delegate such authority.

'(5) COMMENCEMENT OF PROCEEDINGS— The Attorney General shall place an alien detained under paragraph (1) in removal proceedings, or shall charge the alien with a criminal offense, not later than 7 days after the commencement of such detention. If the requirement of the preceding sentence is not satisfied, the Attorney General shall release the alien.

'(6) LIMITATION ON INDEFINITE DETENTION— An alien detained solely under paragraph (1) who has not been removed under section 241(a)(1)(A), and whose removal is unlikely in the reasonably foreseeable future, may be detained for additional periods of up to six months only if the release of the alien will threaten the national security of the United States or the safety of the community or any person.

'(7) REVIEW OF CERTIFICATION— The Attorney General shall review the certification made under paragraph (3) every 6 months. If the Attorney General determines, in the Attorney General's discretion, that the certification should be revoked, the alien may be released on such conditions as the Attorney General deems appropriate, unless such release is otherwise prohibited by law. The alien may request each 6 months in writing that the Attorney General reconsider the certification and may submit documents or other evidence in support of that request.

'(b) HABEAS CORPUS AND JUDICIAL REVIEW—

'(1) IN GENERAL— Judicial review of any action or decision relating to this section (including judicial review of the merits of a determination made under subsection (a)(3) or (a)(6)) is available exclusively in habeas corpus proceedings consistent with this subsection. Except as provided in the preceding sentence, no court shall have jurisdiction to review, by habeas corpus petition or otherwise, any such action or decision.

'(2) APPLICATION—

'(A) IN GENERAL- Notwithstanding any other provision of law, including section 2241 (a) of title 28, United States Code, habeas corpus proceedings described in paragraph (1) may be initiated only by an application filed with—

'(i) the Supreme Court;

'(ii) any justice of the Supreme Court;

'(iii) any circuit judge of the United States Court of Appeals for the District of Columbia Circuit; or

'(iv) any district court otherwise having jurisdiction to entertain it.

'(B) APPLICATION TRANSFER— Section 2241(b) of title 28, United States Code, shall apply to an application for a writ of habeas corpus described in subparagraph (A).

'(3) APPEALS— Notwithstanding any other provision of law, including section 2253 of title 28, in habeas corpus proceedings described in paragraph (1) before a circuit or district judge, the final order shall be subject to review, on appeal, by the United States Court of Appeals for the District of Columbia Circuit. There shall be no right of appeal in such proceedings to any other circuit court of appeals.

'(4) RULE OF DECISION— The law applied by the Supreme Court and the United States Court of Appeals for the District of Columbia Circuit shall be regarded as the rule of decision in habeas corpus proceedings described in paragraph (1)."

APPENDIX E
WAR CRIMES ACT: 18 U.S.C. 2441(SEC. 2441, WAR CRIMES)

(a) Offense.—Whoever, whether inside or outside the United States, commits a war crime, in any of the circumstances described in subsection (b), shall be fined under this title or imprisoned for life or any term of years, or both, and if death results to the victim, shall also be subject to the penalty of death.

(b) Circumstances.—The circumstances referred to in subsection (a) are that the person committing such war crime or the victim of such war crime is a member of the Armed Forces of the United States or a national of the United States (as defined in section 101 of the Immigration and Nationality Act).

(c) Definition.—As used in this section the term "war crime" means any conduct—

(1) defined as a grave breach in any of the international conventions signed at Geneva 12 August 1949, or any protocol to such convention to which the United States is a party;

(2) prohibited by Article 23, 25, 27, or 28 of the Annex to the Hague Convention IV, Respecting the Laws and Customs of War on Land, signed 18 October 1907;

(3) which constitutes a violation of common Article 3 of the international conventions signed at Geneva, 12 August 1949, or any protocol to such convention to which the United States is a party and which deals with non-international armed conflict; or

(4) of a person who, in relation to an armed conflict and contrary to the provisions of the Protocol on Prohibitions or Restrictions on the Use of Mines, Booby-Traps and Other Devices as amended at Geneva on 3 May 1996 (Protocol II as amended on 3 May 1996), when the United States is a party to such Protocol, willfully kills or causes serious injury to civilians.

NOTES

1. The undersigned Chairs and Committee Member, Richard Hartzman.

2. Our Report named the following: White House Counsel, Albert R. Gonzalez; William Haynes, DOD General Counsel; and Legal Adviser to the National Security Council, Richard B. Bellinger, among the presenters in that informative program, who had been involved in the drafting and issuance of the Military Order. It is notable that legislative counsel (who spoke in other parts of the seminar) had not participated in the origins of the Military Order, since Congress had not been consulted. Equally worrying was that the Military Order had been rushed past the expert JAG [Judge Advocate General] attorneys without regard for their views.

3. See letter from Robert E. Hirshon, President, American Bar Association, to William J. Haynes II, General Counsel, U.S. Department of Defense enclosing resolution of the House of Delegates, available at http://www.abanet.org/poladv/letters/107th/militarytrib8c.pdf.

4. Hamdan v. Rumsfeld, 548 U.S. __(2006).

5. Pub. L. No. 109-366, 120 Stat. 2600 (Oct. 17, 2006).

6. This report was prepared by the Committee on Military Affairs and Justice, which was established by the Association of the Bar of the City of New York in 1946. Since that time, it has engaged in study and comment on the military justice system and other legal aspects of military affairs, including the use and regulation of the armed forces. The Committee was involved in the drafting of the Uniform Code of Military Justice.

7. The Order is reproduced in Appendix A.

8. The organization known as al Qaeda is widely believed to be the propagator of many terrorist acts directed toward the United States, including the horrific ones of September 11, 2001 in New York City and Washington, D.C.

9. Military Order, at §2(a).

10. Military Order, at §3(a).

11. Military Order, at §7(b)(2).

12. Military Order, at §3(a).

13. 10 U.S.C. §§801–946 (hereinafter, the "UCMJ").

14. Military Order, at §1(f).

15. As will be explained, events are fast moving and in the course of preparing this Report, it appears as if the Administration may have changed, or may be changing, its position with respect to this issue.

16. U.S. Constitution, Article 1, Section 9, Clause 2.

17. The President has said that al Qaeda operates in no less than 60 nations, including the United States, but because it is believed that Osama bin-Laden, its head, is in Afghanistan, it is that country which is the organization's base. On September 20, 2001, President Bush spoke to Congress: "This group and its leader —a person named Osama bin Laden—are linked to many other organizations in different countries, including the Egyptian Islamic Jihad and the Islamic Movement of Uzbekistan. There are thousands of these terrorists in more than 60 countries. They are recruited from their own nations and neighborhoods and brought to camps in places like Afghanistan, where they are trained in the tactics of terror. They are sent back to their homes or sent to hide in countries around the world to plot evil and destruction. The leadership of al Qaeda has great influence in Afghanistan and supports the Taliban regime in controlling most of that country. In Afghanistan, we see al Qaeda's vision for the world." Quoted on White House Web Site, subsection *America Responds, visited* November 24, 2001.

18. S.J.Res.23, September 18, 2001 (Public Law No: 107-40).

19. United Nations Security Council Resolutions 1368 (September 12, 2001) and 1373 (September 28, 2001).

20. In a proclamation of that date, the President declared that "by virtue of the authority vested in me as President by the Constitution and the laws of the United States, I hereby declare that the national emergency has existed since September 11, 2001, and pursuant to the National Emergencies Act (50 U.S.C. 1601 et seq.), I intend to utilize the following statutes: sections 123, 123a, 527, 2201(c) 12006, and 12302 of title 10, United States Code, and sections 331, 359, and 367 of title 14, United States Code." The President reported this declaration to Congress in a letter dated September 24, 2001: "Pursuant to section 204(b) of the International Emergency Economic Powers Act, 50 U.S.C. 1703(b) (IEEPA), and section 301 of the National Emergencies Act, 50 U.S.C. 1631, I hereby report that I have exercised my statutory authority to declare a national emergency in response to the unusual and extraordinary threat posed to the national security, foreign policy, and economy of the United States by grave acts of terrorism and threats of terrorism committed by foreign terrorists, including the September 11, 2001, terrorist attacks at the World Trade Center, New York, at the Pentagon, and in Pennsylvania."

21. CNN website, http://www.cnn.com/2001/HEALTH/conditions/11/24/connecticut.anthrax/index. html, *visited* November 24, 2001.

22. This report was informed by statements made at a meeting of the ABA Standing Committee on Law and National Security—held in Washington, D.C. on November 29 and 30, 2001. Persons with whom the authors spoke included the White House Counsel, the General Counsel of the Department of Defense, the Legal Adviser to the National Security Counsel, Counsel to the Chairman of the Joint Chiefs of Staff and others in similar capacities. (Hereinafter, references to this event will be to "ABA Meeting.")

23. It has been suggested that the Order may have been issued by the President under his "Executive Powers," such as they are, but its specific designation as a "military order" seems clearly intended to invoke his power as Commander-in-Chief and not as the chief executive officer.

24. *See, e.g.,* 10 U.S.C. §826.

25. 317 U.S. 1 (1942) ("Quirin").

26. President Bush said on November 19: "These are extraordinary times. And I would remind those who don't understand the decision I made [regarding using a military tribunal] that Franklin Roosevelt made the same decision in World War Two. Those were extraordinary times as well." *Bush Defends Military Court Option in U.S. Attacks,* Reuters, Monday, November 19, 2001, 6:06 PM ET, *reprinted at* http:// dailynews.yahoo.com/h/nm/20011119/pl/attack_bush_courts_dc_6.html, *viewed* November 26, 2001.

27. The 1942 order is set forth in Appendix B ("1942 Order").

28. See historical examples from the Revolution, the Mexican War and the Civil War cited in *Quirin, supra,* at notes 9 and 10.

29. "[A]t least since 1886, we have extended to the person and property of resident aliens important constitutional guaranties—such as the due process of law of the Fourteenth Amendment. *Yick Wo v. Hopkins,* 118 U.S. 356. But, in extending constitutional protections beyond the citizenry, the Court has been at pains to point out that it was the alien's presence within its territorial jurisdiction that gave the Judiciary power to act." *Johnson v. Eisentrager,* 339 U.S. 763, 770 (1950). Even in U.S. possessions the right to trial

by jury was not guaranteed and only extended when so provided by Congress. *See e.g., Dorr v. U.S.,* 195 U.S. 138 (1904). Citizens are, however, entitled to trial by jury, even abroad, except in time of war. *See, Reid v. Covert,* consolidated with *Kinsella v. Krueger,* 354 US 1 (1957); *Kinsella v. Singleton,* 361 US 234 (1960); *Grisham v. Hagan,* 361 US 278 (1960); and *McElroy v. Guargliardo,* 361 U.S. 281(1960), which overrule prior UCMJ court martial/commission jurisdiction over US citizen spouses accompanying US forces abroad, invalidating inconsistent provisions of the UCMJ. This is the background for Pub. L. 106-523, 18 U.S.C. 3261 *et seq.,* which creates Article III jurisdiction in such cases to fill the gap. In *Reid v. Covert* the Court allowed court-martial jurisdiction to continue over such persons in time of war, but the Court of Military Appeals limited that jurisdiction to declared war; *U.S. v. Averette,* 19 C.M.A. 363 (1970). *See also, The Military Extraterritorial Jurisdiction Act of 2000: Closing the Gap,* 95 Am. J. Intl. L. 446 (2001).

30. *Id.,* at 29.

31. U.S. Constitution, Article I, Section 8, Clause 9.

32. U.S. Constitution, Article I, Section 8, Clause 10.

33. U.S. Constitution, Article I, Section 8, Clause 14.

34. In addition to more direct authority, Congress has recognized military commissions in passing. The legislative history of the War Crimes Act of 1996 includes the statement by the House Judiciary Committee that such statute "is not intended to affect in any way the jurisdiction of any court martial, military commission, or other military tribunal under any article of the Uniform Code of Military Justice or under the law of war or the law of nations." H.R. Rep. No. 104-698 at 12 (1996).

35. 10 U.S.C. 821.

36. Despite the President's assertion of Section 21 as authority, some commentators argue that such Section allows the President's authority without creating it. The distinction is metaphysical if Congress has the authority, as we believe, to provide preemptively for the rules and regulations of the armed forces and compliance with the laws of nations, including the laws of war, if it chooses to do so. Consequently the terms under which Congress permits the President to act concurrently are equivalent to rules authorizing the President to act. *Compare Youngstown Sheet & Tube Co. v. Sawyer,* 343 U.S. 579 (1952) (the "Steel Seizure Case") where the President was found to have acted directly contrary to the specific intent of Congress in a matter subject to Congressional power.

37. Emphasis supplied.

38. Not long before the adoption of the Constitution, Americans were on the receiving end of the military justice of an occupying power when, during the Revolutionary War, British military tribunals became the default criminal justice system successively in Boston, Newport, New York, Philadelphia and Charleston, some of whose judgments continued to be respected by American authorities after the war. *See generally,* F.B. Wiener, *Civilians under Military Justice,* (Chicago, 1967) at 134.

39. The Department of Defense defines the law of war as follows:

> 3.1. Law of War. That part of international law that regulates the conduct of armed hostilities. It is often called the law of armed conflict. The law of war encompasses all international law for the conduct of hostilities binding on the United States or its individual citizens, including treaties and international agreements to which the United States is a party, and applicable customary international law.

Department of Defense Directive Number 5100.77, December 9, 1998, viewed November 25, 2001 on the Defense Department web site at http://www.dtic.mil/whs/directives/corres/pdf/d510077_120998/ d510077p.pdf (emphasis supplied). The law of war is not, however, coextensive with the broader field of international law or law of nations. For example, money laundering and drug trafficking are the subject of international treaties, but do not relate to the conduct of hostilities.

40. For example, Convention Relative to the Treatment of Prisoners of War, Article 2, opened for signature Aug. 12, 1949, 6 U.S.T. 3316, 75 U.N.T.S. 135.

41. Frederic de Mulinen, *International Committee on The Red of the Red Cross Handbook on the Law of War for Armed Forces* (ICRC 1987), at 3.

42. Part I, Art. 1(1), Protocol Additional to the Geneva Conventions of 12 August 1949, and Relating to the Protection of Victims of Non-International Armed Conflicts (Protocol II), *opened for signature* Dec. 2, 1977, 1125 U.N.T.S. 609.

43. It has been suggested that the limitations on the international law of armed conflict tending to exclude most violence not between nations was deliberately intended to deny belligerent status to dissidents so that national authorities a freer hand in suppressing them. *See generally* George H. Aldrich, *The Law of War on Land,* 94 Am. J. Intl. L. 42 (2000). "Perversely, the application of Protocol II is far too narrow....It is perhaps cynical, but undoubtedly true, that this narrow applicability of Protocol II explains why there are now 147 states party to it." *Id.* at 60.

44. A.G. James Speed, *Opinion on the Constitutional Power of the Military to Try and Execute the Assassins of the President,* Attorney General's Office (Washington, July, 1865). Emphasis supplied.

45. *See, e.g.,* Bob Woodward, *Bin Laden Said to "Own" the Taliban,* The Washington Post, October 11, 2001, at A1.

46. The conceptual difficulty of characterizing this conflict is typified by the fact that although the U.S. may be at war "in Afghanistan", it is not at war "with Afghanistan." Nationals of Afghanistan are not per se "enemy aliens" and may even be allies, without any reliable mechanism, legal or otherwise, to distinguish friend from foe. It is an ambiguous environment in which to apply the black and white distinctions of the classic law of war.

47. Order, at Sec. 2.

48. *See e.g., United States v. Verdugo-Urquidez,* 494 U.S. 259 (1990).

49. *See e.g., Johnson v. Eisentrager,* 339 U.S. 763 (1950).

50. 71 U.S. 2 (4 Wall.) (1866).

51. Whether the Taliban is recognized as the *de jure* government of Afghanistan (which is doubtful considering that that government has been recognized neither by the United Nations nor most of the international community) or as a dissident force being fought by the lawful government, their status for law of war purposes is the same. In the first case, there would be a conflict between states subject to the 1949 Geneva Conventions. In the second, under 1977 Geneva Protocol II, as noted *supra,* they could be deemed dissidents in control of territory of a High Contracting Party and also subject to the protection of that treaty.

52. The Justice Department recently released a partial list of those persons arrested in connection with the anti-terrorist campaign (although not necessarily pursuant to the Order), including, for some of them, the crimes of which they are accused. It is reported that some of the crimes alleged are civilian in nature, even if the larger purpose is to raise money for an organization like al Qaeda. For example: "Three more men on the list were indicted in New Jersey for conspiracy to embezzle, according to Michael Drewniak, a spokesman for the United States Attorney's office in Newark. The men, Hussein and Nasser Abduali and Rabi Ahmed, were charged with conspiring to buy, receive and possess $43,270 worth of stolen corn flakes. All three have been released pending trial." Lewin, *Accusations Against 93 Vary Widely,* New York Times on the Web, November 28, 2001.

53. In his concurring opinion in *Hirayabashi v. U.S.,* 320 U.S. 81 (1943), Justice Murphy said, "We give great deference to the judgment of the Congress and of the military authorities as to what is necessary in the effective prosecution of the war, but we can never forget that there are constitutional boundaries which it is our duty to uphold. It would not be supposed, for instance, that public elections could be suspended or that the prerogatives of the courts could be set aside, or that persons not charged with offenses against the law of war (see Ex parte Quirin, 317 U.S. 1, 63 S.Ct. 2, 87 L.Ed. 3) could be deprived of due process of law and the benefits of trial by jury, in the absence of a valid declaration of martial law." *Id.* at 110.

54. 10 U.S.C. 836.

55. Such procedures had not yet been issued at the time this Report was prepared.

56. Differences between the procedures required by the Order and those assured by the UCMJ include the following:

- Proof beyond reasonable doubt (10 U.S.C. Sec.851(c)), whereas the Order does not specify a standard of proof, which could under minimum standards of the laws of war be less than proof beyond reasonable doubt.

- The right of the defendant to be present at proceedings (10 U.S.C. Sec. 839), whereas the Order allows for the possibility of secret ex parte proceedings (Sec. 4(c)(4)(b).

- Defense role in selection of the court-martial panel, whereas the members of a military commission convened under the Order would not be subject to challenge by the defense.

- Defense right to choose counsel (10 U.S.C. Sec. 838(b)) whereas the Order limits defense counsel to attorneys "subject to this order" (Sec. 4(c)(5).

- Unanimity in applying death sentence (10 U.S.C. Sec. 852(a)), whereas the Order provides for "conviction only upon the concurrence of two-thirds of the members of the commission" (Sec. 4(c) (6).

- - Appellate review of decisions (10 U.S.C. Sec. 866, 867, 867(a), 869), whereas the Order precludes any appellate review by the courts (Sec. 7(b)), and allows review only insofar as the regulations promulgated under the Order may provide as a matter of administration.

57. Military Order, §7(b)(1).

58. UCMJ, §802 (a)(9).

59. The Order provides only that the detainees be treated humanely; given adequate food, water, shelter and medicine, allowed the free exercise of religion, and otherwise be subject to rules to be made by the Secretary of Defense. It even provides that detention may be outside the borders of the United States. Order, at §3. We assume that circumvention of the rights of aliens within the U.S. by arrest and forced removal from the country for delivery to a remote trial location as literally permitted by this section of the Order (*i.e.,* kidnapping) would violate those rights.

60. William Blackstone, *Commentaries,* 3:129–37 (1768), *reprinted in* The Founders' Constitution, Vol. 1, at 324–327 (University of Chicago Press 1987).

61. Joseph Story, *Commentaries on the Constitution,* 3:§§1333-36 (1883), *reprinted in*The Founders' Constitution, supra (hereinafter " Story, *Commentaries on the Constitution*"), at 342.

62. Remarks of Chief Justice William H. Rehnquist, 100th Anniversary Celebration Of the Norfolk and Portsmouth Bar Association, Norfolk, Virginia, May 3, 2000 *available at* http://www.supremecourtus.gov/publicinfo/speeches/sp_05-03-00.html (hereinafter "Rehnquist Remarks").

63. *See, e.g., Wong Wing v. United States,* 163 U.S. 228, 238 (1886) (resident aliens entitled to Fifth Amendment rights); *Kwong Hai Chew v. Colding,* 344 U.S. 590, 596 (1953) (resident alien is a "person" within the meaning of the Fifth Amendment); *Mathews v. Diaz,* 426 U.S. 69, 77 (1976) ("There are literally millions of aliens within the jurisdiction of the United States. The Fifth Amendment, as well as the Fourteenth Amendment, protects every one of these persons from deprivation of life, liberty, or property without due process of law. Even one whose presence in this country is unlawful, involuntary, or transitory is entitled to that constitutional protection.") (citations omitted); *United States v. Verdugo-Urquidez,* 494 U.S. 259 (1990) (distinguishing reach of Fourth Amendment to cover only "the people"—as in "we the people"—from Fifth Amendment's protection of "any person"). *See also United States v. bin Laden,* 132 F.Supp.2d 168, 181 (2001) (a non-citizen whose only connections to the United States are his alleged violations of U.S. law and his subsequent U.S. prosecution is entitled to due process of law under the Fifth Amendment).

64. "In Ex parte Quirin, 317 U.S. 1, we held that status as an enemy alien did not foreclose "consideration by the courts of petitioners' contentions that the Constitution and laws of the United States constitutionally enacted forbid their trial by military commission." Id. at 25. This we did in the face of a presidential proclamation denying such prisoners access to our courts.... [I]n Yamashita v. United States, 327 U.S. 1, we held that courts could inquire whether a military commission, promptly after hostilities had ceased, had lawful authority to try and condemn a Japanese general charged with violating the law of war before hostilities had ceased. There we stated: "[T]he Executive branch of the Government could not, unless there was suspension of the writ, withdraw from the courts the duty and power to make such inquiry

into the authority of the commission as may be made by habeas corpus." Id. at 9." Black, J. dissenting in *Johnson v. Eisentrager,* 339 U.S. 763, 794 (1950).

65. *See, e.g.,* 28 USC 2241(c).

66. *See Ex parte Merryman,* 17 Fed. Cas. 144 (No. 9487), (C.C.D. Md. 1861) (Chief Justice Taney, sitting as a circuit judge, wrote: "I had supposed it to be one of those points in constitutional law upon which there was no difference of opinion,... that the privilege of the writ could not be suspended, except by act of Congress." *Id.* at 148.) After Lincoln ignored the decision and kept Merryman in prison, Congress acted to authorize the suspension of the writ of habeas corpus. *See also,* St. George Tucker, *Blackstone's Commentaries* 1:App.290-92 (1803), *reprinted in* The Founders' Constitution, supra, at 329: "In the United States, [the writ] can be suspended, only, by the authority of congress; but not whenever congress may think proper; for it cannot be suspended, unless in cases of actual rebellion, or invasion." *Accord,* Story, *Commentaries on the Constitution, supra,* at 342 ("It would seem, as the power is given to congress to suspend the writ of habeas corpus in cases of rebellion or invasion, that the right to judge, whether exigency had arisen, must exclusively belong to that body.")

67. The Resolution is set forth in Appendix C.

68. Public Law 107-56. Interestingly, Senator Patrick Leahy, Chairman of the Senate Judiciary Committee, which took the Administration's urgent request for the Act and reported it out rapidly, albeit without significant modification, expressed surprise that the Administration should have requested this Act on an urgent basis, failed to act under it and then issued—without any prior notice to Congress, much less authority from it—the Military Order, which contains very different provisions. Comments by Senator Patrick Leahy made on the television news show *Meet the Press,* November 25, 2001. Perhaps the President's action is not so surprising considering the refusal of Congress to approve the full range of powers sought by the Administration. Having failed to get the desired statutory authority, the President acted as if he did not need it.

69. Section 412 of the USA Patriot Act is reproduced in Appendix D.

70. It should be noted that the USA Patriot Act is viewed by many civil liberties lawyers as "dangerous" in its expansion of the definition of what constitutes terrorism, the basis for an alien's detention and the like. *See, e.g.,* New York Times, November 25, 2001, A1, B4.

71. Nor, for that matter, did "inherent powers never expressly granted but said to have accrued to the office from the customs and claims of preceding administrations" provide the President authority to seize private industry to aid the war effort, *id.,* at 645.

72. *See,* Comments by Assistant Attorney General Michael Chertoff and White House Counsel Alberto Gonzales, ABA Meeting.

73. They may also be less than accurate. It is reported that Attorney General Ashcroft did try to get Congress to suspend the privilege of the writ of habeas corpus when it adopted the USA Patriot Act. Newsweek, Dec. 10, 2001, at 48, reports that the secret first draft of the anti-terrorism bill presented by the Justice Department had a section entitled "suspension of the Writ of Habeas Corpus." Rep. Sensenbrenner (Chairman of the House Judiciary Committee said: "that stuck out like a sore thumb. It was the first thing I [crossed] out." Other claims made by Administration officers likewise do not flow from the text of the Order, *e.g.,* that the Order can provide justice "close to where our forces are fighting," Alberto R. Gonzales, *Martial Justice, Full and Fair,* New York Times, November 30, 2001 ("Gonzales Op-Ed"), whereas the Order can plainly be used for trial in the United States and even provides that the Department of Justice transfer to the Department of Defense subject persons it is detaining; it cannot be imagined that Judge Gonzales is proposing that persons of that group who might be tried under the Order would be shipped to Afghanistan to be close to the combat during their trial. Judge Gonzales also writes that "The order preserves judicial review in civilian courts," whereas Section 7 specifically precludes *any* proceeding or *any* remedy in *any* court, and when asked at the ABA meeting whether this Section meant denial of the writ of habeas corpus, the Assistant Attorney General for the Criminal Division Michael Chertoff said it did not but was intended to "prevent injunctions *and appeals* from military courts," thus at odds with Judge Gonzales' assertions published the next day.

74. 1942 Order.

75. Section 21 provides:

Whenever there is a declared war between the United States and any foreign nation or government, or any invasion or predatory incursion is perpetrated, attempted or threatened against the territory of the United States by any foreign nation or government, and the President makes public proclamation of the event, all natives, citizens, denizens, or subjects of the hostile nation or government, being of the age of fourteen years and upward, who shall be within the United States and not actually naturalized, shall be liable to be apprehended, restrained, secured, and removed as alien enemies. The President is authorized in any such event, by his proclamation thereof, or other public act, to direct the conduct to be observed on the part of the United States, toward the aliens who become so liable; the manner and degree of the restraint to which they shall be subject and in what cases, and upon what security their residence shall be permitted, and to provide for the removal of those who, not being permitted to reside within the United States, refuse or neglect to depart therefrom; and to establish any other regulations which are found necessary in the premises and for the public safety.

76. "The resident enemy alien is constitutionally subject to summary arrest, internment and deportation whenever a "declared war" exists. Courts will entertain his plea for freedom from Executive custody only to ascertain the existence of a state of war and whether he is an alien enemy and so subject to the Alien Enemy Act. Once these jurisdictional elements have been determined, courts will not inquire into any other issue as to his internment. Ludecke v. Watkins, 335 U.S. 160." *Johnson v. Eisentrager,* supra at 775.

77. President Gerald Ford issued a national apology in 1976, calling the actions against Americans of Japanese descent a "setback to fundamental American principles." Presidential Proclamation No. 4417, 41 Fed. Reg. 7741 (1976). The Proclamation formally rescinded Executive Order No. 9066, issued in 1942. Subsequently, compensation was paid to U.S.-citizen detainees.

78. Commission on Wartime Relocation and Internment of Civilians, *Personal Justice Denied* (1982), at 3, 10, cited in Dycus, et. al, eds. *National Security Law,* (2d Ed. 1997), at 572–573.

79. Gonzales Op-Ed, *supra.*

80. ABA Meeting, November 30, 2001.

81. Rehnquist Remarks, *supra.*

82. Because of this conclusion, it is not necessary to determine whether the circumstances permitting suspension of the privilege of the writ of habeas corpus—rebellion or invasion—have occurred and have been found to have occurred by the Congress, although it seems plain that the former event has not and the latter is dubious.

83. It is interesting to note that the delays associated with such challenges do not seem to concern the Administration. The Department of Defense General Counsel, William Haynes, when asked by the Committee at the ABA Meeting whether Section 7 was being interpreted as a prohibition on habeas corpus proceedings responded: "I am sure that this will be challenged when and if this [Order] is employed," concluding that he believed the courts would upheld the President's authority.

84. By comparison in the *Quirin* case, the defendants were acknowledged members of the German military and consequently, without dispute, subject to the claimed jurisdiction of the 1942 commission.

85. 18 USC 2441, set forth in Appendix E.

86. Department of Defense Directive 5100.77, DOD Law of War Program (Dec. 9, 1998).

87. It is not within the purview of this Report to determine or analyze the crimes and/or violations of law, whether they are international or domestic, for which defendants subject to the Order may be tried.

88. *Re G.G.,* unpublished, Military Court of Cassation, Sept. 5, 1997, and *Re N.,* unpublished, Military Court of Appeal, May 26, 2000, http://www.icrc.org/ihl-nat.nsf (visited Dec. 3, 2001). The trial court and intermediate appellate courts were composed of military personnel. The defendants had civilian counsel.

89. It has been argued widely that the use of commissions is necessary to ensure convictions which may not be obtainable in other for a. *See, e.g., Terrorists on Trial—II,* Wall Street Journal Review and Outlook, December 4, 2001: "As recently as 1996, the Clinton Administration rejected Sudan's offer to turn over Osama bin Laden because it didn't think it had enough evidence to convict him in a criminal court. A military tribunal would certainly have come in handy then."

90. Another reason for concern is recognition of terrorists as potentially lawful belligerents. If, for example, some al Qaeda members wearing a uniform and bearing arms were captured while attacking a U.S. military installation (such as U.S.S. Cole or a Marine barracks or the Pentagon), they would be

entitled to treatment as prisoners of war and not criminals once the U.S. government had declared the laws of war to be applicable. Most countries insist on treating terrorists as common criminals and go to great lengths to avoid application of the laws of war. *See,* discussion of the Geneva definitions of armed conflict, *infra.*

91. An end date has been recognized by the Supreme Court as important. *See, e.g., Duncan v. Kahanamoku,* 327 U.S. 304 (1946), which struck down martial law in Hawaii so long after the invasion. There, the defendant had violated a military order covering some of the aspects of daily life, which order remained in place and whose violations were punishable only in military tribunals. In a concurring opinion, Chief Justice Stone noted that the bars and restaurants had reopened, and so the alleged crimes in question (essentially civilian ones), should have been referred to civil courts.

92. *See, War on Terror 'May Last 50 Years,'* BBCi, October 27, 2001, available at http://news.bbc.co.uk/hi/english/uk/newsid_1623000/1623036.stm, *visited* December 4, 2001.

93. *See,* Robinson O. Everett, *Military Justice in the Armed Forces of the United States* (Military Service Publishing Co. 1956): "If an undeclared war suffices to permit trial of a spy by court-martial or by military commission, a subsidiary issue is when that jurisdiction comes to an end. Had there been a declared war, military jurisdiction would continue until there was some formal proclamation of peace." *Id.,* at 30.

94. *See, e.g.,* remarks by the General Counsel of the Department of Defense at the ABA Meeting.

95. *See, e.g.,* the remarks at the ABA Meeting of DoD General Counsel William Haynes; Senior Associate Counsel and Legal Advisor to the National Security Council John B. Bellinger III; and White House Counsel Alberto Gonzales.

96. Rehnquist said:

> The courts, for their part, have largely reserved the decisions favoring civil liberties in wartime to be handed down after the war was over. Again, we see the truth in the maxim Inter Arma Silent Leges —time of war the laws are silent. To lawyers and judges, this may seem a thoroughly undesirable state of affairs, but in the greater scheme of things it may be best for all concerned. The fact that judges are loath to strike down wartime measures while the war is going on is demonstrated both by our experience in the Civil War and in World War II. This fact represents something more than some sort of patriotic hysteria that holds the judiciary in its grip; it has been felt and even embraced by members of the Supreme Court who have championed civil liberty in peacetime. Witness Justice Hugo Black: he wrote the opinion for the Court upholding the forced relocation of Japanese Americans in 1944, but he also wrote the Court's opinion striking down martial law in Hawaii two years later. While we would not want to subscribe to the full sweep of the Latin maxim—*Inter Arma Silent Leges*—in time of war the laws are silent, perhaps we can accept the proposition that though the laws are not silent in wartime, they speak with a muted voice.

Rehnquist Remarks, *supra.*

97. *Steel Seizure Case, supra,* at 635 (1952) (Jackson, J., concurring).

98. *Quoted in* Abraham Sofaer, *War, Foreign Affairs and Constitutional Power: The Origins* (Ballinger 1976), at 215.

99. *See, e.g.,* 33 U.S.C. §381: "The President is authorized to employ so many of the public armed vessels as in his judgment the service may require, with suitable instructions to the commanders thereof, in protecting the merchant vessels of the United States and their crews from piratical aggressions and depredations."

100. This is a particularly specious criticism, since there is no assertion that the Fifth Amendment applies in war to foreign combatants captured and tried abroad.

101. Spain—apparently holding important members of al Qaeda who, the investigating judge there claims, had prior knowledge of the 9/11 attacks—has already said it will not extradite to the US because of the possibility of application of the death penalty here. "The European Union already has a policy stating that no member nation must extradite a suspect to a country unless it gets believable assurances that the death penalty will not be asked for or applied." *Spain Sets Hurdle for Extraditions,* New York Times on the Web, November 24, 2001.

102. Rome Statute Of the International Criminal Court, July 17 1998, UN Doc.A/CONF.183/9* (1998) (opened for signature July 17, 1998).

103. Harold Koh, *We Have the Right Courts for Bin Laden,* New York Times, November 23, 2001.

104. *See* the Classified Information Procedures Act of 1980, 18 U.S.C. App §§1–16.

105. Gonzales Op Ed, *supra.*

106. The concern with respect to the issue that a civilian lawyer who is not cleared to see such information might be hampered in preparing a defense may be addressed either by the clearance of civilian counsel or by the provision of cleared military counsel in those cases where such sensitive material is required to be introduced.

CHAPTER 2

The Legality and Constitutionality of the President's Authority to Initiate an Invasion of Iraq*

PREFACE BY MARK R. SHULMAN

By the spring of 2002, it had become increasingly clear that the Presidential Administration of George W. Bush had decided to topple the Iraqi Ba'athist regime of Saddam Hussein, even at the expense of an all-out war. Rumblings about war had started almost immediately after the attacks of September 11, 2001. Indeed, we now know that President Bush sought to blame Saddam Hussein in the days following 9/11, notwithstanding convincing evidence that the attacks were planned, financed, and conducted by Osama bin Laden's al Qaeda organization without any assistance or support from the Iraqi government. By late December 2001, the Commander of U.S. Central Command, General Tommy Franks, was briefing President Bush on current war plans. Bob Woodward, *Plan of Attack,* 52 (2005). A month later, the President labeled Iraq part of an "axis of evil" suggesting a transnational conspiracy. By the Spring of 2002, rumors of war had grown too loud to ignore, and the Association's Committee on International Security Affairs decided to look into the President's authority to initiate such a war.

The resulting Report took a fresh look at several significant Constitutional issues, some of which have been the subject of vigorous debate for over a century. The delicate balance of power between Congress and the Executive is nowhere more acute than in questions related to the decision to go to war. The addition of the United Nations into the mix has only complicated the issue. Over the decades, the predominant view of jurists has remained that the U.S. Constitution demands Congressional authorization for war, except to repel actual or imminent invasion. However, Presidents had never explicitly accepted this position.

Recently, the U.C. Berkeley law professor John Yoo argued ardently that the Executive has authority to initiate war without seeking Congressional (or UN Security Council) support. Yoo's voluble writings on the topic deployed history, logic, and precedent to find a vast residual authority inherent in the "Unitary Executive." When U.S. Attorney General John Ashcroft appointed Yoo as Deputy Assistant Attorney General in the Justice Department's Office of Legal Counsel, he was better positioned to advocate this position. And he found a willing client in the Bush

Administration. The Committee, therefore, had to consider Yoo's arguments carefully. In the end, as the Report makes clear, the Committee found Yoo's arguments unpersuasive. Instead, the Committee concluded that under U.S. law, absent an actual or imminent attack, explicit Congressional authorization was required before the United States could invade Iraq. At the same time, international law probably required express UN Security Council authorization.

A few weeks after the Committee issued this Report, President Bush did request Congressional authorization. After only cursory debate, Congress issued its unprecedented Joint Resolution to Authorize the Use of Armed Forces Against Iraq on October 2, 2002. At virtually the same time, the Administration launched its campaign for UN support. In the end, the Bush Administration decided not to wait for express UN authorization. And on March 19, the President declared the opening of armed hostilities.

I. INTRODUCTION

The Committee on International Security Affairs of the Association of the Bar of the City of New York ("the Committee") has considered the legal and constitutional aspects of the President's authority to order an invasion of Iraq without Congressional approval, focusing on the scenario of a large-scale invasion proposed by the Bush Administration for the purpose of regime change, without either a prior attack by Iraq on the United States, an imminent threat of such an attack or evidence that Iraq aided in the perpetration of the terrorist attacks of September 11, 2001. Our examination of the Constitution leads us to conclude that an invasion of this nature would constitute a war within the contemplation of the Founders and would thus require prior Congressional authorization. We believe that such an invasion solely on the President's orders would deny Congress its Constitutionally-granted powers and could be justified only by an excessively expansive notion of Presidential authority, one unsupported by the plain text of the U.S. Constitution.

This report addresses the issue of the legality of a Presidentially-initiated, large-scale invasion of Iraq in three steps:

(1) An examination of the Administration's stated rationale for undertaking a large-scale invasion of Iraq;

(2) An analysis of the U.S. Constitution and other relevant law underpinning the respective authority of the Congress and the President to initiate such an invasion; and

(3) The conclusion of the Committee, based upon the foregoing analysis, that such an invasion of Iraq requires prior Congressional authorization.

II. THE WHITE HOUSE IS LAYING THE GROUNDWORK FOR AN INVASION OF IRAQ

Since 9/11, the Administration has taken an increasingly assertive, proactive stance toward Iraq. In October 2001, the White House noted that evidence linked Iraq and the al Qaeda organization which was responsible for the attacks of September 11, 2001, but found nothing specifically linking Iraq to the attacks on the United States.[1] In the State of the Union Address on January 29, 2002, President Bush included Iraq in the "axis of evil," a list of those countries that sponsored terrorists and possessed or were trying to acquire weapons of mass destruction (biological, chemical, or nuclear weapons).[2] He suggested that the United States needed to act quickly against these nations but proposed no specific actions.[3] In March, Vice President Richard B. Cheney made somewhat clearer the Administration's concerns regarding Iraq, a "possible marriage...between the terrorist organizations...and weapons of mass destruction capability, the kind of devastating materials that Saddam used against his own people in "88," although no link to al Qaeda or other terrorist organizations has yet been publicly shown or even claimed by the Administration.[4] Recently, in a speech at West Point, the President made clear that the United States could no longer "wait for threats to fully materialize" but instead "must take battle to the enemy, disrupt his plans, and confront the worst threats before they emerge."[5]

By late January, newspapers had reported that the White House was planning an invasion involving over 200,000 ground troops.[6] By May, the Joint Chiefs of Staff had apparently convinced the Administration, which seemed to regard an offensive as "all but inevitable,"[7] to postpone the proposed invasion of Iraq at least until after the brutal Iraqi summer.

The Administration has also made pronouncements that the invasion of Iraq is designed to replace that country's leadership with one more amenable to the United States' current international goals. Secretary of State Colin Powell said in recent testimony before the House International Relations Committee: "Regime change is something the United States might have to do alone."[8] Defense Secretary Donald Rumsfeld is quoted in June, 2002, in a Defense Department Report document describing his thoughts that the world "would be a safer place if there were a regime change" in Iraq. He pointed out that the United States and a number of its allies, backed by President Bush and the U.S. Congress, have expressed agreement on this because every new day means another opportunity for Iraqi weapons programs to mature further. "To the extent they become more mature,' he said, "obviously, the capabilities both for weapons of mass destruction themselves, as well as the ability to deliver them, evolve as well.'"[9] Finally, in what has been called "one of the strongest and most detailed explanations by a senior U.S. official of the need to oust Hussein,"[10] National Security Advisor Condoleeza Rice made a "moral case" for the invasion of Iraq:

This is an evil man [Saddam Hussein] who, left to his own devices, will wreak havoc again on his own population, his neighbors and, if he gets weapons of mass destruction and the means to deliver them, on all of us. It is a very powerful moral case for regime change...We certainly do not have the luxury of doing nothing...if Saddam Hussein is left in power, doing the things that he's doing now, this is a threat that will emerge, and emerge in a very big way.[11]

Thus, the Administration has made abundantly clear that such an attack is based on long-term foreign policy, if not moral reasons, and not on any concept of defending the United States from an imminent military threat. Regardless of the validity of the rationale set forth by the Administration, a massive campaign against Iraq does not appear to the Committee to be the type of emergency defensive action that is within the exclusive authority of the President to undertake.

III.   THE PRESIDENT DOES NOT HAVE THE AUTHORITY TO ACT UNILATERALLY TO UNDERTAKE THE LARGE-SCALE INVASION CONTEMPLATED

A.   War Powers Clause

The text is simple: Only Congress has the authority to declare war under Article I, Section 8, Clause 11 of the Constitution: "The Congress shall have Power...To declare War...." On this there is no question. Furthermore,

The Founding Fathers drew a distinction between offensive and defensive hostilities.—The records of the convention indicate that this was done to preserve for the executive the power to repel sudden attacks and to avoid the possible implication that Congress was expected to conduct war... [12]

As Louis Fisher notes, the Founders' decision to use the word "declare" instead of "make" left the President the limited and clearly delineated power to "repel sudden attacks" against the United States. [13] The difference between the respective war power authority of the two branches can be explained as the difference between "defensive" military action against actual or imminent attack; and all other military action which constitutes "war" under the Constitution, the former being within the authority of the President as Executive and Commander in Chief, the latter within the exclusive authority of the Congress. [14] The proposed invasion does not come close to the exigent defense against imminent or sudden attack contemplated by the Founders as within the Presidential authority.

B. War Powers Resolution[15]

In response to perceived excesses by Presidents Lyndon B. Johnson and Richard Nixon in initiating and expanding the war in South-East Asia, Congress resolved in 1973 to clarify its sole authority to declare war. The War Powers Resolution (the "WPR") requires the President to report to and regularly consult with Congress after unilaterally choosing to deploy U.S. armed forces. [16] Unless Congress otherwise authorizes the military action, the WPR seeks to require the President to withdraw armed forces within sixty days of deploying them. A Congressional declaration of war or enabling resolution waives these requirements and gives the President the full power to conduct a war. Some argue that the WPR is ineffective or even unconstitutional as it seeks to alter the Constitutional war powers framework and note that no President has recognized its constitutionality. However, in large-scale conflicts, Presidents have sought Congressional authorization, most notably in the most closely analogous military action when President George H.W. Bush sought support of Congress for the Gulf War of 1991.

C. Arguments for Executive Authority to Initiate War

Some writers have argued that the Founders reserved for the President the power to initiate wars and gave Congress the power merely to ratify them, i.e., decide the legal status of the conflict initiated by the President. [17] These writers deny the authority expressly granted to Congress under the Constitution and argue in support of the President's authority to undertake unilateral action by positing that the President has the "inherent executive authority" to initiate wars, as Commander-in-Chief under Article II, Section 2[18] and as part of his generic powers as President. [19] This argument, if accepted, gives the President wide-ranging powers to use force —not just to repel a sudden attack but also to initiate full-scale offensives as part of the war against terrorism. [20] According to this view, Congress has also waived its authority over the years by acquiescing to numerous wars initiated by the President. [21]

These arguments deny or miscast the plain text of the Constitution granting Congress the sole authority to declare war. Conversely, no text gives the President the discretion to deploy U.S. forces without Congressional approval in the absence of a sudden danger to national security, not even for the "moral" reasons or concerns of "emerging" threats cited by the Administration. [22]

Advocates of unilateral executive authority over war powers also claim to bring an originalist understanding to the War Powers clause that contradicts both the text and the clear (originalist) evidence that the Founders wished to prevent the President from having strong war powers. [23] Advocates of inherent executive authority to initiate wars argue that the American conception of executive war powers was largely shaped by Britain, even though the colonies revolted from Britain in part, as a reaction to the excess of British executive power they had experienced.[24] The President's role as Commander-in-Chief emphasizes civilian control over the military and, absent an immediate threat to the nation requiring defense, only gives him the power to execute Congress' decision to commence a war.[25] Many Founders believed war declarations were simply not an executive function.[26]

D. UN or NATO Authorization

Some scholars argue that the President may undertake a military action without Congressional authorization if the UN or NATO has authorized such an action.[27] By this view, the purpose of the "declare war" clause is to ensure that the decision to initiate war does not rest with just one person. UN authorization avoids this problem, perhaps even more effectively than does Congress' authorization, because the Security Council "is far less likely to be stampeded by combat fever than is Congress."[28] As examples, proponents of this view observe that Presidents, on two previous occasions, have deployed U.S. forces pursuant to Security Council authorizations: the Korean War[29] and the 1991 Gulf War.[30]

UN or NATO authorization does not absolve the President of his Constitutional duty to obtain Congress' approval. Whether the Security Council approves of an invasion of Iraq or not,[31] the Constitution requires Congressional authorization for war. Treaty obligations, such as those under the UN Charter or NATO Treaty, are equivalent to federal statutory law[32] and, as such, never trump the Constitution.[33]

Arguments relying on the Korean and Gulf Wars as examples are unconvincing. President Harry S. Truman's order sending U.S. forces to Korea might be viewed as repelling a sudden attack—the North Korean invasion had nearly overrun South Korea, threatening irreparable harm to U.S. security interests.[34] In any case, it appears that President Truman sought UN approval as a fig leaf for acting without Congress; he[35] had already ordered American forces to defend South Korea before obtaining UN authorization[36] and would have done so without receiving it.[37] Likewise President George H.W. Bush, despite obtaining UN authorization, sought and received Congressional approval for the Gulf War.[38]

1. Security Council Resolution 678

The Administration may argue that not only does UN authorization give the President authority to act without Congress, but that specifically, President Bush already has a UN mandate to invade Iraq. This 1990 Resolution states:

The Security Council...Acting under Chapter VII of the Charter...Authorizes Member States co-operating with the Government of Kuwait, unless Iraq on or before 15 January 1991 fully implements Resolution 660 (1990) [calling for Iraq to withdraw from Kuwait] and all subsequent relevant resolutions, to use all necessary means...to restore international peace and security in the area.[39]

Congress stated in PL 102-1 that the President was "authorized to use United States Armed Forces pursuant to United Nations Security Council Resolution 678,"[40] and the subsequent relevant Security Council resolutions referred to in Resolution 660 and thus incorporated into Resolution 678 (including those establishing the Iraq weapons inspection regime), thereby extending Congressional authorization to such subsequent Security Council resolutions. That this is so is indicated by the President's continued reporting to Congress under PL 102-1's reporting requirements regarding the United States' efforts to enforce those subsequent Security Council Resolutions and Congress' acceptance of such reports.[41]

Nonetheless, while it appears that Resolution 678 may still be in effect, and, further, a purely textual analysis of the Resolution may support a broad interpretation of purpose extending even to authorization of force for "regime change,"[42] nonetheless, a review of that and the subsequent resolutions from the Security Council—along with a reading of the debate surrounding the adoption of the Authorization for Use of Force Against Iraq Joint Resolution—suggest that it did not authorize, intend or even contemplate the use of force against Iraq for "moral" reasons or purposes of "regime change." The Committee concludes, therefore, that Resolution 678 does not provide authorization for the invasion contemplated by the Bush Administration.

2.   Security Council Resolution 1373

Even if UN authorization allowed the President to order American forces into hostilities without Congress' approval, Resolution 1373 passed in response to the events of September 11, does not appear to the Committee to authorize the United States to invade Iraq for the purpose of regime change or even moral reasons.[43] In contrast, nothing in the plain, operative text of Resolution 1373 authorizes any state to invade Iraq absent a connection with 9/11.[44] There are also other flaws with citing Resolution 1373 as a blank check (e.g., the phrase "combat by all means" appears in the preamble and is not binding). All this points to the fact that the Resolution 1373 does not authorize the proposed war against Iraq.

E.   1991 and 2001 Joint Resolutions of Congress

Congress has twice issued resolutions that might be used to support a contention that Congress has already authorized a future war against Iraq; yet, neither resolution currently applies. As noted above, President George H.W. Bush sought and received Congressional authorization for undertaking the Persian Gulf War's Operation Desert Storm in January 1991 pursuant to Security Council Resolution 678 in the form of PL 102-1 ("Authorization for Use of Military Force Against Iraq Resolution").[45] While, as explained above, from 1991 to the present three Presidents have continued to report to Congress under PL 102-1 regarding the United States' efforts pursuant to Security Council Resolution 678, and both the U.S. and the British governments take the position that Resolution 678 continues in effect, neither the 1991 Authorization for Use of Military Force Against Iraq Resolution nor Resolution 678 were designed to authorize conquest of Iraq to achieve a change in regime.

More recently, in the immediate wake of 9/11, Congress authorized the President to use armed force against "those nations, organizations or persons he determines planned, authorized, committed, or aided the terrorist attacks on September 11, 2001."[46] This sweeping resolution requires a connection with 9/11 and would only authorize war against Iraq if the President had determined that Iraq had "aided" in perpetrating the attacks. To date, the President has not made such a determination. It is important to note that the United States has not announced any causal link between the events of 9/11 and Iraq; Vice President Cheney has acknowledged as much explicitly.[47] It is thus clear the 2001 Joint Resolution To Authorize The Use Of U.S. Armed Forces Against Those Responsible For The Recent Attacks Launched Against The United States does not extend to authorize war against Iraq for the stated purpose.

F.   Congress' Powers of Appropriation Are Insufficient

Some scholars argue that appropriations are a sufficient check, and the primary one intended by the Founders, against the executive authority to initiate war—Congress may simply refuse funding for further military operations.[48] However, this check will often be useless against the President. Under this theory, Congress may stop military actions once troops have been committed. The action may end, damage may be done, and lives (U.S. and foreign) may be lost well before the withdrawal of funding is effective.[49] It may also be dangerous to withdraw funding once a large ground force has been committed.[50] This view of war powers is backwards. Congress should not be in a position to decide merely how many casualties the United States will accept but rather whether losses need be incurred at all.

G.   Under the Constitution, the Proposed Invasion Is a War

Under the Constitution, President Bush would have the unilateral authority to commit U.S. troops to Iraq if he could show that such an action constituted repelling a sudden or imminent attack or its modern day equivalent. Under the scenario addressed herein, however, the Committee believes he must seek Congressional approval. There are three reasons for this conclusion, which must be read cumulatively:

(1) The scale of the endeavor strongly suggests the action is a "war" under Constitution (although scale alone is insufficient to put the matter into the legislative domain as the type of war requiring Congressional authorization). The United States District Court for the District of Columbia had "no hesitation in concluding that an offensive entry into Iraq by several hundred thousand United States servicemen...could be described as a 'war' within the meaning of [the War Powers Clause]."[51] (Congress is more likely to acquiesce to unilateral executive decisions to deploy relatively small forces, [52] but despite any such acquiescence, Congress cannot waive its Constitutional war powers.)

The deployment of 200,000 or more troops (or, indeed, even a "smaller" invasion in conjunction with massive air attack) is practically and qualitatively different from the scale of other recent U.S. military interventions, except for the Vietnam and Gulf Wars; in each of these two conflicts, the President specifically sought and received Congressional authorization. The Tonkin Gulf Resolution, while passed by Congress as a reaction to largely fabricated events, shows that even President Johnson believed he was Constitutionally compelled to attempt to obtain Congress' authorization before beginning a full-fledged war in Vietnam. President Johnson likely abused his authority to send troops to Vietnam. More important, in the context of this discussion on the separation of war powers, is how he might have abused his authority. President Johnson's actions, if anything, affirmed the legitimacy of the War Powers clause because he actively sought Congressional authorization for the Vietnam War.[53]

(2) The invasion of Iraq for the purpose of regime change is plainly not for the purpose of repelling a sudden or imminent attack, as discussed above. Iraq has not, since the end of the 1991 Gulf War, used force against or directly threatened the United States (aside from attacks on allied airplanes in the no-fly zones). According to the National Security Advisor, any threat that Iraq poses is not of an immediate nature; if it were, the President would have proposed an immediate action, or, already acted on his own authority. To deem an invasion of Iraq repelling a sudden or imminent attack under these circumstances dangerously distorts the intent of the Founders.

(3) In the case of repelling a "sudden attack," or even the modern day equivalent such as disrupting a terrorist operation about to commence, time limitations help to provide an understanding of the boundary between executive and legislative war powers. The President has the authority and obligation to repel sudden attacks because the unitary Executive can react more quickly than Congress. In such cases there is time to deliberate. Perhaps a President who fears that his war plans will be rejected would not want to subject them to Congressional scrutiny. It is in precisely this situation, however, that the decision is not the President's to make alone; he must convince Congress[54] not only of the justness of the cause but the legitimacy of the means.

IV. CONCLUSION

The Committee has set forth its reasoning and conclusion that the President needs Congressional authorization to launch a large-scale invasion of Iraq for the purpose of regime change or on "moral" grounds set forth.[55] Some may disagree with this conclusion. However, when the President seeks to take the nation from a state of peace to a state of war for reasons other than defense against actual or imminent attack, however valid those reasons may be, the Republic deserves—and the Constitution requires—a Congressional debate over whether to authorize such a war. Swift action in defense of the nation and enforcement of legislation are the President's obligations; decision-making from reasoned deliberation and determining America's long-term security interests is Congress'.

Administration officials, former White House officials, members of Congress, and scholars have argued for and against removing Saddam Hussein, and even those who agree he must be ousted, disagree as to whether using ground troops and a massive air assault in a large scale endeavor is the best means.[56] As such, the prudence of offensive military action—from the perspective of U.S. national security—is far from self-evident. This controversy necessarily requires open and public debate about the merits of a war against Iraq to effect regime change. Such deliberation in Congress and amongst citizens—before using force—is the hallmark of a democratic republic, as conceived of by the Founders and written in the Constitution. The President can best facilitate this necessary debate and honor the Constitutional separation of powers by requesting authorization from Congress for his proposed military action before acting.

August 22, 2002

NOTES

* **Committee On International Security Affairs:** Raenu Barod (chair), Igou M. Allbray, John R. Burroughs, John C. Ericson, William V.O. Gnichtel, Kerry J. Houghton, Thomas E. Miotke, Lisa A. Munoz, John V.H. Pierce, Mark R. Shulman.

Mr. Shulman and Lawrence J. Lee, a student at New York University School of Law who will be joining the Committee in September 2002, are the principal authors of this report. Eleven members of the Committee have approved this report. Five members have recused themselves due to conflicts of interest: Nicholas Rostow, Paul W. Butler, Steven C. Krane, Robert J. Cosgrove and Samrat S. Khichi. The Committee is grateful for the considerable input of Stephen J. Shapiro and Miles P. Fischer of the Standing Committee on Military Affairs and Justice.

1. *See* Interview with Richard B. Cheney, Meet the Press, Mar. 24, 2002. With respect to the connection between Iraq and al Qaeda, "We haven't been able to pin down any connection there...We discovered, and it's since been public, the allegation that one of the lead hijackers, Mohamed Atta, had, in fact, met with Iraqi intelligence in Prague, but we've not been able yet from our perspective to nail down a close tie between the al Qaeda organization and Saddam Hussein. We'll continue to look for it."

2. President George W. Bush, State of the Union Address, Jan. 29, 2002, available at http://www.whitehouse.gov/news/releases/2002/01/20020129-11.html. "States like these [North Korea, Iran, Iraq], and their terrorist allies, constitute an axis of evil, arming to threaten the peace of the world. By seeking weapons of mass destruction, these regimes pose a grave and growing danger. They could provide these arms to terrorists, giving them the means to match their hatred. They could attack our allies or attempt to blackmail the United States."

3. *Id.* "Time is not on our side. I will not wait on events while dangers gather. I will not stand by, as peril draws closer and closer. The United States of America will not permit the world's most dangerous regimes to threaten us with the world's most destructive weapons."

4. *See* Interview with Richard B. Cheney, *supra* note 1.

5. President George W. Bush, United States Military Academy Graduation Speech, June 2, 2002.

6. *See generally* Peter Ford, *'Evil axis' and others talk back,* Christian Sci. Monitor, Jan. 31, 2002, at 01, (describing U.S. invasion plans); Ian Bruce, *Pentagon draws up plans for invasion of Iraq,* HERALD (Glasgow), Jan. 31, 2002, at 11 (explaining Pentagon plans to use ground troops to expel Hussein); William Rees-Mogg, *The countdown starts for Operation Saddam,* TIMES (London), Feb. 18, 2002, Features (criticizing White House plans); Eric Schmitt, Cheney, at Marine Base, *Reinforces Bush's Stand On War Against Terror,* N.Y. TIMES, Feb. 19, 2002, at A10 (reporting Cheney's efforts to garner support in the United States for action against Iraq).

7. *See* Scott Ritter, Commentary: *Behind 'Plot' on Hussein, a Secret Agenda: Killing weapons inspections would clear way for war,* L.A. TIMES, June 19, 2002, at B13.

8. *State Department Report: Powell says U.S. is Examining Full Range of Options on Iraq,* Feb. 6, 2002, issued by U.S. Department of State International Information Programs, viewed at http://usinfo .state.gov/topical/pol/arms/02020605.htm.

9. *Defense Department Report: Afghanistan; Iraq, June 17, 2002,* issued by U.S. Department of State International Information Programs, viewed at http://usinfo.state.gov/regional/nea/sasia/afghan/text/ 0617dodrpt.htm.

10. "Rice Lays Out Case for War In Iraq Bush; Adviser Cites 'Moral' Reasons," WASH POST, Aug. 16, 2002, at 1, reported at http://www.washingtonpost.com/wp-dyn/articles/A21333-2002Aug15. html.

11. Rice interview with BBC, reported at http://news.bbc.co.uk/1/hi/world/americas /2193426.stm, Aug. 15, 2002. Brackets in original; emphasis added.

12. R. Turner, THE WAR POWERS RESOLUTION: ITS IMPLEMENTATION IN THEORY AND PRACTICE, (1983), at 17 [emphasis in original].

13. Messrs. Madison and Gerry jointly introduced the amendment to substitute "declare" for "make." They noted the change would "leave to the Executive the power to repel sudden attacks." M. Farrand, The Records of the Federal Convention of 1787 (rev. ed. 1937), at 318, cited in THE CONSTITUTION OF THE UNITED STATES OF AMERICA: ANALYSIS AND INTERPRETATION, Congressional Research Service (1992), at 308, note 1420.

See Louis Fisher, *Sidestepping Congress: Presidents Acting Under the UN and NATO,* 47 Case W. Res. L. Rev. 1237 (1997) (arguing that the constitutional structure adopted by the Framers is "remarkably clear in its basic principles. The authority to initiate war lay with Congress. The President could act unilaterally only in one area: to repel sudden attacks."). A number of leading commentators support this view. *See generally* John H. Ely, WAR AND RESPONSIBILITY: CONSTITUTIONAL LESSONS OF VIETNAM AND ITS AFTERMATH (1993); Louis Henkin, CONSTITUTIONALISM, DEMOCRACY, AND FOREIGN AFFAIRS (1990); Harold H. Koh, THE NATIONAL SECURITY CONSTITUTION: SHARING POWER AFTER THE IRAN-CONTRA AFFAIR (1990); Michael J. Glennon, CONSTITUTIONAL DIPLOMACY (1990); Lori Fisler Damrosch, *Constitutional Control Over War Powers: A Common Core of Accountability in Democratic Societies?,* 50 U. Miami L. Rev. 181 (1995) (arguing that "the body of experience of the mature democracies in their war-and-peace decisions reflects a common core of commitment to democratic accountability."). *See also* S. Con. Res. 133, 107th Cong. (2002) referred to Senate Foreign Relations Committee (expressing "the sense of Congress that the United States should not use force against Iraq, outside of the existing Rules of Engagement, without specific statutory authorization or a declaration of war under Article I, Section 8, Clause 11 of the Constitution of the United States").

14. *See,* e.g., William Whiting, WAR POWERS UNDER THE CONSTITUTION OF THE UNITED STATES (1871), at 38–40: "Congress has the sole power, under the constitution, to make [a] declaration [of war], and to sanction or authorize the commencement of offensive war...But this is quite a different case from a defensive...war. The constitution establishes the mode in which this government shall commence wars, the authority which may authorize, and the declarations which shall precede, any act of hostility; but it has no power to prescribe the manner in which others should begin war against us."

15. *See* 50 U.S.C. 1541–1548.

16. The WPR seeks to prevent the President from abusing both his authority as Commander-in-Chief and his ability to respond more quickly than Congress, as the President may deploy troops and undertake a military action that does not constitute a response to a sudden or imminent attack before Congress can act at all, or he may deploy a sufficient number of troops quickly enough to create a self-fulfilling

prophecy—(that to remove U.S. forces immediately after deploying them would be irresponsible and dangerous). If the President can commit troops offensively and only consult Congress when hostilities become inevitable (i.e., shoot and ask questions later), then Congress has no real war powers. *See* Lori Fisler Damrosch, *The Constitutional Responsibility of Congress for Military Engagements,* 89 Am. J. Int'l L. 58 (1994) (arguing that in the post-Cold War era, it is more important than ever to have "robust parliamentary debate and genuine deliberation" before military action, as required by WPR and the War Powers Clause). *See also* infra Part II.F (arguing that Congressional appropriations or other measures after military deployment are insufficient checks against unilateral action by the President).

17. *See generally* John C. Yoo, *The Continuation of Politics by Other Means: The Original Understanding of War Powers,* 84 Calif. L. Rev. 167 (1996). Yoo argues that the Founders understood declarations of war not as legislative authorization to initiate war but as a mere acknowledgement by Congress that the legal status had changed, from peace to war, between the United States and a hostile state. It alerted all nations that violence committed against hostile states was official and public, not the work of pirates or rebels, and alerts U.S. citizens about the identity of the new enemy. Yoo calls this a Congressional exercise of judicial powers. *See id.* at 205.

18. Some argue that the President has more explicit and unchecked authority to use the armed forces under Article II, Section 2 ("President shall be Commander in Chief of the Army and Navy of the United States, and of the militia of the several states, when called into actual Service of the United States."). *See generally* Robert J. Delahunty & John C. Yoo, *The President's Constitutional Authority to Conduct Military Operations Against Terrorist Organizations and the Nations That Harbor or Support Them,* 25 Harv. J.L. & Pub. Pol'y 487 (2002).

19. *See* Yoo, *supra* note 17, at 252–56 (arguing that President's war powers were continuation of British and colonial traditions and that 18th Century citizens expected a "paternal figure vested with the duty of protecting his fellow citizens.").

20. *See* Delahunty & Yoo, *supra* note 18, at 487 ("The President had the innate power not only to retaliate against any person, organization, or state suspected of involvement in terrorist attacks on the United States, but also against foreign states suspected of harboring or supporting such organizations."). Authors are in the Office of Legal Counsel of the Department of Justice (but do not claim to state official views of the Justice Department).

21. *See* John Yoo, *Clio at War: The Misuse of History in the War Powers Debate*, 70 U. Colo. L. Rev. 1169, 1179 (1999) (arguing that Congress has allowed the President to assume the initiative in war).

22. *See* D.A. Jeremy Telman, *A Truism That Isn't True? The Tenth Amendment and Executive War Power*, 51 Cath. U. L. Rev. 135, 189 (responding to Yoo and others who argue for increased executive war powers by arguing that such powers can only come from a theory of inherent authority because "there is no basis, in the constitutional text, in the writings of the Framers, in political theory, or in the constitutional history of the United States for transferring powers invested in the Legislature to the Executive."). Critics like Yoo read "declare war" out of context, separating from neighboring clauses that clearly enumerate the power to raise, support, and regulate the armed forces (Cl. 12–16), all part and parcel of control when and how the United States goes to war.

23. James Madison said that the Constitution "supposes...that the Executive is the branch of power most interested in war, and most prone to it. It has accordingly, with studied care, vested the question of war in the Legislature." James Madison, Letter From James Madison to Thomas Jefferson, Apr. 2, 1798, in 6 THE WRITINGS OF JAMES MADISON, 311, 312 (Gaillard Hunt Ed., 1906) (cited by Telman, supra note 22, at 152). Furthermore, during the Constitutional Convention, no one even seconded a motion to give the President the power to initiate wars. See 2 RECORDS OF THE FEDERAL CONVENTION OF 1787, (Max Farrand ed., 1937) (cited by Telman, supra note 22, at 152). Finally, Madison argued that the system of checks and balances required that Congress control the decision to initiate war: "Those who are to conduct a war cannot in the nature of things, be proper or safe judges, whether a war ought to be commenced, continued, or concluded." James Madison, *Helvidius No. 1,* in 6 THE WRITINGS OF JAMES MADISON 145 (Gaillard Hunt ed., 1906).

24. *See* Telman, *supra* note 22, at 180 ("Yoo's theory ignores the great efforts expended in the Revolutionary Era to free the United States from the problems associated with the excesses of executive power experienced when the American states had the status of English colonies."). Even Alexander

Hamilton, once an advocate of constitutional monarchy, conceded that the powers granted the President were much inferior to those granted the King of Great Britain, who could declare war and raise and regulate armies. *Id.* at 182.

25. Hamilton argued at the Constitutional Convention that the executive's war time functions were "to have the direction of war when authorized or begun"; nothing in his statement to the Convention indicated that the President should also have the power to decide whether to start a war. 5 DEBATES IN THE SEVERAL STATE CONVENTIONS, ON THE ADOPTION OF THE FEDERAL CONSTITUTION, AS RECOMMEND BY THE GENERAL CONVENTION AT PHILADELPHIA, In 1787, at 205 (Jonathan Elliot ed., 2d ed. 1996).

This paper takes no position with respect to the authority the President may have to employ the armed forces in military operations other than war, such as peacekeeping, disaster relief, peacetime garrisons in foreign bases, training of U.S. and allied forces abroad and the like.

26. Madison, *Helvidius No. 1, supra* note 23, at 148. "A declaration that there shall be war is not an execution of laws: it does not suppose pre-existing laws to be executed: it is not, in any respect, an act merely executive."

27. *See generally* Thomas M. Franck & Faiza Patel, *UN Police Action in Lieu of War: "The Old Order Changeth,"* 85 Am. J. Int'l L. 63 (1991).

28. *Id.* at 74. "The purpose of the war-declaring clause was to ensure that this fateful decision did not rest with a single person. The new system vests that responsibility in the Security Council, a body where the most divergent interests and perspectives of humanity are represented and where five of fifteen members have a veto power." *Id.* As a practical matter of restraining the President, it may be true that the Security Council, made up of different member states with different and often conflicting political interests, is less likely to authorize the use of American force than Congress. Such support seems unlikely under the circumstances.

29. Delahunty & Yoo, *supra* note 18, at 504 ("Perhaps the most significant operation exercised on the President's sole authority occurred during the Korean War, when President Truman ordered United States troops to fight a war that lasted for over three years and resulted in over 142,000 American casualties.").

30. *See* Fisher, *supra* note 13, at 1266 (observing that during the Gulf War, Richard B. Cheney, the Secretary of Defense, argued that Congressional authorization was not necessary for UN-approved actions).

31. Recent history suggests that three of five permanent members (Russia, China, France) of the Security Council would oppose an invasion of Iraq. Richard Butler, THE GREATEST THREAT: IRAQ, WEAPONS OF MASS DESTRUCTION, AND THE GROWING CRISIS OF GLOBAL SECURITY 91, 220–21 (2000) (describing Russian, French, and Chinese support for ending sanctions against Iraq, despite the lack of Iraqi compliance with UN weapons inspection regime, and self-interested political motives for this support).

32. *See* U.S. Const., Art. VI, cl. 2 ("This Constitution, and the Laws of the United States which shall be made in Pursuance thereof; and all Treaties made, or which shall be made, under the Authority of the United States, shall be the supreme Law of the Land").

33. RESTATEMENT (THIRD) OF FOREIGN RELATIONS LAW 111, Comment (a) ("In their character as law of the United States, rules of international law and provisions of international agreements of the United States are subject to the Bill of Rights and other prohibitions, restrictions, and requirements of the Constitution, and cannot be given effect in violation of them.").

34. Truman's advisers believed that the sudden North Korean attack required an immediate U.S. response. "To sit by while Korea is overrun by unprovoked armed attack would start a disastrous chain of events leading most probably to world war." John Foster Dulles & John M. Allison, Telegram to Dean Acheson and Dean Rusk, June 25, 1950 (one day after the North Korean invasion began), *available at* http://www.trumanlibrary.org/whistlestop/study collections/korea/large/week1/elsy 3 1.htm. Truman regarded the Korean invasion as the beginning of general Soviet aggression and expansion in the Far East. See generally Philip C. Jessup, Memorandum of Conversation, June 25, 1950, *available at* http://www.trumanlibrary.org/whistlestop/study collections/korea/large/week1/kw 4 1.htm (summarizing discussion between Truman and his advisers about the Korean situation, its implications for China, Formosa, and Southeast Asia, and plans to strike at Soviet airbases and ships in the Pacific Ocean).

35. Truman, before the Korean War, had agreed that he must seek Congressional authorization before committing U.S. troops to UN or NATO military actions. *See* Fisher, *supra* note 13, at 1245–46 ("After Roosevelt's death, President Truman sent a cable from Potsdam stating that all agreements involving U.S. troop commitments to the United Nations would first have to be approved by both Houses of Congress.). *See also id.* at 1255–56 ("In 1951, during Senate hearings on NATO, [Under Secretary of State Dean] Acheson. . .acknowledged that the treaty does not compel any nation "to take steps contrary to its convictions, and none is obligated to ignore its national interests.").

36. *Id.* at 1261 (indicating that Truman had ordered American support of South Korean forces, in the form of military supplies and air and sea cover, before the Security Council authorized states to repel the invasion by North Korea).

37. *Id.* ("After he left the presidency, Truman was asked whether he had been willing to use military force in Korea without UN backing. He replied, with customary bluntness: "No question about it.'").

38. PL 102-1 (1991).

"Section 2. Authorization for use of United States Armed Forces

(a) Authorization. — The President is authorized, subject to subsection (b), to use United States Armed Forces pursuant to United Nations Security Council Resolution 678 (1990) in order to achieve implementation of Security Council Resolutions 660, 661, 662, 664, 665, 666, 667, 669, 670, 674, and 677."

39. S.C. Res. 678, U.N. Doc. S/RES/0678 (1990).

40. *Id.* [emphasis supplied].

41. *See* e.g., Letter from the President to the Speaker of the House of Representatives and the President Pro Tempore of the Senate January 23, 2002, Office of the White House Press Secretary, January 24, 2002:

Dear Mr. Speaker: (Dear Mr. President:)

Consistent with the Authorization for Use of Military Force Against Iraq Resolution (Public Law 102-1) and as part of my effort to keep the Congress fully informed, I am providing a report prepared by my Administration on the status of efforts to obtain Iraq's compliance with the resolutions adopted by the United Nations Security Council. The last report, consistent with Public Law 102-1, was transmitted on October 11, 2001.

Sincerely,

GEORGE W. BUSH

42. "From a purely textual perspective, that authorization seems to have few, if any, limits. "Area" is undefined and could mean Iraq or the entire Middle East. "Restoring international peace and security' could mean occupying Iraq, removing Saddam Hussein from power, or bombing Iraq's military/industrial capacity." Jules Lobel & Michael Ratner, *Bypassing the Security Council: Ambiguous Authorizations to Use Force, Cease-Fires and the Iraqi Inspection Regime,* 93 Am. J. Int'l. L. 124 (1999), *printed at* http://www.asil.org /ajil/lobel.htm93, at text accompanying footnotes 59 and 60.

43. *Id.*

44. *See* S.C. Res. 1373 resolving (that states shall suppress the financing of terrorist acts (P1), deny other support to terrorists or terrorist groups (P2), cooperate with other states to exchange information, become parties to relevant anti-terrorism treaties, and prevent abuse of asylum laws by terrorists (P3). No part of the text of the resolution urges or condones states to invade other states to prevent terrorism), S.C. Res. 1373, U.N. Doc. S/RES/1373 (2001).

45. Public Law 102 - 1, 2(b) (Joint Resolution to authorize use of military force against Iraq) Jan. 14, 1991. "The President is authorized. . .to use United States Armed Forces pursuant to United Nations Security Council Resolution 678 (1990). . . ."

46. United States Public Law 107-40, 2(a) (Joint Resolution to authorize the use of U.S. Armed Forces against those responsible for the recent attacks launched against the United States) Sept. 18, 2001.

47. *See* note 1.

48. *See* Yoo, *supra* note 17 at 297 ("Recent events [i.e. United States-led military operations in Bosnia] confirm that Congress fully understands that its appropriations power may be used to check executive military operations.").

49. For instance, the Office of the Legal Counsel of the Department of Justice advised President George H.W. Bush that he could send U.S. troops to Somalia on his own authority. 16 Op. Off. Legal Counsel 9

(1992) (cited by Delahunty & Yoo, *supra* note 18, at 500 n.51). After a series of dramatic American set-backs, Congress directed the President to withdraw forces from Somalia pursuant to its authority clarified by the War Powers Resolution. See H.R. Con. Res. 170, 103d Cong., 139 Cong. Rec. 9039 (1993). One might imagine that Congress could have ended the operation in Somalia (a military action far smaller than that contemplated in Iraq) by withdrawing funding instead. Either way, this example suggests that if the power to initiate war lies with the President, Congress has no effective check—it can only limit casualties once hostilities have begun because it cannot stop them from taking place.

50. Yoo concedes that Congress may be reluctant to deny appropriations because of the risk of "creat-ing the impression that they are leaving American troops at the front defenseless," but that "a failure of political will should not be confused with a constitutional defect." Yoo, *supra* note 17, at 299. He assumes that the risk of withdrawing funding as largely a perceptual or political danger, rather than one that may, in fact, involve the lives of deployed troops.

51. *See* Dellums v. Bush, 752 F. Supp. 1141, 1146 (D.D.C. 1990). *See also* Bruce Ackerman, *Commentary: Bush Must Avoid Shortcuts on Road to War: President should not try to sidestep Congress in any action against Iraq,* L.A. Times, May 31, 2002, at B15.

52. Telman, *supra* note 24, at 168. "Although Congress has generally acquiesced in the President's uni-lateral power to commit the Armed Forces to actions of limited scope, that acquiescence in individual cases, no matter how numerous, cannot result in a transfer of war powers from one branch of the federal government to another."

53. Johnson's failing was that he was willing to use false information (allowing the Pentagon to fabri-cate incidents suggesting North Vietnamese provocation) to get such authorization. The President has an obligation to be truthful when exercising his Executive and Commander-in-Chief war powers.

54. If the reasons for a ground invasion depend on top secret intelligence, and public disclosure will compromise intelligence sources, then the President may provide this information to Congress behind closed doors. *See,* e.g., the current Congressional investigation of possible intelligence breakdowns before 9/11, which remained largely closed to the public. Protecting intelligence sources may be a good reason not to reveal secrets but does not justify the President acting without Congress' authorization.

55. The Committee takes no position regarding the validity of those stated reasons.

56. These debates are not a matter of partisan politics. In addition to many Democrats, former senior Republican officials who served during the Gulf War in the Administration of G.H.W. Bush argue against a ground invasion of Iraq. *See* interviews with James Baker and Brent Scowcroft, *Frontline: Gunning For Saddam,* Nov. 8, 2001 (arguing that Saddam Hussein is not the greatest threat to U.S. security and arguing against a ground invasion).

CHAPTER 3

Letter to President Bush re: United Nations Charter Obligations Regarding Iraq

PREFACE BY ALAN R. ROTHSTEIN

In the fall of 2002, with the United States seemingly on the path to war with Iraq, there was substantial debate as to whether the United States was justified in pursuing this course given the role of the United Nations and the United Nations Charter, which the United States ratified. The United States was attempting to work within the UN structure while making it clear that it was prepared to go to war without UN participation, and that such action was consistent with the UN Charter.

The Association's Council on International Affairs drafted a letter for the Association's President, E. Leo Milonas, to send to President Bush, urging that the United States abide by its international obligations under the Charter. The letter argued that the United States had not made the requisite showing of self-defense that would justify its going to war absent authorization by the United Nations Security Council, under Article 51 of the Charter. It therefore urged that the U.S. government obtain authorization from the Security Council before commencing any military action in Iraq.

October 15, 2002

The Honorable George W. Bush
The White House
Washington, DC 20500

Re: <u>*United Nations Charter Obligations Regarding Iraq*</u>

Dear President Bush:

On behalf of The Association of the Bar of the City of New York, I write regarding the international law issues that underlie a possible large-scale military action by the United States in Iraq. We assume that the purpose of such action would be to enforce Iraqi compliance with several United Nations Resolutions and, in particular, to ensure the disarmament of Iraq's weapons of mass destruction.

The Association does not take a position on the issue of whether, as a policy matter, Iraq's violations of these resolutions are most wisely responded to by military action, or by a rigorous policy of containment and inspections. The purpose of this letter is to urge, respectfully, that the United States abide by its international obligations and act in accordance with the United Nations Charter.

Security Council authorization of the use of military force is required under Chapter VII of the UN Charter absent circumstances triggering a nation's inherent right of self-defense, as preserved by Article 51 of the Charter. By its terms, Article 51 permits the use of force in self-defense only in response to an "armed attack." It is generally accepted, however, that this right encompasses traditional definitions of self-defense permitting the use of force against the threat of imminent attack, where, as succinctly stated by Secretary of State Daniel Webster in 1837, the "necessity of that self-defense is instant, overwhelming, and leaving no choice of means, and no moment for deliberation."

We recognize that what constitutes an imminent threat today cannot be limited to what constituted an imminent threat in Secretary Webster's day. We do not presume to pass judgments regarding the significance of any military threat. Nor do we address at this time the broader issues under applicable international legal principles of the standards articulated under the new and recently-released National Security Strategy.

Nevertheless, with regard to Iraq, we believe that the United States, through the information so far made publicly available, has itself not appeared to present the case of an actual or imminent Iraqi attack. In our view, the distinction is not simply a question of uncertainty as to "the time and place of an attack." More fundamentally, the United States has so far not publicly made a claim of any certainty or even probability of an Iraqi attack against the United States that rises to a level of imminence justifying unilateral action at the present time. If there exists information of such a threat, we respectfully urge the administration to demonstrate this case to the international community in connection with any unilateral military action, in order that the United States may proceed within the parameters of international law.

We do not question the grave danger posed by an Iraqi weapons development program, and its threat to international peace and security, particularly in the Middle East. In the absence of an imminent threat, however, it is the Security Council under Chapter VII of the UN Charter that must address this grave danger, not the United States under a claim of unilateral self-defense.

The Security Council expressly found in Resolution 707 that Iraq was in "material breach" of the disarmament Resolution 687 as early as April 18, 1991—only 15 days after Iraq accepted the Resolution. Some could argue that as a result of this "material breach," Resolution 678, which authorized the use of military force in the Gulf War, remains in effect and continues to authorize the use of military force against Iraq.

Nevertheless, existing Security Council resolutions with regard to Iraq do not authorize the use of force by nations to enforce those resolutions. In November 1990, the Security Council adopted Resolution 678 to authorize the use of force against Iraq in response to the invasion of Kuwait. Resolution 678 expressly authorized member states to "use all necessary means to uphold and implement Resolution 660 and all subsequent relevant resolutions and to restore international peace and security in the area." After the coalition forces and Iraq entered into a provisional cease-fire, the Security Council by Resolution 687 declared a formal cease-fire to be effective upon acceptance of the terms of such Resolution by Iraq. The Security Council affirmed prior resolutions, including Resolution 678, subject to this significant limitation: "except as expressly changed below [in this Resolution] to achieve the goals of this Resolution, including a formal cease-fire."

It remains the province of the Security Council to determine what enforcement action is necessary. Under Resolution 687, the Security Council "remain[s] seized of the matter" and may determine "such further steps as may be required for the implementation of the present resolution and to secure peace and security in the area." Subsequent resolutions have condemned Iraq's non-compliance and have imposed additional enforcement measures, but the Security Council has not reauthorized the use of military force under Chapter VII.

The United States helped create the current legal framework governing the use of force by substantially designing, and by signing and ratifying, the United Nations Charter. Under Article 103, the Charter is the cornerstone of international relations, superseding "obligations under any other international agreement." The United States and the member states of the United Nations sought to secure a stable international system based on legal principles. In deference to these principles, President George H.W. Bush revitalized the role of the Security Council when he sought UN authorization to attack Iraq in 1990, in the wake of Iraq's invasion and occupation of Kuwait. The Security Council was finally charged with performing the task signified by its very name—ensuring international peace and security.

To sidestep the Security Council's responsibility at this time would be a setback to the international legal system painstakingly developed since the Second World War. In a conflict to enforce Iraqi compliance with international law, the United States should avoid the risk of being perceived as itself violating generally accepted international legal principles. Moreover, we are concerned that a loose application of these principles by the United States will set a bad precedent for other nations to exploit elsewhere.

The Association supports the Administration's current efforts to work within the United Nations system by seeking adoption of a Security Council resolution to ensure the effective disarmament of Iraq. We agree with your statement to the General Assembly:

The United States helped found the United Nations. We want the United Nations to be effective and respect[ed] and successful. We want the resolutions of the world's most important multilateral body to be enforced. And right now those resolutions are being unilaterally subverted by the Iraqi regime.

In the absence of further facts justifying the use of force in self-defense under Article 51 of the United Nations Charter, the Association of the Bar of the City of New York respectfully urges the government of the United States to obtain authorization of the United Nations Security Council prior to the commencement of any military action in Iraq.

Very truly yours,
E. Leo Milonas

CHAPTER 4

Letter from the Association President to President George W. Bush re Human Rights and Security of Women and Girls in Afghanistan

PREFACE BY ALAN R. ROTHSTEIN

When the United States and coalition forces invaded Afghanistan in November 2001, one of the hoped-for by-products of deposing the Taliban government was the improvement in the condition of women and girls in that country. Females had been deprived of rights by the Taliban government and treated harshly when they sought to exercise those rights. In the aftermath of the overthrow of the Taliban government, however, hope turned to disillusionment. The international community and the central government of Afghanistan were unable to provide the support for a rebirth of women's rights. Several human rights organizations, including Human Rights Watch, issued reports that criticized the United Nations, the United States, and other countries involved in Afghanistan with failing to improve the plight of women and girls.

The Association of the Bar, in a letter to President Bush dated March 10, 2003, sought to focus on specific recommendations for what the President could do to improve the plight of Afghan women and girls. In making these recommendations, the Association was mindful of the deteriorating security situation, particularly outside the capital of Kabul, and the dominance of warlords in many areas of the country, who exercised effective control over wide swaths of territory and over its people. The letter stressed the importance of providing security as an underpinning for achieving success in expanding women's rights.

March 10, 2003

The Honorable George W. Bush
The White House
Washington, DC 20500

Re: Human Rights and Security of Women and Girls in Afghanistan

Dear President Bush:

I am writing on behalf of the Association of the Bar of the City of New York. The Association is an independent non-governmental organization with more than 22,000 members in over

40 countries. Founded in 1870, the Association has a long history of dedication to human rights, notably through its Committee on International Human Rights, which investigates and reports on human rights conditions around the world. The Association, as an organization of lawyers, is particularly interested in the current situation in Afghanistan.

When the United States undertook its mission in Afghanistan, we raised great hopes among all of its citizens—including women and girls—that we would assist them in regaining basic human rights. Indeed, you have spoken out many times in support of the new freedom of Afghanistan's women and girls, and even stressed the importance of this freedom in your recent State of the Union address. We are writing today to express our deep concern about the safety and rights of these women and girls, who are eager to participate as equals in the reconstruction and governance of their country. The dire threat to the security of women and girls in Afghanistan has been made abundantly clear by many recent, independent and reliable sources, including the August 2002 report by the UN Special Rapporteur on Afghanistan, the November and December 2002 reports by Human Rights Watch, and the analysis of the Harvard Program on Humanitarian Policy and Conflict Research, dated January 2003. We urge you to take immediate, strategic and robust action to ensure women's safety and human rights are fully protected.

There is no doubt that the situation for most women and girls in Afghanistan has improved since the fall of the Taliban. However, there are disturbing signs that Taliban-era restrictions are again being promulgated and enforced in several parts of the country—most prominently in districts near Kabul and Kandahar, and in the western province of Herat. In addition, reports indicate that a gravely insufficient number of human rights monitors have been deployed in the countryside, and that women rarely have access to urgently needed services and assistance.

There are credible reports that in Herat, the local governor, Ismail Khan, has censored women's groups, intimidated outspoken women leaders, and sidelined women from his administration. Further, restrictions have been placed on their right to work, so that many women are not able to use their hard-won education. Perhaps most distressing are the physical restrictions on women and girls. Government-enforced limitations on their freedom of movement—including a prohibition on driving and on their being in the presence of unrelated men —mean that women and girls are confined arbitrarily. There are reports of abuses by police in Herat, who have detained women and girls accused of being accompanied by unrelated men and forced them to undergo medical examinations to determine if they have recently engaged in sexual intercourse.

While the violations reported from Herat are deplorable, the worsening situation for women and girls is not limited to that province. Credible reports from across the country indicate that women and girls are facing increasingly harsh restrictions by local leaders. Many women, especially those outside of Kabul, fear abuse by police, troops, and government officials should they attend school or university. Women interviewed by journalists and international workers are not only fearful but also deeply disillusioned; instead of the anticipated improvements in their lives, they are experiencing deteriorating rights.

All of the abuses cited above amount to grave human rights violations. They are also clear threats to the safety and basic security of women and girls in Afghanistan, the backbone of a renewed country. We urge you to work closely with the United Nations and the Government of Afghanistan to press regional leaders such as Ismail Khan to cease immediately the use of decrees and government policies that violate the human rights of women and girls, including their right to bodily integrity and freedom from torture, their right to freedom of expression and equal participation, their freedom of movement and association, and their right to equal treatment, work, and education.

We also call on you to encourage the United Nations Mission in Afghanistan to increase the number of human rights monitors throughout the country, and to offer funding, materials, or technical assistance as needed to support this effort. Human rights monitors should be charged specifically with monitoring violations of the rights of women and girls, as well as other serious abuses, and with publicly reporting on such violations.

Finally, we gratefully acknowledge your support for the Ministry of Women's Affairs and the Independent Human Rights Commission, which will be funded through the Afghan Freedom Support Act. Both the Ministry of Women's Affairs and the Human Rights Commission are in dire need of increased technical and financial assistance, and the promised US funds will go a long way toward ensuring their effectiveness. Money is not enough, however; basic political assistance should be extended to these institutions, and arrangements for their protection should be made by the government and those supporting government institutions.

The United States will make a genuine and concrete difference in the lives of women and girls in Afghanistan by insisting on an end to abuses against women and girls by regional leaders, working with the United Nations to extend the reach of human rights monitors, and supporting the Ministry of Women's Affairs and the Human Rights Commission. Further, by taking these steps, your celebratory words from the State of the Union address—that "today women are free" in Afghanistan—will be supported by the essential complement to freedom: security. Until women are secure in Afghanistan, their freedom will be incomplete.

Thank you for considering our recommendations and concerns. We look forward to your reply.

Respectfully,
E. Leo Milonas
President

CHAPTER 5

Letter to Honorable William J. Haynes II re Comments on Military Commission Instruction —Crimes and Elements for Trials by Military Commissions

PREFACE BY MILES P. FISCHER

"Instruction No. 2,"[1] on which the Association commented with some actual impact, is one of nine Instructions issued by the Department of Defense (DOD) to implement the President's Military Order of November 13, 2003, creating military commissions (MCs). Apart from being the sole substantive guidance for the MCs, Instruction No. 2 is of interest to students of the law of war as a bold attempt at codification of that body of customary law, although it regrettably lacks any citation or reference to customary authority.

Instruction No. 2, as adopted, reflects changes responsive to comments received, including (we are glad to report) some of ours. For example, on a specific offense we questioned how a foreign national owing no duty to the United States could be prosecuted for "aiding the enemy" and proposed requiring such a duty as an element of the offense. Reflecting our suggestion almost literally, the final Instruction added the requirement that "the accused owe allegiance or some duty to the United States of America or an ally or coalition partner." §6B(5)(b)(3).

We also urged greater clarity that the Instruction is declarative of existing customary law. The final Instruction applied that concept to the retroactivity issue, adding that "no offense is cognizable in a trial by military commission if that offence did not exist prior to the conduct in question" and "(B)ecause this document is declarative of existing law, it does not preclude trial for crimes that occurred prior to its effective date." The door seems to be open to defenses challenging whether Instruction No. 2 correctly defined customary law existing at the time of the offense. §3(A).

This amenability of DOD to comments is exceptional. Instruction No. 2 is the only part of the documentation for MCs made available for public comment before adoption. The Military Order itself, Military Commission Order No. 1 thereunder and the other Instructions were all adopted without public comment. However, despite requesting comments on Instruction No. 2, DOD did not take the additional step of making available the comments it received.[2]

Three years later, rereading Instruction No. 2 and the thoughtful views of other known commentators on many implicit issues, we see that even the combined known comments only touched the surface of the innumerable issues presented by this attempted codification of the law of war without indication of supporting authority. A fuller understanding may emerge only after specific allegations of crimes defined by Instruction No. 2 are charged in MCs and litigated before them.[3]

March 21, 2003

Honorable William J. Haynes II
General Counsel
Department of Defense
1600 Defense Pentagon
Washington, DC 20301-1600

Re: Comments on Military Commission Instruction—Crimes and Elements for Trials by Military Commissions (the "Instruction")

Dear Mr. Haynes,

We commend the General Counsel of the Department of Defense for making the Instruction available for public comment. Considering the brief time made available for comments on a subject encompassing nearly the full range of the law of war, we confine our remarks to the following salient points:

The Instruction "provides guidance" and is "declarative" of provisions of the common law of war, "illustrative of applicable principles" and not "an exclusive enumeration". Nonetheless, it is entitled an "Instruction" and purports to "define" the elements of crimes. It should be made clearer that the Instruction is not intended as binding on the members of commissions or defendants with respect to the definition of crimes to the extent that it is determined that a provision is inconsistent with the common law of war, . Moreover, given the authority reserved to the Congress "to *define* and punish...Offenses against the Law of Nations", Article I, Section 8 of the Constitution (emphasis added), language stating that the Instruction "defines" the elements of crimes within the purview of military commissions should be amended in favor of language that characterizes the definitions as reflecting existing common law.

Beyond the classic crimes of the law of war within the traditional jurisdiction of military commissions trying members of an enemy force, the Instructions go on to define "related offenses" of Aiding and Abetting, Solicitation, Accessory after the Fact and Conspiracy. Such offenses are susceptible to expanding the subject matter jurisdiction of military commissions to conduct beyond the established purview of the law of war, especially where the defendant is not a member of an armed enemy. Such expansion would not only exceed the self-limitation of the Military Order to "violations of the law of war and all other offenses triable by military commissions", Military Commission Order No. 1, Section 3B, but, if applied to non-combatant defendants found in the United States, would potentially violate the Constitutional right to trial by jury of civilians not members of an enemy force and triable by the regular courts. See *Ex parte Milligan,* 71 U.S. 2 (1866).

Three provisions are of particular concern with respect to potential overreaching. First, under the Instruction the offense of "terrorism", a relatively new offense to the law of war without substantial customary law, would be committed by causing property damage without regard to conduct causing or threatening loss of life. It is submitted that this offense be limited to the commission of "violent acts or acts dangerous to human life", as in 18 USC §2331. Property damage alone is properly covered by a distinct crime more familiar to the law of war. Secondly, because the offense of "aiding the enemy" would appear to extend to an individual, *e.g.,* a foreign national, owing no duty to the United States; we recommend that there be included a reference to such a duty. Finally, the clause in Paragraph 6.B.6)a(1) of the Instruction referring to persons who "joined an enterprise of persons who shared a common criminal purpose" could improperly extend to ordinary crimes beyond the law of war; it should be deleted or rephrased.

Given the unfamiliar and controversial nature of military commissions, which have not been used in any of America's armed conflicts of the last fifty years, it is respectfully submitted that military commissions will be most effective and attain the greatest legitimacy under the rule of law if they are confined to the trial of defendants who are clearly enemy combatants charged with direct complicity in heinous crimes.

Subject to these comments, we believe that the Instructions will be a useful, and even essential, tool for members of commissions, and prosecutors and defense counsel practicing before them.

Very truly yours,
Miles P. Fischer, Chair
Committee on Military Affairs & Justice
Association of the Bar of the City of New York

NOTES

1. Military Commission Instruction No. 2 Crimes and Elements for Trial by Military Commission, http://www.defenselink.mil/news/May2003/d20030430milcominstno2.pdf; 32 CFR Part 11; 68 Fed Reg 39381, July 1, 2003.

2. The National Institute of Military Justice (NIMJ) published comments made available by commentators, NIMJ, Military Commission Sourcebook (2003), and is suing under the Freedom of Information Act to obtain all comments, NIMJ v. Department of Defense, D.D.C., CA No. 04-0312 (RBW).

3. Whether challenges to charges under Instruction No. 2 can be properly litigated, and if so, publicly known, depends among other things on the limitations posed by the potential secrecy of MC proceedings, restrictions on defense counsel, and the severely limited avenues of appeal characteristic of MCs under the Military Order.

CHAPTER 6

Letter to U.S. Department of Defense Inspector General Joseph E. Schmitz re Enemy Prisoners of War and Other Detainees

PREFACE BY MILES P. FISCHER

Our letter of April 2003 sought (it turned out in vain) the intercession of the Army's Inspector General in enforcing at Guantanamo detainee screening procedures under Army Regulations and the Geneva Conventions. In response, the Inspector General apparently referred the matter to the same civilian General Counsel whose failure to enforce the regulations and treaty inspired our recourse to the Inspector General.

Our letter anticipated a fundamental issue that would be raised in *Hamdan v. Rumsfeld,* 344 F.Supp.2d 152 (D.C.Cir. 2004) and ensuing proceedings up to the appeal to the Supreme Court decided on June 29, 2006. Whether the detainees are entitled to the screening procedures and potentially to status as prisoners of war (POWs) reverberated when some detainees, including Salid Ahmad Hamdan, were charged for trial before military commissions. (POWs can be tried only before the same courts martial as try our own service personnel; any other form of trial would be a grave breach of the Third Geneva Convention where fully applicable and a federal felony under the War Crimes Act.) The Supreme Court found it unnecessary to decide this issue once it held that the present military commissions fail to comply with another provision of the Geneva Conventions, Common Article 3,[1] and the Uniform Code of Military Justice. Thus the POW screening issue and arguable claim to trial by court martial remains undecided.

Our letter did not assume that detainees would, in fact, be entitled to prisoner of war status and thus trial by court martial. Although not discussed in the letter, we found it hard to believe that those accused of membership in al Qaeda could show service in a combatant unit "conducting their operations in accordance with the laws and customs of war,"[2] especially while arguing that they were not combatants at all—all the more reason to hold the required screening proceedings, filter out non-combatants mistakenly brought to Guantanamo, and separate combatants not entitled to POW status (presumably al Qaeda members) from those, if any, entitled to POW status (arguably some Taliban members).

While holding such proceedings would still have left much to criticize at Guantanamo, including the issues decided by the Supreme Court in *Hamdan,* they would certainly have removed a major international complaint against the United States and established a clearer legal basis for the trial of detainees, whether by military commission (if otherwise lawful) or court martial. Unfortunately, the Inspector General, civilian General Counsel, and others in authority did not accept the suggestions of our letter.

April 18, 2003

Inspector General Joseph E. Schmitz
Department of Defense
400 Army Navy Drive
Arlington, VA 22202-4704

Re: Enemy Prisoners of War and Other Detainees

Dear General Schmitz:

The Committee on Military Affairs & Justice of the Association of the Bar of the City of New York is a committee of attorneys, judges and law students engaged on a pro bono basis in matters of policy and law relating to the United States Armed Forces. Our objective is to assist the Association in sharing with its 22,000 members and the general public a balanced view of such matters.

As you know, the legal status of detainees in the custody of the Armed Forces at Guantanamo Bay Naval Station in Cuba is an active concern of bar associations both in this country and in other nations that have ratified the Geneva Convention III Relative to the Treatment of Prisoners of War. The legal status of detainees is also a matter of much public interest and media attention. An article, dated March 24, 2003, in *The New York Times,* reports 21 men detained at Guantanamo Bay were repatriated to Afghanistan by the Armed Forces and 660 others remain in detention at Guantanamo Bay. A subsequent *Times* article of April 8, 2003 reports that officials described detainees as falling loosely into three categories—"people who were probably needlessly detained, a few Qaeda members and a group of people about whom they know little."

It does not appear that those detained by the Armed Forces at Guantanamo Bay have been afforded the right to a formal determination of their status, *if any doubt arises as to their status,* as provided in paragraph (b) of Section 1–6, entitled *Tribunals,* of Army Regulation 190-8 (and identical regulations prescribed by the other services) (the "Regulation") and Article V of such Geneva Convention. In this connection, we have not had a reply to our letter, dated March 7, 2003, to Hon. Steven J. Morello, General Counsel of the Department of the Army, a copy of which is enclosed.

In view of the large number of detainees and the history of releasing some detainees, we believe that it is likely that there remain some detainees concerning whom some doubt exists regarding their legal status. On that basis, the mandate of Section 1-6 (b) is clear: "A competent tribunal shall determine the status of any person...concerning whom any doubt...exists." Moreover, Section 1-6(a) of the Regulation and Article V of such Geneva Convention require that pending such determination, such detainees are to be treated as prisoners of war. This requirement suggests that competent tribunals should be convened at the earliest opportunity in the detention process in order to accord each detainee from the beginning the treatment appropriate to his circumstances.

In making this comment, we do not intend to refer to blanket determinations as to the status of Al Qaeda or the Taliban as entities, but rather to the individual status of detainees as persons who may or may not be "enemy combatants" and members of Al Qaeda or the Taliban. It has been suggested that certain detainees were innocent civilians found on or near the battlefield, exactly the type of person whose status should be considered by a "competent tribunal" under such Geneva Convention and the Regulation.

We are cognizant of the national security considerations affecting the confidentiality of information relevant to the status of detainees and believe that administrative tribunals could function consistently with such considerations.

We appreciate that the Regulation provides for an administrative determination and not for a judicial proceeding, and that administrative proceedings would determine solely the status of detainees and not culpability for any alleged violation of the law of war. We do not express a view as to any possible constitutional requirement of a judicial proceeding to determine the legality of the detention of individuals who may be entitled to constitutional protections based on such factors as citizenship, residence, or place or circumstances of detention.

Accordingly, we wish to call your attention to the apparent violation of the Regulation and such Geneva Convention in the detentions at Guantanamo Bay without the benefit of status determinations by competent tribunals when applicable. On behalf of those detained without the status determinations to which they are entitled, and in the interest of the good repute of the Armed Forces and the rule of law, we ask you to investigate.

Respectfully submitted,
Miles P. Fischer, Committee Chair
Committee on Military Affairs & Justice

NOTES

1. The need for military commissions to comply with international procedural standards under Common Article 3 was argued by the Association in its amicus brief in *Hamdan*.

2. Geneva Convention Relative to Treatment of Prisoners of War, Aug. 12, 1949, 6 USTS 3316, Art. 4, A (2)(d) (setting conditions for POW status of militias and others not forming part of the regular armed forces of a State Party).

CHAPTER 7

Amicus Brief: Jose Padilla v. Donald Rumsfeld

PREFACE BY JOSEPH G. DAVIS

On May 8, 2002, Jose Padilla, an American citizen who was traveling through O'Hare Airport in Chicago on his way back to the United States from Pakistan, was arrested pursuant to a material witness warrant issued by Chief Judge Mukasey of the Southern District of New York. After his arrest, Padilla was transferred to New York and detained there on the basis of the material witness warrant.

On May 15, 2002, Padilla appeared before Chief Judge Mukasey, who appointed Donna R. Newman to represent him. On May 22, Ms. Newman moved to vacate the material witness warrant, raising serious statutory and constitutional challenges to the government's decision to detain Padilla indefinitely without charging him. By June 7, the motion had been submitted for decision. A June 11 conference was scheduled on the motion before Chief Judge Mukasey.

On June 9, 2002, President George W. Bush issued a one-page Order declaring Mr. Padilla an "enemy combatant" and ordering the Secretary of Defense to detain him. In reliance on the President's Order, the United States withdrew the warrant and transferred Padilla from New York to the Consolidated Naval Brig, a high-security military jail in Charleston, South Carolina. One day later, on June 10, 2002, at a news conference called in Moscow, Russia, Attorney General Ashcroft proclaimed that Padilla was a "known terrorist who was exploring a plan to build and explode a radiological dispersion device, or 'dirty bomb,' in the United States."

When Ms. Newman arrived at the June 11 conference with Chief Judge Mukasey, her client had already been transferred to military custody, where the government proposed to hold him indefinitely. Padilla's counsel responded by filing a *habeas corpus* petition as next friend, identifying Secretary of Defense Donald Rumsfeld as Padilla's ultimate custodian, and challenging the legality of the government's continued military detention of Padilla. In opposition to Padilla's *habeas* position, the United States argued that the President had the authority to detain and interrogate Mr. Padilla indefinitely, without access to counsel or any contact outside of his prison.

In a pair of rulings, Chief Judge Mukasey upheld the President's power to detain civilians as enemy combatants, but also held that Padilla had a right under *habeas corpus* to a hearing to challenge his designation as an enemy combatant and his detention by the military. Over the government's objections, the Court also found that Padilla had the right to present facts through counsel. Over Padilla's objection, Chief Judge Mukasey ruled that the President's determination that Mr. Padilla was an enemy combatant was entitled to significant deference and must be upheld as long as the government could provide "some evidence" supporting the Executive's actions. Unwilling to accord Padilla even the minimal procedural protection of access to counsel and to submit its actions even to limited judicial scrutiny under the "some evidence" standard, the United States appealed to the Second Circuit.

ABCNY was closely following the *Padilla* case. All interested Committees were in agreement: The President of the United States did not have the authority to imprison indefinitely an American citizen captured on U.S. soil far from any battlefield without any form of due process. Because Padilla was forcibly removed from the criminal justice system in the Southern District of New York, ABCNY felt a particular obligation to address the far-reaching implications of the Executive's actions.

On July 29, 2003, Willkie Farr & Gallagher LLP filed the brief reproduced below on behalf of ABCNY as *amicus curiae.* ABCNY argued that Padilla had a statutory right to challenge his detention through the writ of *habeas corpus,* that this right necessarily encompassed the right to access to counsel, and that the standard of review of his detention had to be more exacting than the overly deferential "some evidence" standard championed by the government.

On December 18, 2003, the Second Circuit issued a historic ruling declaring that the President did not have inherent Constitutional authority to detain American citizens on American soil outside a zone of combat as an enemy combatant. While this decision was reversed by the United States Supreme Court on the ground that the Southern District of New York did not have statutory jurisdiction over Padilla's custodian after he was transferred to the Naval Brig in South Carolina, the Supreme Court did not rule on the merits of Padilla's detention. With the assistance of Willkie Farr, ABCNY participated as *amicus curiae* in these proceedings and in later proceedings before the Fourth Circuit and Supreme Court, after Padilla's *habeas* petition was re-filed in the District of South Carolina.

When Padilla's case was presented to the Supreme Court for the second time, the government changed tactics. On November 17, 2005, a Grand Jury sitting in the Southern District of Florida indicted Jose Padilla and others for crimes that bore little resemblance to those for which he was detained as an enemy combatant. On November 20, 2005, the President issued an order transferring Padilla to the custody of the Justice Department. Based on these actions, the Supreme Court decided not to review Padilla's South Carolina *habeas* petition. Criminal proceedings against Jose Padilla in Florida continue as of this writing.

What will history recall of the *Padilla* case? Justice Stevens, writing in 2004 for the four members of the Court who dissented from the decision to reverse the Second Circuit on jurisdictional grounds, reasoned that whether Padilla was "entitled to immediate release [was] a question that reasonable jurists may answer in different ways," but that there was "only one possible answer to the question whether he [was] entitled to a hearing on the justification for his detention." He continued:

At stake in this case is nothing less than the essence of a free society. Even more important than the method of selecting the people's rulers and their successors is the character of the constraints imposed on the Executive by the rule of law. Unconstrained Executive detention for the purpose of investigating and preventing subversive activity is the hallmark of the Star Chamber. Access to counsel for the purpose of protecting the citizen from official mistakes and mistreatment is the hallmark of due process.

ABCNY recognized the importance of the *Padilla* case to the rule of law and due process from the outset. Hopefully, the voices of ABCNY and many other members of the Bar who rose up to speak in defense of "the essence of a free society" will be remembered.

United States Court of Appeals for the Second Circuit
Jose Padilla, Donna R. Newman, as Next Friend of Jose Padilla
Petitioner-Appellee-Cross-Appellant,
Against
Donald Rumsfeld,
Respondent-Appellant-Cross-Appellee
On appeal from the United States District Court for the Southern District of New York
Brief for Amicus Curiae Association of the Bar of the City of New York in Support of
Petitioner-Appellee-Cross-Appellant

INTRODUCTION AND ARGUMENT SUMMARY

In this case the Court is asked to decide whether a U.S. citizen apprehended on U.S. soil far from any theatre of war and held by the military as an "enemy combatant" has any meaningful recourse to the courts and access to counsel in defense of his liberty. The government contends that the limited role of an Article III court is to review the Executive's *ex parte* factual determination, confirm that "some evidence" supports the enemy combatant designation and validate the detention. According to the government, neither the detainee's counsel, nor the detainee himself, has any meaningful role to play in that process. The Association of the Bar of the City of New York ("ABCNY") respectfully disagrees, and therefore submits this amicus brief in support of habeas petitioner Jose Padilla.

Never before has the Executive successfully asserted the right to detain indefinitely, without charge or process, someone taken into custody on U.S. soil in a non-combat setting based on the unilateral determination that the detainee is an enemy combatant. Twice in perhaps the darkest moments of this country's history the Executive has made similar attempts. In Ex Parte Milligan and Ex Parte Quirin the Supreme Court twice restrained this overextension of executive power. In no uncertain terms, the Court admonished that the judiciary has the power and the obligation (1) to review *de novo* the Executive's determination that a person detained under those circumstances is an unlawful combatant; and (2) to adjudicate the constitutionality of the detention order and disposition of the detainee. In this amicus brief, ABCNY addresses the first of these two exercises of judicial power and Padilla's right to contest the Executive's determination that he is an enemy combatant.[1]

This is a habeas case. The district court correctly concluded that the writ of habeas corpus demands that Padilla be permitted to present facts in support of his petition and communicate with his counsel. The government concedes Padilla's right to petition for habeas corpus but attempts to eviscerate that right by denying him the ability to present facts and to assist his lawyer and next friend in the presentation of his case. The habeas statutes do not permit such an interpretation of the Great Writ. Rather, they expressly grant petitioner the right to "deny" and "allege" facts, and impose on the court the obligation to "hear and determine" those facts. 28 U.S.C. § 2243. Moreover, and in aid of this right, the district court properly determined that the habeas statutes required the government to grant Padilla access to his counsel for the limited purpose of presenting the petition, and properly invoked the All Writs Act to fulfill its "duty" to "provide the necessary facilities and procedures for an adequate [habeas] inquiry." Harris v. Nelson, 394 U.S. 286, 300 (1969). (See Argument, Part I, infra.)

Though this Court need not invoke it to affirm, the Due Process Clause of the Fifth Amendment also requires that Padilla be given the ability to present facts in aid of his petition and consult with counsel. Padilla's right to communicate with the court and present facts in aid of his petition is the most fundamental of all his Fifth Amendment due process rights. The government's contention that it can hold Padilla incommunicado and that the Court can deny his petition—a petition for his very liberty—while Padilla sits mute in a brig is unprecedented and shocks the conscience. (See Argument, Part II.A, infra.)

Moreover, because the Due Process Clause requires not just access to the courts, but meaningful access, Padilla has the related right to consult with counsel in aid of his petition. The government contends that "[t]here is no basis in historical tradition or practice for recognizing a right of enemy combatants to have counsel for the purpose of challenging their wartime detention." (Gov't Br. at 37.)[2] The government adds that the "Constitution likewise affords no right to counsel...because Padilla is being detained as an enemy combatant and not for any criminal or other punitive purpose." (Id. at 39.) As applied to Padilla and the circumstances of his detention, these contentions are simply false. They are belied by Quirin and Milligan, among other cases, and the well-settled line of authority affording a right to counsel in non-criminal and non-punitive settings when individual liberty and other important interests are at stake. Whatever weight might be given to the Executive's asserted interest in shielding from judicial examination its interrogation of Padilla, its right to continue that interrogation is entirely dependent on the outcome of this proceeding. The Executive's interest therefore must give way to an appropriately defined right to assistance of counsel. (See Part II.B, infra.)

After deciding the procedural issues, the district court also ruled on the standards that would apply to the proceeding. Relying principally on the Fourth Circuit's decisions in Hamdi v. Rumsfeld, the government argued that the courts' power to review the Executive's determination that Padilla is an enemy combatant was limited to a determination of whether "some evidence" supported the designation. The district court, interpreting the government's position to be that Padilla is an unlawful combatant—that is, a combatant not entitled to international law protection as a prisoner of war—essentially agreed.

But Hamdi does not support the district court's ruling, as the Fourth Circuit itself explicitly stated. In Hamdi, unlike here, the petitioner was detained in a foreign theatre of war. According to the Fourth Circuit, this key fact was undisputed and sufficient to support the designation of enemy combatant. While the courts will accord deference to executive decisions concerning the disposition of those already determined to be unlawful combatants, deference does not attach to the unilateral decision to detain a U.S. citizen on U.S. soil far from any active zone of combat. Thus, the "some evidence" standard is incompatible with Milligan and Quirin.

Moreover, the "some evidence" standard has never been applied to test executive jurisdiction on U.S. soil over one who contests that jurisdiction. Rather, as the Supreme Court has held on many occasions, Article III courts should review *de novo* the threshold question of whether executive jurisdiction is appropriate. The Supreme Court consistently has imposed on the government a significant burden to justify restrictions on individual liberty in many and varied contexts. Where, as here, the government seeks to detain a U.S. citizen indefinitely and strip him of his right to due process, even significant concerns of national security cannot justify a burden less substantial than *de novo* review under a clear and convincing evidence standard. The district court thus erred by ruling that it would ratify the Executive's determination if the government could adduce "some evidence" to support it. (See Argument, Part III, infra.)

INTEREST OF AMICUS CURIAE AND SOURCE OF AUTHORITY TO FILE

ABCNY is a professional association of nearly 22,000 attorneys. Founded in 1870, ABCNY has long been committed to studying, addressing, and promoting the rule of law and, when appropriate, law reform. Through its many standing committees, including its Committees on Civil Rights, Federal Courts, Military Affairs and Justice, and Criminal Law, ABCNY educates the bar and public about current issues arising in connection with the "war" on terrorism, the pursuit of suspected terrorists, and the treatment of detainees. While it fully understands the importance of preventing future acts of terrorism, ABCNY believes that the Executive's actions in this and similar cases are dangerously eroding civil liberties and the efficacy of habeas corpus. ABCNY therefore submits this brief in support of Padilla's rights to contest the factual basis for his detention and to meaningful habeas review. All parties have given ABCNY consent to file this brief.

ARGUMENT

I.   The District Court Properly Determined That the Habeas Corpus Statutes Give Padilla the Right to Present Facts Through Counsel Challenging His Detention

A.   Padilla's Right to Petition for Habeas Review Is Undisputed

The government does not dispute directly Padilla's right to petition for habeas review. See Padilla v. Bush, 233 F. Supp. 2d 564, 599 (S.D.N.Y. 2002) ("Padilla I"); Padilla v. Rumsfeld, 243 F. Supp. 2d 42, 53–54 (S.D.N.Y. 2003) ("Padilla II"). Nor could it. The writ of habeas corpus provides the mechanism for reviewing executive detention, Swain v. Pressley, 430 U.S. 372, 386 (1977) (Burger, C.J., concurring), and is the fundamental safeguard against illegal restraint, INS v. St. Cyr, 533 U.S. 289, 301 (2001). The writ's protections are "strongest" when executive detention is challenged, id., because, without judicial scrutiny, such detention "lacks that assurance of legality which has come to be thought of as integral to government under law," Gerald L. Neuman, Habeas Corpus, Executive Detention, and the Removal of Aliens, 98 Colum. L. Rev. 961, 984 (1998). Where, as here, an American citizen is detained under executive authority as an enemy combatant, without judicial or any other process, habeas review is not only appropriate, it is compulsory. See Hamdi v. Rumsfeld, 316 F.3d 450, 464–65 (4th Cir. 2003) ("Hamdi App. III").

B.   The Habeas Corpus Statutes Give Padilla the Right to Present Facts Challenging His Detention as an Enemy Combatant

While the government does not dispute Padilla's right to file a habeas petition, it disputes his right to present facts in support of that petition. It contends that "[t]he habeas statutes do not afford Padilla a free-standing entitlement to raise a factual challenge to his detention." (Gov't Br. at 40.) The district court, correctly, disagreed. See Padilla I, 233 F. Supp. 2d at 600 (finding that "Padilla's right to present facts is rooted firmly in the statutes that provide the basis for his petition").[3]

Padilla petitioned for review pursuant to 28 U.S.C. §§ 2241, *et. seq.*[4] In concluding that Padilla has a statutory right to present facts *in this case,* the district court relied principally on section 2243, which states that "[t]he applicant or the person detained may, under oath, deny any of the facts set forth in the return or allege any other material facts." 28 U.S.C. § 2243. Section 2243 goes on to state that the habeas court "shall summarily hear and determine the facts, and dispose of the case as law and justice require." These provisions grant Padilla the right to raise and support fact-based arguments and require the district court to resolve factual disputes on habeas review. The district court cannot discharge this duty if it only gets to hear the Executive's evidence. See Walker v. Johnston, 312 U.S. 275, 284–85 (1941) (habeas petition could not be adjudicated based on the government's *ex parte* affidavits without opportunity for rebuttal).

Padilla's right to present facts is not discretionary, as the government suggests. (See Gov't Br. at 9.) As the Supreme Court stated over thirty years ago, the writ mandates an opportunity to present evidence in cases where the facts are in controversy, as they are here:

It is now established beyond the reach of reasonable dispute that the federal courts not only *may* grant evidentiary hearings to applicants, but *must* do so upon an appropriate showing.

Harris, 394 U.S. at 291 (emphasis supplied). While a full-blown hearing, replete with the traditional panoply of procedural safeguards, may not be required in every case, the opportunity to present facts cannot be denied. Id. at 298–99. This conclusion applies with extra force where, as here, the petitioner has been detained without any pre-detention process, see Brown v. Allen, 344 U.S. 443, 533 (1953) (Jackson, J., concurring) ("[t]he historic purpose of the writ has been to relieve detention by executive authorities without judicial trial"), and the proof upon which the detention is premised consists solely of a vague affidavit, cf. Blackledge v. Allison, 432 U.S. 63, 82 n.25 (1977) (noting that the disposition of habeas petitions on the basis of affidavits alone is likely to be improper when credibility is at issue).

Unlike the typical habeas petitioner, who has received notice of the charges against him and an opportunity to be heard in his defense, Padilla has not been convicted of any crime, nor has his status been adjudicated in any forum. Rather, the Executive simply declared Padilla an enemy combatant and locked him away without ever giving him the chance to contest the factual basis for his detention. Because Padilla received virtually no process at any time before or after his detention, the habeas statutes compel the conclusion that he be given an opportunity to present facts in his defense. Cf. Harris, 394 U.S. at 298 (petitioners are "entitled to careful and plenary processing of their claims including full opportunity for presentation of the relevant facts").[5]

Ex Parte Bollman is particularly instructive. In Bollman, Chief Justice Marshall addressed the habeas petitions of two prisoners who were accused of conspiring with Aaron Burr to commit treason by levying war against the United States. Bollman, 8 U.S. at 75–76. The petitioners were seized in Pennsylvania and removed to Washington, D.C. based on a warrant issued by the District of Columbia district court on an application by the military. Id. at 75–6 & n.2. The Supreme Court first decided, in the more often quoted section of its opinion, that it had the power to issue a writ of habeas corpus to free the petitioners. Id. at 93–101. The Court then went on to examine, in detail, the evidence of treason proffered against the prisoners, "which the court below ought to have done," according to Justice Marshall. Id. at 114, 114–37. While recognizing that the acts supported by the government's evidence may have been unlawful, id. at 136–37, the Court nevertheless concluded that the evidence, including military affidavits, was insufficient to justify a charge of treason by levying war against the United States and ordered the petitioners set free. Id. at 136. Bollman thus demonstrates that a core function of the writ is to adjudicate, on the facts, the contention of one held prisoner on the word of the Executive that the detention is wrongful—even, or especially, when the charge is levying war against the United States.

In an attempt to avoid the district court's conclusion that Padilla has a statutory right to present facts, the government relies on Hamdi App. III. The government maintains that Hamdi App. III stands for the proposition that, under the habeas statutes, an enemy combatant "has no entitlement to present facts to challenge the basis for his detention nor any entitlement to counsel for that purpose. . . ." (Gov't Br. at 43–44.) The government misconstrues Hamdi App. III on several levels.

First, the Fourth Circuit admonished that its decision does not control, or even apply to, Padilla's situation: "we have no occasion, for example, to address the designation as an enemy combatant of an American citizen captured on American soil or the role that counsel might play in such a proceeding." Hamdi App. III, 316 F.3d at 465.

Second, the Fourth Circuit's decision actually confirms that the right to present facts is available in section 2241 proceedings. Id. at 470 (recognizing that "the ordinary § 2241 proceeding naturally contemplates the prospect of factual development").

Third, and of greatest significance, the Fourth Circuit held that Hamdi was not entitled to the opportunity to present evidence because the key jurisdictional fact underlying his detention was not disputed: "we hold that no evidentiary hearing or factual inquiry on our part is necessary or proper, because it is undisputed that Hamdi was captured in a zone of active combat operations in a foreign country and because any inquiry must be circumscribed to avoid encroachment into the military affairs entrusted to the executive branch." Id. at 473. The court most certainly did not hold that enemy combatants *never* have a right to present facts. Instead, the court limited its decision to the case before it and held that, where the jurisdictional facts that justify an individual's designation and detention as an enemy combatant are undisputed or conceded, there is no right to, or need for, further development of the facts. Id. at 476. In marked contrast to Hamdi's case, the facts underlying Padilla's detention as an enemy combatant are in dispute. In light of that dispute, the habeas statutes mandate that Padilla receive at the very least an opportunity to present facts attacking the credibility and accuracy of the Executive's evidence.

C.   The District Court Properly Directed the Executive to Provide Padilla Access to Counsel for the Purpose of Presenting Facts in Support of His Petition

1.   The appointment of counsel was proper and is not disputed

Notably, the government does not dispute the *appointment* of counsel for Padilla. Rather, the government objects to providing Padilla *access* to counsel, citing concerns about security and the impact that appointed counsel will have on the military's ability to extract information from Padilla. (Gov't Br. at 50–53.) The distinction between appointment of counsel and access to counsel is crucial.

Appointment of counsel in "the interests of justice" was well within the district court's discretion under 18 U.S.C. § 3006A(a)(2)(B). Padilla I, 233 F. Supp. 2d at 600; see also Hodge v. Police Officers, 802 F.2d 58, 60–61 (2d Cir. 1986); Engberg v. Wyoming, 265 F.3d 1109, 1122 (10th Cir. 2001); Winsett v. Washington, 130 F.3d 269, 281 (7th Cir. 1997). The complexity and importance of the statutory and constitutional questions in this case cannot be overstated. The government asserts—and asks this Court to sanction—sweeping authority to hold an American citizen incommunicado for an indefinite period and to interrogate him at length, without criminal charge. The appointment of counsel to represent Padilla would be justified by these circumstances alone. That Padilla is being held incommunicado, with no ability to investigate and present the facts or articulate his legal challenges, intensifies his need for legal representation and buttresses the district court's exercise of discretion. Furthermore, the "public interest" militates in favor of appointment of counsel here. "The public conscience must be satisfied that fairness dominates the administration of justice." Adams v. United States ex rel.

McCann, 317 U.S. 269, 279 (1942). It goes without saying that denying Padilla counsel, and forcing him to advocate on his own behalf, would be neither fair nor just. Indeed, it would be impossible.

2.   The district court properly exercised its authority under the all writs act to order access to counsel

Habeas petitioners have a right to "plenary processing of their claims including full opportunity for presentation of the relevant facts." Harris, 394 U.S. at 298. The district court found that Padilla's right to present the relevant facts would be meaningless without access to counsel:

Padilla's need to consult with a lawyer to help him do what the statute permits him to do is obvious. . . It would frustrate the purpose of the procedure Congress established in habeas corpus cases, and of the remedy itself, to leave Padilla with no practical means whatever for following that procedure.

Padilla I, 233 F. Supp. 2d at 602. Having determined that Padilla's habeas remedy would be lost without access to counsel, the district court properly exercised its discretion under the All Writs Act to order the government to provide such access.

The All Writs Act provides that "all courts established by Act of Congress may issue all writs necessary or appropriate in aid of their respective jurisdictions and agreeable to the usages and principles of law." 28 U.S.C. § 1651(a). The Act "empowers federal courts to fashion extraordinary remedies when the need arises." Pa. Bureau of Corr. v. U.S. Marshals Service, 474 U.S. 34, 43 (1985). The courts should exercise that discretionary power when necessary "to achieve the ends of justice entrusted to [them]." Adams, 317 U.S. at 273. An order issued under the All Writs Act is reviewed for abuse of discretion. Id.

The All Writs Act may be invoked in habeas cases to help the court, *and the petitioner,* investigate and present the facts. Harris, 394 U.S. at 300; United States v. Hayman, 342 U.S. 205, 221 (1952). Indeed, when procedural measures are necessary to ensure that the facts are fully developed and that the habeas proceedings are "fair and meaningful," the Supreme Court has held that "it is the duty of the court to provide the necessary facilities and procedures for an adequate inquiry." Harris, 394 U.S. at 300; see also Hayman, 342 U.S. at 223–24 (holding that the district court erred in conducting an *ex parte* hearing and should have exercised its discretion under the All Writs Act to secure the petitioner's attendance).

Here, the district court appropriately exercised its discretion under the All Writs Act when it commanded the government to afford Padilla access to appointed counsel in aid of his petition. See Padilla I, 233 F. Supp. 2d at 603. The Supreme Court has held that:

[a]n accused must have the means of presenting his best defense. He must have time and facilities for investigation and for the production of evidence. But evidence and truth are of no avail unless they can be adequately presented. Essential fairness is lacking if an accused cannot put his case effectively in court.

Adams, 317 U.S. at 278–79. The Supreme Court's language aptly describes Padilla's situation. Without access to counsel, Padilla will quite literally have no ability to contest the factual basis for his detention. Recognizing as much, the district court ordered access to counsel to ensure that Padilla can exercise his statutory rights in a fair and meaningful way. This constitutes a proper exercise of the district court's authority under the All Writs Act. See United States v. New York Tel. Co., 434 U.S. 159, 175 n.23 (1977) (the All Writs Act authority to issue orders in aid of the court's jurisdiction encompasses the power to issue orders that enable the parties to protect their legal rights).

In exercising its discretion, the district court properly balanced the competing interests at stake and narrowly tailored its order to the facts of this case. See Price v. Johnston, 334 U.S.

266, 284–85 (1948), <u>overruled on other grounds by McCleskey v. Zant</u>, 499 U.S. 467 (1991) (discretion "is to be exercised with the best interests of both the prisoner and the government in mind"). Padilla's interest in having access to counsel is clear: without such access neither he, nor his appointed counsel, will be able to exercise his statutory right to present facts. The Executive's asserted interests are that providing access to counsel will purportedly undermine interrogation efforts and could give rise to security concerns because Padilla may covertly pass messages to al Qaeda through counsel. (Gov't Br. at 50–53.)

The district court thoroughly evaluated these competing interests in the course of ordering access to counsel. In its initial Opinion and Order, the district court addressed the alleged security risks at length:

> Even giving substantial weight, as I do, to the President's statement in the June 9 Order that Padilla is 'a continuing, present and grave danger to the national security of the United States' and that his detention 'is necessary to prevent him from siding with al Qaeda in its efforts to attack the United States,' there has been no fact presented to me that shows that the source of that danger is the possibility that Padilla will transmit information to others through his lawyers. By contrast, Padilla's statutorily granted right to present facts to the court in connection with his petition will be destroyed utterly if he is not allowed to consult with counsel. On the facts presented in this case, the balance weighs heavily in Padilla's favor.

<u>Padilla I</u>, 233 F. Supp. 2d at 604. On the government's Motion for Reconsideration, the district court also comprehensively addressed and dispatched concerns about the impact that giving Padilla access to counsel might have on the military's interrogation efforts. <u>See</u> <u>Padilla II</u>, 243 F. Supp. 2d at 49–54.

Ultimately, the district court tailored its order to minimize the impact on the Executive's interrogation efforts while still providing Padilla a means to effectuate his right to present facts. Specifically, the district court made clear that:

> access to counsel need be granted only for the purposes of presenting facts to the court in connection with this petition if Padilla wishes to do so; no general right to counsel in connection with questioning has been hypothesized here, and thus the interference with interrogation would be minimal or nonexistent.

<u>Padilla I</u>, 233 F. Supp. 2d at 603. The district court's solution was not only proper, but also necessary to effect a meaningful habeas remedy. It should be affirmed.

II.   Padilla Has a Constitutional Right to Present His Case and Consult with Counsel

Although the district court recognized that the Fifth Amendment might provide a constitutional basis for its decision that Padilla is entitled to present facts and consult counsel in support of his habeas petition, it believed that the "nonconstitutional" grounds provided by the habeas statutes and All Writs Act were sufficient to support its ruling. <u>Padilla I</u>, 233 F. Supp. 2d at 601. The court therefore declined to explore an explicitly constitutional basis for its decision. <u>Id.</u> However, should this Court find that the habeas statutes and All Writs Act do not resolve the issue, the Constitution requires that Padilla be permitted both to present facts in aid of his petition and consult with counsel.

No court has ever held that a U.S. citizen detained on U.S. soil outside a theatre of war has no Fifth Amendment right to due process in connection with his habeas petition. On the contrary, as discussed below, the Supreme Court has uniformly granted due process rights to habeas petitioners challenging their status as enemy combatants or military detainees.

The Due Process Clause of the Fifth Amendment gives Padilla the right "to be heard at a meaningful time and in a meaningful manner." <u>Mathews v. Eldridge</u>, 424 U.S. 319, 333 (1976), quoting <u>Armstrong v. Manzo</u>, 380 U.S. 545, 552 (1965). Padilla's due process right to be heard, at a minimum, encompasses the right to present facts in support of his habeas petition.

Moreover, Padilla's right to be heard in a meaningful manner, given the complexity of this case and that his liberty hangs in the balance, encompasses the right to be heard through counsel.

A. *Padilla Has a Fifth Amendment Right to Present Facts in Support of His Habeas Petition*

"The fundamental requisite of due process of law is the opportunity to be heard." Goss v. Lopez, 419 U.S. 565, 579 (1975) (quoting Grannis v. Ordean, 234 U.S. 385, 394 (1914)). Access to the courts is therefore a "fundamental constitutional right." Bounds, 430 U.S. at 828; see also Procunier v. Martinez, 416 U.S. 396, 419 (1974), overruled in part by Thornburgh v. Abbott, 490 U.S. 401 (1989) ("The constitutional guarantee of due process of law has as a corollary the requirement that prisoners be afforded access to the courts in order to challenge unlawful convictions and to seek redress for violations of their constitutional rights"). "Rudimentary due process" requires the right to present arguments and evidence and confront adverse witnesses. Goldberg v. Kelly, 397 U.S. 254, 267–68 (1970). The government's contention that Padilla's habeas petition can be adjudicated without his participation, (Gov't Br. at 14, 40–49), flies in the face of this most basic and fundamental of constitutional tenets.[6]

The government's position is essentially unsupported. The Supreme Court has never accepted the contention that it could adjudicate a habeas petition without giving the petitioner the ability to present facts in support of his case. German saboteurs who landed on Long Island in a submarine wearing German uniforms during World War II were given the right to present facts—undisputed though most of them were—in aid of their habeas petition, through counsel no less. Ex parte Quirin, 317 U.S. 1, 19–20 (1942). Likewise, a Japanese General accused of supervising war crimes in the Philippines was given the right to present facts through counsel. Yamashita v. Styer, 327 U.S. 1, 5 (1946); see also id. at 47 (the Court does not suggest that "it could not ascertain whether conviction is founded upon evidence expressly excluded by Congress or treaty") (Rutledge, J, dissenting). Other detainees were afforded the same ability to present a case. See, e.g., Ludecke v. Watkins, 335 U.S. 160, 173 (1948) (affirming United States ex rel. Ludecke v. Watkins, 163 F.2d 143, 144 (2d Cir. 1947) ("Ludecke, the relator-appellant, made an oral argument and submitted a brief, both of which have been interesting and moving.")); In Re Territo, 156 F.2d 142, 142–3 (1946) (petitioner's case was "tried at the hearing on the order to show cause"); Ex Parte Milligan, 71 U.S. 2, 5–6, 107 (1866); Colepaugh v. Looney, 235 F.2d 429, 431 (10th Cir. 1956) (refusing to "preclude access to the courts for determining the applicability of the laws of war").[7] Padilla, at a minimum, must be afforded those rights.[8]

B. *Padilla's Right to Meaningful Access to the Courts Encompasses the Right to Present His Petition through Counsel*

In determining whether Padilla can receive due process—"the opportunity to be heard at a meaningful time and in a meaningful manner"—without access to his lawyer, the court should examine (1) the private interest that will be affected by official action, (2) the risk of an erroneous deprivation of the interest through the procedures used and the value of additional safeguards; and (3) the government's interest. Mathews, 424 U.S. at 333–35.

1. *Padilla has a fundamental interest in the assistance of counsel*

The Supreme Court has "frequently emphasized" the importance of *provision* of counsel in any case in which an individual may be deprived of his liberty. In Re Gault, 387 U.S. 1, 73 (1967) (Harlan, J, concurring and dissenting in part); see also Gideon v. Wainwright, 372 U.S. 335, 344 (1963), (the "noble ideal" of due process "cannot be realized" absent assistance of counsel); Johnson v. Zerbst, 304 U.S. 458, 462 (1938) (the assistance of counsel is "necessary to insure fundamental human rights of life and liberty"). Indeed, it is well established that the "right to be heard" would be of "little avail if it did not comprehend the right to be heard *by counsel.*" Powell v. Alabama, 287 U.S. 45, 68 (1932) (emphasis added).

The government contends that "because Padilla is being detained under the laws of war rather than under domestic criminal laws, the Constitution affords him no right to counsel." (Gov't Br. at 14.) This is wrong as a matter of constitutional history and theory. First, as noted above, numerous wartime detainees have been afforded the right to counsel.

Second, the right to counsel is not confined to cases arising under the Sixth Amendment in the criminal context. On the contrary, courts have frequently found a due process right to *provision* of counsel under the Fifth Amendment in cases in which the liberty interest in freedom from imprisonment has been implicated. See, e.g., United States v. Perez, 330 F.3d 97 (2d Cir. 2003) (deportation of permanent resident); Haitian Centers Council, Inc. v. McNary, 969 F.2d 1326 (2d Cir. 2000) (repatriation of aliens); Iavorski v. INS, 232 F.3d 124, 128 (2d Cir. 2000) (deportation of aliens); United States v. Budell, 187 F.3d 1 137, 1143 (9th Cir. 1999) (discharge of insanity acquitees); Gault, 387 U.S. at 41 (commitment of juvenile delinquents); Proiect Release v. Prevost, 722 F.2d 960, 976 (2d Cir. 1983) (civil commitment). The Supreme Court has even recognized a due process right to counsel in proceedings where physical liberty is not in issue. See Lassiter v. Dep't of Soc. Servs. of Durham County, 452 U.S. 18, 31–32 (1981) (termination of parental rights) and Goldberg, supra, (termination of welfare benefits).

These cases serve as strong reminders of the critical importance of counsel in proceedings where significant rights are at stake, but the issue here is even more fundamental. The government does not contest appointment of counsel; it contests Padilla's right to consult with counsel. While in some situations there is no right to the *provision* of counsel, see, e.g., Vitek v. Jones, 445 U.S. 480, 482–84 (1980) (plurality opinion) (transfer of prisoner to psychiatric facility), outside the purely administrative contexts of prison and school disciplinary proceedings, cf. Goss, 419 U.S. at 583; Wolff v. McDonnell, 418 U.S. 539, 570 (1974), no case suggests that the government may prevent a detainee from consulting with counsel in connection with a proceeding that may well seal his fate forever.

In fact, the opposite is true. The constitutional requirement of "meaningful access to the courts," Bounds, 430 U.S. at 823, means that reasonable access to appointed or retained counsel (or a surrogate for counsel) cannot be denied:

The constitutional guarantee of due process of law has as a corollary the requirement that prisoners be afforded access to the courts in order to challenge unlawful convictions and to seek redress for violations of their constitutional rights. This means that inmates must have a reasonable opportunity to seek and receive the assistance of attorneys. Regulations and practices that unjustifiably obstruct the availability of professional representation or other aspects of the right of access to the courts are invalid.

Procunier, 416 U.S. at 419 (citations omitted); see also Shaw v. Murphy, 532 U.S. 223, 231 n.3 (2001) (inmates have a right to receive legal assistance from other inmates when necessary to effectuate right of access to courts); Johnson, 393 U.S. at 490 (invalidating prison regulation that barred inmates from providing legal services to other inmates); Coe v. Bell, 89 F. Supp. 2d 962, 967 (M.D. Tenn.), vacated as moot Coe v. Bell, 230 F.3d 1357 (6th Cir. 2000) (death row inmate had constitutional right of access to counsel).

In short, Padilla has a fundamental interest in being permitted to consult with and present his case through counsel.

2. *The risk of error in the absence of consultation with counsel is acute*

Perhaps more fundamentally, given the process insisted upon by the Executive here, the risk of error is acute. The government has sought to justify Padilla's detention based on information derived from unspecified "intelligence sources" and "reports of interviews" with unidentified "confidential informants." (JA 44.)[9] While these confidential sources supposedly are "believed" to have been involved with al Qaeda, the Mobbs Declaration nowhere states that they *in fact* are al Qaeda operatives or provides any facts that would indicate that the information they have provided is trustworthy. (Id.) Quite the contrary, by the government's own admission, these sources "have not been completely candid" and some information they have provided "remains uncorroborated" and may be "part of an effort to mislead or confuse U.S. officials." (Id.) It cannot be gainsaid that there is a risk that Padilla may have been wrongfully imprisoned, given that his detention is based on allegations of admittedly suspect informants providing admittedly suspect information, neither of which has been subjected to any kind of judicial review.

3. *The executive's interests are insufficient to deny access to counsel*

In assessing whether an evidentiary hearing was required prior to termination of disability benefits, the Court in Mathews stated that an examination of "the administrative burden and other societal costs" must be had in order to understand the effect of the procedure. Mathews, 424 U.S. at 347. The ultimate question is "when, under our constitutional system, judicial-type procedures must be imposed upon administrative action to assure fairness[?]" Id. at 348.

The government asserts that denial of access to counsel is required to preserve the Executive's interest in national security by preventing its interrogation process from being jeopardized. The government's affiant states that the military's interrogation techniques "rely in large part on developing and maintaining an atmosphere of trust and dependency." (Gov't Br. at 51 (citing JA 58–59.)) Interposing access to counsel even in a limited manner, the government contends, would jeopardize this relationship and threaten or delay its ability to secure potentially critical intelligence information. (Id. at 51–52.)

Critically, the government's assertions about the need to facilitate the interrogation process assume precisely the fact that Padilla has a right to challenge through habeas—that he is an enemy combatant. If Padilla is not an enemy combatant, any conceivable basis for the government's asserted right to detain and interrogate him as one evaporates.

The assumed force of the government's argument is further blunted by the limited right to counsel granted by the district court. As the district court noted, because no generalized right to counsel and no right to counsel in connection with the interrogation are posited, any interference with the interrogation process would be minimal. Padilla I, 233 F. Supp. 2d at 603. Moreover, the government does not dispute the district court's conclusion that the government's assessment of potential effects on Padilla's interrogation of limited access to counsel "is plausible, it is only plausible." (Gov't Br. at 52–53 (citing Padilla II, 243 F. Supp. 2d at 53).) Indeed, it repeatedly characterizes contact with counsel as a "risk," (id. at 51), that "*could* set back" the interrogation process, (id. at 52 (emphasis supplied)). Even though the Executive's concerns may be speculative, the government asserts they are sufficient to deny access to counsel in light of the assumption it has made that there is no constitutional or other right to counsel. (Id. at 53.) Because, as demonstrated above, its assumption is flawed, the government's conclusion utterly fails.

Padilla's interests in access to counsel are fundamental and undeniable; the Executive's interests, while entitled to due consideration, are at least in part speculative and, therefore, ultimately less convincing. Moreover, Padilla's interests coincide with a broader interest of a lawful society in the legitimacy of executive actions. A principal function of the bar is to provide professional counseling and advocacy to both sides of a dispute. The presence of professional advocates inspires confidence that a court's ruling was made with the benefit of full presentations on each side. The government's plan to denude the process of "adversary argument...embracing conflicting and demanding interests," Flast, 392 U.S. at 97, would undermine the very confidence it should be seeking to engender that the war on terrorism is not incompatible with fundamental protection of individual liberty. The balance of interests favors granting Padilla the right to confer with counsel.

III. Padilla's Petition Should Be Granted Unless the Government Demonstrates by Clear and Convincing Evidence That He Is an Unlawful Combatant

Whether Padilla's right to process arises out of the writ of habeas corpus or the Fifth Amendment, he is entitled to contest the Executive's determination that he is an "enemy combatant." If the Executive or the Federal Government as a whole has the power to detain Padilla, hold him incommunicado and interrogate him without charge, that power is contingent on the jurisdictional fact that the Padilla is an enemy combatant, that is, an unlawful combatant not entitled to prisoner-of-war status.[10] The government contends that the deference owed to the Executive on matters of foreign policy and military affairs reaches so far into the life of a U.S. citizen detained on U.S. soil that the Executive's unilateral determination that the detainee is an enemy combatant can be challenged only under a standard typically used to review hearing decisions of administrative tribunals known as the "some evidence" standard. (Gov't Br. at 44–49.) The district court to a point agreed. See Padilla I, 233 F. Supp. 2d at 605–08. ABCNY respectfully submits that this aspect of the district court's holding was erroneous.

Only two Supreme Court opinions directly address executive power to detain (and try by military commission) as unlawful combatants individuals arrested on U.S. soil in a time of war, but not on a battlefield—Ex Parte Quirin and Ex Parte Milligan. Although the outcome of each case was very different, both decisions recognized that the Great Writ gives a court the power to make a *de novo* factual determination about the initial jurisdictional fact: Is the detainee an unlawful combatant?

In Quirin, the Executive Proclamation pursuant to which the petitioners were detained, tried and convicted by military tribunal expressly "denied access to the courts," and the government contended that the petitioners should have no resort to the courts. 317 U.S. at 23–25. Nevertheless, the Supreme Court held that the Proclamation could not "preclude access to the courts *for determining its applicability to the particular case.*" Id. at 25 (emphasis supplied). The "applicability" of the Proclamation, that is, whether the Quirin petitioners were unlawful combatants, was resolved in the initial per curiam opinion, apparently upon stipulated facts. Id. at 20, 25, 46. Accordingly, the Court stated it had "no occasion now to define with meticulous care the ultimate boundaries of the jurisdiction of military tribunals to try persons according to the laws of war." Id. at 45–46. Nowhere in the opinion does the Court suggest that it would not have had the power to draw those boundaries, or that its power would have been limited to a review of whether "some evidence" supported the Executive's determination that the petitioners were unlawful combatants. On the contrary, the Quirin court recognized that it was precisely those jurisdictional boundaries, drawn by the Milligan court, that distinguished its holding from Milligan:

We construe the Court's statement as to the inapplicability of the law of war to Milligan's case as having particular reference to the facts before it. From them the Court concluded that Milligan, not being a part of or associated with the armed forces of the enemy, was a non-belligerent, not subject to the law of war save as—in circumstances found not there to be present and not involved here—martial law might be constitutionally established.

Id. at 45.[11]

In Milligan the Court was asked to answer three certified questions concerning the trial by military commission of a citizen of Indiana in the middle of the Civil War. 71 U.S. at 8–9. Although an Act of Congress had given the President the power to suspend the writ of habeas corpus, the Act also provided that those held by the President "otherwise than as prisoners of war," would have to be indicted or presented to a judge for discharge or other disposition "according to law." Id. at 5. On October 5, 1864, Milligan, an alleged member of a 100,000-strong secessionist organization, was arrested, tried, convicted and sentenced to death by a military tribunal for plotting to overthrow the government, aiding the rebels and violating the laws of war, among other things. Id. at 6–7.

The Milligan Court rejected the Executive's contention that, even if the Act had been violated (Milligan was never indicted or presented to a judge), the trial of Milligan was justified by executive power to impose martial law.[12] The Court asserted judicial knowledge that in Indiana the Federal authority was always unopposed, and its courts always open to hear criminal accusations and redress grievances; and no usage of war could sanction a military trial there for any offence whatever of a citizen in civil life, in no wise connected with the military service." Id. at 121–22. In short, although the Court recognized the power of the Executive to declare martial law under appropriate circumstances, id. at 126, it made a *de novo* factual determination that even in the dark hours of the Civil War martial law was not appropriate and could not be used to justify Milligan's trial by the military rather than the courts.

Despite their divergent outcomes, Quirin and Milligan thus demonstrate that one who is detained on U.S. soil away from a theatre of war has the right to challenge directly and substantively the Executive's factual determination that he is an enemy combatant. As further demonstrated below, the some evidence test is incompatible with that right, and the district court should have required the government to prove by clear and convincing evidence that Padilla is an enemy combatant.

A. The Executive Must Demonstrate That Padilla Is an Unlawful Combatant

The district court concluded that "when the President designated Padilla an 'enemy combatant,' he necessarily meant that Padilla was an unlawful combatant." Padilla I, 233 F. Supp. 2d at 593. The government has not objected to this conclusion. For purposes of this brief only, ABCNY assumes that the conflict with al Qaeda is governed by the laws of war, such that an unlawful combatant associated with al Qaeda could be considered an unlawful combatant under the laws of war.[13] With that assumption in mind, in order to demonstrate that Padilla is an unlawful combatant, the Executive must demonstrate (1) that Padilla was actively working on behalf of al Qaeda when he was detained; and (2) that his activities were "unlawful" as that term is used to define one who is not a lawful combatant under the Hague and Geneva Conventions. See Padilla I, 233 F. Supp. 2d at 592 93. The government does not appear to disagree that these are the operative elements of the status they seek to impose on Padilla. (See Gov't Br. at 38.)

B. The "Some Evidence" Standard Does Not Apply

The history of the "some evidence" test demonstrates both that it should not be applied to the initial judicial determination whether Padilla is an enemy combatant, and that such determination should be subject to *de novo* review. The test arose in the early part of the 20th century as a standard to be applied to habeas petitions challenging exclusion decisions by immigration officials, principally under the Chinese Exclusion Act. See Gerald L. Neuman, The Constitutional Requirement of 'Some Evidence', 25 San Diego L. Rev. 631, 636–41 (1988). These cases were decided against the background of a long history of judicial deference to congressional and executive authority to regulate aliens not unlike the deference accorded the Executive in military affairs. Accordingly, they are instructive not only because the government has invoked them by contending that the "some evidence" standard applies, but also because they concern the role of the judiciary in reviewing executive determinations regarding significant rights of individuals over whom the Executive has great authority.

Two principles emerge from the "some evidence" cases. First, even those who were conceded to be aliens were entitled to a fair hearing by immigration authorities, and denial of such a hearing would constitute a denial of due process and grounds for issuance of a writ. See, e.g., Kwock Jan Fat v. White, 253 U.S. 454 463–65 (1920). For example, rejecting the petition of an alien named Tisi, the Supreme Court noted:

There is no suggestion that Tisi was not allowed to prepare for the hearing, by prior examination of the written evidence on which the warrant of arrest was issued, or that he was otherwise restricted in the preparation of his defense. The hearing was conducted orally. Tisi was present and he was represented by counsel. He testified fully, and the many witnesses produced by the government were cross-examined by his counsel.

Tisi v. Tod, 264 U.S. 131, 134 (1924). "Upon a *collateral* review in habeas proceedings," that is, only *after* the alien was afforded a sufficient administrative hearing, the "some evidence" standard was applied. United States v. Vajtauer, 273 U.S. 103, 106 (1927) (emphasis added). Thus, it is not surprising that the district court could find no case applying "the 'some evidence' standard to a record that consists solely of the government's evidence, to which the government's adversary has not been permitted to respond." Padilla II, 243 F. Supp. 2d at 54. Because Padilla has had no process—his petition tests a unilateral executive decision, not the outcome of an administrative hearing process—the "some evidence" test is inapplicable.

Second, the Supreme Court consistently distinguished between the Executive's determination concerning exclusion or deportation of the alien, to which it applied the deferential "some evidence" standard of review, and the Executive's determination of the "jurisdictional fact" of alienage, Tisi, 264 U.S. at 133, which a petitioner was entitled to challenge through a *de novo,* judicial hearing of the evidence. Ng Fung Ho v. White, 259 U.S. 276, 284–85 (1922). As the Court stated:

Jurisdiction in the executive to order deportation exists only if the person arrested is an alien. The claim of citizenship is thus a denial of an essential jurisdictional fact. The situation bears some resemblance to that which arises where one against whom proceedings are being taken under the military law denies that he is in military service. It is well settled that in such a case a writ of habeas corpus will issue to determine the status.

Id. at 284 (citations omitted). This distinction is entirely consistent with Milligan and Quirin, and it further demonstrates that Padilla is entitled to a *de novo* determination of the "essential jurisdictional fact" whether he is an enemy combatant.

C.   The Executive Cannot Classify a U.S. Citizen Apprehended on U.S. Soil an Enemy Combatant Absent Clear and Convincing Evidence

"The function of a standard of proof, as that concept is embodied in the Due Process Clause and in the realm of factfinding, is to 'instruct the factfinder concerning the degree of confidence our society thinks he should have in the correctness of factual conclusions for a particular type of adjudication.'" Cruzan v. Dir. Mo. Dept. Health, 497 U.S. 261, 282 (1990) (citations omitted). The degree of confidence in turn depends on the interests at stake on each side of the dispute. See Cruzan, 497 U.S. at 280–87; Addington v. Texas, 441 U.S. 418, 423–33 (1979); Cooper v. Oklahoma, 517 U.S. 348, 362–69 (1996); Heller v. Doe, 509 U.S. 312, 332 (1993).

"In cases involving individual rights, whether criminal or civil, '[t]he standard of proof [at a minimum] reflects the value society places on individual liberty.'" Addington, 441 U.S. at 425 (quoting Tippett v. Md., 436 F.2d 1153, 1166 (4th Cir. 1971)). Indeed, in non-criminal cases, the Supreme Court "has mandated an intermediate standard of proof—'clear and convincing evidence'—when the individual interests at stake in a state proceeding are both 'particularly important' and 'more substantial than mere loss of money.'" Cruzan, 497 U.S. at 282, quoting Santosky v. Kramer, 455 U.S. 745, 756 (1982). The clear and convincing evidence standard, required in many circumstances implicating fundamental individual liberties—such as civil commitment proceedings, deportation proceedings, denaturalization proceedings and proceedings for the termination of parental rights, id.—is the standard most appropriate to test the Executive's contention that Padilla is an enemy combatant.

This proceeding will govern some of Padilla's most fundamental rights. First, Padilla's liberty interest is at stake: "Freedom from imprisonment, from government custody, detention, or other forms of physical restraint—lies at the heart of the liberty that the [Due Process] Clause protects." Zadvydas v. Davis, 533 U.S. 678, 690 (2001). The government seeks the right to detain Padilla, at a minimum, "during wartime." (Gov't Br. at 2.) In a "war" against such an elusive and ephemeral "enemy" as al Qaeda, this effectively means indefinite detention. Indeed, Padilla already has been in military custody, incommunicado, for over a year.

Second, should a court determine that Padilla is indeed an enemy combatant, the government could assert a right to try Padilla by invoking new and as yet untested military tribunal procedures, as it apparently intends to apply to non-citizen enemy combatant detainees. See Military Order of November 13, 2001, 66 Fed. Reg. 57,833 (Nov. 13, 2001). If this occurs, Padilla could ultimately lose his right to trial by jury and many of the other constitutional and statutory rights afforded to a criminal defendant. Cf. Department of Defense, Military Commission Order No. 1 (Mar. 21, 2002), 41 I.L.M. 725 (establishing military commissions to try non-citizen detainees and allowing ex parte presentations to the commission).

Third, much like the stigma of a criminal conviction or even involuntary civil commitment, the Executive's decision to brand Padilla an "enemy combatant"—a traitor to his country—carries a severe stigma. See In re Winship, 397 U.S. 358, 363–64 (1970) (proof beyond a reasonable doubt is required in criminal cases, in part, because of the "certainty" that conviction will stigmatize the defendant); Addington, 441 U.S. at 425–26 (recognizing that the stigma of involuntary commitment "can have a very significant impact on the individual"). A decision of this court affirming the Executive's determination will only lend the weight of judicial authority to that stigmatization.

The government's countervailing interests are also undeniably important, but ultimately insufficient to justify a standard of proof more lenient than clear and convincing evidence. The government argues: "Because the President's determination that Padilla is an enemy combatant represents a core exercise of the Commander-in-Chief authority, that determination is entitled to great deference." (Gov't Br. at 14.) For this proposition it relies principally on the decisions in Hamdi. (Id. at 45–46.) This reliance is entirely misplaced.

The Fourth Circuit determined that Hamdi was captured "in Afghanistan during a time of active military hostilities." Hamdi App III, 316 F.3d at 460. "To compare this battlefield capture to the domestic arrest in Padilla v. Bush is to compare apples and oranges," as the author of the Hamdi III decision bluntly stated. Hamdi v. Rumsfeld, No. 02-7338, WL 21540768, at *3 (4th

Cir. 2003) ("Hamdi App. IV") (Wilkinson, J., concurring in denial of reh'g *en banc*).[14] The Fourth Circuit's opinion is expressly and forcefully limited to the treatment of an enemy combatant who was concededly "captured in a zone of active combat operations abroad." Hamdi App. III, 316 F.3d at 476. The court noted:

> We earlier rejected the summary embrace of a sweeping proposition—namely that, with no meaningful judicial review, any American citizen could be detained indefinitely without charges or counsel on the government's say-so. But Hamdi is not 'any American citizen alleged to be an enemy combatant' by the government; he is an American citizen captured and detained by American allied forces in a foreign theatre of war during active hostilities and determined by the United States military to have been indeed allied with enemy forces.

Id. (internal citations omitted). Padilla, of course, *is* prototypically "any American citizen alleged to be an enemy combatant by the government." He was not captured in a foreign war zone; indeed, he was not "captured" at all, but taken into custody after he was arrested on a material witness warrant. Thus, the Fourth Circuit's observations about "the murkiness and chaos that attend armed conflict," id. at 473, have no relevance here.

Despite the significant differences between the capture of Hamdi and the detention of Padilla, ABCNY recognizes the force of the government's arguments concerning deference to the Executive's powers as Commander-in-Chief. One cannot dispute that imposing *de novo* review under any kind of meaningful standard will require the Court to evaluate facts that implicate serious intelligence, military and foreign policy matters. (See Gov't Br. at 46–47.) But a constitutional government that wages war to protect and preserve a way of life must find a way to accommodate individual liberties so essential to its character. As Quirin and Milligan demonstrate, in cases involving detention on U.S. soil outside a war zone, that accommodation under our Constitution occurs through meaningful participation of the judiciary.

Fortunately, the courts have significant experience discharging their role as Article III adjudicators using procedures that safeguard sensitive factual inquiries implicating military and foreign affairs. For example, the courts have long presided over trials involving espionage offenses. See 18 U.S.C. §§ 792 *et seq.* The Classified Information and Procedures Act, 18 U.S.C. App. 3, in fact sets forth a detailed procedure for cases involving classified information. Although separately constituted by statute, the Foreign Intelligence Surveillance Court, which is routinely asked to determine whether a suspect is an agent of a foreign power, likewise demonstrates that Article III courts can and do handle matters involving sensitive issues of foreign affairs and the collection of intelligence information. See, 50 U.S.C. §§ 1801 *et seq.* Furthermore, if necessary and under the proper conditions and restraints, a court can even consider information *ex parte,* as the government's submission of classified versions of the Mobbs and Jacoby Declarations demonstrate. While the government's interests in intelligence operations and safeguarding sensitive matters of military and foreign affairs are great, there is sufficient precedent to demonstrate that the courts can accommodate them.

"Due process commands that no man shall lose his liberty unless the Government has borne the burden of. . .convincing the factfinder of his guilt." Winship, 397 U.S. at 364 (internal citations omitted). In Winship, the Supreme Court re-affirmed that criminal conviction requires proof beyond a reasonable doubt of every element necessary to constitute the crime. Id. Padilla in one sense has more at stake than a criminal defendant—not just his liberty and the stigma of being branded a traitor, but also, potentially, his right to the very process Winship guarantees. On the other hand, society has a very strong interest in waging a war against a known terrorist enemy. Requiring the government to demonstrate by clear and convincing evidence that Padilla is an enemy combatant strikes an appropriate balance between the significant and competing interests of individual liberty and protection from terrorist threat.

CONCLUSION

For these reasons, ABCNY respectfully submits that if the Court finds that the Executive *may* have had the power to detain Padilla as an unlawful combatant affiliated with al Qaeda, it should remand the matter to the district court to determine whether that power was lawfully exercised as follows:

(1) Padilla is entitled to present facts in support of his petition at a hearing;

(2) Padilla is entitled to consult with counsel in a manner consistent with reasonable national security and intelligence concerns;

(3) At Padilla's hearing, the government will bear the burden of demonstrating by clear and convincing evidence that Padilla is an unlawful combatant working on behalf of al Qaeda.

Dated:	New York, New York	Respectfully Submitted,
	July 29, 2003	WILLKIE FARR & GALLAGHER
		Benito Romano, Esq.
		Joseph G. Davis, Esq.
		Mary Eaton, Esq.
		Attorneys for the Association of the Bar of the
		City of New York

NOTES

1. ABCNY takes no position on the constitutionality of the detention order.

2. "Gov't Br." refers to the Brief of Respondent-Appellant Donald Rumsfeld.

3. Of course, even absent the discrete rights that the habeas statutes create, a prisoner has a constitutional right of access to the courts for the purpose of assailing his detention through the writ of habeas corpus. See Bounds v. Smith, 430 U.S. 817, 821–22 (1977); Johnson v. Avery, 393 U.S. 483, 485 (1969). The Executive cannot limit or withhold that right. Ex Parte Hull, 312 U.S. 546, 549 (1941) (holding that "the state may not abridge or impair petitioner's right to apply to a federal court for a writ of habeas corpus"); Johnson, 393 U.S. at 485 (stating that "it is fundamental that access of prisoners to the courts for the purpose of presenting their complaints may not be denied or obstructed"). (See also Part II, infra.)

4. 28 U.S.C. § 2241 authorizes the federal courts to grant writs of habeas corpus to prisoners who, like Padilla, are "in custody under or by color of the authority of the United States," id. at (c)(1), as well as to those who are "in custody in violation of the Constitution or laws or treaties of the United States," id. at (c)(3). Other provisions of the habeas statute, particularly 28 U.S.C. § 2243, establish the procedures to be followed in section 2241 cases.

5. Other provisions of the habeas statute confirm Padilla's right to present facts and the district court's obligation to review the factual predicate for Padilla's detention as an enemy combatant. See e.g., 28 U.S. C. § 2246 (identifying methods for the habeas court to take evidence); 28 U.S.C. § 2247 (stating that documentary evidence "shall" be admissible in habeas cases); 28 U.S.C. § 2248 (directing the habeas court to accept the government's allegations as true unless the court "finds from the evidence that they are not true"). The Executive cannot unilaterally suspend the operation of these statutes and prevent Padilla from presenting facts in support of his petition, just as it cannot suspend the Great Writ itself. See Ex Parte Bollman, 8 U.S. 75, 101 (1807) (holding that Congress alone holds the power to suspend writ and the act that implements it); Ex Parte Merryman, 17 F. Cas. 144, 148–49 (1861) (rejecting executive authority to suspend the writ).

6. Indeed, were the Court to deny Padilla the right to present facts in support of his petition—facts that right now are in his possession alone—it would place itself in the position of ruling on a dispute without the benefit of a fully adversarial proceeding, in violation of the prohibition against advisory opinions. A federal court may not validate an executive action without that "'clear concreteness provided when a question emerges precisely framed and necessary for decision from a clash of adversary argument exploring

every aspect of a multifaceted situation embracing conflicting and demanding interests.'" Flast v. Cohen, 392 U.S. 83, 96–97 (1968) (quoting United States v. Fruehauf, 365 U.S. 146, 157 (1 961)). More generally, a federal court's jurisdiction extends only to cases or controversies, which "implies the existence of present or possible adverse parties, *whose contentions are submitted to the court for adjudication.*" Muskrat v. United States, 219 U.S. 346, 357 (1911) (emphasis supplied). Despite the vigorous and admirable efforts of Padilla's next friend and counsel, it is impossible to know whether the issues presented by the habeas petition they have filed are "precisely framed," because without access to Padilla the Court cannot be assured that the facts relevant to his petition have been aired. The Court cannot and should not exercise its Article III powers to validate the detention of Padilla unless Padilla himself is permitted to submit his contentions to the court.

7. Although the Fourth Circuit appears to have held otherwise, Hamdi App. III, 316 F.3d at 473–76, Hamdi App. III is distinguishable on two significant grounds. The Fourth Circuit viewed the operative facts as undisputed, id. at 473; Padilla's next friend has made no such concession. Moreover, based on the purportedly undisputed facts, the Fourth Circuit concluded that Hamdi was an enemy combatant captured in a "zone of active combat operations." Id. This fact, which the Fourth Circuit viewed as crucial to its decision, see id. at 474, 476–77, likewise makes Hamdi App. III inapplicable to this case. In addition, for the reasons stated above, and those outlined by Judge Motz in Hamdi App. IV, ABCNY respectfully suggests that the decision in Hamdi App. III to adjudicate the petition without hearing directly from the petitioner was error.

8. The government's position also trespasses on Padilla's First Amendment right to petition the court. The First Amendment's Petition Clause guarantees Padilla a right of access to the courts. See U.S. Const. Amend. I (prohibiting infringements on right to "petition the Government for a redress of grievances"); BE & K Const. Co. v. NLRB, 536 U.S. 516, 525 (2002) ("The right of access to the courts is...one aspect of the right of petition" under the First Amendment.) (quotations omitted). "The right to petition government for redress of grievances is 'among the most precious of the liberties safeguarded by the Bill of Rights.'" Franco v. Kelly, 854 F.2d 584, 589 (2d Cir. 1988) (quoting United Mine Workers v. Il. State Bar Ass'n, 389 U.S. 217, 222 (1967)). Hence, the right of access to the court is not satisfied by merely opening the courtroom doors. Rather, as the Supreme Court has held, "meaningful access to the courts is the touchstone." Bounds, 430 U.S. at 823 (internal citations omitted). Incommunicado detention, with no ability to draft a petition or communicate with next friend or counsel can hardly be described as meaningful access.

9. Citations to "JA" refer to the Joint Appendix filed by the parties.

10. The government has no power to detain Padilla as an "enemy" or unlawful combatant unless laws of war apply to his detention.

11. Cf. Padilla I, 233 F. Supp. 2d at 594 ("Because the Quirin court *found* that the German saboteurs were not only attempting to harm the United States during an armed conflict but doing so as persons associated with an enemy's armed forces, the Court concluded that the saboteurs, unlike Milligan, could be treated as unlawful combatants" (emphasis supplied).

12. The government argued that "jurisdiction is complete under the laws and usages of war." Id. at 121.

13. If the laws of war do not apply, Padilla is at best an alleged criminal, and his detention is patently unlawful. ABCNY notes that the government's position with respect to the laws of war is, at best, inconsistent. On the one hand, the government contends that the "laws" of war apply, but on the other that the entire enemy force with whom we are at war is "unlawful." See id. (noting government's position that neither al Qaeda nor the Taliban are lawful combatants). If so, presumably there would be nothing to stop the Executive from "declaring war" on any form of international criminal organization—or on any international political organization with views hostile to the U.S.—and treating its members as unlawful combatants subject to seizure, indefinite detention and military trial, an outcome that is certainly unconstitutional.

14. Judges of the Fourth Circuit dissenting from the decision not to grant rehearing of the Hamdi App. III ruling disagreed whether that fact had been sufficiently established. See Hamdi App. IV, No. 02-7338, 2003 WL 21540768, at *15–34.

CHAPTER 8

An Act to Amend the Agriculture and Markets Law, in Relation to Unlawful Tampering with Animal Activities

PREFACE BY MARIANN SULLIVAN

Terrorism can harm us in numerous ways, not the least of which is in creating an atmosphere in which legitimate dissent may be squelched in the name of fear. The Committee on Legal Issues Pertaining to Animals was confronted with what appeared to be an example of an attempt to use post-9/11 fears in an inappropriate fashion when a bill was introduced in the New York State legislature that was ostensibly designed to strengthen the hand of law enforcement in fighting "terrorism" motivated by environmental or animal rights philosophies. In fact, the bill went far beyond any legitimate law enforcement concerns and, if enacted, would have, instead, stifled protected speech and characterized as "terrorists" legitimate, mainstream organizations advocating for the protection of animals and the environment. Moreover, while the right to express opinions should be protected regardless of whether they are persuasive or popular, it was clear to the Committee that, in this case, much of the criticism of environmental degradation and cruelty to animals that would have been stifled by this bill is both accurate and extremely alarming.

After the bill came to the Committee's attention, research revealed that it was part of a national post-9/11 movement to enact similar legislation around the country as part of the "war on terrorism." While that movement was led by the National Sportsmen's Alliance, the bills, which were also promoted by the American Legislative Exchange Council, did not deal exclusively, or even primarily, with hunting issues, and appeared to have been influenced by industries vulnerable to criticism on environmental and animal welfare grounds, in particular, agribusiness.[1]

The New York bill, as introduced, was certainly not difficult to criticize, as it was written so broadly and was so blatantly unconstitutional that it would arguably have labeled as a "terrorist" organization the Committee itself. And, as the Committee pointed out, all of the activities that were rendered illegal by the bill that could arguably deserve attention from law enforcement were already illegal under New York's Penal Law. Indeed, in 2005, several animal protection advocates who publicized a videotape they had taken after entering an egg production factory farm in upstate New York, from which they removed several sick and dying hens, were charged with felony burglary. Although two pled guilty to reduced charges, the one who proceeded to trial was acquitted of burglary and petit larceny, but nevertheless received six months of imprisonment for three counts of simple trespass. This appears to be exactly the type of activity toward which the bill is targeted, and this prosecution clearly shows that law enforcement is not without weapons to zealously defend animal use industries from animal advocates.

However, in spite of its blatant unconstitutionality and redundancy, the Committee believed that the bill could not be ignored. Similar, but somewhat toned-down, versions of this bill have been introduced in a variety of state legislatures, and versions have passed in California and Oklahoma. In Missouri and Illinois, only last-minute conference committees prevented the passage of bills prohibiting photography of animal facilities, such as puppy mills and factory farms, even from a legal vantage point, a provision that was also contained in the New York bill. And, the New York bill, even in spite of widespread criticism, was reintroduced in the Assembly in the current session, where it was referred to, and currently remains in, the Agriculture Committee.

These bills are appearing at a time when there is growing public concern regarding animal suffering and environmental degradation, particularly as they relate to conditions on factory farms. These proposed laws, which are clearly unnecessary to combat real terrorism, or even real crimes, have the potential to prevent the legitimate investigation of, dissemination of information about, and debate over the conditions in which animals are kept, by the billions, by an industry that is virtually unregulated on animal welfare grounds. That this should be part of the legacy of 9/11 is anathema, and the Committee strongly felt that it must be actively opposed.

Re: A. 4884   Assemblymember Smith
S. 2996   Senators Kuhl, Alesi, Larkin,
                                               Maziarz, McGee, Mendez, Rath,
                                               Volker, Wright

An Act to amend the agriculture and markets law, in relation to unlawful tampering with animal activities

This Bill is Disapproved

This bill proposes an amendment to Section 378 of the Agriculture and Markets Law, which already sets forth criminal penalties for certain acts in relation to animal research, including stealing animals, appropriating confidential material and releasing animals exposed to infectious agents, and creates a private right of action for its violation. If enacted, this proposed amendment will vastly expand the acts which are made illegal and vastly expand, beyond animal research, the animal related activities that are shielded by the law. Many of the acts that this bill seeks to criminalize are already crimes under New York State law, primarily in the nature of trespass and property damage. This bill would provide for additional, and very substantial, penalties for these crimes when they are "politically motivated," which, according to this bill, renders them terrorist acts. The bill also seeks to criminalize certain acts, if politically motivated, which are not already crimes under New York state law and, further, seeks to criminalize the donation of money to or other support of organizations which commit prohibited acts. Because the bill is both very broad and very vague, it appears that it would criminalize many activities that are protected by the Constitution, including many forms of legitimate protest.

First, this bill would greatly expand the types of "animal activities" that are to receive special treatment, including limitations on protest and criticism, under the law. In addition to three activities which quite clearly involve animals, i.e., hunting, fishing and trapping, it also includes a number of activities which may, or may not, involve animals, including food production, clothing manufacturing, agriculture, recreation and entertainment. It also, oddly, includes activities which do not appear to be significantly related to animal use, including camping and traveling. It is unclear under what circumstances such activities would come within the proposed law. Moreover, the definition contains a catchall provision, i.e., "any other services involving the use of animals" with no indication as to what is meant by "services" or, again, what would constitute a sufficient connection to the "use of animals."

The bill goes on to define an "animal or ecological terrorist organization":

(j) "Animal or ecological terrorist organization" means any association, organization, entity, coalition, or combination of two or more persons with the primary or incidental purpose of supporting any politically motivated activity through intimidation, coercion, fear, or other means that is intended to obstruct, impede or deter any person from participating in a lawful animal activity, animal facility, research facility, or the lawful activity of mining, foresting, harvesting, gathering or processing natural resources.

Simplified, this section labels as a terrorist organization any two people who, through any means, support politically motivated activity intended to deter someone from participating in any lawful "animal activity" (as described above) or various activities related to natural resources. This definition is broad enough to encompass organizations such as The Sierra Club and the American Society for the Prevention of Cruelty to Animals. Indeed, it might make this Committee a "terrorist organization." Virtually all political and social advocacy is an attempt to "obstruct," "impede" or "deter" some activity or conduct, such as through education, persuasion or legislative change. Moreover, by using the terms "intimidation," "coercion" and "fear" to define the proscribed methods, rather than the proscribed intent, the terms become completely subjective. Legislative action may "coerce" change, people who are the subject of protests are often "intimidated" by the disapproval of their fellow citizens, and people who are informed that there is opposition to their positions may be "fear[ful]" of the ramifications. In this context, these words are so subjective as to be meaningless. But even if those words adequately defined methods of seeking change that should render one a "terrorist," the bill goes on to include the use of any "other means" as well.

The limitation that the activity which is sought to be deterred must be "lawful" does not effectively limit the scope of this definition. Much political advocacy is directed at activities that are lawful, but nevertheless objectionable to the particular advocates, in the hopes of changing the law and/or educating the public or the person involved in the activity.

Moreover, the bill's singling out as "terrorism" of activity that is "politically motivated," does not serve to legitimately focus on terrorist activity. While some terrorists may be politically motivated, that obviously does not make anyone who is politically motivated a terrorist. Indeed, politically motivated activity is at the core of the fundamental freedoms of speech, association and assembly guaranteed by the First Amendment. It is necessary to the successful functioning of a democracy.

It is also troubling that this bill seeks to introduce a definition of terrorism that is not content neutral, but seems to be aimed at setting a lower bar for labeling those in the animal rights or environmental movements as terrorists than is set for those whose political motivation is for a different cause. In this context, it is worth noting that federal criminal law dealing with "terrorism" (see 18 USC 2331 et seq.) as well as those sections of New York's penal law setting forth the crime of "terrorism" (§ 490.00 et seq.) do not attempt to label any entity with a targeted ideology as a "terrorist organization." Instead, these laws define what activities constitute "terrorism" and uniformly identify as a "terrorist" any individual, entity or organization which engages in those activities with the requisite intent, i.e., to intimidate or influence a civilian population or a government. That is the essence of what separates terrorism from other sorts of violent crime.

This bill, on the other hand, seeks to extend the definition of "terrorism" to virtually any politically motivated crime (as well as heretofore non-criminal activities), not where those crimes are targeted at the government or the populace, but where they are targeted at private entities that are the subject of criticism from particular advocacy groups. Of course, crimes that are politically or philosophically motivated are properly considered crimes, and should be prosecuted as such. They are not necessarily terrorism. If terrorist acts were committed in the name of the animal rights or environmental movements, they are already subject to prosecution under existing federal and state laws.

The bill at issue, after defining who is a terrorist, goes on to list the activities which it would prohibit. Though stated much more vaguely than similar sections in the Penal Law, many of the prohibited actions set forth in the bill appear to be targeted at activities that are already prohibited under New York law, including various forms of larceny (Penal Law § 155.00 et seq.), trespass (Penal Law § 140.00 et seq.), burglary (Penal Law § 140.20 et seq.), criminal mischief (Penal Law § 145.00 et seq.), criminal tampering (Penal Law § 145.14 et seq.), reckless endangerment of property (Penal Law § 145.25), and unlawful tampering with animal research (Agriculture and Markets Law § 378). Interestingly, the activities would not fit within the definition of the crime of terrorism (Penal Law § 490 et seq.), which not only requires a specific intent not required here,[2] but is limited to "specified offense" which are much more narrow in scope (*see* Penal Law § 490.05(3)) than the ones set forth herein. By and large, the activities prohibited by this bill also fall far short of the serious nature ("dangerous to human life") of the activities which, if properly motivated, may be deemed to be "domestic terrorism" in the federal law dealing with terrorism.[3] Indeed, this bill focuses primarily on non-violent crimes, and does not even target either murder or kidnapping, which are probably the two crimes most frequently associated with actual terrorism.

While most of the activities prohibited by the bill are already illegal, section (v) specifically defines activity which is not currently a crime, i.e., "entering an animal or research facility to take pictures by photograph, video camera, or other means with the intent to commit criminal activities or defame the facility or its owner." This provision would criminalize even legal entry into a facility if it is for the purpose of taking photographs or making a video recording to "defame" the facility or its owner. In light of the fundamental First Amendment interests involved, defamation has always been a civil matter, not a criminal offense. Moreover, this section goes well beyond the proscriptions of civil law and seeks to criminalize the *intent* to defame. This section appears to create a substantial risk that its effect would be to inhibit investigative reporting and whistle-blowing regarding the cruel treatment of animals.

Furthermore, the activities which would be made crimes under this bill include a catch-all provision, which is so broad, and so vague, that it could clearly include legitimate protest activity, i.e., "interfering with any lawful animal activity or the lawful use of a natural resource or its byproduct." Since legitimate protest is, by definition, designed to "interfere" with the activity it is focused against, the effect of this section would be to criminalize virtually all protest in the area of animal rights and environmental protection. Furthermore, the term "byproduct" of a "natural resource" is undefined and would appear to encompass virtually anything. Moreover, as noted above, the definition of "animal activity" is extraordinarily broad.

In addition to criminalizing (or further criminalizing) these activities, the bill seeks to criminalize the provision of material or financial support to "encourage, plan, prepare, carry out, publicize, promote or aid" any of these activities. This section appears to be targeted at donors and other supporters of animal and environmental protection organizations, though it would also include persons who rent cars or hotel rooms, or provide meals to people who then carry out one of the prohibited activities. First, as noted, many of the activities which are prohibited would normally be assumed to be legal and/or are otherwise clearly protected by the Constitution. Moreover, this section does not require that the donor, or other supporter, intend or even know that the support will be used for these acts. This section would likely have a chilling effect on donors to legitimate organizations performing legitimate activities. Not only would it be difficult for a donor to know whether an activity that an organization is performing fits within the very vague definitions of this bill, but he or she could be held criminally liable even if unaware of the activity. And, the mischief the act would cause if used to prosecute rental car companies, hotels and restaurants, all within the content of the bill, is obvious.

The penalties set forth by this bill are very significant. On the assumption that the bill's reference to "third degree felony" is meant to be a Class C felony, this would mean that a court could sentence a person convicted under this section, if they were a first felony offender, to an indeterminate sentence of up to 5 to 15 years in prison. Since the crime is defined separately and with additional elements from the underlying criminal act, that sentence could likely be made to run consecutively to any sentence imposed for an underlying act.

Moreover, the bill takes the extraordinary step of setting up a website for the keeping and public dissemination of a database containing information about persons who have been convicted of these offenses (including donors). The only thing remotely comparable to this proposal is the requirement that sexual predators and child molesters register to advise people in their neighborhood of their presence (*see* Correction Law § 168-a et seq.). There is no comparable provision for numerous other serious crimes, including murder, rape, arson, kidnapping, robbery, or burglary.

In conclusion, this bill does not appear to be sincerely targeted at fighting terrorism. It is certainly unconstitutional in many respects because of its effect on legitimate protest activities. To the extent it seeks to criminalize activities which may legitimately be classified as crimes, it is unnecessary, as it is redundant of other laws, both state and federal. Moreover, it appears to be an attempt to impose a singular definition of terrorism based on the political beliefs of two groups, i.e., the animal protection movement and the environmental movement. This Committee strongly recommends that the bill be opposed.

NOTES

1. For an extended discussion of these bills, see E.C. Eddy, "Privatizing the Patriot Act: The Criminalization of Environmental and Animal Protectionists as Terrorists," 22 *Pace Environmental Law Review* 261 (2005).

2. ...intended to

(I) intimidate or coerce a civilian population;

(ii) influence the policy of a unit of government by intimidation or coercion; or

(iii) affect the conduct of a unit of government by murder, assassination or kidnapping...

(Penal Law § 490.05(1)(a)).

3. The term "domestic terrorism" means activities that:

(A) involve acts dangerous to human life that are a violation of the criminal laws of the United States or any State;

(B) appear to be intended:

(I) to intimidate or coerce a civilian population;

(ii) to influence the policy of a government by intimidation or coercion; or

(iii) to affect the conduct of a government by mass destruction, assassination or kidnapping; and occur primarily within the territorial jurisdiction of the United States.

(18 USC § 2331)

CHAPTER 9

The Indefinite Detention of "Enemy Combatants": Balancing Due Process and National Security in the Context of the War on Terror

PREFACE BY THOMAS H. MORELAND

Few actions by the Bush Administration pursuant to the war on terror have caused more controversy than its indefinite detention of Jose Padilla. Padilla, a U.S. citizen seized at a Chicago airport in 2002, has remained in military custody pursuant to a determination by President Bush that Padilla was an "enemy combatant" allied with al Qaeda. Although the conduct of which Padilla is suspected would violate the criminal laws, and many other accused terrorists have been prosecuted under those criminal laws, Padilla has been detained without charges. His *habeas* petition challenging his detention puts dramatically at issue the relative powers and responsibilities of the three branches of the U.S. government to balance the interests of national security and civil liberties in the context of the war on terror.

The following Report by the Association's Committee on Federal Courts* contained below analyzes the indefinite detention of enemy combatants as an exercise of the President's war powers, under Article II of the U.S. Constitution, and as a possible violation of core due process rights. In essence, it concludes that the President's war powers, at least absent specific Congressional authorization, do not authorize the indefinite detention of American citizens seized on American soil, and that such detention violates core due process values. This Report was first issued on February 6, 2004, and the revised version that follows was issued on March 18 of the same year.

The Second Circuit, relying principally on the absence of Congressional authorization, invalidated Padilla's detention in its 2003 decision reported at 352 F.3d 695. The U.S. Supreme Court reversed, but on the grounds that the venue of Padilla's *habeas corpus* petition had been improper. 542 U.S. 426 (2004). The petition was then refiled in the District of South Carolina, where Padilla is now detained. District Judge Floyd granted the petition, *Padilla v. Hanft,* 2005 U.S. Dist. Lexis 2921, February 28, 2005. Also finding a lack of Congressional authorization for the detention, the court held that to sustain the detention based on the President's alleged inherent authority as Commander-in-Chief would "offend the rule of law and violate this country's constitutional tradition…" On September 9, 2005, the Fourth Circuit reversed an opinion by Judge Floyd. *Padilla v. Hanft,* 2005 U.S. App. Lexis 19465. The Fourth Circuit did not address the President's inherent powers. Rather it found the detention had been authorized by Congress in its September 18, 2001, Authorization for Use of Military Force Joint Resolution, which authorized the President to use "all necessary and appropriate force" against those responsible for the September 11, 2001, terrorist attacks. The Fourth Circuit found there to be no meaningful distinction between the detention of an armed citizen seized on a foreign battlefield, as in *Hamdi v. Rumsfeld,* 124 S. Ct. 2633 (2004), and the detention of an unarmed citizen seized in the United States and determined by the President, such as was Padilla, to be actively conspiring with al Qaeda.

The U.S. Supreme Court will have an opportunity to address the merits of the Fourth Circuit's decision. While so far only Padilla and one other American citizen have been apprehended in the United States and detained as enemy combatants, the legal principle involved is potentially of far broader application. The indeterminate duration of the war on terror, and the Administration's view that the "battlefield" embraces the entire United States, places at risk in the United States even the most basic of individual rights when opposed by the asserted dictates of national security.

EXECUTIVE SUMMARY

The President, assertedly acting under his "war power" in prosecuting the "war on terror," has claimed the authority to detain indefinitely, and without access to counsel, persons he designates as "enemy combatants," an as yet undefined term that embraces selected suspected terrorists or their accomplices.

Two cases, each addressing a habeas corpus petition brought by an American citizen, have reviewed the constitutionality of detaining "enemy combatants" pursuant to the President's determination:

- *Hamdi v. Rumsfeld*, 316 F.3d 450 (4th Cir. 2003), cert. granted, 124 S. Ct. 981 (Jan. 9, 2004) (No. 03-6696), concerns a citizen seized with Taliban military forces in a zone of armed combat in Afghanistan;
- Padilla ex. rel. Newman v. Bush, 233 F. Supp. 2d 564 (S.D.N.Y. 2002), rev'd sub nom., Padilla ex. rel. Newman v. Rumsfeld, 352 F.3d 695 (2d Cir. 2003), cert. granted, 124 S. Ct. 1353 (Feb. 20, 2004) (No. 03-1027), concerns a citizen seized in Chicago, and suspected of planning a terrorist attack in league with al Qaeda.

Padilla and Hamdi have been held by the Department of Defense, without any access to legal counsel, for well over a year. No criminal charges have been filed against either one. Rather, the government asserts its right to detain them without charges to incapacitate them and to facilitate their interrogation. Specifically, the President claims the authority, in the exercise of his war power as "Commander in Chief" under the Constitution (Art. II, § 2), to detain persons he classifies as "enemy combatants":

- indefinitely, for the duration of the "war on terror";
- without any charges being filed, and thus not triggering any rights attaching to criminal prosecutions;
- incommunicado from the outside world;

- specifically, with no right of access to an attorney;
- with only limited access to the federal courts on *habeas corpus,* and with no right to rebut the government's showing that the detainee is an enemy combatant.

These detentions, effected unilaterally by the executive without congressional authorization and not subject to meaningful judicial review, violate core due process rights under the Constitution, including:

- the right not to be detained except pursuant to a statute authorizing the detention;
- the right not to be detained without the prompt proffer of specific criminal charges;
- the right to test the legality of the detention in the federal courts through the writ of habeas corpus at a meaningful evidentiary hearing;
- the right to consult with and to be represented by counsel concerning the detention, and in connection with a habeas corpus hearing challenging it.

The holding of persons incommunicado in this country, without charges, indefinitely and based solely on the executive's decision, has nothing in common with due process as we know it. Though effected in the perceived interest of national security, these detentions are alien to America's respect for the rule of law. Until now, no court has ever sustained the assertion of such unilateral detention powers by a President, even in times of war.

The President's war power is insufficient to justify such detentions, in derogation of core due process rights. The only Supreme Court precedent said to establish this detention power, Ex parte Quirin, 317 U.S. 1 (1942), did not. Quirin involved only the question of whether saboteurs, members of the German army, could be tried before a military commission for alleged war crimes, as Congress had authorized. In sustaining the prompt trial by commission of the saboteurs, who were represented by counsel, Quirin said nothing supporting the executive's unauthorized, indefinite and incommunicado detentions now at issue.

Apart from the absence of judicial support, recognizing an essentially unlimited and unilateral executive power to detain would have serious negative consequences for our country. The sharp departure from the rule of law inherent in such detentions would threaten many adverse effects beyond the violation of the detainees' rights.

There is a significant risk that persons will be detained erroneously, since they would be permitted no access to counsel or opportunity to rebut their classification as enemy combatants. This risk of error is all the graver because of the obvious potential for ethnic-based actions against men of Middle Eastern extraction, already evidenced in fact in immigration contexts, given the distinct ethnic cast of the terrorists apprehended to date.

Recognition of this unlimited detention power would impose an intolerable pressure on criminal defendants accused of terrorist-related crimes. They could be threatened, if they refuse to plead guilty, with removal from the criminal justice system, and indefinite detention with no access to a lawyer and no opportunity to contest their guilt. This is precisely the fate, to date, of one civilian non-combatant, suspected of providing (but not proven to have provided) logistical support for al Qaeda, who was designated as an enemy combatant and transferred to military jurisdiction shortly before he was to be tried on criminal charges. Al-Marri v. Bush, 274 F. Supp. 2d 1003 (C.D. Ill. 2003).

There is also the danger of further extensions of the war power to curtail other civil liberties. A jurisprudence that holds that the domestic war on terror is indistinguishable from the "total war" circumstances of World War II and the Civil War, and on that basis defers to the President all decisions on the best means to prosecute the war on terror within the United States, leaves the door wide open to an almost unlimited expansion of executive power. Why should the First

Amendment right of free speech, or the Fourth Amendment right to be free of unreasonable searches, be any less subordinate to the President's war power than the core due process right to remain free of unilateral executive detention? Pick your favorite constitutional amendment or right: its survival during the war on terror cannot be assumed if the legitimacy of these indefinite detentions is sustained.

Nor can the assertion of this detention power be comfortably assumed to be only a temporary departure from the rule of law. The war on terror is likely to be a prolonged, if not a permanent feature of our times. Thus, extraordinary departures from due process justified by the existence of this war may prove to be enduring features of the constitutional landscape, not short-term measures easily reversed.

The fact that the administration concedes that *habeas corpus* petitions can be brought on behalf of the detainees provides cold comfort for due process rights, if the basic principle of the detentions is upheld. This is especially so if, as the administration contends, no rebuttal in court is to be permitted to its claim, supported only by "some evidence," that the detainee is an enemy combatant. The Great Writ, under these restrictions, becomes perilously close to an empty gesture.

Finally, to sustain these lawless executive detentions would undermine the position of the United States in promoting the rule of law abroad, and would provide encouragement and cover for repression around the globe. If the United States feels justified in departing from the rule of law in combating terrorism at home, notwithstanding our strong tradition of constitutionalism, regimes in other countries with no such tradition may see such conduct as justifying crackdowns against political dissidents.

We do not question that the President has the power to treat aspects of the war on terror as a "war," a political question traditionally held unreviewable by the courts. Further, the President's war power, coupled with his primacy in the realm of foreign affairs, rightly afford the President a wide discretion in prosecuting the war on terror abroad, a discretion which supports at least the initial detention of Hamdi in Afghanistan in a zone of armed combat.

But no such near total deference is appropriate with respect to the President's actions at home, where due process and the rule of law prevail. The executive's authority to launch military campaigns against al Qaeda and Iraq cannot be conflated with an unlimited power to take actions in this country, in alleged pursuit of the same war on terror, that trammel on core due process rights. The Constitution makes the President the Commander in Chief of the Armed Forces, not Commander in Chief of all persons within the United States.

We do not say that due process is unyielding in the face of dire circumstance. To the contrary, it can accommodate a short-term departure from its usual strictures in an imminent emergency created by terrorism, in which immediate action is essential and can be taken only by the executive. But claims of such a crisis-borne necessity must be scrutinized by the courts, and a heavy presumption weighs against them to the extent they would suspend core due process rights.

No such general claim of necessity can be sustained with respect to the detentions of suspected terrorists in the United States. The criminal laws provide ample means for prosecuting such suspects and imposing heavy sentences upon their conviction, including the death penalty (and using the prospects of such sentences to plea bargain as a means of extracting information). Nor need a criminal prosecution wholly preempt an interrogation for intelligence purposes, if appropriate safeguards are put in place to insure that the fruits of the interrogation are not used against the defendants at the criminal trial.

The absence of Congressional authorization for these detentions further undermines their legitimacy. In other instances of disputed domestic exercises of the President's war power, including Quirin, the courts have looked to whether Congress, the other political branch, had authorized the challenged action. Here Congress has not authorized indefinite detentions. The Joint Resolution of September 2001, authorizing the President to use "all necessary and appropriate force" against al Qaeda, through the "United States Armed Forces," cannot reasonably be read as approving the suspension of basic due process rights in the United States, as distinguished from the use of military force abroad. In the USA Patriot Act passed a month later, which contains numerous expansions of executive power to combat terrorism, Congress notably did not authorize any detentions of citizens, and imposed a seven-day limitation (absent the commencement of removal proceedings) on the detention of aliens suspected of terrorism, a limitation inconsistent with the indefinite detentions now defended. Further, given that neither the Joint Resolution nor the President's war power justifies indefinite detentions, such detentions of citizens also violate 18 U.S.C. § 4001(a), prohibiting detentions of citizens "except pursuant to an act of Congress," as the Second Circuit has now held in Padilla.

There are, to be sure, limits on Congress's own war powers, to the extent legislation would seek to supplant core due process rights. But if Congress did authorize limited and conditional detentions, in specifically defined circumstances, and subject to meaningful judicial review, such a statute would command greater deference than the executive's unilateral assertion of an unlimited detention power.

In addition to its claimed detention power, the administration asserts that alien enemy combatants may be tried at the President's discretion before special military commissions, rather than in Article III courts applying the extensive procedural protections accorded under the Constitution to defendants in criminal prosecutions. Quirin and existing statutory authorization do provide some support for the use of such commissions to prosecute violations of the law of war. Assuming that some enemy combatants could be so charged, nonetheless the use of military commissions should be minimized because of the several advantages offered by criminal prosecutions in the federal courts. Because of the public access to such federal court trials, the procedural safeguards they embrace, and the independence of the federal judiciary, the fairness of such trials and the justness of their verdicts is much more likely to be accepted, in this country and abroad, than would be the case with military trials controlled by the executive. The federal courts have successfully tried numerous terrorism cases. They should be the preferred forum for future terrorism cases.

The war on terror has created many challenges for our country. Not the least is the challenge to preserve the rule of law in acting against enemies that respect no laws. The Constitution is not a "suicide pact," as a Supreme Court justice once famously declared. But neither is it a mere compact of convenience, to be enforced only in halcyon days of civic tranquility. It should take far more than the monstrous brutality of a handful of terrorists to drive us to abandon our core constitutional values. Insistence on the rule of law will not undermine our national security. Abandoning the rule of law will threaten our national identity.

I. INTRODUCTION

Especially since the attacks of September 11, 2001, the United States has viewed itself as engaged in a "war on terror" against the forces of al Qaeda and its adherents, and other terrorist groups, both abroad and at home. The measures taken in response to the threat of terrorism have raised many issues concerning the proper balance between national security and individual liberties. This report addresses, in particular, the role the federal courts should play in striking this balance with respect to the detention and trial of suspected terrorists or their accomplices, designated as "enemy combatants" by the executive branch.

A. Hamdi and Padilla: the President's War Power Trumps Due Process

To date, the constitutionality of detaining "enemy combatants," pursuant to the President's unilateral determination, has been reviewed in two cases, each addressing a habeas corpus petition brought by an American citizen:

- Hamdi v. Rumsfeld, 316 F.3d 450 (4th Cir. 2003) ("Hamdi"), reh'g and reh'g en banc denied, 337 F.3d 335 (4th Cir. 2003), cert. granted, 124 S. Ct. 981 (Jan. 9, 2004) (No. 03-6696);
- Padilla ex. rel. Newman v. Bush, 233 F. Supp. 2d 564 (S.D.N.Y. 2002) ("Padilla"), adhered to on recons. sub nom., Padilla ex. rel. Newman v. Rumsfeld, 243 F. Supp. 2d 42 (S.D.N.Y. 2003), rev'd, 352 F.3d 695 (2d Cir.) ("Padilla Cir."), cert. granted, 124 S. Ct. 1353 (Feb. 20, 2004) (No. 03-1027).

In addition, one alien, a student from Qatar, Ali Saleh Kahlah al-Marri, has been designated as an enemy combatant and transferred to military jurisdiction, shortly before he was scheduled to be tried on criminal charges. See Al-Marri v. Bush, 274 F. Supp. 2d 1003 (C.D. Ill. 2003) ("Al-Marri") (habeas petition dismissed in view of transfer of petitioner to military custody in South Carolina). If the reported facts concerning al-Marri are correct, he is a civilian suspected of providing logistical support for terrorists, specifically helping "other members of al Qaeda 'settle' in the United States."[1]

Padilla and Hamdi, both American citizens, were seized under different circumstances, ultimately declared "enemy combatants," and given over to the custody of the Department of Defense, where they have been held incommunicado, without any access to legal counsel, for well over a year at this point. Padilla at 571–72, 574; see Hamdi at 460.

No criminal charges have been filed against either Hamdi or Padilla.[2] The government disclaims, for now, any interest in pursuing the two "primary objectives of criminal punishment: retribution or deterrence." Padilla at 600, quoting Kansas v. Hendricks, 521 U.S. 346, 361–62 (1997). Rather, the government asserts its right to detain them without charges indefinitely, for the duration of the war on terror, to serve two different purposes: to prevent them from returning to the enemy, and to facilitate their interrogation in the hope of obtaining information to thwart additional terrorist acts. Padilla at 573–74; Hamdi at 465–66.

A brief comparison of Hamdi and Padilla, and of the al-Marri detention, arising as they do out of different factual settings, will help illuminate some of the issues presented by "enemy combatant" detentions.[3]

Hamdi, according to the government's allegations that the Fourth Circuit viewed as indisputable, was "captured in a zone of active combat in a foreign theater of conflict," namely Afghanistan. Hamdi at 459. He allegedly was captured by the Northern Alliance forces, together with other members of a Taliban fighting unit, while in possession of a weapon. The Northern Alliance forces handed Hamdi over to the American armed forces in the fall of 2001. The Department of Defense thereafter has held him in Afghanistan, Guantánamo Bay, Cuba, and ultimately, commencing in April 2002, in Naval Brigs in Virginia (id. at 460, 477) and, commencing July 2003, South Carolina. Brief for the Respondents in Opposition at 4–5, Hamdi v. Rumsfeld (U.S., No. 03-6696) ("Resp'ts Hamdi Brief"). It is not clear when and by whom Hamdi was formally declared to be an "enemy combatant." Compare Hamdi at 461 (Hamdi was so designated "by our Government") with Resp'ts Hamdi Brief at 4 ("the United States military determined that Hamdi is an enemy combatant").

Padilla was arrested in May 2002 by Department of Justice personnel when he arrived at a Chicago airport. The arrest was pursuant to a material witness warrant issued by the Southern District of New York, pursuant to 18 U.S.C. § 3144, to enforce a subpoena to secure Padilla's testimony before a grand jury in the Southern District. Padilla at 568–69. A lawyer appointed to represent Padilla, after consulting with him, filed a petition for a writ of habeas corpus challenging his detention as a material witness. After the motion had been fully submitted, the government suddenly withdrew its grand jury subpoena and transferred Padilla to the custody of the Department of Defense in South Carolina, pursuant to his designation by President Bush, himself, as an "enemy combatant." Id. at 571–74.

To support the classification of the petitioners as enemy combatants, in each case the government presented an affidavit or declaration by Special Advisor to the Undersecretary of Defense for Policy, Michael Mobbs, reciting the circumstances under which each petitioner had been detained and at least some of the alleged facts said to support his designation as an enemy combatant. In Hamdi's case, the evidence was basically his capture, bearing a weapon, as a part of the Taliban fighting forces in Afghanistan. Hamdi at 461, 472. In Padilla's case the facts alleged included his contacts with a senior al Qaeda lieutenant in Afghanistan, allegedly proposing to steal radioactive material so as to build and detonate a "dirty bomb" in the United States, and other contacts with al Qaeda, including training and alleged instructions to journey to the United States to "conduct reconnaissance and/or conduct other attacks on their behalf." Padilla at 572–73.

Both the Hamdi circuit court and the Padilla district court recognized, as the government ultimately conceded, the availability of habeas corpus as a procedural remedy to test the legality of the detentions of these American citizens.[4] But, as a matter of substance, both upheld the constitutionality of the detentions, if the classification of the detainee as an "enemy combatant" were established, as proper exercises of the President's war power as Commander in Chief under Article II, section 2, of the Constitution. Neither court viewed the detainee's U.S. citizenship to limit the President's power to detain them.[5]

The Second Circuit, in its recent decision reversing Padilla, disagreed. It held that, absent explicit congressional authorization, the President's war power did not extend to the detention of American citizens on American soil, removed from any zone of armed combat. Padilla Cir. at 710–18. It also found Padilla's detention to violate 18 U.S.C. § 4001(a), which prohibits the detention of a citizen "except pursuant to an act of Congress." Id. at 718–24.

To sustain the enemy combatant classification, the Padilla district court would have required that the government adduce "some evidence" supporting the classification, while permitting the petitioner to rebut this showing. Padilla at 608. On its interlocutory appeal to the Second Circuit, the government urged that Padilla "has no entitlement to present facts to challenge the basis for his detention," because the "some evidence" standard "turns exclusively on the facts presented by the Executive. . . ." Opening Brief of Respondent-Appellant at 43, 45.

In Hamdi no rebuttal was permitted and Hamdi's counsel was not permitted to consult with him to determine if any rebuttal was feasible: the court found the Mobbs declaration sufficient given that (in its view) the facts supporting Hamdi's classification were beyond dispute. Thus while in its earlier remand decision the Fourth Circuit had refused to sustain the classification "on the government's say so", declining to accept the government's determination as "the first and final word" on the subject, its ultimate resolution based exclusively on the Mobbs declaration—consistent with the government's "no rebuttal" position in the Padilla appeal—seems to have done precisely that in the military battlefield context before it.

Neither Hamdi nor the Padilla district court attempted an all-purpose definition of "enemy combatant," and the administration also seems not to have gone beyond the facts of the individual cases to articulate a generally applicable definition. In Padilla's case, his alleged role in planning a bomb attack bore obvious analogy to the German saboteurs seized as illegal combatants in the World War II case of Ex Parte Quirin, 317 U.S. 1 (1942) ("Quirin"). To the Fourth Circuit, Hamdi's classification as an enemy combatant was self-evident based on his alleged capture while fighting with Taliban forces against the Northern Alliance, America's ally.

Neither Hamdi nor the Padilla district court held that the detainee had a due process right to consult with counsel in connection with the habeas proceeding. In Padilla, however, Judge Mukasey ordered that such consultation be allowed, as a matter of discretion, in part because Padilla had already consulted with his appointed counsel when he had been held as a material witness. The government vigorously resisted this order, resulting in an interlocutory appeal to the Second Circuit, which found Padilla's detention itself to be unconstitutional.

As the Supreme Court is poised to review the Hamdi and Padilla rulings, we offer a review of these decisions, and an analysis of the interests and values at stake.

In different ways, and in different factual contexts, Hamdi and the Padilla district court held that certain basic limits on the power of the executive branch, treated as unquestioned "rights" in most contexts, are of limited or no applicability to accused terrorists. These holdings suggest that a system largely separate from Article III courts and the due process rights they enforce, but rather based on the war power of the President—though still subject to some review via habeas corpus—is appropriate to deal with terrorism. Under this system, "enemy combatants" as determined by the executive branch may be held indefinitely, without charges, perhaps with no access to a lawyer (as in Hamdi), and subject to aggressive interrogation, until the end of the "war on terror." This "enemy combatant" classification can embrace a U.S. citizen seized abroad during a military campaign and accused of fighting with enemy forces (Hamdi), a U.S. citizen accused of planning sabotage in the United States (Padilla), and, given the reported facts concerning al-Marri, a civilian non-combatant perhaps accused of providing logistical support for terrorists in the United States.[6]

The Second Circuit's opinion reversing Padilla does not speak directly to the constitutional rights of detainees to due process. But it does squarely hold that indefinite detentions are not within the President's unilateral war power, to the extent that the person detained is "an American citizen seized on American soil outside a zone of combat." Padilla Cir. at 698. The opinion necessarily does not address the President's powers with respect to non-citizens, such as al-Marri, or with respect to citizens seized abroad or in zones of combat, such as Hamdi.

B.   Questions Presented

Since the war on terror has no foreseeable end, it becomes vital to reexamine the role of the federal courts, and the core principles they generally enforce, in the context of terrorism. What is the appropriate role for the courts, the President and Congress with respect to the detention and prosecution of alleged terrorists, given a proper application of the separation of powers doctrine in the light of the war power of the President and the Due Process Clause? Is it likely that denying basic due process rights to alleged terrorists would do lasting damage to those rights traditionally accorded to all persons within the reach of the Constitution? Is it unwise to apply to terrorism the due process limitations on executive power that apply in criminal proceedings? Instead, should the courts find that the President, under his war power, possesses the discretion to fight the war on terror through whatever means he deems appropriate, including here the unlimited detention and interrogation of suspected terrorists? Should the answer to this detention issue depend on whether, for example, the suspect is a citizen, or was arrested, or is detained, in the United States or abroad?

In this report we will:

• restate the basic substantive and procedural "rights" of detainees, outside of the war context;

- examine the precedents construing the war power of the President (and/or Congress), and the extent to which those powers have been held to limit or preempt basic due process rights, including in Padilla and Hamdi;
- analyze the potential damage to civil liberties inherent in upholding the constitutionality of unilateral and indefinite executive detentions of "enemy combatants" in the United States;
- set forth our own analysis of why the President's war power should not be construed to embrace such detentions, at least absent express authorization by Congress; and
- weigh the practical and policy advantages and disadvantages of the federal courts as a trial venue for alleged terrorists, as compared with military commissions, to the extent the use of commissions would be constitutional.

II. THE CORE PRINCIPLES OF INDIVIDUAL LIBERTY AND DUE PROCESS

It is asserted by the administration that, on its determination that an individual is an "enemy combatant", that person may be detained:

- indefinitely, for the duration of the "war against terror";
- without any charges or proceedings being filed, and thus not triggering any rights attaching to criminal prosecutions;
- incommunicado from the outside world;
- specifically, with no right of access to an attorney;
- with only limited access to the federal courts, and no right to rebut the government's showing that the detainee is an "enemy combatant."

Our core constitutional principles of due process and individual liberty prohibit such indefinite and incommunicado detentions in times of peace. After discussing these clear peacetime principles, we will proceed to consider the possible limitation or inapplicability of those principles in the context of the "war on terror."

A. Substantive Rights

1. *No Arbitrary Detentions; The Rule of Law*

The Constitution with its Bill of Rights defines the balance between governmental authority and individual liberty in the United States.

The United States is entirely a creature of the Constitution. Its power and authority have no other source.

Reid v. Covert, 354 U.S. 1, 5–6 (1957) (Black, J., plurality opinion).

Early on, the Supreme Court sounded the rule of law as central to the Constitution:

The government of the United States has been emphatically termed a government of laws, and not of men. Marbury v. Madison, 5 U.S. 137, 163 (1803).

Fundamental to our constitutional scheme is the principle that a person can be detained by the government only pursuant to a valid law, and upon a judicial determination that sufficient cause exists to believe it has been violated. The Constitution prohibits detentions based only on the executive's subjective determination.

From at least the Magna Carta of 1215, a major stream in the history of English-speaking peoples has been the increasing protection of individuals from such arbitrary exercises of executive power. The Magna Carta recognized the right to be free from intrusions on personal security "except by the legal judgment of [one's] peers or by the law of the land." The Magna Carta, though initially benefiting only a narrow class of English barons, recognized that even the King was subject to a superior law. The rule of law was gradually extended to protect the rights of commoners. By the time of Edward III, the right to "due process of law" was recognized as protecting personal liberty. See Ingraham v. Wright, 430 U.S. 651, 673 n.41 (1977). Key later developments included the work of Sir Edward Coke in the early 17th century, and the enactment of the English Habeas Corpus Act of 1679 and Bill of Rights of 1689, the latter declaring the supremacy of Parliament and its laws over the power of the crown.

The founding fathers "were opposed to governments that placed in the hands of one man the power to make, interpret and enforce the laws." Duncan v. Kahanamoku, 327 U.S. 304, 322 (1946). The Fourth Circuit, in its Hamdi decision, well articulated the fear of arbitrary governmental power, and specifically unrestrained executive detentions, as a central focus of the Constitution:

The Constitution is suffused with concern about how the state will yield its awesome power of forcible restraint. And this preoccupation was not accidental. Our forebears recognized that the power to detain could easily become destructive "if exerted without check or control" by an unrestrained executive free to "imprison, dispatch or exile any man that was obnoxious to the government by an instant declaration that such was their will and pleasure." 4 W. Blackstone, Commentaries on the Laws of England 349–50 (Cooley Ed. 1899) (quoted in Duncan v. Louisiana, 391 U.S. 145, 151 (1968)).

Hamdi, 316 F.3d at 464.

The rule of law finds its most explicit constitutional formulation in the Fifth Amendment's guarantee that no person may be "deprived of life, liberty, or property without due process of law…." The "touchstone of due process is protection of the individual against arbitrary action of government." Wolff v. McDonnell, 418 U.S. 539, 558 (1974). The right to due process has both substantive and procedural aspects:

The Due Process Clause of the Fifth Amendment provides that "No person shall…be deprived of life, liberty, or property, without due process of law…." This Court has held that the Due Process Clause protects individuals against two types of government action. So-called "substantive due process" prevents the government from engaging in conduct that "shocks the conscience," Rochin v. California, 342 U.S. 165, 172 (1952), or interferes with rights "implicit in the concept of ordered liberty," Palko v. Connecticut, 302 U.S. 319, 325–326 (1937). When government action depriving a person of life, liberty, or property survives substantive due process scrutiny, it must still be implemented in a fair manner. Mathews v. Eldridge, 424 U.S. 319, 335 (1976). This requirement has traditionally been referred to as "procedural" due process.

United States v. Salerno, 481 U.S. 739, 746 (1987).

Due process requires an express statutory basis for detentions. Common law crimes, recognized in England, were held incompatible with our Constitution in United States v. Hudson, 11 U.S. 32 (1812). Much more recently, in 1971, Congress acted to rescind the Emergency Detention Act and to prevent any conduct similar to the internment of Americans of Japanese ancestry during World War II. Its remedy was to enact 18 U.S.C. § 4001(a), which provides:

No citizen shall be imprisoned or otherwise detained by the United States except pursuant to an Act of Congress.

The Fourth Amendment protects not only against unreasonable searches for evidence, but also against arbitrary arrest and detention, in these words:

The right of the people to be secure in their persons, houses, papers and effects, against unreasonable searches and seizures, shall not be violated, and no Warrants shall issue but upon probable cause, supported by Oath or affirmation, and particularly describing the place to be searched, and the persons or things to be seized.

The "Fourth Amendment requires a judicial determination of probable cause as a prerequisite to extended restraint of liberty following arrest." Gerstein v. Pugh, 420 U.S. 103, 114 (1975);[7] County of Riverside v. McLaughlin, 500 U.S. 44 (1991) (Fourth Amendment requires prompt judicial determination of probable cause, within 48 hours of arrest, as prerequisite to extended pretrial detention following a warrantless arrest). "Probable cause exists if the facts and circumstances known to the officer warrant a prudent man in believing that the offense has been committed." Henry v. United States, 361 U.S. 98, 102 (1959).

The requirement that probable cause be promptly determined to justify a detention is not limited to the context of criminal prosecutions.[8] It also applies to detentions for investigatory purposes, even where there is no intention of charging the detainee with a crime. Davis v. Mississippi, 394 U.S. 721, 726–27 (1969); see Dunaway v. New York, 442 U.S. 200, 214–16 (1979); cf. United States v. Verdugo-Urquidez, 494 U.S. 259, 264 (1990) (Rehnquist, C.J., plurality opinion) (the Fourth Amendment is violated "at the time of an unreasonable governmental intrusion," and "whether or not the evidence is sought to be used in a criminal trial....").

2. No Indefinite Detentions (with Rare Exceptions)

While recognizing exceptions, the Supreme Court has declared that "[i]n our society liberty is the norm, and detention prior to trial or without trial is the carefully limited exception." Salerno, 481 U.S. at 755 (emphasis added). See also id. at 749 (recognizing a "'general rule' of substantive due process that the government may not detain a person prior to a judgment of guilt in a criminal trial"); accord Foucha v. Louisiana, 504 U.S. 71, 83 (1992) ("our present system..., with only narrow exceptions and aside from permissible confinements for mental illness, incarcerates only those who are proved beyond reasonable doubt to have violated a criminal law"); Addington v. Texas, 441 U.S. 418, 425 (1979) ("This Court repeatedly has recognized that civil commitment for any purpose constitutes a significant deprivation of liberty that requires due process protection"); see Petition of Brooks, 5 F.2d 238, 239 (D. Mass. 1925) ("There is no power in this court or in any other tribunal in this country to hold indefinitely any sane citizen or alien in imprisonment, except as a punishment for crime").

Though from a dissenting opinion, the following comment on indefinite detentions likewise states the law of the land:

Fortunately, it still is startling, in this country, to find a person held indefinitely in executive custody without accusation of crime or judicial trial. Executive imprisonment has been considered oppressive and lawless since John, at Runnymede, pledged that no free man should be imprisoned, dispossessed, outlawed or exiled save by the judgment of his peers or by the law of the land.

Shaughnessy v. Mezei, 345 U.S. 206, 218 (1953) (Jackson, J., dissenting from opinion upholding indefinite detention of an excludable alien, held at the border, based on confidential information the Attorney General refused to disclose, even in camera).

The Supreme Court recently declared that "[a] statute permitting indefinite detention of an alien would raise a serious constitutional problem." Zadvydas v. Davis, 533 U.S. 678, 690 (2001) (construing statute to authorize detention of removable aliens only for a "reasonable time," to avoid constitutional question presented by unlimited detention).[9] The Court explained:

Freedom from imprisonment—from government custody, detention, or other forms of physical restraint— lies at the heart of the liberty [the Due Process] Clause protects. See Foucha v. Louisiana, 504 U.S. 71, 80 (1992). And this Court has said that government detention violates that Clause unless the detention is ordered in a *criminal* proceeding with adequate procedural protections, see *United States v. Salerno,* 481 U.S. 739, 746 (1987), or, in certain special and "narrow" nonpunitive "circumstances," *Foucha, supra,* at 80, where a special justification, such as harm-threatening mental illness, outweighs the "individual's constitutionally protected interest in avoiding physical restraint." *Kansas v. Hendricks,* 521 U.S. 346, 356 (1997).

Id., 533 U.S. at 690.

Kansas v. Hendricks, cited by the Court, upheld the constitutionality of indeterminate civil commitments when a continuing condition of mental illness precluded release, in the interests of the detainee or of public safety. The Kansas statutory scheme passed muster, in important part, because the detainee was guaranteed periodic review by a court to determine whether the condition justifying the detention persisted. Hendricks, 521 U.S. at 364 (annual judicial hearing and finding required to continue commitment).

Dangerousness is the other basis on which the Court has found preventive detention consistent with due process. To pass muster, the detention must serve regulatory rather than punitive purposes: "For under the Due Process Clause, a detainee may not be punished prior to an adjudication of guilt in accordance with due process of law." Bell v. Wolfish, 441 U.S. 520, 535 (1979). Prior to trial, bail can be denied under the Bail Reform Act of 1984, 18 U.S.C. §§ 3141, 3142, after an adversary hearing, on a finding upon "clear and convincing evidence" that no conditions of release "will reasonably assure...the safety of any other person and the community."[10] This provision was upheld as a permissible "regulation", and not a punitive measure, in United States v. Salerno, 481 U.S. 739, 746–48 (1987).[11] See United States v. El-Hage, 213 F.3d 74, 80 (2d Cir. 2000), cert. denied, 531 U.S. 881 (2001) (pretrial detention of 30–33 months did not violate due process given, inter alia, gravity of charges against defendant, accused of playing a vital role in al Qaeda, which poses "a substantial threat to national security"). Similarly in Schall v. Martin, 467 U.S. 253 (1984), the Court upheld a statute permitting "a brief pretrial detention" of a juvenile—for a maximum of 17 days (id. at 270)—on a finding that there was a "serious risk" he might commit a crime before the return date. Again, this holding was premised on the conclusion that this statute served the legitimate regulatory and nonpunitive purpose of "protecting both the community and the juvenile himself from the consequences of future criminal conduct." Id. at 264.

In its 2001 Zadvydas opinion, the Supreme Court summarized its preventive detention cases, to the extent based on the dangerousness of the detainees, as follows:

...we have upheld preventive detention based on dangerousness only when limited to specially dangerous individuals and subject to strong procedural protections.

Zadvydas v. Davis, 533 U.S. at 690–91.[12]

There is one 1909 case in which no such "strong procedural protections" were present. The Governor of Colorado detained a union leader for two and one-half months during a "state of insurrection" created by labor strife, until "fears of the insurrection were at an end." Moyer v. Peabody, 212 U.S. 78, 84–85 (1909). After the unionist had been released, he brought suit for damages, claiming the Governor's actions had violated his due process rights. The Court, based on findings that the Governor had acted in good faith, though "without sufficient reason," found no constitutional violation and affirmed dismissal of the damage suit. Justice Holmes' language for the majority was expansive:

When it comes to a decision by the head of the State upon a matter involving its life, the ordinary rights of individuals must yield to what he deems the necessities of the moment. Public danger warrants the substitution of executive process for judicial process....This was admitted with regard to killing men in the actual clash of arms; and we think it obvious, although it was disputed, that the same is true of temporary detention to prevent apprehended harm.

Id. at 85 (citation omitted).[13]

Moyer seems to stand alone in approving an indefinite detention by a local official. See, generally, Note, Riot Control and the Fourth Amendment, 81 Harv. L. Rev. 625, 632–35 (1968). However, it may have some continued relevance to the war on terror.[14]

B.   Procedural Rights

1.   Right to a Hearing

A constitutional right without a remedy for its violation would be antithetical to our system of government under law. The rule of law would mean little

if the laws furnish no remedy for the violation of a vested legal right.

Marbury v. Madison, 5 U.S. 137, 167 (1803).

The nature of the procedural remedy available to contest a detention is governed by the due process clause. Procedural due process is not a rigid concept. "Due process is flexible and calls for such procedural protections as the particular situation demands." Morrissey v. Brewer, 408 U.S. 471, 481 (1972); see Gilbert v. Homar, 520 U.S. 924, 930 (1997). But while flexible, the courts have evolved certain basic concepts that provide a baseline of individual rights in most circumstances.

The "fundamental right of due process," the Supreme Court has held, "is the opportunity to be heard 'at a meaningful time and in a meaningful manner.'" Mathews v. Eldridge, 424 U.S. 319, 333 (1976), quoting Armstrong v. Manzo, 380 U.S. 545, 552 (1965). See Nat'l Council of Resistance v. Dep't of State, 251 F.3d 192, 208–09 (D.C. Cir. 2001) (designation of terrorist organizations); cf. Yakus v. United States, 321 U.S. 414, 433 (1944) (in context of wartime price control regulations, due process requires that those affected by an administrative order be afforded "a reasonable opportunity to be heard and present evidence").

When the Due Process Clause requires a hearing, "it requires a fair one, one before a tribunal which meets at least currently prevailing standards of impartiality." Wang Yang Sung v. McGrath, 339 U.S. 33, 50 (1950). The particular kind of hearing required will vary in accordance with the relative gravity of the private and public interests at stake in the governmental action challenged. See generally Henry J. Friendly, Some Kind of Hearing, 123 U. of Pa. L. Rev. 1267 (1975).

A person cannot be detained, for more than a short period of time, without being afforded a hearing concerning the legality of his detention. Aside from the immigration context, a detention requires an evidentiary hearing, generally to be conducted by the courts, rather than by an administrative agency, or subject to prompt review by the courts. See Zadvydas v. Davis, 533 U.S. at 692 (noting constitutional problem posed by unreviewable agency determinations affecting fundamental rights). In the criminal context, the initial hearing after an arrest is nonadversarial, conducted by a magistrate to determine probable cause, but the Sixth Amendment's guarantee of a "speedy and public trial" dictates that a full blown evidentiary hearing will soon follow.

2.   Habeas Corpus: The Right of Access to the Federal Courts

The fundamental procedural remedy to obtain a hearing to test the legality of a detention is the writ of habeas corpus. 28 U.S.C. § 2241. The federal courts have jurisdiction to hear claims that a person is being held "in custody in violation of the Constitution or laws...of the United States." 28 U.S.C. § 2241(c)(3). See Harris v. Nelson, 394 U.S. 286, 290–91 (1969):

The writ of habeas corpus is the fundamental instrument for safeguarding individual freedom against arbitrary and lawless state action.

If the petition makes specific allegations of fact that, if true, would invalidate the detention, "it is the duty of the court to provide the necessary facilities and procedures for an adequate inquiry" into those facts. Id., 394 U.S. at 300.

The writ, with origins as early as the 14th century in England, was first codified in the English Habeas Corpus Act of 1679, 31 Car. II, c. 2. See generally R.J. Sharpe, The Law of Habeas Corpus (1976). This Act required the jailer, on service of the Writ, to produce the prisoner (except in cases of treason or felony), and to "certify the true causes of his detainer or imprisonment," which led to the release of the prisoner on bail unless the detention was upon a legal process, by a court of jurisdiction, for an offense "for which by the law the prisoner is not bailable...."

The "Great Writ" was guaranteed by the Constitution in Article I, section 9:

The privilege of the Writ of Habeas Corpus shall not be suspended, unless when in Cases of Rebellion or Invasion, the public Safety may require.[15]

Again the Fourth Circuit's decision in Hamdi well states the role of the writ in our system:

In war as in peace, habeas corpus provides one of the firmest bulwarks against unconstitutional detentions. As early as 1789, Congress reaffirmed the courts' common law authority to review detention of federal prisoners, giving its explicit blessing to the judiciary's power to 'grant Writs of Habeas Corpus for the purpose of an inquiry into the cause of commitment' for federal detainees. Act of Sept. 24, 1789, ch. 20, § 14, 1 Stat. 81–82. While the scope of habeas review has expanded and contracted over the succeeding centuries, its essential function of assuring that restraint accords with the rule of law, not the whim of authority, remains unchanged.

Hamdi, at 464–65.

More concisely put:

The historic purpose of the writ has been to relieve detention by executive authorities without judicial trial. Brown v. Allen, 344 U.S. 443, 533 (1953) (Jackson, J., concurring), quoted in Zadvydas v. Davis, 533 U.S. at 699.

See also INS v. St. Cyr, 533 U.S. 289, 301 (2001):

At its historical core, the writ of habeas corpus has served as a means of reviewing the legality of Executive detention, and it is in that context that its protection has been strongest.

3.   Right to Consult an Attorney (and Usually to Be Represented by One)

The right to file a writ of habeas corpus provides basic access to the federal courts to test the legality of a detention.[16] But for that right of access and any consequent right to a hearing to be meaningful, legal representation is often a near necessity. The "right to be heard would be, in many cases, of little avail if it did not comprehend the right to be heard by counsel." Powell v. Alabama, 287 U.S. 45, 68–69 (1932).

In criminal prosecutions in federal courts, the Sixth Amendment's guarantee of the accused's right "to have the Assistance of Counsel for his defense" long has been construed to require "the appointment of counsel in all cases where a defendant is unable to procure the services of an attorney...." Betts v. Brady, 316 U.S. 455, 464 (1942).[17]

The constitutional right to legal representation by governmental detainees not charged with a crime is measured by the Due Process Clause.[18] The general test of due process rights outside the criminal and military justice contexts, including whether a right to appointed counsel should be afforded, turns on the three-part balancing test articulated in Mathews v. Eldridge, 424 U.S. 319, 335 (1976). The private interests and the government interests at stake must be weighed, together with the risk of "an erroneous deprivation" of the private interest absent the additional procedural safeguard sought.

While the Mathews v. Eldridge balancing test can require some nice judgments, it seems clear—war power issues aside—that a person faced with a significant period of physical detention has a due process right to counsel to test the legality of the detention. The "fundamental fairness" required by due process requires the appointment of counsel for any indigent litigant who "may lose his physical liberty if he loses the litigation." Lassiter v. Dep't of Social Servs., 452 U.S. 18, 25 (1981) (adopting a case-by-case approach to the right to appointed counsel in parental termination proceedings). It is "the defendant's interest in personal freedom, and not simply the special Sixth and Fourteenth Amendments right to counsel in criminal cases, which triggers the right to appointed counsel...." Id. See In re Gault, 387 U.S. 1, 41 (1967) (since juvenile delinquency proceeding, though civil, may result "in commitment to an institution in which the juvenile's freedom is curtailed," due process mandates appointment of counsel).

Generally, cases concerning a due process right to counsel have focused on the right to appointed counsel, at government expense. But occasionally the right to have retained counsel participate in hearings has been discussed. In the context of welfare benefit termination proceedings, "the recipient must be allowed to retain an attorney if he so desires." Goldberg v. Kelly, 397 U.S. 254, 270 (1970). But the direct participation of even retained counsel may be prohibited in certain proceedings which have only limited consequences, or where an informal, non-adversarial hearing system furthers important governmental interests.[19] Even in these situations where counsel may not attend a hearing, there seems no question that consultation with retained counsel outside the hearing room is permissible. The concept of incommunicado detentions appears to be without precedent, at least outside of the law of war.

4. Additional Rights in Criminal Prosecutions

In the context of criminal prosecutions, additional fundamental rights apply. The Fifth Amendment secures the right against double jeopardy and self-incrimination. The Sixth Amendment provides other critical rights:

In all criminal prosecutions, the accused shall enjoy the right to a speedy and public trial, by an impartial jury...and to be informed of the nature and cause of the accusations; to be confronted with the witnesses against him; to have compulsory process for obtaining witnesses in his favor, and to have the assistance of counsel for his defense."[20]

The Supreme Court articulated this litany of a criminal defendant's rights in Herrera v. Collins, 506 U.S. 390, 398–99 (1993):

A person when first charged with a crime is entitled to a presumption of innocence, and may insist that his guilt be established beyond a reasonable doubt. In re Winship, 397 U S 358 (1970). Other constitutional provisions also have the effect of ensuring against the risk of convicting an innocent person. See, e.g., Coy v. Iowa, 487 U.S. 1012 (1988) (right to confront adverse witnesses); Taylor v. Illinois, 484 U.S. 400 (1988) (right to compulsory process); Strickland v. Washington, 466 U.S. 668 (1984) (right to effective assistance of counsel); Winship, supra (prosecution must prove guilt beyond a reasonable doubt); Duncan v. Louisiana, 391 U.S. 145 (right to jury trial); Brady v. Maryland,... [373 U.S. 83 (1963)] (1968) (prosecution must disclose exculpatory evidence); Gideon v. Wainwright, 372 U.S. 335 (1963) (right to assistance of counsel); In re Murchison, 349 U.S. 133, 136 (1944) (right to "fair trial in a fair tribunal").[21]

All of these rights apply only to criminal defendants, and therefore do not apply to detainees against whom no criminal charges have been filed. However, as discussed above, due process precludes more than a brief detention without the proffer of charges. Thus the government is put to a prompt choice: it must either release a detainee, or institute criminal charges and thereby trigger the application of the Fifth and Sixth Amendment rights of a criminal defendant.

C.   The Applicability of Core Principles Abroad: To Citizens, but Generally not to Foreign Nationals

To what extent does the application of due process rights turn on whether the detainee is seized in the United States or abroad, or on where the detainee is held subsequent to his initial detention?

Broadly speaking, citizens have the same rights abroad, with respect to actions taken by agents of the United States, as they would with respect to such actions taken within the country. The constitutional rights of citizens—or at minimum those rights deemed "fundamental"— apply anywhere in the world, though always subject to a review of what due process requires under the "particular situation" presented. See United States v. Verdugo-Urquidez, supra, 494 U.S. at 275–78 (Kennedy J., concurring); Reid v. Covert, 354 U.S. 1 (1957) (plurality would so hold with respect to all constitutional rights; concurring opinions would limit to fundamental rights).

In contrast, foreign nationals subject to detention or other action abroad by United States agents generally do not enjoy constitutional protection,[22] including the right to present a habeas corpus petition. The leading case is Johnson v. Eisentrager, 339 U.S. 763 (1950). The petitioners were German nationals convicted of violating the law of war in World War II by furnishing intelligence to Japanese forces in China. They were convicted by a military commission sitting in China with that government's permission, following which petitioners were sent to Germany to serve out their sentences in a military prison. From Germany they filed petitions for writs of habeas corpus, claiming that their right to due process under the Fifth Amendment had been violated. See id. at 765–66.

The district court dismissed the petitions, but the Court of Appeals reversed, holding that any person, including an enemy alien, deprived of his liberty anywhere in the world under the purported authority of the United States is entitled to the writ if he can show his imprisonment to be illegal under any constitutional right. See id. at 767. The Supreme Court reversed the Court of Appeals. The Court wrote:

We are cited to no instance where a court, in this or any other country where the writ is known, has issued it on behalf of an alien enemy who, at no relevant time and in no stage of his captivity, has been within its territorial jurisdiction. Nothing in the text of the Constitution extends such a right, nor does anything in our statutes.

Id. at 768.

It is, principally, on the precedent of Johnson that the alien suspected terrorists and Taliban fighters held at Guantánamo Bay, Cuba, allegedly outside the sovereign territory of the United States, have been held without any access to U.S. courts via habeas corpus proceedings. Coalition of Clergy v. Bush, 189 F. Supp. 2d 1036 (C.D. Cal.), vacated in part, 310 F.3d 1153 (9th Cir. 2002). But the contrary result was reached in Gherebi v. Bush, No. CV-03-01267 (9th Cir. Dec. 18, 2003), distinguishing the legal status of Guantánamo Bay from that of the prison in Germany involved in Johnson. On November 10, 2003, the Supreme Court granted certiorari in two cases to consider the question of whether "United States courts lack jurisdiction to consider challenges to the legality of the detention of foreign nationals captured abroad in connection with hostilities and incarcerated at the Guantánamo Naval Base, Cuba." Al Odah v. United States, 321 F.3d 1134 (D.C. Cir. 2003), cert. granted, 2003 WL 22070725 (No. 03-343); Rasul v. Bush, 215 F. Supp. 2d 55 (D.D.C. 2002), aff'd, 321 F.3d 1134 (D.C. Cir.), cert. granted, 72 U.S.L.W. 3323 (No. 03-334).

D. The Rights of Foreign Nationals in the United States

To what extent do the substantive and procedural due process rights reviewed above apply to foreign nationals detained in the United States? Do they have the same rights as citizens? See generally David Cole, Enemy Aliens, 54 Stan. L. Rev. 953, 978-85 (2002).

Generally, there is no distinction between the procedural due process rights of citizens and those of aliens who are within the jurisdiction of the United States.[23] Procedural due process rights apply to any alien who has entered the country, legally or illegally. Zadvydas v. Davis, 533 U.S. 678, 693–94 (2001); see, e.g., Reno v. Flores, 507 U.S. 292, 306 (1993); Wong Wing v. United States, 163 U.S. 228, 238 (1896); Yick Wo. v. Hopkins, 118 U.S. 356, 369 (1886); Patel v. Zemski, 275 F.3d 299, 307 (3d Cir. 2001).[24]

In contrast to these procedural protections applicable to aliens, their substantive rights to remain in the country are subject to almost unlimited restriction or termination by Congress —"plenary power"—and correspondingly little judicial review:

Courts have long recognized the power to expel or exclude aliens as a fundamental sovereign attribute exercised by the Government's political departments largely immune from judicial control.

Shaughnessy v. United States ex rel. Mezei, 345 U.S. 206, 210 (1953) (upholding indefinite detention of removable alien held at border, based on national security grounds not disclosed by Attorney General).[25] The Supreme Court has observed that "Congress regularly makes rules [governing aliens] that would be unacceptable if applied to citizens," Matthews v. Diaz, 426 U.S. 67, 80 (1976), a proposition "firmly and repeatedly endorsed," most recently in Demore v. Kim, 538 U.S. 510, 128 S. Ct. 1708 (2003) (case involved "lawful permanent resident"). Further, "when the Government deals with deportable aliens, the Due Process Clause does not require it to employ the least burdensome means to accomplish its goal." Id., 128 S. Ct. at 1720. The rationale for the great discretion accorded Congress with respect to legislation concerning the exclusion or departure of aliens—and the deference accorded to the executive in implementing such legislation—is that "any policy toward aliens is vitally and intricately interwoven with contemporaneous policies in regard to the conduct of foreign relations, the war power and the maintenance of a republican form of government." Id., 128 S. Ct. at 1716 (quoting Mathews, 426 U.S. at 81 n.17, quoting Harisiades v. Shaughnessy, 342 U.S. 580, 588–89 (1952).

Specifically, the Court in Demore recognized that "[d]etention during removal proceedings is a constitutionally permissible part" of the deportation process." Id., 128 S. Ct. at 1721–22. The Court sustained the constitutionality of 8 U.S.C. § 1226(c), which requires that deportable aliens convicted of aggravated felonies be detained during "the limited period" of removal proceedings, regardless of whether they constitute a flight risk or threat to the community.[26] The Court contrasted the "limited" and finite period of detention occasioned by removal proceedings— about 47 days on average, plus another four months in the event of an appeal (id., 128 S. Ct. at 1721)—with the "indefinite" and "potentially permanent" detention held constitutionally suspect in Zadvydas of an alien already found to be removable, but not removable as a practical matter. Id., 128 S. Ct. at 1720. In Zadvydas, the Court had found that such continued detention "no longer bear[s] [a] reasonable relation to the purpose for which the individual [was] committed." Id., quoting Zadvydas, 533 U.S. at 690, quoting Jackson v. Indiana, 406 U.S. 715, 738 (1972).

Thus an alien can be deported on any ground sanctioned by Congress, but is entitled to procedural due process with respect to such deportation proceedings. While detention is permissible for the "limited period" during which removal proceedings are pending, this detention must be based on specific charges warranting removal by statute, and on which a hearing will be held resulting in removal if sustained. An indefinite detention without charges would appear no more constitutional for an alien within the country than for a citizen.

E. Hierarchy of Rights

We believe that the above discussion confirms that there is a hierarchy of rights recognized in times of peace, firmly imbedded in our constitutional structure and case law. These rights include, with respect to citizens or aliens detained in the United States or its sovereign territory:

- the right not to be detained except pursuant to a statute authorizing the detention;
- the right (subject to inapplicable exceptions noted above) not to be detained without the prompt proffer of specific criminal charges;
- the right to test the legality of the detention in the federal courts through the writ of habeas corpus and, where the matter has not been previously adjudicated, at a meaningful evidentiary hearing;
- the right to consult with and to be represented by counsel concerning the detention, and in connection with a habeas corpus hearing challenging it.

Our system precludes—again, before considering the implications of the war powers— indefinite detentions without charges, with the detainee held incommunicado without access to a lawyer. Further, the legality of any detention should be testable through the writ of habeas corpus made effective through the assistance of counsel, at least where the detainee is able to retain counsel.

III. POSSIBLE LIMITATIONS AND EXCEPTIONS TO CORE DUE PROCESS RIGHTS, BASED ON THE WAR POWERS

We now review the possible restraints and limitations upon the above core due process values and rights when the President acts in the exercise of his war-making power under Article II of the Constitution. Do the precedents require or suggest that the core rights discussed above, at the heart of our self-identity as a society existing under the rule of law, are inapplicable to persons designated "enemy combatants" by the President, as Commander in Chief prosecuting the war on terror? To what extent can the President so act without congressional authorization? Are these questions for the courts, or rather for the political process?

A. The War Powers

Article I, section 8, of the Constitution grants Congress the power to "provide for the common Defense and general Welfare of the United States...To declare War, grant letters of Marque and Reprisal, and make Rules concerning Captures on Land and Water; To raise and support Armies...and To provide and maintain a Navy." Article II, section 2, declares that "the President shall be Commander in Chief of the Army and Navy of the United States, and of the Militia of the several states, when called into the actual Service of the United States."

The Constitution is held to invest "the President, as Commander in Chief, with the power to wage war which Congress has declared, and to carry into effect all laws passed by Congress for the conduct of war and for the government and regulation of the Armed Forces, and all laws defining and punishing offences against the law of nations, including those which pertain to the conduct of war." Quirin, 317 U.S. at 26. But the scope of the President's powers as Commander in Chief is not clearly defined by Article II, section 2: "These cryptic words have given rise to some of the most persistent controversies in our constitutional history." Youngstown Sheet &. Tube Co. v. Sawyer, 343 U.S. 579, 641 (1952) (Jackson, J., concurring). Few cases—other than Hamdi and Padilla—have considered the authority of the President to detain "enemy combatants" or similar individuals. However, a review of the main stress periods faced by the country reveals some limited case law construing the President's war power and discussing the role of the courts in reviewing exercises of that power.

B. An Historical Perspective

1. Cases before the Civil War

Before the Civil War the government used military forces on a number of occasions as a domestic policing force, seizing and holding rebellious or otherwise threatening citizens by a process neither commenced nor supervised by the civilian courts. See Ex parte Milligan, 71 U.S. 2, 50–53 (1866) ("Milligan") (referring to instances of military arrests during Revolutionary War, Shay's Rebellion, and Gen. Andrew Jackson's occupation of New Orleans). The early Supreme Court opinions that discussed the degree of deference owed the President in a national security crisis did not directly address the executive's power to deprive individuals of their liberty. Nonetheless, those decisions concerned related problems occasioned by coercive executive action, and they provided a portion of the analytical framework that has been followed in later cases governing the seizure of individuals suspected of posing a threat to public safety in times of crisis.

The first of these decisions was triggered by President Madison's call-up of the state militias during the War of 1812. Martin v. Mott, 25 U.S. 19 (1827). That step was authorized by a 1795 statute permitting the President to activate the state militias for duty in time of "imminent danger of invasion" or insurrection. Mott had refused to report for militia duty, and as a result was court-martialed, fined and then sentenced to prison by the military authorities when he failed to pay the fine. He sought relief from the civilian courts, in which, among other things, he challenged the validity of the call-up order.

The Supreme Court rejected the notion that the civilian courts may review the President's decision, instead characterizing the President's power as "exclusive" and his decision as "conclusive upon all other persons." Id. at 30. In reaching this conclusion, the Court emphasized not only the wording of the statute, which it read as conferring unlimited discretion on the President to determine whether the danger of invasion existed, but also the impracticality of vesting final authority on that question in the courts. Speed was key:

The power itself is to be exercised upon sudden emergencies, upon great occasions of state, and under circumstances which may be vital to the existence of the Union. A prompt and unhesitating obedience to orders is indispensable to the complete attainment of the object. The service is a military service, and the command of a military nature; and in such cases, every delay, and every obstacle to an efficient and immediate compliance, necessarily tend to jeopardize the public interests. Id.

According to the Court, any other interpretation of the President's powers would undermine his authority, delegated by Congress, to "regulat[e] the militia and to command[] its services in times of insurrection and invasion." Id. at 30 (quoting The Federalist No. 29).

Apart from the dangers posed by delay inherent in any resort to the courts, the Supreme Court noted other potential inadequacies of the court processes as an instrument of review in such an emergency. Thus, it observed that the grounds for the President's decision "might be of a nature not constituting strict technical proof" and that the disclosure of such information "might reveal important secrets of state, which the public interest, and even safety might imperiously demand to be kept in concealment." Id. at 31.[27]

The inclination of the Supreme Court to defer to the President during a military confrontation, both for constitutional and for practical reasons, was subsequently reiterated in Luther v. Borden, 48 U.S. 1 (1849). The case arose out of the so-called Dorr's Rebellion in Rhode Island. The narrow issue in Luther involved a claim for trespass asserted by a Rhode Island resident in the wake of a state militia's entry into his home during an armed confrontation between two political factions, each claiming to represent the state government. The principal holding of the Court concerned its interpretation of the so-called Guarantee Clause of the Constitution (Art. IV, § 4), which it viewed as leaving to the political branches of the federal government the determination of which faction was the legitimate government of the state. Id. at 41–43.

The Court noted that, under the Guarantee Clause, the Congress is responsible for determining the legitimate government of each state, and has specific responsibility for ensuring the protection of such government against "invasion" and, on request of the state legislature or governor, against "domestic violence". Congress in turn had delegated to the President, by the Act of 1795, the authority to decide whether to call out the militias of the various states to protect a state government against "insurrection" as well as "invasion". Id. at 42–43 (citing Act of Feb. 28, 1795). This constitutional and statutory arrangement required the President to decide which competing faction is the legitimate state government, since that would be a predicate to his determination whether to provide federal protection upon the request of the ostensible state authorities. Id. at 43. Once the President made that decision, practical limitations precluded judicial review:

After the President has acted and called out the militia, is a Circuit Court of the United States authorized to inquire whether his decision was right? Could the court, while the parties were actually contending in arms for the possession of the government, call witnesses before it and inquire which party represented a majority of the people? If it could, then it would become the duty of the court (provided it came to the conclusion that the President had decided incorrectly) to discharge those who were arrested or detained by the troops in the service of the United States or the government which the President was endeavoring to maintain. If the judicial power extends so far, the guarantee contained in the Constitution of the United States is a guarantee of anarchy, and not of order.

Id. The judicial process was manifestly inadequate to decide these sorts of issues in the midst of conflict:

When citizens of the same State are in arms against each other, and the constituted authorities unable to execute the laws, the interposition of the United States must be prompt, or it is of little value. The ordinary course of proceedings in courts of justice would be utterly unfit for the crisis.

Id. at 44.

Having concluded that the courts have no role to play in reviewing a President's recognition of a state faction "when the conflict is raging," the Luther Court went on to conclude, as a logical extension, that such judicial power also cannot be constitutionally invoked "when the contest is over." Id. at 43. In short, this type of decision was left to the unreviewable discretion of the political branches of Government.[28] Significantly, the court likened the power of the President to choose among competing state factions to his unquestioned authority to determine which foreign governments to recognize. Id. at 44.

2. Civil War Cases

Prior to the Civil War, such matters as the applicability of the Bill of Rights in wartime were "unstudied in law schools, ignored in universities, and unknown in West Point," since such questions had not previously arisen. Harold Hyman, A More Perfect Union: The Impact of the Civil War and Reconstruction on the Constitution 66 (1973) ("Hyman"). Early in the War, President Lincoln declared martial law to be applicable to citizens engaging in disloyal conduct, thus subjecting them to prosecution by courts martial or military commission, and, at the same time, suspending the writ of habeas corpus for such individuals. See Milligan, 71 U.S. at 15–16 (quoting Proclamation dated Sept. 24, 1862).[29] Persons suspected of disloyalty or at least sympathy towards the Confederacy were arrested by federal military and local authorities. These individuals were typically not processed through any civilian court, but rather were either released after subscribing to a loyalty oath, or tried by a military commission, or simply held under some other ad hoc arrangement. See, e.g., Ex parte Vallandigham, 68 U.S. 243, 244–47 (1863). Trials by commission are said to have been extremely rare, in areas where the regular courts were functioning, "since the normal method of dealing with persons suspected of treasonable activity was arrest without warrants, detention without trial, and release without punishment...." Clinton Rossiter, The Supreme Court and the Commander in Chief 28 (1951) ("Rossiter"). Where the military authorities did not trust the civil courts, the practice was "to keep the suspects locked up until the danger had passed." Id. at 36.[30]

While a number of individuals swept up by these measures challenged their detentions in the courts,[31] few challenges resulted in judicial decisions. The Supreme Court, in Ex parte Vallandigham, supra, held itself without jurisdiction to review proceedings before military commissions. See Hyman at 261–62.

One decision of note, though of little practical consequence, was rendered early in the war by Chief Justice Taney, sitting in his capacity as circuit judge. Ex parte Merryman, 17 F. Cas. 144 (1861). The petitioner, a civilian seized by the military in Baltimore,[32] sought release by a habeas petition. Justice Taney ordered the United States Marshal to produce Merryman, but the Marshal proved incapable of doing so because the military authorities in Baltimore would not surrender their prisoner. Id. at 147–48. Taney settled for issuing an opinion in which he held that Merryman's detention violated due process and that the courts had the authority to so rule.

Taney first held that the President himself was not authorized to suspend the writ, a power assigned by the Constitution exclusively to Congress. Id. at 148–50. He then went much further, holding that, regardless of whether the writ was suspended by Congress, the President lacked the authority to arrest a private citizen—that is, "a party not subject to the rules and articles of war"—without judicial process. Id. at 149. The only pertinent authority of the President was to "take care that the laws are faithfully executed", which required him to come to the aid of the judiciary, not to bypass it.[33]

The fact that the country faced a military emergency was, in Justice Taney's view, inconsequential for this point: "I can see no ground whatever for supposing that the president, in any emergency, or in any state of things, can authorize the suspension of the privileges of the writ of habeas corpus, or the arrest of a citizen, except in aid of the judicial power." Id. The federal courts and criminal justice system were functioning, without "the slightest resistance or obstruction," and "there was no reason whatever for the interposition of the military." Therefore the controlling requirements of the Constitution, including due process and the right to a public trial "in a court of justice" still applied, precluding petitioner's seizure and detention by the military. Id. at 152. To Taney, this conclusion flowed from English constitutional law as well as from the Fifth Amendment's guarantee of due process. Id. at 149–50 (citing inter alia "the great habeas corpus act", 31 Car. II).

The full Court gave a broader reading to the President's war power the next year in The Prize Cases, 67 U.S. 635 (1862). An executive order imposing a maritime blockade on a number of Confederate states had led to the seizure of numerous ships and their cargoes. In upholding the President's powers against the claims of cargo and ship owners—including some who disclaimed any sympathy for the Confederate secession—the Supreme Court emphasized traditional principles of international law regarding an executive's powers in wartime, as well as the President's statutory power to use the military to defend against invasion or insurrection. Id. at 668 (citing Acts of Feb. 28, 1795 and March 3, 1807). There had been no formal declaration of war by Congress, but a state of war plainly existed, a war "all the world acknowledges to be the greatest civil war known in the history of the human race...." Id. at 669. The Court emphasized that the determination of what measures were required to counter the insurrection was left to the judicially unreviewable discretion of the President:

Whether the President in fulfilling his duties, as Commander-in-chief, in suppressing an insurrection has met with such armed hostile resistance, and a civil war of such alarming proportions as will compel him to accord to them the character of belligerents, is a question to be decided by him, and this Court must be governed by the decisions and acts of the political department of the Government to which this power was entrusted. 'He must determine what degree of force the crisis demands.' The proclamation of blockade is itself official and conclusive evidence to the Court that a state of war existed which demanded and authorized a recourse to such a measure under the circumstances peculiar to the case.

Id. at 670 (emphasis in original).[34] Thus, although the Court, echoing Merryman in this respect, defined a civil war in terms of hostilities that prevented the functioning of the "Courts of Justice" (id. at 667–68), it effectively left to the executive the determination of whether such a state of war existed, as well as the degree of force to be used in responding to the insurrection.

3.   After the Civil War: Milligan

A year after the Civil War, the pendulum swung back toward a narrow reading of the President's war power in Milligan. During the War, Milligan had been arrested by order of the commander of the military district of Indiana, tried before a military commission for crimes relating to his membership in a secret organization sympathetic to the Confederacy, found guilty and sentenced to be hanged.[35] Milligan then proceeded by petition for a writ of habeas corpus in the federal circuit court, challenging the authority of the military to try him given his status as a citizen of a non-belligerent state.

The government, in its brief, boldly asserted that the Bill of Rights was inoperable in wartime:

[T]hese provisions of the Constitution, like all other conventional and legislative laws and enactments, are silent amidst arms, when the safety of the people becomes the supreme law.

Quoted in Rehnquist at 21.

The Supreme Court, however, upheld Milligan's challenge to his conviction, holding that the military commission had no jurisdiction to try and convict a civilian resident of a non-belligerent state. The constitutional guarantees against trial and punishment except in accordance with the Bill of Rights were unaffected by the War: "The Constitution of the United States is a law for rulers and people, equally in war and in peace, and covers...all classes of men at all times, and under all circumstances." Id. at 120–21. The fact of civil disorder only emphasized the need to preserve these protections:

[I]f the society is disturbed by civil commotion—if the passions of men are aroused and the restraints of law weakened, if not disregarded—these safeguards need, and should receive, the watchful care of those intrusted with the guardianship of the Constitution and laws.

Id. at 121–22.[36]

The Court summarily rejected the contention that the military commission could try Milligan "under the law and usages of war," holding that such law and usages "can never be applied to citizens in states [such as Indiana] which have upheld the authority of the government, and where the courts are open and their process unobstructed." Id. at 121. Cf. Caldwell v. Parker, 252 U.S. 376, 386–87 (1920) (soldier may be prosecuted in state court, since local courts were open and functioning; military law did not supplant them in wartime). If citizens in non-battlefield states plotted to aid the enemy, they could be arrested and held for trial in the regular courts, which must be deemed adequate to deal with such criminal conduct. Milligan at 126–27. Only in battlefield areas—where the civilian courts were effectively closed—could the military substitute its processes for those of the courts, and only until those courts resumed operation. Id. at 127.

The Milligan holding thus limited the executive's power to proceed by military commission. But the Court in dictum went further, stating that even Congress could not, consistent with the Constitution, authorize the use of military commissions in the fashion that led to Milligan's conviction. Id. at 122. In contrast, four justices in a concurring opinion concluded to the contrary:

We cannot doubt that, in such a time of public danger, Congress had power, under the Constitution, to provide for the organization of a military commission, and for trial by that commission of persons engaged in this conspiracy.

Id. at 140.[37]

Several Reconstruction cases offered the Supreme Court the opportunity to expand upon its holding in Milligan, but those cases were decided solely on jurisdictional grounds.[38] Some later decisions by state courts and lower federal courts upheld military trials of civilians in the context of violent labor unrest and declarations of martial law by Governors. But the "basis of those decisions was definitely held erroneous in Sterling v. Constantin, 287 U.S. 378 [1932], where the Court said: 'What are the allowable limits of military discretion and whether or not they have been overstepped in a particular case, are judicial questions.' Id. at 401." Duncan v. Kahanamoku, 327 U.S. 304, 321 n.18 (1946). See p. 18, n.13, supra, discussing Sterling.

4.   World War II: Quirin

World War I did not result in any Supreme Court decision directly focusing on our subject,[39] but the extent of the President's (and Congress's) war powers was revisited in a number of decisions during and after World War II.

In Ex parte Quirin, 317 U.S. 1 (1942) ("Quirin"), the Court upheld the President's use of a military commission to try enemy saboteurs who had been arrested by the FBI after entering the country surreptitiously and in civilian garb for the purpose of carrying out acts of sabotage, operating under German military command. The FBI turned these "illegal belligerents" (id. at 35) or "unlawful combatants" (id. at 31) over to the military for trial before a military commission, pursuant to a Presidential order. The order seemed at odds with the Milligan holding, for clearly the civilian courts were open and functioning. Id. at 23–24. But unlike Milligan, which concerned actions taken by military commanders, the commission reviewed in Quirin had been specifically authorized by the President, and the President, in turn, had been generally authorized by Congress to convene military commissions to try offenses against the law of war. Id. at 26–27.

At the close of the evidentiary presentation before the commission, the saboteurs sought a writ of habeas corpus in federal district court, contending that the commission had no jurisdiction to try them. In opposition the government contended that the petitioners, as illegal combatants, had no right to habeas review by the courts.[40] Alternatively the Government contended that the President had permissibly exercised his powers as Commander in Chief in ordering a military trial for violations of the law of wars. The Court phrased the "question for decision" before it as follows:

whether the detention of petitioners by respondent for trial by Military Commission, appointed by Order of the President of July 4, 1942, on charges proffered against them purporting to set out their violations of the law of war and of the Articles of War, is in conformity to the laws and the Constitution of the United States. Id. at 18–19.[41]

The answer was affirmative, because violations of the law of war[42] were, by long tradition, triable by a military commission, as authorized by Congress and ordered by the President.

Petitioners had contended that their seizure by civilian authorities within the United States entitled them (or at least the one said to be an American citizen) to a jury trial, under the Fifth and Sixth Amendments. The Court, however, held that pre-existing law at the time of the adoption of these Amendments allowed the use of military commissions for violations of the law of war and that the Amendments did not specifically overrule that legal tradition. "We must conclude that § 2 of Article III and the Fifth and Sixth Amendments cannot be taken to have extended the right to demand a jury to trials by military commission, or to have required that offenses against the law of war not triable by jury at common law be tried only in the civil courts." Id. at 40.[43]

Quirin addressed, albeit briefly, the specific issue of whether a United States citizen could be tried as an unlawful combatant. One of the saboteurs (Haupt) claimed to be a United States citizen, and argued that his citizenship made it improper for him to be tried by a military commission rather than a civil court. The Court rejected this argument:

Citizenship in the United States of an enemy belligerent does not relieve him from the consequences of a belligerency which is unlawful because in violation of the law of war. Citizens who associate themselves with the military arm of the enemy government, and with its aid, guidance and direction enter this country bent on hostile acts, are enemy belligerents within the meaning of the Hague Convention and the law of war. . . . It is as an enemy belligerent that petitioner Haupt is charged with entering the United States, and unlawful belligerency is the gravamen of the offense of which he is accused.

Id. at 37–38. See Colepaugh v. Looney, 235 F.2d 429, 432 (10th Cir. 1956) (citing Quirin, and holding a military commission had jurisdiction to try a citizen illegal combatant who had secretly landed in Maine from German submarine).

a.   Lawful vs. Unlawful Combatants

The Quirin Court recognized a fundamental distinction under the law of war between lawful and unlawful combatants, a distinction first codified in 1863 in the so-called Lieber Instructions.[44] Lawful combatants are members of an organized army who, if captured in an armed conflict, are entitled to be treated as prisoners of war. Their conduct as combatants is deemed to be lawful and not subject to punishment. Unlawful combatants, in contrast, are not members of a duly organized national military force, do not wear uniforms or other distinctive insignia and do not bear arms openly. As such, if captured, they are not entitled to be treated as prisoners of war and may be tried for violating the law of war:

By a long course of practical administrative construction by its military authorities, our Government has likewise recognized that those who during time of war pass surreptitiously from enemy territory into our own, discarding their uniforms upon entry, for the commission of hostile acts involving destruction of life or property, have the status of unlawful combatants punishable as such by military commission. This precept of the law of war has been so recognized in practice both here and abroad, and has so generally been accepted as valid by authorities on international law that we think it must be regarded as a rule or principle of the law of war recognized by this Government by its enactment of the Fifteenth Article of War.

Quirin, 317 U.S. at 35–36 (footnote omitted). See Spencer J. Crona & Neal A. Richardson, Justice for War Criminals of Invisible Armies: A New Legal and Military Approach to Terrorism, 21 Okla. City U. L. Rev. 349, 360–61 (1996).

The Third Geneva Convention of 1949,[45] in Article 4, defines persons entitled to treatment as prisoner of war[46] as members of the armed forces of a belligerent nation, or of militia and other volunteer corps, including organized resistance movements, provided they are commanded by a person responsible for his subordinates; bear a fixed distinctive sign recognizable at a distance; carry arms openly; and conduct their operation in accordance with the laws and customs of war. By inference, unlawful combatants, a term not used in the Third Geneva Convention, are combatants not satisfying those conditions. Cf. Quirin, 317 U.S. at 35 (by defining lawful combatants entitled to prisoner of war status, the Government "has recognized that there is a class of unlawful belligerents not entitled to that privilege....").

b.   Military Commissions: Quirin v. Milligan

It is not easy to harmonize the holdings of Quirin and Milligan with respect to the constitutionality of the use of military commissions in the United States.[47] Milligan certainly suggested that a citizen could never be tried by military commission when the civilian courts were open and functioning. However, Quirin distinguished Milligan on the ground that, unlike the Quirin saboteurs, who were "enemy belligerents" acting pursuant to orders from the German military and intelligence authorities (id. at 45–46), Milligan was not a combatant: he had not been "a part of or associated with the armed forces of the enemy," and, hence, was a "non-belligerent, not subject to the law of war.... (id. at 45).[48]

Another distinction is that Quirin relied on congressional authorization for the use of military commissions,[49] while there had been no such authorization in Milligan (though the majority in Milligan opined that such authorization would have been unavailing—see p. 45, above).

Aside from these distinctions, Quirin also appears to reflect a greater deference to the political branches in the midst of a war, in contrast to Milligan's vigorous assertion of judicial authority after the Civil War had ended. Quirin may reflect in part "the reluctance of courts to decide a case against the government on an issue of national security during a war." Rehnquist at 221.

Regardless of the cogency of Quirin or Milligan, it is important to note that neither addresses whether a President has authority to detain enemy combatants indefinitely, without charges. The question did not arise, for in each case the purpose of the detention was to proceed—even with precipitous speed—with a military trial on proffered charges.

5.   World War II: Hirabayashi and Korematsu

The other major war powers landmarks of World War II reflected extremely broad deference to the President and Congress. In Hirabayashi v. United States, 320 U.S. 81 (1943), and Korematsu v. United States, 323 U.S. 214 (1944), the Court faced challenges to the wartime restrictions imposed by the government on American citizens and residents of Japanese ancestry. The Congress and the President had delegated to the military the authority to exclude from any militarily sensitive area any category of persons deemed a potential threat. The military in turn had declared the entire Pacific Coast to be a sensitive area, and excluded all persons of Japanese ancestry from portions of those areas—choosing to confine those residents in camps—and placed curfews on their out-of-doors activities in other areas. Hirabayashi was convicted of violating militarily-imposed curfew regulations, and Korematsu of refusing to comply with so-called exclusion regulations, which effectively confined Japanese-Americans to detention camps for the duration of military hostilities with Japan.

The Court upheld both convictions and the validity of these national-origin-specific regulations, and did so in terms of broad deference to the war-making powers of Congress and the President. In Hirabayashi, while acknowledging that distinctions based on national origins are "odious", 320 U.S. at 100, the Court nevertheless went on to note that the country was in the midst of a national emergency, and that the political branches had the authority and obligation to take whatever measures they thought necessary to protect against feared invasion or sabotage:

Since the Constitution commits to the Executive and to the Congress the exercise of the war power in all the vicissitudes and conditions of warfare, it has necessarily given them wide scope for the exercise of judgment and discretion in determining the nature and extent of the threatened injury or danger and in the selection of the means for resisting it. Where, as they did here, the conditions call for the exercise of judgment and for the choice of means by those branches of the Government on which the Constitution has placed the responsibility of warmaking, it is not for any court to sit in review of the wisdom of their action or substitute its judgment for theirs.

320 U.S. at 93 (internal citations omitted). This substantial deferral to the judgment of the executive branch and Congress was based on a broad reading of the war powers, referred to as "the power to wage war successfully." Id. at 92 (quoting Charles Evans Hughes, War Powers Under the Constitution, 42 A.B.A. Rep. 232, 238). The Court held that it need satisfy itself only that the military authorities had "a reasonable basis for the actions taken" (id. at 101), which basis it found by relying on stereotypical characterizations of the Japanese-American community and the unquestioned fact that Japan was waging a war of aggression against the United States. Given "the facts and circumstances with respect to the American citizens of Japanese descent residing on the Pacific Coast",[50] it was rational to suspect a greater loyalty to the enemy among Americans of Japanese ancestry than among others. Id. at 102.

The next year the Court followed further along the same path in upholding in Korematsu the exclusion of all people of Japanese ancestry from large areas of the Pacific Coast and relegating them to detention camps. 323 U.S. at 217–18 (relying on Hirabayashi). Although the Court conceded that exclusion from one's home and community is a far greater deprivation than was inflicted by the Hirabayashi curfew (confinement for ten hours at night in one's home), its foreshortened analysis rested on the same forgiving formula that allowed the executive very broad discretion to protect national security in a crisis:

As in the Hirabayashi case, we cannot reject as unfounded the judgment of the military authorities and of Congress that there were disloyal members of that population, whose number and strength could not be precisely and quickly ascertained. We cannot say that the war-making branches of the Government did not have ground for believing that in a critical hour such persons could not readily be isolated and separately dealt with, and constituted a menace to the national defense and safety, which demanded that prompt and adequate measures be taken to guard against it.

Id. at 218.[51]

6.   Youngstown (The Steel Seizure Case)

In Youngstown Sheet & Tube Co. v. Sawyer, 343 U.S. 579 (1952) ("Youngstown"), the Court rejected President Truman's claimed exercise of his war power during the Korean War in seizing steel mills to ensure against disruption of production resulting from labor unrest.

The Court rejected the notion that "broad powers in military commanders engaged in day-to-day fighting in a theater of war" translated into a right of the President "to take possession of private property in order to keep labor disputes from stopping production." Id. at 587 (holding that President could not so act without congressional authorization).

This rhetorical limitation of the war power to battlefield decisions is, in general tenor, in some tension with the Court's sensitivity in Korematsu to the dangers lurking on the home front. Youngstown probably owes something to the less threatening nature of the Korean conflict, and particularly the absence of any suggestion that the enemy, rather than inflexible corporate management, posed a threat within the country.

It also is significant that in Youngstown, unlike in Quirin, Hirabayashi and Korematsu, the President had acted without any congressional authorization, and, in the view of several justices, even contrary to the evident intent of Congress in the Taft-Hartley Act. Id. at 598-604 (Frankfurter, J., concurring). Justice Jackson's concurring opinion argued persuasively that, as a general matter, a President's power is at a maximum when exercised in a manner expressly authorized by Congress, in a "zone of twilight" if taken in the absence of congressional authorization, and at "its lowest ebb" when incompatible with congressional will. Id. at 635–38.

Youngstown has been called "perhaps the Court's most important attempt to fit the needs of executive branch decisionmaking at times of crisis within our constitutional tradition," Neal K. Katyal & Lawrence H. Tribe, Waging War, Deciding Guilt: Trying the Military Tribunals, 111 Yale L.J. 1259, 1273 (2002) ("Katyal & Tribe"), and "a landmark case affirming not only that the President must obey the law but that in general he may act only on the basis of statutory authority." David Currie, The Constitution of the United States 40 (2d ed. 2000). These accolades more properly belong to Justice Jackson's concurring opinion, which has proven widely influential. E.g., Dames & Moore v. Regan, 453 U.S. 654, 668–69 (1981) (adopting the three-tier Jackson analysis of Presidential power). As will be seen, the Second Circuit's opinion reversing Padilla relies heavily on that concurrence and its distinction between the war power of the President at home and his war power abroad.

7.   Hamdi and Padilla: Indefinite Detentions under the President's War Power

The Hamdi and Padilla courts were required to apply the above limited case law on the President's war power to the declared "enemy combatants" before them, both United States citizens. Recall: Hamdi allegedly had been captured in a zone of armed combat in Afghanistan, carrying a gun and in the company of other Taliban fighters, while Padilla was seized in Chicago and ultimately accused of conspiring with al Qaeda operatives abroad to build and detonate a "dirty bomb" in this country. Counsel for each detainee urged that due process barred their indefinite and incommunicado detentions, while the government urged that the President's war power permitted them, based on the government's hearsay representation of the basic facts justifying the detainee's "enemy combatant" status.

As Judge Mukasey noted in Padilla, "it would be a mistake to create the impression that there is a lush and vibrant jurisprudence governing these matters There isn't." Padilla, 233 F. Supp. 2d at 607. Applying this sparse jurisprudence, and faced with very different factual contexts, Hamdi and the Padilla district court reached somewhat different results, but both sustained the constitutionality of indefinite detentions of "enemy combatants." The Second Circuit, reversing Padilla, held the detention of Padilla unconstitutional.

In Hamdi the petition was denied without an evidentiary hearing, the Fourth Circuit finding that the government's representation of the facts, indisputable in the court's view, was sufficient to justify the enemy combatant classification without the need for further inquiry (or permitting

Hamdi any access to counsel), given the deference due the President's exercise of his war power.

In Padilla Judge Mukasey, while similarly according great deference to the President's war power, withheld ruling on the merits of the petition before him. Instead, he granted Padilla a limited right to consult with his counsel for the purpose of submitting a rebuttal to the Mobbs declaration (Padilla at 599–602), which rested on hearsay reports from "unnamed confidential sources" concerning Padilla's alleged contacts with al Qaeda operatives. Id. at 573. Padilla's "right to present facts" was found "firmly rooted" in the habeas statute, 28 U.S.C. § 2241, and related statutes. Id. at 599. However, the court held that the government ultimately need meet only a low "some evidence" standard to justify Padilla's continued detention. Id. at 608. The Second Circuit did not reach these questions, since it held the President without power to detain Padilla in the first place.

Before turning to our own analysis of the issues posed by enemy combatant detentions, we review the manner in which Hamdi and the two Padilla courts dealt with those issues.

a.   Separation of Powers; Deference to Political Branches

The Hamdi circuit court and Padilla district court opinions share much in common. In particular, both decisions place heavy stress on the need for the courts to defer to the political branches in the exercise of their war-making powers, and to avoid any intrusion that would hamper the effective discharge of those powers.

In dismissing Hamdi's petition, the Fourth Circuit stressed the battlefield context of his classification: "an American citizen captured and detained by American allied forces in a foreign theater of war during active hostilities and determined by the United States military to have been indeed allied with enemy forces." Hamdi at 476. The court rejected any "broader categorical holdings on enemy combatant designations" (id. at 465), and disclaimed "placing our imprimatur upon a new day of executive detentions." Id. at 476.[52] It specifically distinguished the Padilla situation, i.e., "the designation as enemy combatant of an American citizen captured on American soil or the role that counsel might play in such a proceeding." Id. at 465.

Hamdi proceeds to analyze at some length what it believes would be unacceptable intrusions in the conduct of military field operations were military commanders required to litigate back in the United States over the factual circumstances of a detainee's capture, detention and interrogation. Id. at 469–71. Because of the deference due to "executive branch decisions premised on military determinations made in the field," and "because Hamdi was indisputably seized in an active combat zone abroad," the Hamdi court did not require any supplementation (or permit any rebuttal) to the Mobbs declaration. Id. at 473. It was persuaded that "a factual inquiry into the circumstances of Hamdi's capture would be inappropriate," and "would entail an unacceptable risk of obstructing war efforts authorized by Congress and undertaken by the executive branch." Id. at 474–75.[53] The Constitution required deference:

The constitutional allocation of war powers affords the President extraordinarily broad authority as Commander in Chief and compels the courts to assume a deferential posture in reviewing exercises of this authority.

Id. at 474.

The Hamdi court's deference to the executive hence was the product of both institutional deference, which it believed was required by the Constitution's separation of powers, and practical considerations that it found powerfully supported the necessity of such deference in the factual context presented.

In Padilla, which did not involve an overseas military campaign, the practical considerations played much less of a role in the court's analysis. "The prospect of courts second-guessing battlefield decisions...does not loom in this case." Padilla, 243 F. Supp. 2d at 57. In fact, Judge Mukasey noted that federal judges do have the expertise to make and review the sort of factual determinations on which Padilla's classification as an enemy combatant rested. Padilla at 608. However, the court found deference required by the Constitution's separation of powers. It was beyond the appropriate scope of the court's "commission" to consider de novo whether the enemy combatant classification had properly been applied to Padilla:

The "political branches," when they make judgments on the exercise of war powers under Articles I and II, as both branches have here, need not submit those judgments to review by Article III courts.

Id. at 607.

This observation did not lead the court to deny all review, but rather to craft a highly deferential scope of review. The court's commission, it held, extended "only to deciding two things:"

(i) whether the controlling political authority—in this case, the President—was, in fact exercising a power vouchsafed to him by the Constitution and the laws; that determination in turn, is to be made only by examining whether there is some evidence to support his conclusion that Padilla was....engaged in a mission against the United States on behalf of an enemy with whom the United States is at war, and (ii) whether that evidence has not been entirely mooted by subsequent events

Id. at 608.[54]

The Second Circuit, on appeal, answered the constitutional question in the negative, holding the President did not have the power, absent express congressional authorization, to detain an American citizen on American soil.

The Hamdi court, while recognizing that the government urged the "some evidence" standard, found it unnecessary to decide that question. It held that, in response to a habeas petition challenging a detention as unlawful, the courts should appropriately "ask that the government provide the legal authority upon which it relies for the detention and the basic facts relied upon to support a legitimate exercise of that authority." Hamdi at 472. It found the requisite legal authority in the "executive's...power to detain under the war powers of Article II," and the basic facts adequately set forth in the Mobbs declaration. Id. at 472–73.

b. Existence of a State of War

None of the three courts viewed itself as entitled to second-guess the government's position that the "war on terror" invoked the President's "war power." All courts treated the question of whether a state of war existed and determinations as to its cessation to be political matters essentially within the authority of the President and/or Congress and not the courts. Padilla at 588–91; Padilla Cir. at 712; Hamdi at 476.

Both Padilla courts placed important reliance for this point on The Prize Cases. Padilla at 589, 595–96; Padilla Cir. at 712. None of the courts placed any significance on the unconventional nature of the war on terror as compared to previous wars, involving massed troops of opposing sovereign states. None found it necessary to probe the question of when the war on terror might come to an end. Hamdi and the Padilla district court expressly found that it plainly had not, given the continued presence of United States troops in Afghanistan. Padilla at 590; Hamdi at 476. Padilla held expressly that the challenge to the alleged indefinite nature of the detention was premature. Padilla at 590–91.[55]

c. Detention of U.S. citizens Arrested on U.S. Soil

The Padilla district court posed as the "central issue" before it this question:

whether the President has the authority to designate as an unlawful combatant an American citizen, captured on American soil, and to detain him without trial.

Padilla at 593. In reaching an affirmative answer to this question, the Padilla court placed heavy stress on Quirin. Since the Court in Quirin drew no distinction between the alleged American citizen and the other German saboteurs,

it matters not that Padilla is a United States citizen captured on United States soil.

Id. at 606.

In relying on Quirin, the court adopted as well its limitation of Milligan to "non-belligerent [s]." Quirin, 317 U.S. at 45. The Padilla court held petitioner within the reach of Quirin, not Milligan, since he, "like the Quirin saboteurs, is alleged to be in active association with an enemy with whom the United States is at war." Padilla at 594. See also id. at 608 (relevant showing is whether "Padilla was...engaged in a mission against the United States on behalf of an enemy with whom the United States is at war").

It is on this point that the Second Circuit reversed. Drawing heavily on Justice Jackson's Youngstown concurrence, the Court held that the detention of a citizen was in violation of an express statute, 18 U.S.C. § 4001(a), and hence involved an exercise of Presidential power at its lowest ebb, i.e., Jackson's third category. The President's war power did not support the detention in the United States because the Constitution allocated to Congress, not the President, emergency powers to act in this country, and Congress had not authorized the detention, distinguishing Quirin and The Prize Cases where such authorization had been present. Padilla Cir. at 710–24. Surprisingly, the infringement of individual due process rights inherent in the detention was not a main focus of the opinion.

d. Access to Counsel

As noted, the Padilla district court did not dismiss the writ but rather authorized further proceedings in which Padilla could attempt to rebut the allegations in the Mobbs declaration, and communicate with his counsel for the limited purpose of preparing such a rebuttal. This result proceeded in part from a recognition that normally the purpose of a habeas petition is to allow the presentation of facts (Padilla at 599–602), and the court's view that "Padilla's need to consult with a lawyer to help him do what the statute permits him to do is obvious." Id. at 602. The court, in its opinion on reconsideration, rejected the government's argument that the "some evidence" standard meant that Padilla need be given no opportunity to respond to the government's allegations in support of its enemy combatant classification. Padilla, 243 F. Supp. 2d at 54–56.

The court found it unnecessary to determine whether Padilla had a due process right to counsel. Rather, it authorized counsel as a discretionary matter pursuant to the All Writs Act, 28 U.S.C. § 1651(a), finding that counsel's participation would aid the court in ruling on the merits of the habeas petition, and that its exercise of discretion could be at least informed by the Sixth Amendment right-to-counsel jurisprudence. Padilla at 602–03. The court rejected the government's position that Padilla's contact with counsel would interfere with its ongoing interrogation of Padilla, finding any such interference "would be minimal or nonexistent" since the court was permitting only limited consultations to facilitate the presentation of the facts in the habeas proceeding. Id. at 603. The court also noticed that Padilla, unlike Hamdi, already had consulted with counsel when earlier held as a material witness, and thus there was "no potential prophylactic effect of an order barring access by counsel." Id. at 605.[56]

The Second Circuit had no need to reach the right-to-counsel issue, but Judge Wesley, in dissent, made plain his lack of sympathy for the government's position:

No one has suspended the Great Writ. See U.S. Const. art. I, § 9, cl. 2. Padilla's right to pursue a remedy through the writ would be meaningless if he had to do so alone. I therefore would extend to him the right to counsel as Chief Judge Mukasey did. [citation omitted]. At the hearing, Padilla, assisted by counsel, would be able to contest whether he is actually an enemy combatant thereby falling within the President's constitutional and statutory authority.

Padilla Cir. at 732–33.

The Hamdi court, given its conclusion that the Mobbs declaration was not subject to challenge, never expressly addressed the right-to-counsel issue, nor the government's related claim that its ability to interrogate Hamdi would be harmed if, as a result of contacts with counsel, the detainee was placed in an "adversary relationship with the captor." Hamdi at 466 n.4. The court noted that "a capable attorney could challenge the hearsay nature of the Mobbs declaration and each and every paragraph for incompleteness or inconsistency", but found that such "instinctive skepticism, so laudable in the defense of criminal charges," would risk a "constitutionally problematic intrusion into the most basic responsibilities of a coordinate branch." Id. at 473.[57]

*e. Congressional Authorization or Prohibition: The Joint Resolution and 18 U.S.C. §
4001(a)*

Both Hamdi and the Padilla district court rejected, while the Second Circuit adopted, petitioners' arguments based on 18 U.S.C. § 4001(a), which provides that "No citizen shall be imprisoned or otherwise detained by the United States except pursuant to an Act of Congress". Judge Mukasey found that § 4001(a) did in fact unambiguously require congressional authorization for "enemy combatant" detentions, and the Second Circuit agreed. But while Judge Mukasey found that Congress had provided such authorization in the Joint Resolution adopted by Congress on September 18, 2001, Authorization for Use of Military Force, Pub. Law 107-40 § 2(a), 115 Stat. 224 (2001) (the "Joint Resolution"), the Second Circuit held it had not.

The Joint Resolution, fully titled "To authorize the use of the United States Armed Forces against those responsible for the recent attacks launched against the United States," empowers the President:

to use all necessary and appropriate force against those...organizations or persons he determines planned, authorized, committed or aided the terrorist acts that occurred on September 11, 2001...in order to prevent any future acts of international terrorism against the United States by such...organizations or persons.

Because Padilla was alleged "to have been an unlawful combatant in behalf of al Qaeda," itself deemed responsible for the September 11 attacks, Judge Mukasey held the detention of Padilla authorized by the Joint Resolution and thus in compliance with 18 U.S.C. § 4001(a). Padilla at 596–98.

The Second Circuit, reversing, construed the Joint Resolution only to authorize combat abroad and, possibly, detentions in a battlefield context. It relied on the Supreme Court's opinion in Ex parte Endo for the proposition that the Joint Resolution should be construed to impose no greater restraint on citizens than "clearly and unmistakably indicated" by its language. Padilla Cir. at 723, quoting Endo, 323 U.S. at 300.

The Hamdi court was unwilling to read 18 U.S.C. § 4001(a) as potentially applicable to Hamdi, believing the statute was not intended to override the "well established precedent" authorizing the capture and detention of enemy combatants as an inherent part of warfare. Hamdi at 468. But, in the alternative, the Fourth Circuit also held that the Joint Resolution authorized the detention. Id. at 467.

f. The Geneva Convention

Hamdi and the Padilla district court treated differently the Third Geneva Convention. Padilla held that the detainee's designation as an "enemy combatant," if sustained, meant that he was an "illegal combatant," and thus would not be within the protections of the Geneva Convention as a prisoner of war. Padilla at 592–93, 599. The Hamdi court found the distinction between lawful and unlawful combatants irrelevant to the case before it, since either could be detained under the authority of Quirin. Hamdi at 469. It held, further, that the Geneva Convention afforded no private right of action to any detainee, but rather was enforceable only through diplomatic and reciprocal measures between the warring parties. Id. at 468–69.[58] The Second Circuit had no need to reach this question.

IV.   WAR POWERS AND DUE PROCESS: INDEFINITE U.S. DETENTIONS BY UNILATERAL EXECUTIVE ACTION VIOLATE THE CONSTITUTION

We turn now to our own analysis of how the competing considerations of due process and the war power should be applied in the unique and present circumstances of the "war on terror." Our conclusion, in agreement with the Second Circuit's but for somewhat different reasons, is that the Constitution does not permit the President unilaterally, without congressional authorization, to effect indefinite and incommunicado detentions of suspected terrorists seized in the United States.[59] The serious negative consequences of recognizing such an executive power— damaging the rule of law in ways not easily confined to terrorism, opening the door to other abuses of due process, and offering an invitation by example to repressive regimes around the globe—strongly supports not giving the war power such an expansive reading. The limited war power jurisprudence does not justify indefinite detentions in this country of either citizens, as the Second Circuit has now held, or non-citizens, at least until and unless Congress addresses and affirms the President's claim that the national security requires such extraordinary departures from long accepted due process standards.

Much the same could be said with respect to the use of military commissions, based solely on the President's determination of who should be so tried, and in the absence of specific congressional authorization. However, the constitutional question is a closer one. Quirin and the generally worded statute on which it relied do support the use of such commissions to prosecute violations of the law of war. But in any event, after reviewing the military commission orders promulgated for enemy combatant trials, we urge that the use of military commissions be minimized. There are important advantages offered by criminal prosecutions in the federal courts, which have successfully tried many terrorism cases. The most important is that the enhanced fairness of such civilian proceedings will result in a likely greater acceptance in this country and abroad of the justness of their results (see pp. 129–35, below).

A.   The Serious Negative Consequences of Recognizing a Unilateral Executive Power to Detain

As we show below, the less than "lush" war power jurisprudence surveyed above does not resolve how to balance the war power and due process in the context of indefinite detentions and the war on terror. Before further discussing this sparse case law, therefore, we look at the possible consequences, legal and practical, of a decision sustaining the constitutionality of such executive detentions. Those serious negative consequences, as we see them, argue strongly against interpreting the war power precedents to sanction the detentions.

1.   The Sharp Departure from the Rule of Law

Indefinite detentions constitute a sharp departure from core due process principles and the rule of law. The detentions have no finite term, and may continue for as long as the war on terror, which has no foreseeable end. They are effected solely by the executive, without any "probable cause" or other judicial finding. The executive expressly disclaims any intention of bringing charges against the detainees, and thus rules out any assessment by some neutral decision-maker of guilt or innocence. The detainees are isolated, including from any relatives or attorneys, thus precluding any factual challenge by the detainees to the claimed basis for their classification as "enemy combatants". Further, the executive urges that, on any habeas corpus petition brought by a "next friend" of the detainee, no rebuttal should be permitted to its enemy combatant classification.

The holding of persons incommunicado, without access to an attorney, without charges or statutory basis, indefinitely and based solely on the executive's subjective determination, has nothing in common with due process as we know it. The policy has an almost medieval ring to it, harkening back to the days when the sovereign recognized no limitations on its power to detain subjects for whatever reason, uncontrolled by any superior rule of law.

Nor has the term "enemy combatant" even been defined, or limited to persons suspected of planning or carrying out terrorist attacks. Padilla may fit that description as an alleged saboteur. But al-Marri, a civilian in this country legally, seems suspected of providing logistical support for al Queda sleeper cells: presumably criminal activity, if proven, but not "combatant" activity under any likely definition of the term. The scope of the indefinite detentions, in the executive's conception, thus appears to extend to any person believed—on the basis of "some" hearsay—to have provided some form of assistance to al Qaeda, e.g., any form of "material support or resources" to a designated terrorist organization, such as "expert advice or assistance," "currency" or "lodging", 18 U.S.C. § 2339B(g)(4).[60] If the courts sustain the constitutionality of such detentions, the technique may be used against far more people than the three so detained in this country (so far as is known) to date.[61]

Already the use of such a technique by the government appears to have had an impact well beyond the persons detained. It opens the door to the intimidation of non-detainees. Defendants or potential defendants facing charges in criminal proceedings can be threatened, should they not plead or otherwise cooperate, with indefinite detention as enemy combatants terminating their due process rights, as indeed happened to al-Marri on the brink of his criminal trial. Wholly deprived of any protection of the rule of law, or of the interposition of judge and jury, such persons would be subject to an intolerable pressure well beyond the pressure of a criminal prosecution.

We are not sanguine about the practical ability of the courts to cabin the use of such indefinite detentions on a case-by-case basis, if the general technique is accepted as constitutional. While the courts could review evidence concerning whether an alleged terrorist is one in fact, even here the courts' ability to provide meaningful review is dependent on the burden of proof applied to the government. The "some evidence" standard found applicable in Padilla to review of enemy combatant determinations may not provide meaningful review.[62] Surely it will not if, as the government contends, the detainee is not permitted to consult counsel or rebut the government's minimal required showing. Padilla, 243 F. Supp. 2d at 54–56 (rejecting this government contention).

But assuming that the enemy combatant classification is sustained, questions concerning the length and conditions of incommunicado detentions designed to facilitate interrogation may not be subject to effective control by the courts. Our whole tradition is opposed to coerced confessions, including by extended detentions designed to extract information. Once that Rubicon is crossed, the courts are poorly positioned to second-guess executive decisions as to the utility or necessity of extracting information from a particular detainee, or the tactics—including the length and conditions of the detentions—best calculated to perform the extraction.[63] These are largely subjective judgments, based on experience and hunches, informed by whatever has been gleaned from interrogations of other detainees, classified intelligence intercepts and other non-evidentiary information. The courts, on such matters of tactical judgment, would "tend to defer to the executive's assumed greater knowledge and expertise." Katyal & Tribe, 111 Yale L.J. at 1275. Cf. Korematsu v. United States, 323 U.S. 214, 245 (1943) (Jackson, J., dissenting): "In the very nature of things, military decisions are not susceptible of intelligent judicial appraisal."

Nor can the public through the political process, rather than the courts, reasonably be expected to rein in executive excess. That may be a practical possibility in the context of exercises of the President's war power that impact widely on many citizens, such as mobilization, the draft, rationing or higher taxes.[64] But where the exercise of the war power focuses on a discrete minority—the Japanese-Americans in World War II or Arab-Americans and other Muslims in the war on terror—it is unrealistic to expect too much of the political process.[65] The public at large, in the context of the traumatic events of September 11 and continuing acts of lawless terrorism around the world, cannot be expected sua sponte to impose due process constraints on the President's efforts to prevent future terrorist attacks.[66]

Further, the prospects of any political restraint are minimized if the President's war power is found to justify indefinite detentions unless Congress affirmatively passes legislation to prohibit them. Political inertia weighs against such legislation. However, if affirmative congressional authorization is deemed necessary (at a minimum) to sanction such detentions, as we believe and the Second Circuit has held, at least a debate on the wisdom and necessity of such measures is assured.

2. The Risk of Error

If such an extraordinarily lawless system could be confined to actual terrorists—lawless in their very essence—at least a certain symmetry would result. But no such limitation can be expected, for the executive branch, of course, like any human institution, is susceptible to error in its detention decisions. The dangers of ethnic profiling are all too apparent in the context of terrorism investigations. In recent times, most international terrorists have been Arabs or other Muslims. Striking the balance between security and individual rights is not an abstract proposition in this context. An estimated 1,200 non-citizens, mostly from the Middle East or South Asia, reportedly were secretly detained after 9/11, of whom only four were subsequently indicted for terrorism-related crimes. Human Rights Watch website (hrw.org/un/chr.59/counter-terrorism-bck4.htm (Dec 17, 2003)).[67] See United States v. Awadallah, 349 F.3d 42, 78 (2d Cir. 2003) (Straub, C.J., concurring) (referring to "the waves of anti-Muslim sentiment that...followed September 11"); cf. United States v. Alameh, 341 F.3d 167, 172–74 (2d Cir. 2003) (percentage of Middle Eastern men charged under certain immigration statutes said to increase from 15% before 9/11 to 85% thereafter, though court questioned reliability of these statistics).

We do not believe the country would tolerate today, as did the Court in Korematsu, a wholesale round-up of Arabs or Muslims based on a claim that "there [are]...disloyal members of that population," and on a judgment that "such persons could not readily be isolated and separately dealt with...." Korematsu, 323 U.S. at 218. No one has urged any such wholesale detentions.[68] But targeted detentions, limited in number, can be based on "some evidence" that later proves to be faulty. See In re Application of United States for Material Witness Warrant, 214 F. Supp. 2d 356, 358–60 (S.D.N.Y. 2002) (recounting filing of material witness warrant application and criminal charges against Egyptian national following September 11, 2001, based on what proved to be false information provided to government and on an allegedly coerced confession). Indeed, the narrower the scope of court review, the greater the likelihood of such error.

The chance of error inevitably is magnified if detainees, as urged by the government, are held incommunicado, with no opportunity to consult an attorney or to rebut the executive's allegations advanced to justify the detention.

3. The Long-Term and Expandable Nature of the War on Terror

The threat to due process posed by indefinite detentions is all the greater because of the likely prolonged nature of the war on terror, which creates a risk that such extraordinary measures adopted in its context may prove to be permanent features of the constitutional land-scape.

In the past, occasional departures in wartime from due process standards have been tolerated in the expectation that, when war ended, the peacetime contours of due process would be resuscitated. Thus, President Lincoln, defending his policy of military arrests of civilians during the Civil War, emphasized the temporary nature of these measures:

I am unable to appreciate the danger...that the American people will by means of military arrests during the rebellion lose the right to public discussion, the liberty of speech and the press, the law of evidence, trial by jury and *habeas corpus* throughout the indefinite peaceful future which I trust lies before them, anymore than I am able to believe that a man could contract so strong an appetite for emetics during temporary illness as to persist in feeding upon them during the remainder of his healthy life.

Edward S. Corwin, <u>Total War and the Constitution</u>168–69 (1947) ("Corwin").[69]
Others have found Lincoln's optimism as to the temporary nature of war measures misplaced:

The Court has had little success in preventing the precedents of war from becoming the precedents of peace. We might even go so far as to say that the court has made a positive contribution to the permanent peacetime weakening of the separation of powers, the principle of non-delegation, the Fifth Amendment, and the necessary and proper clauses applicable limits to governmental power. Rossiter at 129.

Justice Jackson, in his <u>Korematsu</u> dissent, feared that the Court's ruling in that case would lie "like a loaded weapon ready for the hand of any authority that can bring forward a plausible claim of an urgent need." 323 U.S. at 246.

But whatever the merits of this debate in the context of "temporary" wars, the war on terror shows few signs of being temporary. There is certainly little expectation that it will be over anytime in the near term. And its scope is expandable, based on the determinations of the President and/or Congress. It is not limited to al Qaeda, as in the Joint Resolution. It has been said by the President to embrace the former Hussein regime in Iraq, Palestinian terror groups and the Abu Sayyaf Group in the Philippines. Numerous other suspected terrorist organizations presumably are within its potential scope: 36 have been designated by the United States. U.S. Dep't of State Press Statement, Oct. 3, 2003.

Accordingly, we must assume a substantial possibility that we will have to live with the war on terror for many years, if not indefinitely. If that is the case, we may not safely await a foreseeable post-crisis period during which the previous contours of due process will be restored. Departures from core due process principles in the context of the war on terror may well be long-lived, not short-term measures easily reversed. This makes all the more important a careful consideration of the relevant constitutional values before due process rights are set aside in obeisance to proclaimed wartime necessity.

4. The Potential Extension of Anti-Terrorism Measures to Other Criminal Activity

In theory tactics justified in the war against terror, such as indefinite detentions, might be confined to that context. Terrorism is distinguishable, to some significant degree, from other types of criminal activity. But a bright line between terrorism and other types of criminal activity will not be easy to maintain. If such tactics are deemed constitutionally acceptable with respect to terrorism, and effective in practice, there will be pressure to employ similar tactics with respect to other types of suspected criminal activity.

The Bush administration, arguing for a broadening of the USA PATRIOT Act, has urged that law enforcement agencies be afforded "the same tools to fight terror that they [already] have to fight other crime,"[70] but the dynamic will work in the other direction as well. The two rationales for the detentions of suspected terrorists—to facilitate their interrogation and to incapacitate them (preventive detention)—are not limited to terrorism. Compelling arguments for extracting information from detainees surely could be made in the context of investigations of international drug dealing, serial murders or rapes, or even child abuse. Nor can the rationale of preventive detention logically be limited to terrorism. Undoubtedly, any United States Attorney's office could point to many persons of interest believed to a moral certainty by prosecutors to have committed or to be planning to commit serious crimes, but who have not been arrested because the evidence gathered to date is not deemed sufficient to satisfy "probable cause" or to secure a conviction. If such deficiencies of proof do not preclude the detention of suspected terrorists—if "some evidence" is enough to detain them indefinitely—pressures may build to use preventive detention in other contexts to lock up other persons suspected of other serious criminal activity, based on "some" evidence falling well short of proof of their guilt.[71]

One possible such context is the so-called "war on drugs," which also involves both domestic law enforcement and military efforts abroad, here in aid of governments battling local drug lords, particularly in Colombia and, in the past, in Peru. See, e.g., Thomas Powers, War and its Consequences, N.Y. Review of Books, March 23, 2003, at 19, c. 4 (discussing Dana Priest, The Mission: Waging War and Keeping Peace with America's Military (2003)). In this context, if the war on terrorism leads to a socially accepted notion that constitutional norms are reserved solely for peacetime, we may see a willingness to accept more extreme and potentially extra-constitutional measures in dealing with suspected drug dealers domestically, particularly if they are linked to foreign groups or governments and if the threat they pose to our social fabric is viewed as sufficiently acute.

Granted, it could be argued that the war powers, however expansively construed, could never justify indefinite detentions in pursuit of some rhetorical "war on drugs" or "war on child abuse." But if the focus is on due process, the forecast is more worrisome. If due process is deemed not to preclude indefinite detentions in the context of the domestic war on terror, because of the exigencies and urgencies it presents in the sole judgment of the President, there is reason to fear it might not preclude such detentions in the context of other alleged criminal activity.[72] Our core due process principles should not be subject to this risk.

5. Further Extensions of the War Power

If the unilateral war power of the President is sufficient to displace due process with respect to the rights of detainees, might it also be held to trump other constitutional rights, such as free speech under the First Amendment? A separation of powers jurisprudence that places in the executive plenary power to determine the means best suited to prosecute the war on terror offers no comforting reassurance on this score.[73] To vindicate the use of the war power domestically to justify indefinite detentions may open the door to other executive acts heretofore believed beyond the pale, particularly if the courts accept the administration's position that the United States should be viewed as a "battlefield" in the war on terror. N.Y.L.J. Nov. 18, 2003, p. 1, c. 3 (quoting argument of government counsel to Second Circuit in Padilla appeal, Nov. 17, 2003).

6.   The Encouragement of Repressive Regimes Abroad

Another negative consequence of indefinite detentions is the encouragement or "cover" they could provide for repressive regimes abroad to oppress their non-terrorist dissidents. If the United States feels justified in departing from the rule of law in combating terrorism at home, notwithstanding our strong tradition of constitutionalism, other countries with no such tradition may see such conduct as justifying crackdowns against their citizens for opposition political activity. We will be in a poor position to complain of arbitrary executive detentions by these regimes, bypassing their judicial systems, if we have engaged in much the same conduct ourselves.

This effect, according to Human Rights Watch, is already occurring:

Over the past two years, numerous governments throughout the world have enacted laws that unduly expand government powers of detention and surveillance. Some governments have pointed to the erosion of civil liberties in the United States after September 11 to deflect criticism of their own rights abuses. www.hrw.org.press (Sept. 30, 2003).[74]

B.   The War Powers Jurisprudence Does Not Support Unilateral Executive Detentions in the United States

The negative consequences of sustaining executive detentions, as just reviewed, argue against construing the Constitution to permit such detentions. We now look again at the few relevant war power case precedents. In our view, they provide no definitive answer to the constitutional question, but surely do not require that the detentions be sustained.

1.   The Padilla Analysis: Based on Scant Precedent from "Total War" Contexts

At base, the Padilla district court's affirmance of the President's indefinite detention power rests on two cases:

- Quirin, for the proposition that in times of war even United States citizens captured in the United States may be detained as illegal combatants;

- The Prize Cases, for the proposition that the question of whether we are at war is a political question within the President's unreviewable discretion.

While relevant, neither case can bear the weight assigned to it, and each case was decided in the very different circumstances of the Civil War (The Prize Cases) and World War II (Quirin).

Quirin is cited in Padilla as virtually the only precedent supporting the constitutionality of the indefinite "enemy combatant" detentions. It is a weak reed for it involved no such detention.[75] In passing dictum the Quirin court did observe that the petitioners in that case (including a citizen), seized in the United States as unlawful combatants, were "subject to capture and detention," like prisoners of war, 317 U.S. at 31. But the issue before the court was not the President's "wartime detention decisions," Hamdi II, 296 F.3d at 282, but rather the President's order that the saboteurs be tried before a military tribunal for war crimes. The constitutionality of that order, supported by congressional authorization as well as a congressional declaration of war, was sustained. Quirin—"just another of the isolated cases...that deal with isolated events and have limited application" (Padilla, 243 F. Supp. 2d at 57)—does not speak to the constitutionality of domestic detentions of suspected illegal combatants, held indefinitely with no tribunal passing upon the question of guilt or innocence.

Nor is there other case authority supporting such detentions. The cases do support use of military commissions to prosecute illegal combatants (Quirin), or legal combatants who have committed war crimes. In re Yamashita, 327 U.S. 1 (1946). Clearly the detention of prisoners of war (legal combatants) is permitted for the duration of a war, subject to the observation of the conditions protective of the POWs in the Third Geneva Convention. But no cases are found addressing the detention without charges of alleged illegal combatants seized in this country.[76]

Nor should the power to try illegal combatants before a military commission, sustained on the record before it by Quirin, potentially leading even to the imposition of the death penalty, be viewed as embracing indefinite detentions as a lesser exercise of the war power. A trial before a military commission provides an assessment of guilt or innocence on specific charges, and thereby provides some protection against arbitrary or erroneous executive detentions.

In a sense, to be sure, detention of an individual without charges is more arbitrary than detention on charges to be tried before a tribunal.

Rehnquist at 50. Certainly many detainees might prefer to be merely held rather than promptly tried by a military commission and, if convicted, punished or even executed. But our concern is not honoring the preference of the detainees, but rather respecting the values of the Constitution.

The Prize Cases likewise provide no compelling precedent in the domestic war on terror. They sustained only Lincoln's power as Commander in Chief to respond with appropriate military force, as he judged it, to the indisputable rebellion of the South. The absence of a declared war between two sovereigns did not mean there was in fact no war. A state of war plainly existing, the President's power to prosecute the war through such military measures as he deemed appropriate—here through a blockade of enemy ports—was undeniable.

But the military decisionmaking discretion of the President sustained in The Prize Cases should not be taken to constitutionalize indefinite detentions, effected far from any military battlefield, simply because the President proclaims that we are in a "war" and deems the detentions helpful in its prosecution. Surely, at minimum, such a fundamental departure from due process should not be seen as an unreviewable wartime measure, based on the military precedent of Abe Lincoln's 1861 blockade.

2. A Different Analysis for a Different Type of "War"

Given that the result reached by the Padilla district court is not compelled by the few precedents it cites, and that it has troubling implications for due process rights in the United States, we look again at the war power precedents, and separation of powers principles. We agree with the Second Circuit's decision reversing Padilla: those precedents can and should be read in a way that does not grant the President unilateral power to override core due process principles whenever he declares his actions are part of the war on terror.

a. The Differing Nature of Wars: "Total War" Precedents Should Not Govern the War on Terror at Home

As already noted, there is no specific case support for unilateral executive detentions in the United States. The cases supporting an expansive construction of the President's war power generally, such as The Prize Cases, Korematsu and Quirin, were decided in the very different "total war" circumstances of the Civil War and World War II, which should not control the balance between due process and the war power in the quite different setting of the domestic war on terror. Further, the President's actions sustained in these cases were supported by congressional authorization, while indefinite detentions are not.

The cases involving the President's war power are few in number, and are all but silent in construing the limits or contours of those powers. This post-World War II summary of the case law remains accurate today:

[T]he Court has refused to speak about the powers of the President as commander in chief in any but the most guarded terms. It has been respectful, complimentary, on occasion properly awed, but it has never embarked on one of those expansive flights of dicta into which it has been so often tempted by other great constitutional questions.

* * *

[I]t has fixed neither the outer boundaries nor the inner divisions of the President's martial authority, and has failed completely to draw the line between his powers and those of Congress....

Rossiter at 4–5.

It has been equally rare for the courts to balance purported exercises of the war powers against the due process rights of individuals affected by such actions. Generally the courts have viewed the invocation of the war powers as a black-and-white proposition: if the war powers are found properly invoked, a due process analysis attempting to limit the means or methods by which such powers are exercised is seldom to be found.

This all-or-nothing approach reached its zenith in the World War II cases reviewed above. In Quirin and Yamashita, with respect to military commissions, and Hirabayashi and Korematsu with respect to the Japanese exclusions, once the action was held within the scope of the war powers there was no further consideration by the majority of whether due process might limit the scope or exercise of the powers.

The contrast between this extreme deference to the President's war powers and the due process jurisprudence prevailing in times of peace led one post-World War II commentator to conclude that there are really "two Constitutions—one for peace, the other for war." Rossiter at 129. In times of war, according to this analysis, the courts recognized the futility of any judicial restraint on the President's freedom of action in prosecuting the war:

The government of the United States, in a case of military necessity proclaimed by the President, and a fortiori when Congress has registered agreement, can be just as much a dictatorship, after its own fashion, as any other government on earth. The Supreme Court of the United States will not, and cannot be expected to, get in the way of this power (id. at 54).

Rather, the only realistic curb on the use of the war powers was executive self-discipline:

Most important, the defense of the Constitution rests at bottom exactly where the defense of the nation rests: in the good sense and the good will of the political branches of the national government, which for most martial purposes must mean the President and his military commanders (id. at 131).[77]

Applying the Rossiter analysis to the war on terrorism would lead to the conclusion that it is both inappropriate and futile for the courts to review now, save perhaps in the most cursory fashion, any decision by the President of how to fight terrorism at home or abroad. Any bold judicial pronouncements applying due process to limit overzealous executive action would come only later, following the example of Milligan, after terrorism is licked.[78]

But this declaration of judicial impotence seems overdrawn, at least, in the context of something less than the "total war" circumstances confronting the courts during the Civil War and World War II. Even in the midst of the actual hostilities of the Korean War, the Supreme Court, in Youngstown, rejected President Truman's attempted invocation of his war power to justify his seizure of the steel mills.[79] The court was unanimous that

the President's action could not be justified as an exercise of his military power as Commander in Chief of the armed forces.

Indeed, the case should serve as a particularly valuable precedent in precluding an extensive interpretation of the President's autonomous military powers as a basis for executive control of the internal economy when the country is not in a state of declared war and not threatened with imminent invasion.

Kauper, The Steel Seizure Case: Congress, the President and the Supreme Court, 51 Mich. L. Rev. 141, 175 (1952).

Viewed against the general sweep of the thin war powers jurisprudence, the World War II near "total deference" cases are the exception rather than the rule with respect to exercises of the war power in the United States.[80] Nor have the decisions by the Supreme Court in Quirin, Hirabayashi and Korematsu—which exhibited the greatest deference to the executive as crisis manager—well stood the test of time. The Japanese exclusion cases are almost universally condemned. Quirin also has been called into serious question. Another reason not to follow blindly the lead of the World War II precedents is the emergence, in the years since World War II, of a jurisprudence far more vigorous in recognizing and protecting individual rights from excessive governmental action. Katyal & Tribe, 111 Yale L.J. at 1303–04.[81] We trust that today neither the executive nor the courts would countenance the wholesale ethnic-based military orders upheld in Korematsu and Hirabayashi. See generally, E. Muller, 12/7 and 9/11: War, Liberties, and the Lessons of History, 104 W. Va. L. Rev. 1 (2002) (favorably comparing the Bush administration's policies toward Arab Americans after 9/11 with the Roosevelt administration's actions against ethnic Japanese during World War II).

Short of the most pressing emergency circumstances, there should be room to balance civil liberties and national security, i.e., to analyze whether the necessities of national security truly require limiting or abandoning core due process principles. But to achieve such a balance, the courts must go beyond the "yes" or "no" question of whether a state of war exists. The courts recognize the President's power to commit the nation's military forces to combat, though the power to declare war (and finance it) remains with Congress. But this Commander-in-Chief power should not be construed to carry with it the inherent authority to depart from due process at home. Wars and armed conflicts are of too varying kinds, and the war on terror specifically is too multi-faceted, to equate the power to activate the Armed Forces, or even to declare war, with a power to override fundamental individual rights and liberties.

The Padilla district court decision appears to treat the "war on terror" as no different from the Civil War or World War II, in terms of a separation of powers analysis, thus compelling judicial deference to the President's actions as Commander in Chief in pursuit of that war, wherever prosecuted, with the courts without power to "review the level of force selected." Padilla, 533 F. Supp. 2d at 589, quoting Campbell v. Clinton, 203 F.3d 19, 27 (D.C. Cir. 2000) (Silberman, J., concurring).[82] To the contrary, wars or armed conflicts are of different kinds, particularly as they concern the exercise of the President's war power in this country. One size does not fit all. World War II should not be equated, with respect to the scope of the President's war power at home, with our military invasion of Grenada (or Iraq). World War II, a war declared by Congress, was a "total war" fought for national survival, with extensive domestic impacts. It involved a general mobilization of domestic industry for the war effort, a draft, rationing, etc. Grenada, of course, was not even a blip on the domestic screen. The war on terror is no such minor matter, but neither does it, by its nature, involve the military in domestic affairs to the extent required in World War II or, even more so, the Civil War fought on American soil.

As the nature of a war changes, so too should the permissible scope of the President's war power at home and its balance with due process. Youngstown shows that at a minimum. While the power to wage war is "the power to wage war successfully," what may be necessary for success in the context of one war may be gratuitous in another—or at least not so necessary as to sacrifice our core due process principles.

The relevant question, then, is not whether the war on terror is truly a "war," but rather what kind of war it is. Does it exhibit the conditions that, in past conflicts, have justified expansive interpretations of the war power? The war on terror, in fact, has many different aspects involving widely differing circumstances, ranging from the military campaign in Afghanistan to domestic law enforcement efforts to root out "sleeper cells." To use the Afghanistan campaign to justify limits on due process at home—on the ground that the "war on terror" embraces both venues—is dangerous and unnecessary business in the context of due process. The words of Justice Jackson, concurring in *Youngstown*, are salient here:

...[N]o doctrine that the Court could promulgate would seem to me more sinister and alarming than that a President whose conduct of foreign affairs is so largely uncontrolled, and often even is unknown, can vastly enlarge his master over the internal affairs of the country by his own commitment of the Nation's armed forces to some foreign venture.

343 U.S. at 642.[83]

Any analysis of the balance between the war power and due process should distinguish between the two principal theaters of the war on terror, domestic and foreign. The rule of law speaks very differently to these two venues, as do the justifications typically advanced in support of an expansive reading of presidential power in wartime.

b.   The War on Terror Abroad: Broad Presidential Discretion, and Maximum Judicial Deference

The courts are most deferential to exercises of the war power when the President is acting in a military context, as Commander in Chief, or as the architect of foreign policy, and especially "in time of war and of grave public danger." See, e.g., Quirin, 317 U.S. at 25 (detention and trial of saboteurs ordered by President in the exercise of his powers as Commander in Chief should not "be set aside by the courts without the clear conviction that they are in conflict with the Constitution or the laws of Congress constitutionally enacted"). Such judicial deference, strongest when Congress has specifically authorized the challenged action, appears to follow from the courts' acceptance of two related notions. First, that military and foreign affairs are seen as areas in which the President is constitutionally vested with unique authority and possesses presumed expertise. See, e.g., Chicago & Southern Air Lines v. Waterman Steamship Co., 333 U.S. 103, 111 (1948); United States v. Curtiss-Wright Export Corp., 299 U.S. 304, 319 (1936). Second, the courts view themselves as particularly ill-equipped to make decisions in these areas, because they require policy judgments not within the judges' special knowledge and because decisions often must be made rapidly and in a manner that court processes are not designed to accommodate. In addition, judicial deference is also heightened by the fact that the President and Congress are the "political" branches, and thus charged with making life-and-death decisions in times of crisis. As the one unelected branch, the judiciary is properly reluctant at such times to take positions that either potentially threaten, or may be seen as threatening, national survival.

The Fourth Circuit in Hamdi articulated the reasons for this deference in the context of overseas conflicts in these words:

Through their departments and committees, the executive and legislative branches are organized to supervise the conduct of overseas conflict in a way that the judiciary simply is not. The Constitution's allocation of the warmaking powers reflects not only the expertise and experience lodged within the executive, but also the more fundamental truth that those branches most accountable to the people should be the ones to undertake the ultimate protection and to ask the ultimate sacrifice from them.

Hamdi III, 316 F.3d at 463. The very notion of a court attempting to adjudicate facts that may be concealed by the fog of foreign wars suggests caution. Hence we see the courts reluctant to become involved in cases that may call upon them to decide factual and policy-laden questions that are either not susceptible of direct proof by competent evidence, or that may require, for proper illumination, substantial disruption of military or other national security activities by the executive branch.

These justifications for extreme judicial deference speak most strongly to the overseas and military aspects of the war on terror. The military campaigns in Afghanistan and Iraq squarely implicate the President's powers as Commander in Chief. Their international aspects speak to the President's primacy in foreign affairs. The need for speedy executive action in response to terrorist-inspired crises abroad is self-evident. The need broadly to gather information (often not of evidentiary quality) from a wide variety of sources, including foreign intelligence services, is one that only the executive can meet.

For these reasons, an expansive view of the President's powers to pursue the war on terror abroad is justified. Further, the exercise of such powers abroad rarely will implicate due process concerns in view of the traditionally limited role of due process outside the country. The Hamdi decision, in these respects, was an easier one than Padilla.[84]

c.   The War on Terror at Home: Due Process Still Applies

But when the focus is shifted to the detention of alleged enemy combatants seized in this country, such as in Padilla and now al-Marri, the case for deference to the President's unilateral war power becomes problematic. In this context, the President's foreign affairs primacy is of lesser moment. Nor is the President's role as a military commander dominant, for the domestic war on terror seems closer to a law enforcement effort than to a military campaign.[85] Most suspected terrorists detained in this country in fact have been prosecuted through the criminal justice system.[86] Nor does the war on terror at home, as a general matter, involve an emergency requiring action so hasty as to preclude the use of judicial processes, though particular crises may occur that do so temporarily (as in the immediate aftermath of 9/11). Speed surely is not the essence of the indefinite detentions, which are expressly intended to be long-term.

There is a vital line to be drawn between the exercise of the President's war power at home versus abroad. In the words of an FBI agent engaged in anti-terrorism investigations:

Inside the borders of the United States, there is the rule of law. We had U.S. citizens. I was not just going to go up and scoop them off the street. N.Y. Times, The First Home-Front Battle in the War on Terror, Oct. 16, 2003, E8, c.3, 8 (quoting special agent Peter Ahearn on why he had not acted to seize the "Lackawanna Six" in the absence of sufficient evidence for an arrest).

A protest might be raised to the distinction of the war on terror abroad from the war on terror at home on the ground that it is all one war waged by the same enemy: an international conspiracy that respects no national boundaries. But while the war may be one, due process operates (generally) only at home, not abroad. The constitutional calculus is different, and it must be if the war on terror is not to swallow domestic liberties whole.

The contrary view of an undifferentiated global war on terror, with America viewed as part of the "battlefield," would hold all civil liberties hostage to the Commander in Chief's unilateral military judgment as to the "level of force" required to combat al Qaeda or other terrorists. With the President possessed of unreviewable powers to determine (i) when we are "at war," (ii) the dimensions of the "battlefield," and (iii) the "level of force" to be used, the elements of a "constitutional dictatorship," in Rossiter's phrase,[87] would be in place. The courts must abandon their role as protectors of core due process rights if they take Quirin and The Prize Cases to justify such an extreme result.

The Second Circuit did not. In reversing Padilla it drew a clear distinction between exercises of the war power abroad and at home. Again turning to Justice Jackson's concurrence in Youngstown, it cited his articulation (343 U.S. at 644) of the "Constitution's policy that Congress, not the Executive, should control utilization of the war power as an instrument of domestic policy." Padilla Cir. 713. The separation of powers as enforced by the courts, in sum, requires congressional authorization for Presidential action at home, as distinguished from his action abroad, which the courts generally will not scrutinize. Cf. United States v. Verdugo-Urquidez, 494 U.S. 259, 275 (1990) (any restrictions on actions by American armed forces abroad "must be imposed by the political branches through diplomatic understanding, treaty, or legislation," and not by the courts).

3.   The Claimed Necessity for Indefinite Detentions

The exigencies of the war on terror at home surely warrant some deference by the courts to the executive's anti-terror initiatives, and the "flexible" nature of due process permits it. Such measures as heightened screening of luggage at airports and the use of police checkpoints during terrorism alerts are two examples of reasonable restrictions of liberty that should cause little pause. But the question of necessity cannot be left entirely in the hands of the executive branch, given its institutional need to place primary emphasis on national security. Political realities almost compel the President, by virtue of his role, to tilt the balance between national security and the due process rights of suspected terrorists strongly in favor of national security. He may be held responsible by the voters if he fails to prevent another terrorist attack, but likely not for any violation of due process in the course of seeking to prevent such an attack.

Chief Justice Rehnquist, writing in his private capacity as historian, sees the need for "more careful" judicial review of exercises of the war powers based on claims of necessity:

It is all too easy to slide from a case of genuine military necessity, where the power sought to be exercised is at least debatable, to one where the threat is not critical and the power either dubious or non-existent.

  * * *

It is neither reasonable nor is it remotely likely that civil liberty will occupy as favored a position in wartime as it does in peace-time. But it is both desirable and likely that more careful attention will paid by the courts to the basis for the government's claims of necessity as a basis for curtailing civil liberty. The laws will thus not be silent in time of war, but they will speak with a somewhat different voice.

Rehnquist at 224–25.

The courts, to be sure, are not ideally positioned to judge the military necessity of particular exercises of a President's claimed war power. But they are familiar with and responsible for enforcing due process principles. When a President's actions so sharply depart from core due process principles as do indefinite detentions, a heavy burden is fairly placed on the executive to justify the necessity of such unilaterally adopted measures.

With these observations in mind, we turn to the two bases on which the executive has claimed a necessity to employ indefinite detentions: to incapacitate suspected terrorists, and to interrogate them.

a.   Incapacitation. Achieved Well by the Criminal Justice System

The first rationale is simply incapacitation: detaining a suspected terrorist prevents him from committing further acts of terrorism.[88] But so, too, does a successful criminal prosecution followed by a sentence commensurate with the crime. Accordingly, indefinite detentions could be justified on this rationale only if we lack confidence in the ability of the Justice Department, juries and judges to prosecute, convict and sentence terrorists. No such lack of confidence is warranted in light of the record of Article III courts in handling terrorist cases to date.

Are there an appreciable number of cases in which there exists "some evidence" that a suspect is a terrorist, but not enough to convict him of terrorism "beyond a reasonable doubt"? We have not heard of such an argument being seriously advanced. If there is any basis for it, it should be presented to Congress for it to consider whether legislation permitting indefinite detentions under some circumstances is justified.

b. Intelligence Gathering: Prosecutions Need Not Short Circuit the Process

The more serious alleged need for indefinite, incommunicado detentions is to facilitate intelligence-gathering interrogation designed to extract information helpful in preventing future terrorist attacks. It is with respect to this alleged need that the question of how to balance due process and security is most acutely posed, in the context of executive detentions.

It seems apparent, if press reports can be believed, that interrogations of al Qaeda leaders and some lower level operatives have yielded some valuable information concerning ongoing terrorist plots. The professed purpose of these enemy combatant detentions is indeed to extract information, rather than to impose a penalty for past conduct. To require prompt trials of the detainees on charges, the government urges, will defeat this purpose: a criminal proceeding, with its requirement that the defendant have access to counsel and to information in the possession of the government that is pertinent to his defense, may interfere with the continuity of debriefing of terrorist suspects, including both the defendant and others.

The premise for this point is summarized in a declaration submitted by the government on its re-argument motion in Padilla. In that declaration, an official from the Defense Intelligence Agency ("DIA") summarized the technique of debriefing favored by the DIA in this context. As quoted by Chief Judge Mukasey, the government represented:

DIA's approach to interrogation is largely dependent upon creating an atmosphere of dependency and trust between the subject and the interrogator. Developing the kind of relationship of trust and dependency necessary for effective interrogations is a process that can take a significant amount of time. There are numerous examples of situations where interrogators have been unable to obtain valuable intelligence from a subject until months, or even years, after the interrogation process began.

  Anything that threatens the perceived dependency and trust between the subject and interrogator directly threatens the value of interrogation as an intelligence-gathering tool. Even seemingly minor interruptions can have profound psychological impacts on the delicate subject-interrogator relationship. Any insertion of counsel into the subject-interrogator relationship, for example—even if only for a limited duration or for a specific purpose—can undo months of work and may permanently shut down the interrogation process. Therefore, it is critical to minimize external influences on the interrogation process.

Padilla, 243 F. Supp. 2d at 49.

The interference posited by the government could come in two ways. First, once criminal charges are filed the interrogation process could come to an immediate halt since the defendant must be warned of his rights to silence and to counsel.[89] Second, the defendant might seek and obtain court authorization to contact other detainees who may be undergoing such interrogation, and such contacts could imperil the gathering of information even from individuals who are being held abroad, outside of the criminal justice system.

Although these concerns are not fanciful, there are at least some potential avenues for dealing with them. First, in many instances, the government might most effectively obtain information from a detainee by pursuing criminal charges, having counsel assigned and then allowing the attorney to seek to persuade his client to cooperate in exchange for leniency. See Padilla, 243 F. Supp. 2d at 51–53 (suggesting the same scenario). In fact, the Department of Justice touts its success at obtaining information from accused terrorists in precisely this manner:

- **[W]e are gathering information by leveraging criminal charges and long prison sentences.** When individuals realize that they face a long prison term, they often try to cut their prison time by pleading guilty and cooperating with the government. Since September 11, we have obtained criminal plea agreements from more than 15 individuals, who must, and will continue to, cooperate with the government in its terrorist investigations.

- These individuals have provided critical intelligence about al Qaeda and other terrorist groups, safehouses, training camps, recruitment, and tactics in the U.S., and the operations of those terrorists who mean to do American citizens harm.

- One individual has given us intelligence on weapons stored here in the United States.

- Another cooperator has identified locations in the U.S. being scouted or cased for potential attacks by al Qaeda.

(Dept. of Justice Website, Jan. 30, 2004: www.lifeandliberty.gov/subs/a_terr.htm) (emphasis in original).

Second, since there is little doubt that after arrest accused terrorists will be subject to pre-trial preventive detention, while they are so detained the government could possibly subject them to an intelligence-gathering process, and yet protect its ability to prosecute, by having the interrogation conducted by someone who is involved solely in intelligence-gathering and will be walled off from any participants in any subsequent criminal proceeding. See, e.g., Padilla, 243 F. Supp. 2d at 51 (citing cases).[90] The privilege against self-incrimination is an evidentiary one: a "fundamental trial right," the violation of which "occurs only at trial." United States v. Verdugo-Urquidez, 494 U.S. at 264. It is not offended by questioning if the fruits are not used at trial. Therefore, so long as the interrogation is isolated from the criminal proceeding, with no information elicited from the suspect introduced at trial against the suspect or made available to the prosecuting attorneys, due process and the right to assistance of counsel may be flexible enough to permit some interrogation of suspected terrorists. The precise extent to which such interrogations might be permitted is not a question we need answer for the purpose of this discussion, except to note that such interrogation is not necessarily precluded if due process, as we urge, is construed to prevent indefinite and incommunicado detentions in service of the domestic war on terror.

The danger of interference with other ongoing interrogations is not entirely speculative, as illustrated by the case of Zacarias Moussaoui, the accused "twentieth hijacker". Moussaoui has successfully sought from the trial court some form of access to Ramzi Bin Al-Shibh, an allegedly high-level al Qaeda operative recently seized in Pakistan and now being held and interrogated overseas. The government's refusal to permit such access has resulted in the dismissal of portions of the indictment and the preclusion of the death penalty, a ruling now on appeal. United States v. Moussaoui, 282 F. Supp. 2d 480 (E.D. Va. 2003), appeal pending, No. 03-4792 (4th Cir.).

We do not know the eventual fate of the Moussaoui prosecution, but it appears to present quite a unique circumstance: a charge of conspiracy to commit a specific act (the 9/11 attacks), supported by (it would appear) scant evidence, and with the defendant able credibly to identify another suspect in a position to refute the charge. There are likely to be very few similar cases, in part because the argument for the necessity of access to another detainee will not appeal to most courts. Moreover, even if some access is deemed necessary, the less intrusive approach may involve either providing defense counsel with some of the fruits of the other suspect's interrogation or, still more likely, having the trial judge review those fruits and, if they are helpful to the defendant, grant relief comparable to what is authorized by the Classified Information

Procedures Act, 18 U.S.C. App. 3, § 1 et seq., as a substitute for production of classified information.

While we recognize that the above measures fall short of the unlimited opportunity for interrogation desired by the executive, they accommodate the proclaimed need to some degree. If due process is to be bent further, perhaps to the breaking point, we submit that statutory authority is required at a minimum based on a showing of compelling necessity found persuasive by Congress.

4. Emergencies

While we conclude that indefinite detentions in this country should not be held within the executive's war power, absolutism is not necessary or prudent in this context. Due process is not unyielding in the face of dire emergency. It can accommodate transient, short-term departures from its normal strictures in truly emergency situations, requiring immediate action to protect the nation's security that only the executive is capable of initiating. Temporary detentions by the executive in such emergency circumstances might pass due process muster in "the particular situation" presented. Morrissey v. Brewer, 408 U.S. at 481.

The Second Circuit appears to disagree, holding that "the Constitution lodges these [emergency] powers with Congress, not the President," again relying on the Jackson concurrence in Youngstown. Padilla Cir. at 714–15.[91] We do not agree with this total negation of a President's ability to act swiftly in a dire emergency at home under his war power given the possibility—not so remote in light of 9/11—of an unpredictable circumstance in which awaiting congressional action would be folly and reliance on criminal procedures futile.

But to say that the domestic war on terror presents such circumstances of emergency necessity in general—throughout its indeterminate duration and wherever prosecuted—would be not only contrary to fact but deeply threatening to our core due process values. The courts cannot abdicate meaningful review of Presidential claims of emergency circumstances and remain true to their role as protectors of constitutional liberties.

C.   The Necessity of Congressional Authorization

1.   A Clear If Not Loud Message: Congress Counts

The question of the extent to which due process should yield to the demands of the war on terror is not an easy one. But when the President's actions at home so clearly conflict with core due process principles, we do not believe that the President's war-making power alone should be held sufficient to sustain those actions under the Constitution. Rather, we believe that congressional authorization is essential for any indefinite domestic detentions conceivably to pass constitutional muster, given that they depart so sharply from core due process principles. Striking the balance between national security and due process rights cannot and should not depend on the courts' naked review of unilateral executive actions, not supported by the other political branch.

One fairly consistent theme that runs through the relatively sparse relevant case law is that the courts are more willing to approve the President's actions in the United States pursuant to his war powers when there has been specific congressional authorization for those actions. See, e.g., Martin v. Mott, 25 U.S. 19 (1827) (President's activation of state militias authorized by 1795 statute); Luther v. Borden, 48 U.S. 1, 42–43 (1849) (citing same statute); Quirin, 317 U.S. 1 (1942) (use of military commissions to try unlawful combatants seized in U.S.); Hirabayashi v. United States, 320 U.S. 81 (1944), and Korematsu v. United States, 323 U.S. 214

(1944) (congressional authorization found for the curfew and relocation orders imposed by the executive branch on Japanese resident aliens and citizens).[92]

In contrast, several important cases have struck down executive action in the United States as beyond the President's war power, in the absence of specific congressional authorization. See Milligan, 71 U.S. 2 (no congressional authorization for use of military commissions in areas in which civil courts were functioning; four concurring justices in Milligan would have affirmed the challenged military commissions had they been authorized by Congress); Youngstown, 343 U.S. 579 (no congressional authorization for seizure of steel mills). The absence of congressional authorization, in fact, is the principal basis of the Second Circuit's invalidation of citizen detentions in its Padilla decision.[93]

It is true that the presence or absence of congressional authorization has not been the central focus of the above-cited Supreme Court decisions. The clearest expression of the importance of congressional action is probably Justice Jackson's concurring opinion in Youngstown, heavily relied upon the Second Circuit's Padilla opinion, in which he urged that the presumption in favor of the constitutionality of presidential action is strongest when the action is supported by specific congressional authorization. There is compelling wisdom in this observation. It is consistent with a sensitive application of the separation of powers doctrine for the courts to show greater deference to action authorized by both of the political branches of government, rather than to action taken by the executive alone.

The sharp departure from due process inherent in indefinite detentions should require, at minimum, affirmative congressional authorization after consideration of the difficult relevant policy considerations. There is, we recognize, a rational basis for some special treatment of terrorist activities under the law, for terrorism, to some degree, can be distinguished from other types of criminal activity. International terrorism represents an organized and violent conspiracy directed against the United States, as distinguished from other criminal activity, which is typically more private and limited in its objectives. As September 11 demonstrated, terrorism can cause a uniquely grave impact on the national sense of well-being as well as terrible loss of life. The demonstrated willingness of religious fanatics to engage in suicidal attacks places their actions beyond the normal variety of criminal conduct, and beyond the likely deterrent capacity of any threat of punishment by our criminal justice system.

In criminal prosecutions, the requirement that the government prove guilt beyond a reasonable doubt is "designed to exclude as nearly as possible the likelihood of an erroneous judgment," and thereby "our society imposes almost the entire risk of error upon itself." Addington v. Texas, 441 U.S. 418, 424–25 (1979). With respect to terrorism, when the consequence of error may be not just the acquittal of a defendant but the perpetration of further terrorist acts, the graver risk of error may argue against reading the Constitution to impose the "entire risk of error" on society. Cf. Kennedy v. Mendoza-Martinez, 372 U.S. 141, 160 (1963) (the Constitution "is not a suicide pact"; case involved compulsory military service).

Congress is in a position to weigh the interests of due process and national security in this context. It "can see the problem whole," not limited to the President's necessary emphasis on national security or by the courts' necessary focus on individual cases. Katyal & Tribe, 111 Yale L.J. at 1275. Specifically, it can explore through hearings and debate the extent to which indefinite detentions are necessary to facilitate the interrogations of terrorists, and the degree to which such interrogations are essential in preventing future terrorist attacks. It can consider ways in which such interrogations can be facilitated without wholesale departure from the rule of law and due process.[94]

There are, it is important to note, constitutional limitations on what Congress itself can authorize in the war on terror. See Humanitarian Law Project v. Ashcroft, No. CV 03-6107

(C.D. Cal. Jan. 22, 2004) (invalidating section of USA Patriot Act as unconditionally vague); cf., e.g., Reid v. Covert, 354 U.S. 1 (1957) (ruling unconstitutional, as violative of Article III and the Fifth and Sixth Amendments, the congressionally-authorized use of courts marshal to try dependents of military personnel abroad on capital charges). To the extent legislation abrogates core due process principles in authorizing enemy combatant detentions, its constitutionality cannot be assumed.[95] But no question: the judgment of both political branches as to the necessity of enemy combatant detentions, and their appropriate extent and limitations, would carry a stronger presumption of constitutionality than does unilateral executive action.

If legislation in this area is deemed desirable, it could and should address the circumstances (if any) warranting detentions without charges, and the appropriate role of the courts in reviewing such detentions.[96] Among the many relevant questions:

- What type of activity is sufficient to warrant detention (as distinguished from a trial on criminal charges), e.g., should only direct involvement in a violent terrorist plot be sufficient or should providing logistical support for a terrorist organization also be sufficient, as the administration seems to believe?

- What standard of proof concerning the detainee's activities must the government meet in court to justify the detention (e.g., "some evidence," probable cause, clear and convincing evidence)?

- What type of hearing should the courts conduct to test the government's justification (a full adversary proceeding or something less rigorous)?

- Is the detainee to be afforded the right to counsel by statute, as is the case in proceedings under the Alien Terrorist Removal Act, 8 U.S.C. § 1534(c)(1)?

- For what purposes can the detention be continued (e.g., preventive detention, ongoing interrogation), and what standard of proof applies to such a showing by the government?

- For how long can the detention be continued before additional justification must be presented by the government in court?

- Are the rules for detention to be different for citizens and non-citizens?[97]

There is a risk that the Second Circuit's opinion in Padilla, relying as it does on a statute prohibiting the detention (only) of citizens, and deciding as it must only the case before it, involving a citizen, might encourage arbitrary distinctions between citizens and non-citizens. Any such bright line distinctions are to be avoided. They would violate the equal protection and due process rights of aliens, and encourage additional discrimination against Arabs and Muslims.

Nor would such distinctions make sense. Padilla and Hamdi, both citizens, probably have less attachment to this country than millions of Arab-Americans who have lived here for many years. Any detentions, if at all justified outside the criminal justice system, should be based on individualized considerations, and not ethnic stereotyping or arbitrary citizen vs. non-citizen categories.

2.   Congress Has Not Authorized Indefinite Detentions

a.   The Joint Resolution Does Not

We agree with the Second Circuit that the Joint Resolution of September 18, 2001, does not constitute authorization for indefinite enemy combatant detentions in the United States. The Joint Resolution broadly authorizes the President to use "all necessary and appropriate force" against terrorist organizations (and their members) responsible for the September 11 attacks. By its title it speaks expressly of "Military Force" and "the use of the United States Armed Forces," and its text specifies that it constitutes authorization, under sections 5(b) and 8(a)(1) of the War Powers Resolution, 50 U.S.C. § 1544(b), 1547(a)(1), for the use of the United States

Armed Forces. This generally worded enactment, speaking most directly (and perhaps exclusively) to military action abroad, should not be sufficient to suspend or abridge basic due process rights of individuals detained in the United States.[98] Specific congressional legislation addressing the enemy combatant context, and invoking Congress' own war powers, properly would elicit greater judicial deference, though not an abdication of the courts' role to pass on the constitutionality of legislation.

b. The USA PATRIOT Act Does Not, and by Implication Restricts Detentions

Legislation more specific than the Joint Resolution is found in the USA PATRIOT Act, Pub. L. No. 107-56, 115 Stat. 272 (2001), but it does not support detentions of an extended or indefinite nature, and its detention provisions do not apply at all to U.S. citizens. The statute authorizes only the detention for up to seven days of an alien "the Attorney General has reasonable grounds to believe" is engaged in activity that "endangers the national security," following which the Attorney General must either commence removal proceedings or release the detainee. Title IV, §§ 411-12, codified at 8 U.S.C. § 1226a(a)(3) and (5) (2001).

Further, "[i]f an alien is finally determined not to be removable", then the detention "shall terminate." 8 U.S.C. § 1226a(a)(2). If the alien is found to be removable, but cannot be removed, then but only then is the Attorney General authorized to detain such an individual for successive six-month periods until the alien either is removed or is no longer a threat to "the national security of the United States or the safety of the community or any person." Id. § 1226a(a)(6).

Thus the PATRIOT Act authorizes continuing detentions of aliens only if a) they are adjudged to be removable, pursuant to proceedings which must be commenced within 7 days of detention; b) they cannot be removed; c) and they pose a threat to national security.[99] The designation of an individual as an "enemy combatant" is not a substitute for a final order of removal. Therefore, it cannot be said that Congress authorized such indefinite detentions in the PATRIOT Act.

c. 18 U.S.C. § 4001(a) Prohibits Detentions Not within the War Power

The Second Circuit held that the detention of citizens as enemy combatants is prohibited (since not authorized by the Joint Resolution) by 18 U.S.C. § 4001(a), which provides:

No citizen shall be imprisoned or otherwise detained by the United States except pursuant to an Act of Congress.

This statute was passed in 1971 to preclude any detentions analogous to the widely condemned removals of Japanese citizens in World War II upheld in the Korematsu case. In our view, this generally worded statute, enacted in a context far removed from terrorism, should not be construed to abrogate any long-standing war power of the President.[100] But, as argued above, such power does not include indefinite detentions in the United States, and to that extent the statute does have force.

V. MILITARY COMMISSIONS: THEIR USE IN THE WAR ON TERROR SHOULD BE MINIMIZED

If we are correct in arguing that accused terrorists seized in the United States and citizens seized abroad must be tried (or released),[101] the question of the trial tribunal becomes ripe.

The President's Military Order issued on November 13, 2001 (the "PMO"),[102] authorized the trial by military commission of non-citizens—whether seized at home or abroad—accused of being members of al Qaeda or committing or aiding terrorist acts. In July 2003 six detained "enemy combatants" were designated as subject to the PMO, but no commissions have yet been scheduled.

As a matter of constitutional law, we believe the President's war power alone would be insufficient to override the Sixth Amendment right of suspects seized in this country to a "speedy and public trial before an impartial jury." But, unlike with respect to indefinite detentions, there is express congressional authorization for the use of military commissions to try offenses violating the law of war: the same statute on which the Quirin court relied.

Quirin, although it has been questioned,[103] stands as precedent authorizing the use of military commissions to try violations of the law of war, even by a United States citizen seized in the United States. It is true that the statute on which Quirin relied, Article 15 of the Articles of War, was general. It merely confirmed, without defining, the pre-existing jurisdiction of military commissions to try "offenders or offenses that by statute or by the law of war may be tried by military commissions...." It was arguably inadequate to support the result reached in Quirin, for there was little precedent for the use of military commissions outside occupied territories or theaters of active combat, or in any area where the civilian courts were functioning. However, Congress reenacted Article 15 in 1950 as part of the Uniform Code of Military Justice. 10 U.S. C. § 821.[104] That congressional action, with knowledge of the Quirin precedent, can fairly be read as endorsing Quirin's view that Congress has authorized the use of military commissions in the United States to prosecute violations of the law of war.[105]

Thus, given Quirin, we do not say "never" with respect to the use of military commissions to prosecute alleged violators of the law of war seized in the United States. We note, however, that whether acts of terrorism by non-state actors violate the law of war is far from clear. Neither customary international law nor any treaties to which the United States is a party recognize a state of war or "armed conflict," thereby implicating the law of war, in the absence of any organized armed forces. An international terrorist conspiracy, though subject to criminal prosecution, is not easily viewed as governed by the law of war. See generally, Congressional Research Service, Terrorism and the Law of War: Trying Terrorists as War Criminals Before Military Commissions, CRS 10–17 (Dec. 11, 2001); Nat'l Inst. of Military Justice, Annotated Guide, Procedures for Trials by Military Commission of Certain Non-United States Citizens in the War Against Terrorism 9–10 (2002) ("NIMJ Guide"). For a thorough discussion of this and related issues concerning the use of military commissions in the war on terror, see Association of the Bar of the City of New York, Inter Arma Silent Leges: In Times of Armed Conflict, Should the Laws be Silent? A Report on The President's Military Order of November 13, 2001 Regarding "Detention, Treatment, and Trial of Certain Non-Citizens in the War Against Terrorism" ("City Bar Report").

But assuming that, to some extent, the use of military commissions to try suspected terrorists would be constitutional, we urge that they be sparingly used, given the competence and advantages of the federal court forum.

As a practical matter, the federal courts have proven their ability effectively to try terrorists, aided by the enactment in 1980 of the Classified Information Procedures Act, 18 U.S.C. App. 3, § 1 et seq. ("CIPA"), which protects national security information in the context of such trials.

As a policy matter, trials in Article III courts serve the national interest by providing a public determination of guilt or innocence by an impartial jury overseen by an independent judge. The far greater likely acceptance of the fairness of such trials more than compensates for any marginal increase in the protection of classified information, or any higher likelihood of convictions, that may be available in military commissions controlled by the executive branch.

A. Military Justice System (Courts Martial)

Since September 11th, both courts-martial and military commissions have been proposed as venues for trying terrorists. These proposals often conflate two very different mechanisms. Each system has a unique function, constitutional foundation and relationship with what this report has labeled "core values". See NIMJ Guide 78–80. While in general the federal judiciary has had minimal contact with and oversight of these forms of military justice, civilian and military judicial structures have interacted in important ways.

1. Constitutional and Statutory Basis

The United States Constitution empowered the Congress to create a military justice system, including a courts-martial system. This congressional power springs from Article I, section 8, clause 1 (to "provide for the common defense") and clause 11 ("To make Rules for the Government and Regulation of the land and naval Forces."). Statutory authority for courts-martial derives from the Articles of War, initially adopted by the Second Continental Congress in 1775 (NIMJ Guide 78), its numerous amendments,[106] and the Uniform Code of Military Justice ("UCMJ"), enacted by Congress in 1950, which in part codifies the Articles of War. 10 U.S.C. §§ 801–950.

The UCMJ amended the Articles of War to create the system of military courts-martial in existence today.[107] It authorizes the President (and the Secretary of Defense) to convene courts-martial (Article 22(a)(1)(2)) and to compel, insofar as the President considers "practicable," the enforcement of civilian standards of criminal procedure.[108] The Supreme Court has upheld the constitutionality of this delegation of power.[109]

Both the Articles of War and the UCMJ reflect the initial conception of the military justice system as primarily a system for disciplining soldiers, and only secondarily a venue for trying non-military personnel.[110] But the UCMJ contains provisions that give courts-martials jurisdiction over non-servicemen in narrow circumstances.[111] Most notably, the UCMJ provides that courts-martial have jurisdiction, concurrent with military tribunals and commissions (Article 21), "to try any person who by the law of war is subject to trial by a military tribunal and may adjudge any punishment permitted by the law of war" (Article 18), and also jurisdiction over prisoners of war (Article 2(a)(9)). In practice, however, these functions have generally been fulfilled by special military commissions.

2. Protection of Core Values and Judicial Oversight

The Due Process Clause is applicable to legislation dealing with military affairs, though the courts afford great deference to Congress given its "plenary control" over the military under the Constitution (Art. I, § 8). Weiss v. United States, 510 U.S. 163, 176–77 (1994), quoting Chappell v. Wallace, 462 U.S. 296, 301 (1983).

The UCMJ contains many provisions recognizing rights also enforced in civilian courts:

By enacting the Uniform Code of Military Justice in 1950, and through subsequent statutory changes, Congress has gradually changed the system of military justice so that it has come to more closely resemble the civilian system. Weiss, 510 U.S. at 174.

Thus the UCMJ includes a prohibition on compulsory self-incrimination (Article 31), and a right to be represented by civilian counsel or military counsel of one's own selection (Article 38), and imposes a burden of proof on the United States to establish guilt beyond a reasonable doubt (Article 51). The UCMJ also establishes an appeals court of five civilian judges, the United States Court of Appeals for the Armed Forces, which is located within, but independent of, the Department of Defense (Articles 59–76).[112]

The most widely criticized weakness of the courts-martial system has been its lack of independence from the military command structure. Courts-martial judges have significantly less independence than civilian judges since their selection, as well as many pre-trial procedural decisions, are made by commanding officers, who often also have initiated the prosecutions.[113]

In general, the military justice system has not been the subject of significant judicial oversight. Most procedural issues and appeals have been dealt with by the Court of Appeals for the Armed Forces. However, the federal courts have intervened to adjudicate the overlapping or conflicting jurisdictions of the courts-martial and civilian courts in the context of habeas petitions.[114] A series of post-World War II cases ruled that courts-martial jurisdiction could not be extended to non-military personnel, including discharged soldiers,[115] civilian employees of the military overseas (for capital offenses),[116] and civilian dependents of overseas military personnel.[117] With respect to members of the Armed Forces, in 1987 the Supreme Court overruled its 1969 decision that had limited the jurisdiction of courts-martial to crimes committed by military personnel that had a relationship to their military service (a "service connection").[118]

The federal courts have heard habeas petitions from courts-martial rulings and on occasion intervened in the procedural area of courts-martials. For instance, in Loving v. United States, 517 U.S. 748 (1996), the Supreme Court held that Supreme Court jurisprudence on the death penalty applied to the military court system. At the same time, the Court endorsed the power of the President to circumscribe courts-martial procedural rules (a power delegated to him under the UCMJ).

In summary, while the traditional role of the military justice system has been to discipline soldiers and other individuals working for or under the control of the military, it could nonetheless be used as a tool for prosecuting terrorists for offenses violating the "law of war", under the jurisdiction accorded by Article 18. While the courts-martial's lack of independence presents a risk of manipulation by military commanders, the UCMJ and the Manual for Courts-Martial offer significant protection to core values.

B. Special Military Commissions

1. *Constitutional and Statutory Basis*

Military commissions, as Quirin observed, have a long history of use both in this country and elsewhere in the world. See Quirin, 317 U.S. at 35–36. They have been the historic and traditional venue for the trial of war crimes. See Wedgwood, 96 Am. J. Int'l L. at 332.[119]

The historical precedent for the use in the United States of special military tribunals (hereinafter "military commissions"), extends back to the Revolutionary War trial of Major John Andre.[120] While the Constitution makes no mention of military commissions, Presidential authority to establish them is traceable to the Commander in Chief war power clause of Article II, section 2. During the occupation of parts of Mexico during the Mexican American War, military commissions were set up to try civilian offenses committed in the occupied territory, and "councils of war" were set up to try violations of the law of war.[121] During the Civil War, the use of military commissions flourished, with over 4000 trials covering both violation of the laws of war and ordinary crimes.[122] President Lincoln declared a state of martial law throughout the country in 1862, and set up tribunals to try both military personnel and civilians.

During World War II, as most notably upheld in Quirin, military commissions were once again put into place to try spies and enemy combatants both on American soil and abroad, in

Germany, Japan and other countries occupied by the Allies. The year after World War II ended, the Court again upheld the use of a military commission in In re Yamashita, 327 U.S. 1 (1946). Japanese General Tomoyuki Yamashita, though captured as a lawful combatant, was accused of committing war crimes: failure to take steps to prevent the commission of atrocities by Japanese troops under his command during the U.S. Army's retaking of the Philippines. 327 U.S. at 16. The Court affirmed the authority of military commissions to try offenses against the law of war, even after active hostilities had ceased.[123] It further held, based on congressional grants of power in the Articles of War and the Espionage Act of 1917, that proceedings before military tribunals were free from review by the Supreme Court, save only inquiry as to whether the trial was within the authority of the military power.

In Madsen v. Kinsella, 343 U.S. 341 (1952), the Supreme Court surveyed the history of military commissions as follows:

Since our nation's earliest days, such commissions have been constitutionally recognized agencies for meeting many governmental responsibilities related to war. They have been called our common law war courts. They have taken many forms and borne many names. Neither their procedure nor their jurisdiction has been prescribed by statute. It has been adopted in each instance to the need that called it forth....

Id. at 348 (footnotes and citation omitted).

In Madsen, the wife of an American officer stationed in occupied Germany was tried by the United States Court of the Allied High Commission for Germany for murdering her husband and was convicted. The Supreme Court upheld the High Commission Court's authority, stating that the establishment of a military tribunal in an occupied country after the cessation of hostilities was within the President's authority, absent any attempt to limit that authority by Congress:

In absence of attempts by Congress to limit the President's power, it appears that, as Commander-in-Chief of the Army and Navy of the United States, he may, in time of war, establish and prescribe the jurisdiction and procedure of military commissions and of tribunals in the nature of such commissions, in territory occupied by Armed Forces of the United States. His authority to do so sometimes survives cessation of hostilities. The President has the urgent and infinite responsibility not only of combating the enemy but of governing any territory occupied by the United States by force of arms. The policy of Congress to refrain from legislating in this uncharted area does not imply its lack of power to legislate.

Id. at 348–49 (emphasis added).

The UCMJ, the Constitution, and federal jurisprudence limit the subject matter jurisdiction of military tribunals to violations of the law of war, with the narrow exception, as affirmed by *Madsen*, of the temporary use of tribunals to try civilian offenses during military occupation by United States forces abroad. See American Bar Association Task Force on Terrorism and the Law, Report and Recommendations on Military Commissions, Army Law 8, 12–13 (March 2002); City Bar Report at 10–14.[124] If, then, the President seeks to prosecute suspected terrorists before military commissions, one necessary role for the federal courts will be to review whether the actions charged constitute violations of the law of war, a question not free from doubt in the context of stateless terrorism.

2. The Enemy Combatant Commission Orders

Language in the Manual for Courts-Martial suggests that, barring other regulations set forth by the President or Congress, the UCMJ governs military commissions.[125] However, the Bush administration chose to promulgate specific procedures to govern the trial of any suspected terrorists, initially in the PMO issued November 13, 2001, and, later, in Military Commission Order No. 1 issued on March 21, 2002, by the Department of Defense (the "DOD Order"). See generally NIMJ Guide (comprehensive analysis of the DOD Order).

The PMO presented an array of potential due process issues.[126] This is foreshadowed in Section 1(f) of the PMO, stating "it is not practicable to apply in military commissions under this order the principles of law and the rules of evidence generally recognized in the trial of criminal cases in the United States district courts." The PMO provided for preventive arrest,[127] seemingly indefinite detention,[128] suspension of the exclusionary rule,[129] and exclusive jurisdiction, the latter provision perhaps intended to prohibit habeas corpus relief.[130] Under the PMO, a detainee could be convicted, and even sentenced to death, on secret evidence (§ 4(c) (4)), and on a vote of only two-thirds of the members of the commission (§ 4(c)(6) and (7); conviction could be premised on evidence well short of proof beyond a reasonable doubt; the decision was to be rendered, not by a jury of the detainee's peers, but by military officers subject to executive command; and the trials could be closed to the public (§ 4(c)(4)). In the opinion of this Association, the framework set forth in the PMO was inconsistent with the procedural protections of the UCMJ, thereby violating the requirement of UCMJ Article 36 that procedural changes made by the President "not be contrary or inconsistent with this chapter [the UCMJ]." City Bar Report at 18.

The March 2002 DOD Order responded to numerous complaints about the lack of protection of core values in the PMO. For instance, the DOD Order articulates a presumption of innocence, a right to counsel, a right to cross-examine witnesses, and a right not to testify during trial with no adverse inference to be drawn. § 5 ("Procedures Accorded the Accused"). It also establishes a procedure for limited appeals to a review panel appointed by the "Appointing Authority" (§ 6H(4) and (5)), defined as "the Secretary of Defense or a designee." § 2.

However, the DOD Order does little to answer concerns that the commission structure lacks independence, fails to provide some very basic protections for 'core values', and falls substantially short of the procedural safeguards embodied in the UCMJ. For instance, the Order gives the President, the Secretary of Defense or their designee control over the appointment of tribunal members (§ 4A) and members of the review panel (§ 6H(4)), and the authority to review the rulings of the review panel (§ 6H(5) and (6)). The DOD Order's guarantee of a right to civilian counsel is conditioned on such counsel being approved by the government, and their employment at no government expense. (§ 4(C)(3)). The DOD Order allows for public hearings (§ 5O), but also empowers the Appointing Authority to close those hearings for security reasons and to exclude the accused and civilian defense counsel from closed hearings in certain circumstances. § 6B(3). It further authorizes the government to withhold information "concerning... national security interests" (§ 6D(5)), or "state secrets." § 9.[131] It does not supersede (see § 7B) the terms of the PMO providing for preventive arrest, indefinite detention, suspension of the exclusionary rule and exclusive jurisdiction § 6(b).

Thus from the standpoint of due process values, the DOD Order, while a significant improvement from the PMO, still stops considerably short of the procedural protections available in Article III courts, or even those available in courts-martial under the UCMJ. See NIMJ Guide 80–83.

VI.   THE ADVANTAGES AND DISADVANTAGES OF THE FEDERAL COURT FORUM

Our review of legal and historical precedent suggests that the government, consistent with the Constitution, may have the authority to try suspected terrorists for violations of the law of war, in the United States or elsewhere, before military commissions. We turn to the question of whether such an approach, to the extent constitutional, is desirable public policy, and, if so, in what circumstances.[132]

The principal articulated argument for avoiding the civilian courts is that both procedural and substantive legal requirements applicable in these courts pose significant practical problems for the war on terrorism. In substance, the proponents of alternative remedies suggest that the civilian courts are not equipped to handle cases of this sort without endangering either national security or the participants in the proceeding. See, e.g., Ruth Wedgwood, After September 11, 36 New Eng. L. Rev. 725, 728 (2002); Wedgwood, 96 Am. J. Int'l L. at 330–32 (2002). This argument rests on explicit or implicit assumptions about how the civilian legal system works and what its limitations may be in dealing with the prosecution of terrorists. To test these assumptions, we look to the courts' experience in dealing with similar types of cases, and also assess the procedures available to the courts under current law to protect national security and other vital interests in the context of terrorism prosecutions.

A. The Feasibility of Criminal Prosecutions of Terrorists in Article III Courts

As an initial matter, we note that the criminal justice system today clearly has the statutory authority to deal with acts of terrorism. This has not always been the case. During the Civil War, one reason for the frequent resort to military commissions was that few if any criminal statutes reached the actions of Confederate sympathizers and activists. See, e.g., Hyman at 65–75. Prosecutors lacked any legal basis for charging many such suspects with serious and provable criminal violations. Absent clear proof of violent activity, the only available legal theory was treason, and that charge carries with it a very difficult, constitutionally mandated burden of proof.[133] See Hyman at 94–95. See generally United States v. Rahman, 189 F.3d 88, 111–12 (2d Cir. 1999).

In contrast, the current federal criminal code is well stocked with provisions criminalizing a significant array of activities that are said to bear the hallmark of terrorist intent. As recent prosecutions illustrate, the potential legal charges are many and varied.

For example, the defendants in the Rahman prosecution faced charges of seditious conspiracy, 18 U.S.C. § 2384; illegal use of explosives to destroy property, 18 U.S.C. § 844(i); conspiracy to kill foreign officials, 18 U.S.C. §§ 1416–17; and the use of violence or other criminal acts to assist a racketeering organization, 18 U.S.C. § 1959. See Rahman, 189 F.3d at 126. In the embassy bombing case, the defendants were charged, inter alia, with possession of firearms in a federal facility, 18 U.S.C. § 930; dealing in, possessing or distributing explosives without a license, 18 U.S.C. § 842; murder within the territorial jurisdiction of the United States, 18 U.S.C. § 1111; destruction of national-defense materials, premises or utilities, 18 U.S.C. § 2155(b); the killing of a United States official or employee in the course of his official functions, 18 U.S.C. § 1114; maiming within the territorial jurisdiction of the United States, 18 U.S.C. § 114; malicious destruction of government property, 18 U.S.C. § 844(f)(1); and use of explosives against United States nationals, 18 U.S.C. §§ 844(n) & 2332(b). See, e.g., United States v. Bin Laden, 92 F. Supp. 2d 189, 192, 198, 201–04 (S.D.N.Y. 2000); United States v. Bin Laden, 160 F. Supp. 2d 670, 672 n.1 (S.D.N.Y. 2001). Other recent prosecutions have featured charges of fraud in connection with the possession or use of identification documents, visas and passports, 18 U.S.C. §§ 1546(a), 1028(a)(6), see United States v. Koubriti, 199 F. Supp. 2d 656, 658 (E.D. Mich. 2002), and providing material support and resources to a registered terrorist organization, 18 U.S.C. § 2339B. See United States v. Sattar, No. 02 CR 395, 2002 WL 1836755 *1 (S.D.N.Y. Aug. 12, 2002).[134]

The federal courts have had significant experience trying terrorists, with a high rate of convictions.[135] Since criminal prosecutions in Article III federal courts are a readily available option for proceeding against accused terrorists, we turn to the question of whether such prosecutions are preferable to the use of military commissions. We start with the evident benefits of such an approach, and then address the principal articulated drawbacks.

B.   The Benefits of Using Article III Courts to Deal with Terrorism Offenses

The considerations militating in favor of using the federal courts to deal with criminal conduct that involves terrorist aims or methods are easy to cite and compelling in their simplicity.

1.   Justice

As we have noted earlier in this report, our Constitution—as interpreted by the Supreme Court—embodies a set of requirements that evolve from the twin concepts that the government may not seize an individual and hold him against his will absent evidence of criminal conduct or some other constitutionally cognizable basis for detention (the substantive due-process principle) and that any such detainee is entitled to certain procedural protections to ensure that his loss of liberty is justified by governing legal rules (the procedural due-process principle). In substance, any person seized by the government is presumed to be entitled to be restored to freedom, and the government must persuade a neutral decision-maker that the detainee is permissibly deprived of his liberty for whatever length of time and under whatever circumstances may be involved.

The rules that ordinarily apply to enforce this principle in the context of criminal prosecutions include a host of requirements to ensure both a tolerable level of reliability to the process and respect for the dignity and presumptive autonomy of the individual. Each of the procedural protections offered by the Constitution adds a quantum of assurance of both fairness to the detainee and reliability in the result of the process. Collectively, they reflect our society's understanding of what is required to ensure that individuals are not held by the government without basis and that the factual and legal validity of the asserted bases for detention are reliably judged. They are recognized by our society as necessary to protect a detainee's liberty interest when he is faced with the prospect of prolonged detention because of alleged misconduct.

It seems self-evident that the same protections should presumptively extend to those individuals whom the government has seized and proposes to detain for an extended, and perhaps indefinite, period of time because they are suspected of having engaged in conduct intended to further terrorist aims, thus violating applicable criminal laws. Such a presumption serves the precise goals of honoring the substantive and procedural due-process principles to which we have adverted.

Many of the protections afforded in the civilian criminal process are denied in the context of military commissions, even under the DOD Order, as discussed above. To the extent such protections are denied, so too is justice as our society traditionally defines it under the Constitution.[136]

In short, the demand for a just result is a persuasive reason for resorting to the Article III forum in which the full panoply of rights are available to a detainee, unless there are compelling reasons for depriving him of some of those protections. These considerations justify a presumption in favor of resorting to the civilian courts.

2.   Appearance of Fairness

As we have suggested, the protections for the detainee that are recognized by the Supreme Court in the context of criminal proceedings form the basis of a regime acknowledged by our society as necessary to ensure fair procedure and a reliable result in determining criminal liability. In view of this societal consensus, these protections provide not merely the substance of fairness to the detainee—both a fair process and, hopefully, a just result—but also the appearance of fairness. In short, they lend legitimacy both to the process and to its outcome.

The significance of this consideration extends beyond the boundaries of our society. Just as the use of indefinite detentions may encourage repression abroad, so too may any prominent resort to military commissions. Our leaders have not been shy in trumpeting the civic virtues of our constitutional system to other nations, including those with little, if any, tradition of respect for individual autonomy and limitation on government authority. Necessarily, the manner in which our government actually conducts itself in dealing with perceived misconduct both by citizens and by foreigners—including acts that may be considered threats to our civil peace and security—offers the world a strong indicator as to whether our system of self-governance actually adheres to the high standards that we profess to honor.

3. Maintaining the Health of the Bill of Rights Generally

For many of the reasons cited above with respect to indefinite detentions, the unnecessary bypassing of the criminal justice system in dealing with accused terrorists would create the risk of weakening our observance of core due process principles in other areas protected by the Bill of Rights. By the same token, if we can adhere to pre-existing rigorous norms of procedural fairness even in a time of fear and potentially serious threats to our national security, we reinforce the strength of those shared values in all contexts. In short, we diminish the temptation to cut corners in connection with both procedural and substantive requirements of regularity and fairness in all circumstances. If—despite the severity of the threat—we avoid ad hoc solutions designed to achieve an easy result in terms of the government's ability to ensure security, we will inevitably reinforce adherence to those norms in the face of other, and hopefully less extreme, circumstances.

4. Public Participation in the Process

In summarizing the various protections offered by the civilian criminal justice system, we have mentioned, among others, the right to a trial by a jury of the defendant's peers and the right to a public trial. These guarantees are deemed to offer some affirmative assurance as to the fairness of the process to the detainee, but they also serve another function, which benefits society as a whole.

The openness of the process gives the public itself the assurance that this aspect of governance is carried out in a manner consistent not only with constitutional norms, but with society's expectations. As the Supreme Court has recently noted, "[t]ransparency is essential to maintaining public respect for the criminal justice system, ensuring its integrity, and protecting the rights of the accused." Smith v. Doe, 528 U.S. 84, 99 (2003). Thus, the guarantee of a public trial is not merely a benefit to the defendant, but also a benefit to the public at large. Indeed, the courts have recognized that the principle of public access to the proceedings of the courts has a basis in the First Amendment.

Apart from the benefits of such access for purposes of public observation and monitoring, the direct participation of the community in the process, as jurors or potential jurors, offers further assurance that the government, when exercising its most coercive function, operates only with the consent and at the behest of the public. In effect, the executive branch is held to account for its actions in a very direct and public fashion. Moreover, when a verdict is rendered by a jury of citizens chosen from the community, it most consistently reflects the voice and judgment of that community, not only on the alleged actions of the defendant, but also on the conduct of the government.

Resort to the civilian courts ensures such participation to a far greater degree than other proposed means of handling detainees. The guarantee of a public trial in the civilian courts is not absolute, but the court is required to minimize any closure to the narrowest possible scope consistent with any compelling need for closed proceedings. See, e.g., Waller v. Georgia, 467 U.S. 39, 48 (1984); Ayala v. Speckard, 131 F.3d 62, 68-69 (2d Cir. 1997) (en banc), cert. denied, 524 U.S. 958 (1998). Moreover, the right to a jury trial on criminal charges filed in federal court remains inviolate, and thus ensures direct public participation in the process.

In a period when the government may seek, presumably for legitimate reasons, to exert its coercive authority to the greatest extent that may be consistent with constitutional limitations, the participation of the public, both as observer and as fact-finder, will serve to legitimize defensible applications of government powers. In this respect, it bears emphasis that the trust presumably desired by the executive branch must be earned, and that a failure to shine a light on government processes is conducive to abuse. See generally NLRB v. Robbins Tire & Rubber Co., 437 U.S. 214, 242 (1978) (describing policy underlying Freedom of Information Act). See also Jane Mayer, Annals of Justice: Lost in the Jihad, The New Yorker, 50, 57–59 (March 10, 2003) (recounting circumstances in which John Walker Lindh was allowed to plead to lesser charges); Al-Najjar v. Reno, 97 F. Supp. 2d 1329, 1352–61 (S.D. Fla. 2000) (rejecting INS detention order against suspected terrorist sympathizer, which was based on ex parte and hearsay evidence), vac. as moot, 273 F.3d 1330 (11th Cir. 2001).

Viewed in this context, a decision to use the civilian courts brings with it the evident advantage that public participation is assured. In contrast, military commissions lack equivalent protections, and are in fact designed to exclude them. For the reasons noted, such a choice would bring with it a serious cost in terms of both the regularity of the process and public acceptance of its legitimacy.

C. Possible Drawbacks to the Use of Article III Courts

Having taken account of the advantages to be derived by a consistent adherence to the processes of the civilian courts in dealing with terrorism detainees, we address those points principally made in favor of military commissions, and offer, if not a rebuttal, at least a context in which to assess them.

The principal difficulties cited by critics of the use of the civilian judicial process include i) the danger of detainees obtaining access to classified or otherwise sensitive information, ii) possible leakage of such information to the public through its compelled disclosure at a public trial or through intentional or inadvertent revelation by defense counsel, iii) the stringency of the standards for admission of relevant evidence, iv) the threat of physical harm to the civilian participants in the trial (including, presumably, jurors, judges and prosecutors), v) juror intimidation by fear of terrorist retaliation, and vi) the administrative and fiscal burden of these types of cases on the judicial system. We address each of these issues in turn.

1. Detainees' Demand for Access to Sensitive Information and the Conduct of the Trial

The defendant in a criminal proceeding is constitutionally entitled to see potentially exculpatory information, Brady v. Maryland, 373 U.S. 83, 84-87 (1963), and is also permitted, as a matter of discovery, to see a variety of other information pertinent to the prosecutor's case, including statements by witnesses. See 18 U.S.C § 3500; Fed. R. Crim. P. 16. In the trial of an accused terrorist, even good-faith requests by defense counsel for such information might pose the hazard that a defendant will obtain access to sensitive information that, if revealed to others in a position to act on it, could cause serious harm to national security. Moreover, there may be circumstances in which a defendant exercises his right to discovery for purposes antithetical to its governing purpose, which is the assurance of a fair trial. Thus, the defendant may seek sensitive and arguably relevant data precisely because it may be helpful to those of his conspirators who are still at liberty. In other circumstances, he may seek the most sensitive information arguably available in order to place the government on the horns of a dilemma, in which it must choose between (1) risking the dangerous disclosure of secret information (either to the defendant or at trial or both) as the price of prosecution and (2) foregoing prosecution.

Obviously these dangers would be entirely avoided by subjecting the detainee to a court process in which he is not entitled to disclosure of information by the prosecutor, in which evidence deemed necessary for proof of guilt can be disclosed ex parte by the government to a reliable set of military judges, and to which the public, including the press, has no access.

The concern with disclosure of sensitive information to a defendant accused of threatening national security is not a new phenomenon. Indeed, from the earliest espionage cases, it appears that the government has been compelled to address the question of how to obtain convictions consistent with legal requirements while protecting national security.[137] Ultimately in 1980 Congress addressed concerns about the potential for abuse of classified information by defendants in criminal prosecutions by enacting the CIPA. See generally Timothy J. Shea, CIPA Under Siege: The Use and Abuse of Classified Information in Criminal Trials, 27 Am. Crim. L. Rev. 657 (1990). The CIPA is designed to ensure a fair trial while at the same time minimizing the risk that a defendant can disclose classified information, whether as part of an effort to present a defense at trial or as a tactic to preclude his prosecution (euphemistically referred to as "greymail"), or even as part of an effort to assist enemies of the country. See, e.g. United States v. Pappas, 94 F.3d 795, 799 (2d Cir. 1996) (quoting United States v. Wilson, 571 F. Supp. 1422, 1426 (S.D.N.Y. 1983)). The pertinent provisions impose a series of procedural requirements on a defendant who proposes to use classified information in his defense and authorize several forms of remediation by the court to harmonize the conflicting legitimate interests of the defendant and the government.[138]

The statute addresses three circumstances in which the question of disclosure of classified information may arise. First, the defendant may seek production of such information from the government and may propose to use it at trial. Second, the defendant may already be in possession of classified data, and may wish to use it at trial. Third, the government may find it necessary to use such information as evidence.

To deal with any of these circumstances, the government may demand a pre-trial conference to consider matters related to the use of classified information in the case. These issues include discovery, the defendant's obligation to provide notice of his intent to use such information at trial, and the conducting of hearings to determine whether and in what circumstances classified information must be produced to the defendant or may be used at trial. See Shea, 27 Am. Crim. L. Rev. at 662–64.

With respect to discovery, the CIPA entitles the government, on an ex parte submission, to seek an order excusing it from disclosing classified information to the defense. See, e.g., United States v. Rezaq, 156 F.R.D. 514, 525–26, vac. in part, 899 F. Supp. 697 (D.D.C. 1995). The statute gives the court three options in ruling on the government's request: first, to conclude that the classified information is not sufficiently relevant to require its disclosure (e.g., United States v. Fowler, 932 F.2d 306, 310 (4th Cir. 1991)); second, even if some disclosure is deemed necessary, to authorize the government to substitute for the classified information either a summary of it or "a statement admitting relevant facts that the classified information would tend to prove" (CIPA § 4; see, e.g., United States v. Rezaq, 134 F.3d 1121, 1142 (D.C. Cir.)); or third, to conclude that the latter substitutes are not adequate to protect the defendant's interests (see, e.g., United States v. Fernandez, 913 F.2d 148, 150 (4th Cir. 1990)), in which event the court has broad discretion to enter a protective order conditioning the discovery required on compliance with terms that ensure against improper use of the sensitive information. CIPA § 3.[139]

The CIPA further provides that if the defendant wishes to use classified information at trial or intends to cause it to be disclosed (presumably by questioning government witnesses), he must notify the prosecutor and the court at least thirty days before trial and identify the information in question. CIPA, § 5(a). See, e.g., United States v. Wilson, 750 F.2d 7, 8 (2d Cir. 1984), cert. denied, 479 U.S. 839 (1985). In response, the government may request an in camera hearing on "the use, relevance, or admissibility of classified information" (§ 6(a)), and, in support of a motion to limit or exclude classified information at trial, may submit an affidavit by the Attorney General, to be reviewed in camera and ex parte if the government requests,[140] "certifying that disclosure of classified information would cause identifiable damage to the national security of the United States and explaining the basis for the classification of such information." § 6(c).

In deciding whether to permit the use of classified information at trial, the courts have generally held that CIPA does not change the law on privilege or admissibility, but requires the trial judge to apply a balancing test, weighing the relevance and probative weight of the information, the public interest in its non-disclosure,[141] and the adequacy of a summary or statement in lieu of its use. See, e.g., United States v. Smith, 780 F.2d 1102, 1107 (4th Cir. 1985); United States v. Yunis, 924 F.2d 1086, 1095 (D.C. Cir. 1991) (citing United States v. Sarkissian, 841 F.2d 959, 965 (9th Cir. 1988). See also United States v. Rahman, 870 F. Supp. 47, 50–51 (S.D.N.Y. 1994). But see United States v. Baptista-Rodriguez, 17 F.3d 1354, 1164 (11th Cir. 1994).

If the court authorizes the disclosure at trial, the government may request that instead the court permit a summary or statement admitting relevant facts to be substituted, and the court must grant the motion if the summary or statement will provide the defendant "with substantially the same ability to make his defense as would disclosure of the specific classified information." § 6(c)(1);[142] see, e.g., Rezaq, 134 F.3d at 142–43. If the court denies the government's substitution motion, the Attorney General can still block the disclosure by filing an affidavit objecting to it. CIPA, § 6(e)(1). The resulting limitation on the defense, however, requires that the court dismiss the indictment,[143] unless it concludes "that the interests of justice would not be served by dismissal" (id.), in which event the court has broad discretion in designing an appropriate remedy.[144]

The statute also deals with trial procedure. See, e.g., United States v. O'Hara, 301 F.3d 563, 567 (7th Cir.). It authorizes the court to minimize the use of classified materials at trial by admitting only selected parts of a document or by requiring the deletion of classified portions "unless the whole ought in fairness to be considered." CIPA, § 8(b). The government may object to any question or line of inquiry by the defense on the ground it will lead to the unauthorized disclosure of classified information, in response to which objection the court must ensure against such unauthorized disclosure, such as by requiring an explanation by the defense as to the nature of the information it seeks to elicit. § 8(c).

The CIPA also requires the Chief Justice, in consultation with specified executive branch agencies, to issue procedural rules to protect against the unauthorized disclosure of classified information through the courts. § 9(a). Those rules, issued in 1981 by then-Chief Justice Burger, require, inter alia, the appointment of a court security officer to supervise security measures, the identification of secure quarters within the courthouse in which proceedings concerning classified information are to take place, and security investigations and clearances for any court personnel who may have access to such information. Security Procedures Published By the Chief Justice of the United States for the Protection of Classified Information, ¶¶ 3–4 ("Security Procedures"), reprinted following 18 U.S.C.A. App. 3, § 9 (West 2000).[145]

The requirements imposed by CIPA and the rules of the Chief Justice have been repeatedly upheld as constitutional. See, e.g., Wilson, 750 F.2d at 9 (upholding requirement that defendant notify government of his intention to use classified information); United States v. Lee, 90 F. Supp. 2d 1324, 1326–28 (D.N.M. 2000); United States v. Poindexter, 725 F. Supp. 13, 31-35 (D.D.C. 1989) (same); United States v. Collins, 603 F. Supp. 301, 303–06 (S.D. Fla. 1985) (upholding provisions authorizing court to substitute admission or summary for original document); United States v. Wilson, 571 F. Supp. 1422, 1426–27 (S.D.N.Y. 1983) (definitions not void for vagueness); United States v. Joliff, 548 F. Supp. 229, 231–32 (D. Md. 1981) (upholding discovery limitations); United States v. Smith, 899 F.2d 564, 569-70 (6th Cir.), cert. denied, 498 U.S. 848, reh. denied, 498 U.S. 848 (1990) (upholding rules of Chief Justice). The provisions of CIPA have been consistently applied by the federal courts in a variety of prosecutions, including cases involving charges of terrorism. E.g., Rezaq, 134 F.3d at 1142–43 (upholding substitution order in aircraft piracy case); Bin Laden, 58 F. Supp. 2d at 115–17, 121–23 (requiring security clearances for defense counsel and imposing stringent rules for handling classified materials in terrorism case); Rahman, 870 F. Supp. at 52 (authorizing summary of pertinent part of classified document in terrorism prosecution). See also United States v. Bin Laden, 2001 WL 66393, * 2–4 (S.D.N.Y. Jan. 25, 2001).

Based on this body of experience, we are aware of no indication that the statute, reasonably interpreted by federal judges, is inadequate to the task of protecting national security interests while affording defendants a fair trial. Indeed, the recent experience of the Southern District of New York in hosting a series of trials involving al Qaeda defendants suggests that available procedures can minimize the dangers of either public disclosure or defendant misuse of classified information.

We particularly note that periodic review of classified information was required in the recent prosecution of defendants in the embassy bombing case in the Southern District of New York. The district court ordered that all defense counsel be subjected to security checks; directed that to the extent that the defense required access to classified information, the documents were to be shown only to counsel and not to the defendants; conducted in camera reviews and ex parte hearings, as necessary; and determined on an item-by-item basis whether disclosure of classified data was required. E.g., Bin Laden, 58 F. Supp. 2d at 115–17, 121–23; Bin Laden, 2001 WL 66393, *4–7. Further, a number of testifying witnesses possessed highly sensitive information (including not only law-enforcement agents, but also one or more formerly highly placed members of al Qaeda who were cooperating with the government), and the district court supervised the questioning to avoid disclosing any such information not clearly necessary for the defense. We have no reason to believe at this point that this manner of proceeding was inadequate either to safeguard sensitive information or to ensure a fair trial for all of the defendants.

In reaching these conclusions, we recognize that the CIPA does not remove all risks in the prosecution of terrorists. The statute itself creates the possibility that an indictment charging an alleged terrorist suspect with heinous crimes could be dismissed if the court ordered disclosure of sensitive information and the government declined. The Moussouai case demonstrates, in analogous circumstances, the potential of such an outcome.[146]

Nonetheless, the CIPA gives the courts broad discretion to find other alternatives that, in most if not all circumstances, should give adequate assurance to the government that its interest in protecting the public will not be significantly threatened by the need to disclose classified information as a condition for prosecuting the detainee. We are confident that, given the importance of permitting such prosecutions to go forward, the courts will continue to make every effort to design procedures that would provide reasonable assurance that the legitimate concerns of the government are met.

Finally, we view the CIPA and other governing law as likely to be adequate to deal with the concern that if classified information must be used at trial, it will filter out to terrorist groups or others who could make use of it to harm this country. The potential sources of such disclosure presumably are members of the public and the press who attend the trial, and the jurors.[147] But the long-recognized authority of the court to protect sensitive information even at trial suggests that this concern does not pose an irremediable problem.

As noted, the Supreme Court has explicitly recognized that an otherwise public trial may be closed for as long as necessary to avoid disclosure of information that could cause public injury. This principle has most commonly been applied to protect the identity of undercover agents in narcotics prosecutions. Brown v. Artuz, 283 F.3d 492, 498–500 (2d Cir. 2002); Bowden v. Keane, 237 F.3d 125, 127 (2d Cir. 2001). Nonetheless, it plainly would extend to portions of a terrorism or other criminal trial in which sensitive information must be disclosed or national security concerns are present. E.g., Abu-Jamal v. Horn, 2001 WL 1609690, *87–90 (E.D. Pa. Dec. 18, 2001); United States v. Poindexter, 732 F. Supp. 165, 167–69 (D.D.C. 1990); see generally Noble, The Independent Counsel Versus the Attorney General in a Classified Information Procedures Act—Independent Counsel Statute Case, 33 B.C.L. Rev. 539, 585–90 (1992).

Similarly, although the jurors could be exposed to such information if it was received in evidence, there are precautions available to minimize the risk that they will disclose what they have seen. First, as noted, the CIPA allows the court to mask classified data through the substitution of summaries or findings, so that actual disclosure of highly sensitive information to the jury is unlikely. Second, the voir dire process is likely to weed out individuals who might pose a possible risk of disclosing very sensitive information. Third, although the rules promulgated by the Chief Justice specify that security clearances for jurors are not required, neither the statute nor the rules preclude a thorough background check of potential jurors, up to and including an inquiry at the level of a security investigation. Between these forms of assurance and the court's authority to instruct the jurors that they are not to make any such disclosure, on pain of potential criminal prosecution, again we view the cited danger as in the realm of fairly remote speculation.[148]

2. Stringency of Evidentiary Rules

Another criticism of the use of civilian courts is the suggestion that the rules of evidence applicable in federal court are too stringent to permit proper proof of guilt when dealing with an organization as shadowy and difficult to track as al Qaeda. In general terms, the stated concern is that information that may be quite compelling may be found inadmissible in a civilian court because of the restrictions on hearsay, authentication requirements (for example, how to establish chain of custody for objects found on a foreign battlefield) and the possible effect of the exclusionary rule for illegal searches. Since a military commission may be empowered to consider such evidence, albeit with the discretion to discount its weight if there are serious questions about its reliability, proponents of that approach suggest that the commission will be a better tool for dealing with the threat of organizations that are based overseas and have far-flung and very secretive means of operating. See, e.g., Wedgwood, 96 Am. J. Int'l L. at 330–31.

We do not doubt that lowering these evidentiary barriers would make successful prosecution of suspects somewhat easier. To the extent that some of the cited rules are designed to ensure reliability, however, we question whether sacrificing that goal is necessarily desirable.

In any event, we believe that the concern that the Federal Rules of Evidence will prevent successful prosecutions in cases in which the government has persuasive evidence of guilt is overstated. For example, the rules governing authentication give the trial court significant discretion, and if the evidence in question is probably what it purports to be, then the court is likely to treat chain-of-custody issues with some flexibility. See, e.g., United States v. Tropeano, 252 F.3d 653, 660 (2d Cir. 2001); United States v. Bin Laden, 2001 WL 276714, *1–2 (S.D.N.Y. March 20, 2001).

As for the hearsay rule, apart from the numerous specific exceptions found in Fed. R. Evid. 803 and 804, the catch-all provisions of Rule 807 allow for admission of a statement that would otherwise be barred if the statement "is offered as evidence of a material fact" and "is more probative on the point for which it is offered than any other evidence which the proponent can procure through reasonable efforts" and, finally, if "the general purposes of these rules and the interests of justice will best be served by admission of the statement into evidence." This provision also gives the court ample latitude, and if the statement in question is deemed to bear indicia of reliability and it is relevant to a material issue, it will presumably be admitted.[149]

With regard to the possibility of Fourth or Fifth Amendment suppression due to irregularities in evidence-gathering overseas, the courts have recognized that information-gathering in foreign countries may not permit all of the formalities that pertain to police searches or investigations here. For example, in the embassy bombing case, the defendants sought to suppress statements that they had made to law enforcement agents in Kenya because they were not supplied with lawyers at the time and were informed that none were available there but that they could receive help if they confessed. The court denied suppression. In doing so, it held that the American agents had undertaken reasonable measures in view of all of the circumstances when questioning the defendants, and that in general terms a defendant being interrogated in Kenya by Kenyan law enforcement agents is not entitled to the same protections as would apply if he were in the United States or being questioned overseas under the supervision of American agents. United States v. Bin Laden, 132 F. Supp. 2d 168, 185–89 (S.D.N.Y. 2001). Similarly, when defendants sought to suppress the fruits of electronic surveillance and searches of a residence undertaken overseas, the court held that foreign intelligence surveillance is not governed by a warrant requirement, and it denied the motion, holding that both the electronic surveillance and the residential searches had been reasonable. United States v. Bin Laden, 126 F. Supp. 2d 264, 277 (S.D.N.Y. 2001); United States v. Bin Laden, 160 F. Supp. 2d 670, 678–79 (S.D.N.Y. 2001).

In short, although the federal rules of evidence may make proof somewhat more difficult in some circumstances, they are unlikely to pose a serious obstacle to the successful prosecution of a strong case. This is evident from the convictions secured in the various World Trade Center and related prosecutions, e.g., United States v. Salameh, 152 F.3d 88 (2d Cir. 1998); United States v. Youssef, 327 F.3d 56 (2d Cir. 2003); United States v. Rahman, 189 F.3d 88 (2d Cir. 1999); the embassy bombing case, see, e.g., United States v. Bin Laden, 2001 WL 1160604 (S.D.N.Y. Oct. 2, 2001); United States v. Bin Laden, 156 F. Supp. 2d 359, 361 (S.D.N.Y. 2001); and other terrorism cases in which defendants have ultimately pled to serious charges despite possible difficulties of proof. See, e.g., United States v. Lindh, 227 F. Supp. 2d 565 (E.D. Va. 2002); Another Man in Buffalo Case Pleads Guilty to Qaeda Link, N.Y. Times, March 25, 2003, at D7, c. 5.

3. Possible Harm to Trial Participants

Another concern voiced by proponents of alternatives other than civilian court trials is the danger of retaliation against the participants in such a trial. E.g., Wedgwood, 96 Am. J. Int'l L. at 331. The implied assumption is that military prosecutors and judges are more used to taking physical risks and can more readily be protected.

We understand that the judges who have presided at terrorism trials have been offered continued security protection after the completion of the trials, and that some have accepted.

Theoretically the same danger might be found in cases involving other types of charges of organized mayhem, including gang cases, organized-crime cases and drug prosecutions. Indeed, the few incidents of actual violence directed at federal judges have taken place in a variety of settings. These include the murder of a judge in the Southern District of New York following an unfavorable decision in a civil case brought by the daughter of the assailant; the bombing death of a federal appellate judge in Georgia; and the shooting of a judge in Texas at the behest of a convicted drug dealer. See Zagel & Winkler, The Independence of Judges, 46 Mercer L. Rev. 775, 830–31 (1995).

As for risks to jurors or prosecutors, this concern seems quite speculative. The use of anonymous juries seems adequate to shield jurors. We know of no evidence that prosecutors are significantly more at risk in handling terrorism cases than in pursuing drug, gang or organized crime cases. In fact, the general animus of terrorist groups toward American society generally may make it less likely, than with other criminal suspects, that their confederates would seek vengeance against specific federal actors.

In sum, the danger posed by participation in a terrorist trial is not a compelling argument for denying this class of detainees the same procedural protections as have been afforded to all criminal defendants under the Constitution.

4. Juror Intimidation

A related potential area of concern is based on the perception that trial participants may face threats of retaliation from terrorist groups. Regardless of whether that is a realistic possibility, it might be argued that the perception of such a threat exposes jurors—who have no training or perspective to deal with the fear—to subtle pressures to alter their analysis of the evidence.

It is certainly conceivable that some potential jurors may be fearful of serving and, if left on the jury, might tailor their verdict to some degree to accommodate that fear. This is a concern in other types of case as well, however, particularly in prosecutions of organized-crime figures and possibly some other cases involving violence-prone defendants who belonged to criminal organizations. See, e.g., United States v. Ruggiero, 928 F.2d 1289, 1300–02 (2d Cir. 1991). In those cases, the problem is dealt with in two ways: first, by careful and searching voir dire, with ample opportunity for both sides to exercise peremptory challenges and with heightened sensitivity by the court to challenges for cause, and, second, by the availability of anonymity for jurors.

We recognize that this may not be a perfect solution. A recent article that was based on interviews with a number of jurors who had participated in the embassy-bombing trial suggested that at least one may have been partly influenced by a personal concern for safety in assessing the death-penalty question, although apparently not the issue of guilt. See Weiser, A Jury Torn and Fearful in 2001 Terrorism Trial, N.Y. Times, Jan. 5, 2003 at 1 (reprinted at http://www.why-war.com/news/2003/01/05/ajuryfor.html). Nonetheless, perfection is obviously not a tenable standard on which to base the decision as to how we are to treat detainees in the current circumstances, since none of the other proposed solutions even approach that lofty criterion.

In truth, we are left with a variety of quite imperfect approaches, but the highly subjective concern with the mental processes of jurors seems a very weak reed on which to rest a serious deviation from accepted standards of procedural fairness.

5. Administrative and Fiscal Burdens

A further concern that has been voiced at the use of the civilian courts is related to the security issues. Simply stated, the argument, as we understand it, is that the procedures for ensuring that the national security is adequately protected and that the participants are secure will prove too cumbersome and delay resolution of the charges. See, e.g., Byard Q. Clemmons, The Case for Military Tribunals, 49 The Federal Lawyer 27, 31 & nn.51–52 (2002). This concern is that the financial and administrative headaches of managing a Rube Goldberg set of procedures will put an excessive strain on the courts.

We view this concern as entirely unpersuasive. First, compared to the wealth of other legal proceedings handled by the federal courts—some of them of great length and complexity— terrorism trials are a minor drain on the courts' resources. Second, the considerations going to the fairness of our treatment of detainees and the legitimacy for which our society should properly strive in its handling of proceedings involving charges of serious crimes plainly outweigh dollar-and-cents calculations. If the war on terrorism is of sufficient moment, our country is capable of paying for it. Third, the speed with which verdicts are rendered is not a determinant of the fairness of the result nor should it dictate the availability of fundamental due process protections to a defendant.

D.   On Balance: Maximize Use of the Federal Court Forum

The case for using the federal courts as the preferred forum for the trial of terrorism cases is in our view compelling. Conceivably there may be exceptional circumstances from time to time that would warrant proceeding before a military commission. But as a general matter, the powerful benefits derived from the transparency and perceived fairness of federal court trials will strongly militate in favor of that venue.

We note that with the recent capture of Saddam Hussein, the Administration has been careful to emphasize the importance of a transparent and open trial proceeding that will give the world confidence that justice has been served at the end of the process. These same considerations are what impels us to recommend the use of the federal courts to try domestic terrorism cases.

VII.   CONCLUSION

While to date only three enemy combatants are known to have been detained in the United States, the importance of the issues discussed in this report extend well beyond those three individuals. It must be expected that there will be further terrorist attacks against the United States, and also further suspected terrorists apprehended before they have been able to put their plans into effect. The precedents set with respect to the three existing cases will influence the treatment of such later cases, and more generally the degree to which our country preserves its due process values while it maintains its homeland security.

The issues are not easy ones, and the dearth of case law and practical experience truly on point is striking. But the fundamental due process principles that form the rule of our law under the Constitution are not obscure. In our view, those basic principles cannot be set aside and avoided, in the context of terrorism, without doing likely permanent damage to the constitutional values we honor in all other circumstances.

The Constitution is not a "suicide pact", as a Supreme Court Justice once famously declared. But neither is it a mere compact of convenience, to be enforced only in times of civic tranquility. It should take far more than the monstrous brutality of a handful of terrorists to drive us to abandon our core constitutional values. We can effectively combat terrorism in the United States without jettisoning the core due process principles that form the essence of the rule of law underlying our system of government.

Insistence on the rule of law will not undermine our national security. Abandoning the rule of law will threaten our national identity.

February 6, 2004
(revised March 18, 2004)

NOTES

* **Committee on Federal Courts:** Thomas H. Moreland (chair; subcommittee member), Jill S. Abrams, Stuart M. Altman, David JB Arroyo, Carmine D. Boccuzzi, Francisco E. Celedonio (subcommittee member), Lewis Richard Clayton (abstained from consideration of this report), Eric O. Corngold (abstained from consideration of this report), James L. Cott (abstained from consideration of this report), Michael H. Dolinger (subcommittee member), Thomas A. Dubbs, Martin D. Edel, William C. Fredericks, Barry S. Gold, Thomas H. Golden, Rita W. Gordon, Marc L. Greenwald, Caitlin J. Halligan, Lynne Troy Henderson (subcommittee member), Fran M. Jacobs, Lowell Johnston, Bruce Robinson Kelly, Lynn Mary Kelly, Richard Mancino (subcommittee member), Michael B. Mushlin, Lynn K. Neuner, Katherine Huth Parker, Douglas J. Pepe, Amy Rothstein, Gail P. Rubin, Peter Salerno, Wendy H. Schwartz, Alexandra Shapiro (abstained from consideration of this report), James A. Shifren (subcommittee member), Ellen B. Unger, Alan Vinegrad, Hilary M. Williams, and Victor Worms.

1. The New York Times reported as follows concerning al-Marri:

Mr. Marri 37, came to the United States a day before the 9/11 attacks on a student visa. He was held in December 2001 as a material witness in the Sept. 11 investigation and later charged with lying to the F.B.I. in an interview and credit card fraud.

Officials said the recent information from Qaeda operatives in American custody, including Khalid Shaikh Mohammed, pointed to Mr. Marri as a "sleeper" operative assigned to help other members of al Qaeda "settle" in the United States. Mr. Marri visited a Qaeda training camp in Afghanistan and met with Osama bin Laden, officials said. Eric Lichtblau, Wide Impact From Combatant Decision Is Seen, N.Y. Times, June 25, 2003, at A14.

In the same article, the purpose of the detention was described as follows:

Administration officials said the decision to imprison...al-Marri in a brig in South Carolina...was intended in part to try to cull more information from him about possible links to al Qaeda. That avenue would probably have been foreclosed if Mr. Marri's case had gone to trial the next month.

"This way," an administration official said, "we'll obviously be able to continue to interrogate him. We may be able to obtain valuable intelligence from him." (Id.).

It appears al-Marri was arrested as a material witness by FBI agents in Peoria, Illinois, at the direction of the U.S. Attorney's Office for the Southern District of New York, and transferred to New York. He was formally arrested on a complaint charging him with credit card fraud in January 2002. In February an indictment was returned with additional charges, none expressly tied to terrorism. Ultimately he was scheduled to be tried on these charges in Peoria on July 21, 2003. On June 23 President Bush designated him an enemy combatant. The indictment thereupon was dismissed and he was "immediately transferred into military custody and transported to the Naval Consolidated Brig in Charleston, South Carolina, where he continues to be held." Al-Marri, 274 F. Supp. 2d at 1004–05. In the cited order, al-Marri's subsequent habeas corpus petition was dismissed by the Central District of Illinois for improper venue, given al-Marri's transfer to South Carolina and the general rule that "habeas cases should be brought in the district of confinement." Id. at 1009–10.

2. Padilla's alleged conduct as a saboteur undoubtedly violated numerous criminal statutes directed against terrorist acts and conspiracies. Hamdi's criminal liability as a Taliban foot soldier is less clear.

3. For a more complete analysis of the Padilla and Hamdi decisions see [discussion below].

4. The government initially contested Hamdi's right to bring the writ. It argued, in the Fourth Circuit's words, that the federal courts "may not review at all its designation of an American citizen as an enemy

combatant" because "[the government's] determinations on this score are the first and final word." Hamdi v. Bush 296 F.3d 278, 283 (4th Cir. 2002). The Fourth Circuit refused to dismiss the habeas petition on this ground and remanded it to the District Court, declining to embrace by such a dismissal "a sweeping proposition, namely that, with no judicial review, any American citizen alleged to be an enemy combatant could be detained indefinitely without charges or counsel on the government's say so" (id.). After the Fourth Circuit's remand, apparently the government revised its position and did not dispute Padilla's or Hamdi's right to bring a habeas petition.

5. Both Padilla and Hamdi are American citizens. Padilla grew up in Chicago and New York, and then moved to Egypt after serving a prison sentence (Padilla at 572). Hamdi was born in this country, but moved to Saudi Arabia as a young child. (Hamdi at 460).

6. Alternatively, such suspected "enemy combatants," or at least the foreign nationals among them, may be tried at the President's discretion before special military commissions, rather than in Article III courts, which apply the extensive procedural protections accorded under the Constitution to defendants in criminal prosecutions.

So far no trials before military commissions have been ordered, though detailed rules to govern such trials have been promulgated. Those rules do not provide for such military trials of citizens.

7. The procedure used to determine probable cause, though it need not be adversarial in nature, "must provide a fair and reliable determination of probable cause as a condition for any significant pretrial restraint of liberty, and this determination must be made by a judicial officer either before or promptly after arrest". Id., 420 U.S. at 125.

8. Though concerned with a criminal prosecution, the Gerstein court pointed out "consequences of prolonged detention" that are not limited to the criminal context: confinement "may imperil the suspect's job, interrupt his source of income, and impair his family relationships." Id., 420 U.S. at 114.

9. The Court distinguished Shaughnessy v. Mezei as involving the indefinite detention of an alien held at the border, and therefore not subject to the due process protection afforded to aliens within the United States. 533 U.S. at 692–93. See p. 29 n.23. The Supreme Court recently has granted certiorari in a case challenging the indefinite detention of an illegal immigrant from Cuba who cannot be removed to Cuba. Benitez v. Wallis, 337 F.3d 1289 (11th Cir. 2003), cert. granted, 72 U.S.L.W. 3460 (U.S. Jan. 16, 2004) (No. 03-7434).

10. The "clear and convincing evidence" standard is required by 18 U.S.C. § 3142(e). However, cutting the other way, under § 3142(f) there is a "presumption," subject "to rebuttal," that the conditions justifying detention exist if the judicial officer finds "probable cause to believe" that the detainee has committed certain serious enumerated crimes: crimes of violence, serious drug offences, repeat offenses, and crimes for which the sentence can be life imprisonment or the death penalty. See United States v. Millan, 4 F.3d 1038, 1047 (2d Cir. 1993) (citing presumption, inter alia, in sustaining pre-trial detentions that to date of decision had exceeded two years).

11. The test distinguishing permissible regulatory from impermissible punitive confinement looks at the apparent statutory purpose, and also asks whether that alleged non-punitive purpose is rationally assignable to the detention, and whether the detention is excessive in relation to such purpose. Salerno, 481 U.S. at 746–47; Schall v. Martin, 467 U.S. 253, 269 (1984).

12. To anticipate the later portions of this report, we note the Court observed that terrorism might justify a different result:

Neither do we consider terrorism or other special circumstances where special arguments might be made for forms of preventive detention and for heightened deference to the judgments of the political branches with respect to matters of national security.

Id. at 696.

13. In Sterling v. Constantin, 387 U.S. 378 (1932), the Court cited Moyer for the proposition that the executive (the President or a Governor) has discretion "to determine whether [there existed] an exigency requiring military aid" to suppress insurrection and disorder, and possesses "a permitted range of honest judgment as to the measures to be taken in meeting force with force...." Id. at 399–400.

But the Sterling Court upheld a lower court injunction against action by the Governor of Texas to enforce through the national guard a state order limiting the production of oil, a restriction the federal court had ruled arbitrary and a violation of due process. The Governor had justified this action as required by "military necessity" due to an alleged state of insurrection in the East Texas area affected by the order. The Court, based on the factual record compiled below, in essence held this justification a pretext advanced in bad faith—there was no actual or threatened insurrection—and therefore beyond the "permitted range of honest judgment" accorded to the Governor in responding to disorder. Id. at 399–404.

14. In its 1987 Salerno decision, the Supreme Court cited Moyer for this rather sweeping dictum:

... in times of war or insurrection, when society's interest is at its peak, the Government may detain individuals whom the Government believes to be dangerous.

Salerno, 481 U.S. at 748.

15. Some do not believe that the Constitution's prohibition of the suspension of the writ is equivalent to a constitutional mandate that the writ be recognized in the first place. The question has been academic, since Congress as one of its first acts gave statutory recognition to the writ in the Judiciary Act of 1789. William H. Rehnquist, All the Laws But One: Civil Liberties in Wartime 37 (1988) ("Rehnquist").

16. As noted above, there seems to be no dispute that alleged enemy combatants detained in the United States have the procedural right to challenge their detention by means of a habeas corpus petition. The areas of procedural controversy concern the nature of the hearing to be afforded such petitioners: whether detainees have a right to counsel in connection with the hearing and a right to rebut at the hearing the government's showing that they are enemy combatants, and what showing is required by the government to justify the detention.

17. Gideon v. Wainwright, 372 U.S. 335 (1963), applied the same per se requirement to the states, through the Due Process Clause of the Fourteenth Amendment, rejecting the case-by-case approach of Betts v. Brady. See also Argersinger v. Hamlin, 407 U.S. 25 (1972).

After a conviction at a trial at which that right to counsel (and other procedural protections) has been respected, the prisoner does not have a right to appointed counsel when pressing a habeas or other collateral attack on the conviction. Coleman v. Thompson, 501 U.S. 722, 752–57 (1991); Pennsylvania v. Finley, 481 U.S. 551, 555–58 (1987); Murray v. Giarratano, 492 U.S. 1 (1989) (Finley rule applies to death penalty case). But no court appears to have denied petitioner the right, in connection with such collateral attacks, to appear through retained or pro bono counsel. Further, the government has some duty to facilitate a petitioner's pro se efforts to pursue a habeas petition. Bounds v. Smith, 430 U.S. 817, 828 (1977) (right of access to courts requires prison authorities to provide facilities to enable prisoners to prepare meaningful legal papers).

18. Statutes have extended a right to counsel in some circumstances where due process might or might not so require. Somewhat ironically, in light of the executive's refusal to afford "enemy combatant" suspected terrorists access to counsel, accused terrorists are guaranteed by statute the right to appointed counsel in proceedings under the Alien Terrorist Removal Act. 8 U.S.C. § 1534(c)(1).

19. For example, in school suspension hearings, in which the maximum suspension was 10 days, the Court did not construe due process to require that the student be afforded "the opportunity to secure counsel. ..." Goss v. Lopez, 419 U.S. 565, 583 (1973); see also Wolff v. McDonnel, 418 U.S. 539, 570 (1974) (no right to retained or appointed counsel in prison disciplinary proceedings); see Walters v. Nat'l Ass'n of Radiation Survivors, 473 U.S. 305 (1985) (statute prohibiting more than de minimis attorneys' fees in veterans benefit hearings upheld); Middendorf v. Henry, 425 U.S. 25 (1976) (a soldier faced with a summary court martial has no right to be represented by retained counsel; defendant could obtain counsel by demanding special court martial, thereby risking greater penalties if convicted).

The Court has twice declined to address whether a parolee, in a revocation hearing, "is entitled to the assistance of retained counsel," or to appointed counsel if indigent. Morrissey v. Brewer, 408 U.S. 471, 489 (1972); Gagnon v. Scarpelli, 411 U.S. 778, 783 n.6, 783–91 (1973) (adopting a case-by-case approach with respect to a right to appointed counsel, in probation revocation hearings, while not deciding whether parolee "has a right to be represented at a revocation hearing by retained counsel" under circumstances in which indigent parolee would not be entitled to appointed counsel).

20. The public, including the media, has a First Amendment right of access to criminal trials independent of the accused's Sixth Amendment right to a "public trial." Richmond Newspapers, Inc. v. Virginia, 448 U.S. 555 (1980). That public right of access has been extended to pretrial criminal proceedings,

Press-Enterprise Co. v. Superior Court, 478 U.S. 1 (1986), and, by circuit court authority, to civil trials, e.g., Westmoreland v. CBS, 752 F.2d 16, 23 (2d Cir. 1984), and, with the courts divided, to some administrative proceedings. Compare Detroit Free Press v. Ashcroft, 303 F.3d 681 (6th Cir. 2002) (recognizing right of access, subject to case-by-case determination, to deportation hearings), with North Jersey Media Group, Inc. v. Ashcroft, 308 F.3d 198 (3d Cir. 2002) (finding no such right of access), cert. denied, 123 S. Ct. 2215 (2003).

21. The requirement that the state prove guilt in a criminal case "beyond a reasonable doubt," expressly held a requirement of due process by In re Winship, 397 U.S. 358, 364 (1970), has been said to be "bottomed on a fundamental value determination of our society that it is far worse to convict an innocent man than to let a guilty man go free." (Id. at 372) (Harlan, J., concurring).

More expansively, the procedural protections of criminal law are sometimes said to reflect the sentiment that it is "better that 10 guilty persons escape than that one innocent suffer." However, the quoted sentiment is from Blackstone. 4 W. Blackstone Commentaries § 358.

22. See United States v. Verdugo-Urquidez, supra, 494 U.S. at 274–75 (search of Mexican national's home in Mexico by United States agents was not subject to Fourth Amendment's prohibition of unreasonable searches).

23. In stark contrast, procedural due process rights do not apply to aliens who have been excluded and held at the border (and therefore not deemed to have entered the country):

> . . .an alien seeking initial admission to the United States requests a privilege and has no constitutional rights regarding his application, for the power to admit or exclude aliens is a sovereign prerogative. Landon v. Plasencia, 459 U.S. 21, 32 (1981).

"Whatever the procedure authorized by Congress is, it is due process as far as an alien denied entry is concerned." United States ex rel. Knauff v. Shaughnessy, 338 U.S. 537, 544 (1950). Even such a detained and excluded alien, however, has the right to file a habeas proceeding to challenge his detention. Ekiu v. United States, 142 U.S. 651, 660 (1892).

24. Most constitutional rights have been held applicable to resident aliens, whether legal or illegal:

> [P]ersons who are not citizens receive the protection of all of the civil liberties guaranties of the constitution, and its amendments, except for the privileges and immunity clauses." R. Rotunda and J. Nowak, Treatise on Constitutional Law 528 (3d Ed. 1999).

See United States v. Verdugo-Urquidez, 494 U.S. 259, 271 (1990) (listing cases extending rights to aliens); Harisiades v. Shaughnessy, 342 U.S. 580, 586–87 n.10 (1952) (listing the respects in which the alien is not "conceded legal parity with the citizen", such as the right to vote and hold public office).

To be distinguished are "enemy aliens"—citizens of a country with whom the United States is engaged in a declared war—whom the President may detain or deport pursuant to the Enemy Alien Act, 50 U.S.C. §§ 21–24. Ludecke v. Watkins, 335 U.S. 160 (1948).

25. For a critical view of this "plenary power" doctrine, see Louis Henkin, The Constitution and United States Sovereignty: A Century of Chinese Exclusion and its Progeny, 100 Harv. L. Rev. 853 (1987).

26. Justice Kennedy, providing the fifth vote in a 5 to 4 decision, in a concurring opinion stated that due process required, as a condition to continued detention, that the alien be afforded a hearing at which the government would need to meet a "minimal, threshold burden" of showing there was "at least some merit" to its claim that the alien was within the class subject to mandatory detention, and that, consistent with Zadvydas, the alien "could be entitled to an individualized determination as to his risk of flight and dangerousness if the continued detention became unreasonable and unjustified." (Demore, 128 S. Ct. at 1722).

27 The concern about the release of state secrets is relevant to the current debate over whether terrorist suspects should be tried in Article III courts or by military commissions.

28. It bears noting, however, that the Court then acknowledged, albeit in dictum, some legal limits to the military authorities' power to intrude on the property and liberty of civilians, even during a period of civil unrest or insurrection. The Court said the state militia members "were justified in breaking and entering the plaintiff's house" if they acted upon "reasonable grounds." Id. at 45–46. The Court went on to specify that "[n]o more force. . .can be used than is necessary to accomplish the object," and that if "the

power is exercised for the purposes of oppression, or any injury willfully done to person or property, the party by whom or by whose order it is committed would undoubtedly be answerable," id. at 46, though the Court did not specify in what forum or at whose behest. See also Mitchell v. Harmony, 54 U.S. 115, 134–35 (1851) (claim in trespass sustained against lieutenant-colonel in army for seizure of private goods to facilitate lawful U.S. military expedition in Mexico; such seizures lawful only if officer has "reasonable ground for believing" they are required by an "immediate and impending" danger).

29. There was substantial political opposition to President Lincoln's wartime measures: "evidence from secession notwithstanding...educated Americans were convinced that Americans lived always under a rule of law." Hyman at 67. By the end of the war, it is said that the public seemed supportive of Lincoln's position that wartime necessity did not permit strict observance of peacetime legal restrictions on executive action. Id. at 131–40.

30. In 1863 Congress regularized Lincoln's procedures to a degree by formal legislation. It authorized the President to suspend the writ whenever during "the present rebellion" he judged that the public safety so required, while requiring that "political prisoners," as listed by the Secretaries of State and War within 20 days of their detention, be released unless indicted by a succeeding grand jury. Milligan, 71 U.S. at 114–15; see generally Hyman at 249–56. Excluded in practice from these lists of political prisoners were civilians facing courts-martial or military commission trials for military offenses, including guerrillas, saboteurs and spies, the closest analogues to today's terrorists. Hyman at 253–54.

31. It quickly became customary, and later official policy, to allow "prisoners who could afford the luxury to enjoy access to lawyers". Hyman at 82.

32. Merryman was accused of trying to block the passage of Union troops by railway from the north to the beleaguered Washington, D.C.

33. Chief Justice Taney's narrow view of the President's wartime powers may be viewed as in some tension with the general tenor of the Supreme Court's analysis in Luther, which Taney also authored. His hostility to the increase in federal power in service of the Union cause, and his enduring sympathy for states rights, is well documented. Hyman at 256–60.

34. The Court indicated that legislative recognition of a state of war was not required, but observed that if such congressional assent were needed, it could be found in many pieces of legislation enacted since the start of the war to assist in its prosecution. Id. at 670.

35. Lambdin P. Milligan, a well-known lawyer sympathetic to the Confederate cause, was convicted and sentenced to death for planning and organizing an attack upon the Democratic convention which was to be held in Chicago in 1864. Rehnquist at 21–23; Alex Abella & Scott Gordon, Shadow Enemies 140 (2002) ("Shadow Enemies").

36. The Court's clarion words echoed those of Milligan's brief, authored by future President James Garfield. Of a decision favorable to Milligan, he wrote:

> It will establish forever this truth, of inestimable value to us and to mankind, that a republic can wield a vast engine of war without breaking down the safeguards of liberty; can suppress insurrection, and put down rebellion, however formidable, without destroying the bulwarks of law; can by the might of its armed millions, preserve and defend both nationality and liberty. Quoted in Rehnquist at 23.

37. The majority's dictum against congressional power was highly controversial, regarded "as a gratuitous salvo against the plans of the Radicals for congressional reconstruction...." Rossiter at 30–31.

38. See Ex parte McCardle, 74 U.S. 506 (1868) (challenge by civilian facing military commission in Mississippi; Court holds it lacks appellate jurisdiction under Judiciary Act of 1867 in view of 1868 repeal of jurisdiction); Ex parte Yerger, 75 U.S. 85 (1868) (challenge by civilian held for military tribunal; Court finds continuing appellate jurisdiction under 1789 Judiciary Act).

To the extent that these jurisdictional decisions have relevance to our inquiry, they emphasize the strong reluctance of the Supreme Court to treat even a congressional enactment as effectively depriving the court of habeas appellate jurisdiction. See e.g., Yerger, 75 U.S. at 94–98, 100–02; Sandoval v. Reno, 166 F.3d 225, 231–32 (3d Cir. 1999) (discussing McCardle and Yerger). See also Felker v. Turpin, 518 U.S. 651, 660 (1996).

39. Decisions after the termination of hostilities in World War I did uphold the power of the political branches to decide when the consequences of the war, and therefore the need for wartime emergency statutes, had expired. See, e.g., Hamilton v. Kentucky Distilleries & Warehouse Co., 251 U.S. 146 (1919). See generally Note, Judicial Determination of the End of the War, 47 Colum. L. Rev. 255 (1947).

40. The Government's position was clearly stated in its brief:

"The fact is that ordinary constitutional doctrines do not impede the Federal Government in its dealings with enemies." [citations omitted]

The President's power over enemies who enter this country in time of war, as armed invaders intending to commit hostile acts, must be absolute. 317 U.S. at 12.

41. The district court had denied leave to file a petition, and the case was then heard within a few days by the Supreme Court. The Court announced its decision on the day after oral argument had been completed, summarily ruling against the petitioners on the merits. Id. at 11. At the same time it promised a written decision, which it issued several months later, after sentence had been pronounced by the Commission and a number of the detainees had been executed.

42. The law of war is a centuries' old branch of international law that "prescribes the rights and obligations of belligerents," and which "define[s] the status and relations not only of enemies—whether or not in arms—but also of persons under military government or martial law and persons simply resident or being upon the theatre of war, and which authorizes their trial and punishment when offenders." William Winthrop, Military Law and Precedents 773 (2d ed. 1920). "Such laws and customs would especially be taken into consideration by military commissions in passing upon offences in violation of the laws of war." Id. at 42.

43. The Court read the Constitution in this light even though the Amendments do contain a specific exception for "cases arising in the land and naval forces," and do not otherwise restrict the scope of the grand jury and civil jury guarantees for any other persons. Id. at 41–44. The Court held: "We cannot say that Congress in passing the Fifth and Sixth Amendments intended to extend trial by jury to the cases of alien or citizen offenders against the law of war otherwise triable by military commission, while withholding it from members of our own armed forces.. . ." Id. at 44.

44. See Instructions for the Government of Armies of the United States in the Field, promulgated as General Orders No. 100 by President Lincoln, April 24, 1863, reprinted in The Laws of Armed Conflicts 3 (D. Schindler & J. Toman, eds., 1988). The Lieber Instructions were prepared by Francis Lieber, then a professor of Columbia College. They became a strong influence on later codifications of the law of war by other states and international tribunals.

45. Convention (III) Relative to the Treatment of Prisoners of War, signed at Geneva, August 12, 1949 (consented to by the United States Senate on July 6, 1955, with reservations). 6 U.S.T 3316, 75 U.N.T.S. 136 ("Third Geneva Convention").

46. Prisoners of war are entitled to various rights and privileges as set forth in the Third Geneva Convention. As lawful combatants they are not subject to prosecution and "shall be released and repatriated without delay after the cessation of active hostilities." Art. 18. See Ruth Wedgwood, al Qaeda, Terrorism and Military Commissions, 96 Am. J. Int'l L. 328, 333 (April 2002) (hereafter cited as "Wedgwood").

47. The Supreme Court's decision in Duncan v. Kahanamoku suggests that Milligan remained good law after Quirin, to the extent that Milligan prohibits the trial of civilians by military commission for actions not constituting violations of the law of war. The majority opinion cited Milligan with approval (id. at 322, 324), and Justice Murphy, concurring, expressly reaffirmed Milligan's "open court" rule (id. at 328–35).

48. But see Mudd v. Caldera, 134 F. Supp. 2d, 138, 145–47 (D.D.C. 2001), appeal denied, 309 F.3d 819 (D.C. Cir. 2002) (military commission had jurisdiction to try Dr. Samuel Mudd for aiding and abetting assassination of Lincoln, a military offense violating the law of war; Quirin does not limit the jurisdiction of military commissions to persons acting under direction of enemy armed forces).

49. Quirin found it did not need "to determine to what extent the President as Commander in Chief has constitutional power to create military commissions without the support of Congressional legislation," for "here Congress has authorized trial of offenses against the law of war before such commissions." 317 U.S. at 29.

50. The Court referred to the asserted facts, inter alia, that (i) "social, economic and political conditions which have prevailed since the close of the last century, when the Japanese began to come to this country in substantial numbers, have intensified their solidarity and have in large measure prevented assimilation as an integral part of the white population," (ii) many children of Japanese parentage were sent to after-school Japanese language training, sometimes at schools "generally believed to be sources of Japanese nationalistic propaganda, cultivating allegiance to Japan," and (iii) Japan recognized dual citizenship. Id. at 96–97.

51. Korematsu, widely condemned in retrospect, was not without vigorous dissents. Justice Murphy, for one, opined that the exclusion order "'goes over the very brink of constitutional power' and falls into the ugly abyss of racism." Id. at 233.

It also bears noting that, on the same day it upheld the exclusion order in Korematsu on constitutional grounds, the Court, in Ex parte Endo, 323 U.S. 283 (1944), construed the regulations governing the relocation centers to require the release of "citizens who are concededly loyal." Id. at 297.

52. The Fourth Circuit's opinion, in fact, is notable for its several rhetorical flourishes recognizing the importance of civil liberties and the writ of habeas corpus, even in times of war. It was emphatic that "the detention of United States citizens must be subject to judicial review" by means of the writ of habeas corpus, consistent with the writ's "essential function of assuring that restraint accords with the rule of law, not the whim of authority. . . ." Id. at 464–65. See also:

> The duty of the judicial branch to protect our individual freedoms does not simply cease whenever our military forces are committed by the political branches to armed conflict. Id. at 464.

53. The court vigorously criticized the district court's orders in connection with that court's plan to conduct an evidentiary hearing on the legality of the detention, i.e., that Hamdi have unmonitored access to his court-appointed lawyer and that the government disclose detailed information concerning Hamdi's seizure and interrogation. The Fourth Circuit found those orders, which it had earlier stayed, unacceptably to intrude into the President's authority and to show insufficient deference to the war-making powers of the two political branches. Id. at 462, 469–71.

54. In United States v. Lindh, 212 F. Supp. 2d 541 (E.D. Va. 2002), the District Court was similarly deferential to the President's finding that an American citizen fighting with the Taliban and captured in Afghanistan was an 'unlawful combatant' and so not subject to immunity from prosecution as a prisoner of war under the Geneva Convention. The court found that "conclusive deference, which amounts to judicial abstention, is plainly inappropriate." Id. at 556–57. The court proceeded to examine the President's finding in light of Geneva Convention Article 4, which sets forth the criteria for determining unlawful combatant status, and held that the Taliban forces were unlawful as lacking a command structure, distinctive uniforms and compliance with the law of war. Id. at 557–58.

55. Padilla did refer to Padilla's potential ability to demonstrate, at some point in the future, that the evidence used to support his enemy combatant classification had been "entirely mooted by subsequent events." Id. at 608. This may envision a possible showing that operations against al Qaeda had ended, or that "the operational capacity of al Qaeda [had been]. . .effectively destroyed" (id. at 590), or that Padilla's usefulness as a source of intelligence had been exhausted, at which point continuing the detention might no longer bear "a reasonable relation to the purpose for which the individual [was] committed." Zadvydas, 533 U.S. at 690.

Judge Wesley's dissenting opinion in the Second Circuit strikes a somewhat similar note with respect to the purpose of the detention:

> Certainly, a court could inquire whether Padilla continues to possess information that was helpful to the President in prosecuting the war against al Qaeda. Presumably, if he does not, the President would be required to charge Padilla criminally or delineate the appropriate process by which Padilla would remain under the President's control. See, e.g., Zadvydas v. Davis, 533 U.S. 678 (2001).

Padilla Cir. at 733.

56. As to the government's argument that Padilla might use his lawyer to pass messages to terrorists—echoing charges in an unrelated pending case—the court found, after reviewing the sealed Mobbs declaration, that such conjecture amounted to only "gossamer speculation." Id. at 604. It noted that the military

would be able to monitor the attorney-client communications, so long as the monitors were insulated from any further involvement with court proceedings. Id. The court cited in this regard the procedures for monitoring attorney-client communications recently promulgated at 28 C.F.R. § 501.3(a).

57. Since these decisions, in December 2003 the government announced it would permit Hamdi to consult with his attorneys. The Department of Defense announced on December2, 2003, that Hamdi "will be allowed access to a lawyer" because it had "completed its intelligence collection with Hamdi." Its press release billed this decision as a matter of discretion," and "not required by domestic or international law . . . ." The government, in its unsuccessful brief in opposition to Hamdi's petition for a writ of certiorari, described the new position in these words:

> As a matter of discretion and military policy, the Department of Defense (DOD) has adopted a policy of permitting access to counsel by an enemy combatant who is a United States citizen and who is detained by the military in the United States, when DOD has determined that such access will not compromise the national security of the United States, and when DOD has determined either that it has completed intelligence collection from the enemy combatant or that granting access to counsel would not interfere with such intelligence gathering. In accordance with DOD's policy and the military's ongoing evaluation of Hamdi's detention, DOD has determined that Hamdi may be permitted access to counsel subject to appropriate security restrictions. See http://www.dod.gov/releases/2003/ nr20031202-0717.html.

Resp't Hamdi Brief at 25–26 n.11.

58. As a practical matter the Hamdi court's holding would mean that the Geneva Convention is unenforceable in the war on terror, since neither the defeated and dissolved Taliban nor the terrorist organization al Qaeda is capable of diplomacy.

The Lindh court held, consistent with Padilla, that the Geneva Convention was enforceable by the defendant before it, but that he was an unlawful combatant and thus not entitled to immunity from prosecution under the Convention. Lindh, 212 F. Supp. 2d at 553.

59. Some urge that the principles of international law should be applied by American courts in reviewing or limiting the purported exercise of the war power by the President. See Jordan J. Paust, Judicial Power to Determine the Status and Rights of Persons Detained Without Trial, 44 Harv. Inter. L.J. G4 (2003). But the invocation of "customary international law" as part of American law is problematic, for there often is no clear consensus on its content. See generally Flores v. Southern Peru Cooper Corp., 343 F.3d 140 (2d Cir. 2003) (construing the Alien Tort Claims Act's embrace of torts "committed in violation of the law of nations," 28 U.S.C. § 1350). No principles of customary international law—"those rules that States universally abide, or to which they accede, out of a sense of legal obligation and mutual concern" (id. at 158)—appear to either clearly permit or prohibit the detention of illegal combatants in the context of the war on terror. Like the law of war, customary international law speaks with an especially uncertain voice in the context of stateless terrorism. See Paust, supra, at G11 n.30.

60. The Central District of California recently enjoined the enforcement of the "expert advice and assistance" clause of the cited section of the USA PATRIOT ACT, finding it to be unconstitutionally vague. Humanitarian Law Project v. Ashcroft, No. CV 03-6107 (C.D. Cal. Jan. 22, 2004). For an analogous holding by the Southern District of New York.

61. It may well be that the "enemy combatant" detentions have been infrequently employed in the United States to date because the executive has been able to detain other suspects in other ways. Numerous aliens have been detained on immigration charges and a lesser number have been detained as "material witnesses," Padilla's initial status, under 18 U.S.C. § 3144. Further, a large group of alleged "enemy combatants" seized abroad is being held at the Guantanamo Bay Naval Base in Cuba, detentions which present distinct issues not addressed in this report.

62. The usual predicate for the "some evidence" standard is a review of administrative fact-finding. In that context, "some" evidence can be "meager" evidence. See Superintendent v. Hill, 472 U.S. 445, 457 (1985) (review of prison disciplinary decision). The "some evidence" standard "is not intended as a substantive check on the accuracy of administrative fact-finding." Butler v. Oak Creek-Franklin School District, 172 F. Supp. 2d 1102, 1118 (E.D. Wis. 2001) (school disciplinary hearing).

63. Truly extreme instances of abuse might be held to violate substantive due process, but the vagueness of that standard makes it a poor vehicle for controlling exercises of the war power.

64. Compare this observation by Justice Stewart, concurring in the "Pentagon Papers" case, commenting on the Executive's "enormous powers in the two related areas of national defense and international relations":

> In the absence of the governmental checks and balances present in other areas of our national life, the only effective restraint upon executive policy and power in the areas of national defense and international affairs may lie in an enlightened citizenry—in an informed and critical public opinion which alone can here protect the values of democratic government.

New York Times Co. v. United States, 403 U.S. 713, 728 (1971).

65. Cf. Graham v. Richardson, 403 U.S. 365, 372 (1971):

> Aliens as a class are a prime example of a "discrete and insular" minority . . . for whom . . . heightened judicial solicitude is appropriate. (citations omitted).

66. In a poll conducted for National Public Radio in November 2001, the respondents were equally divided—48% to 48%, with 4% "don't know"—on whether the government should have the authority to "detain terrorist suspects indefinitely without charging them." NPR/Kaiser/Kennedy School Survey on Civil Liberties, available at www.npr.org/programs/specials/poll/civilliberties/civillibertiesstaticresults_4.html.

67. The government's secret detentions of these unidentified aliens, most held on immigration charges, have (so far) been upheld by the courts. Center for National Security Studies v. United States Department of Justice, 331 F.3d 918 (D.C. Cir. 2003), cert. denied, No. 03-472 (Jan. 12, 2004). Compare, in the non-immigration context, the comment that "secret arrests" represent a "concept odious to a democratic society." Morrow v. District of Columbia, 417 F.2d 728, 741–42 (D.C. Cir. 1969).

68. However, nationality-based immigration policies have been implemented. See David Stout, Ridge Moves to Tighten Security Ahead of an Iraq War, N.Y. Times, WYSIWYG//12/ http://www.nytimes.com/2003/03/18/politics/18CND-Home.htm (noting new order by Homeland Security Department to detain all persons seeking political asylum if they arrived from any of 34 countries).

69. Similarly, President Roosevelt in World War II, in announcing to Congress that he would impose stringent ceilings on food prices if Congress failed to act, proclaimed:

> When the war is won, the powers under which I act automatically revert to the people—to whom they belong.

Quoted in Edward S. Corwin, The War and the Constitution: President and Congress, 37 American Political Science Review 18, 19 (1943).

70. Remarks of President Bush, Sept. 10, 2003, at FBI Academy, Quantico, Virginia (White House website).

71. Salerno opens the door to preventive detentions in the context of pre-trial detentions, but still subject to both a prior probable-cause finding and the speedy trial guarantee of the Sixth Amendment.

72. Concerns of this nature informed Justice Jackson's dissent in Korematsu. Citing Cardozo's reference to "the tendency of a principle to expand itself to the limits of its logic" (Nature of the Judicial Process 51), Jackson argued that the Court should not lend its imprimatur to a military decision, reasonable as such but unconstitutional in principle, since the Court's ruling would have a "generative power of its own," beyond that of the military order. Korematsu, 323 U.S. at 246.

73. Compare Center for National Security Studies v. United States Dep't of Justice, 331 F.3d at 932 (D.D.C. 4003) (reversing decision under FOIA requiring disclosure concerning post 9/11 detainees: "the courts must defer to the executive on decisions of national security"), with United States v. Moussaoui, 336 F.3d 279, 282 (4th Cir. 2003) (Wilkins, C.J., concurring in denial of rehearing en banc) ("Siding with the Government in all cases where national security concerns are asserted would entail surrender of the independence of the judicial branch and abandon our sworn commitment to the rule of law").

74. Examples from the Human Rights Watch website of such statements include:

On December 16, 2001, [Egyptian] President Mubarak asserted that new U.S. policies "prove that we were right from beginning in using all means, including military tribunals....There is no doubt that the events of September 11 created a new concept of democracy that differs from the concept that Western states defended before these events, especially in regard to the freedom of the individual," Mubarak said.

In comments to a Washington Post columnist in November 2002, Eritrea's Ambassador to the United States justified his government's arrest of journalists by claiming that detention without charge was consistent with the practices of democratic countries. He cited the roundup of material witnesses and aliens suspected of terrorist activities in the United States as proof.

www.hrw.org/campaigns/september11/opporrtunismwatch.htm (Dec. 17, 2003).

75. In addition, as Judge Mukasey observed, neither Quirin nor any other case addresses the appropriate standard of review with respect to the classification of a particular person as an illegal combatant. Padilla necessarily covered new ground in holding that such classifications are subject to judicial review only on a deferential "some evidence" standard.

76. The absence of case law does not end the inquiry, for "practical construction"—action on the ground—may constitute relevant precedent. See Quirin, 317 U.S. at 35–36 (relying on the practice of military authorities recognizing illegal combatants); see also Hyman at 558–59 (bemoaning distorted "case-centered" historical analysis). Justice Frankfurter, in his Youngstown concurrence, would recognize an "executive construction of the Constitution," (Youngstown, 343 U.S. at 613), citing United States v. Midwest Oil Co., 236 U.S. 459 (1915), but only on a showing of "a systematic, unbroken, executive practice, long pursued to the knowledge of the Congress and never before questioned...." (Youngstown, 343 U.S. at 610–11).

The only apparent candidate for such an "executive construction" with respect to detentions appears to be Lincoln's policy during the Civil War, when military detentions of alleged Confederate sympathizers are said to have been frequent.

However, the dramatically different circumstances of the Civil War, an armed rebellion on American soil, minimize the relevance of any such precedents to the domestic war on terror. Further, Lincoln's unique actions hardly meet the Frankfurter test of a "systemic unbroken" practice "long pursued," and in fact were sharply questioned at the time and invalidated in the only two court decisions on point, Merryman and Milligan.

77. Edward S. Corwin, writing in 1947, came out at about the same place:

The restrictive clauses of the Constitution are not, as to the *citizen at least,* automatically suspended, but the scope of the rights to which they extend is capable of being reduced in face of the urgencies of war, sometimes even to the vanishing point, depending on the demands of the war. Theoretically these will be determined by the President and then Congress, subject to judicial review; actually the Court will not intrude its veto while war is flagrant.

Corwin at 131.

78. Milligan, decided the year after the Civil War ended, emphasized, with surprising candor, that the Court was able to address the question before it dispassionately precisely because the war had concluded:

During the late wicked Rebellion, the temper of the times did not allow that calmness in deliberation and discussion so necessary to a correct conclusion of a purely judicial question. *Then,* considerations of safety were mingled with the exercise of power; and feelings and interests prevailed which are happily terminated. *Now* that the public safety is assured, this question, as well as all others, can be discussed and decided without passion or the admixture of any element not required to form a legal judgment. 71 U.S. at 109 (italics in original).

As Rossiter observes:

It is one thing for a court to lecture a President when the emergency has passed, quite another to stand up in the middle of the battle and inform him that he is behaving unconstitutionally.

Rossiter at 38.

The hazard in the latter course is illustrated by Justice Taney's 1861 decision in Merryman, in the early days of the Civil War, ruling Lincoln's suspension of habeas corpus unconstitutional: the President simply ignored the ruling in his conduct of the war. Hyman at 89.

79. The Court offered no explanation for its conclusion that the President's war power, absent congressional authorization, did not embrace the seizure of domestic industries. The conclusion seemed obvious to the Court, but for reasons it chose not to articulate.

This assertion of judicial power in Youngstown must have surprised Rossiter, who only the year before had written as follows concerning a President's power to seize industries to aid the war effort:

Nor can there be any doubt that under the conditions of modern war the President has a broad constitutional power to seize and operate industrial facilities in which production has been halted, a power which, like his other powers of martial law, is virtually impossible to define or control.

Rossiter at 63.

80. At the other extreme, the insistence of Milligan that war and peace make no difference in constitutional terms also finds little echo in the caselaw (or common sense). Milligan's words are clarion: the Constitution "is a law for rulers and people, equally in war and in peace, and covers...all classes of men at all times, and under all circumstances." Milligan, 71 U.S. at 120–121. But no case has adopted Milligan's view that it is constitutionally impossible even for Congress and even in emergency circumstances to adopt wartime measures that limit individual rights in a way not limited in peacetime. Due process is not so rigid:

Early constitutional absolutism is replaced by constitutional relativity; it all depends—a result that has been definitely aided in the case of substantive rights by the modern conception of due process of law as 'reasonable law'—that is to say, what the Supreme Court finds to be reasonable in the circumstances.

Corwin at 80.

81. Louis Henkin, writing in 1972, pointed out the transformation in the role of the Constitution, as applied by the Supreme Court, with respect to individual rights. While "there was hardly a case during more than a hundred years [after adoption of the Constitution] in which the courts invalidated federal action on the ground that it violated an individual's constitutional rights"—Dred Scott (recognizing the property rights of the slave owner) being the only such pre-Civil War case—more recently for the courts "the Constitution has become primarily a bulwark for the individual against government excess." Louis Henkin, Foreign Affairs and the Constitution 251–52 (1972).

82. In Campbell, a group of Congressmen challenged President Clinton's authority to direct American armed forces to participate in the NATO military campaign in Yugoslavia, in the absence of a congressional declaration of war or authorization under the War Powers Resolution (50 U.S.C. § 1541 et seq.). The court held the plaintiffs lacked standing and Judge Silberman, concurring, also added that "what constitutes a war" was a non-justifiable political question.

83. Admittedly, the Korean War, which Justice Jackson addressed, did not involve attacks on American soil. Nor is the labor-management context of Youngstown closely analogous to Padilla, involving seizure of a suspected terrorist as he entered this country. But, on the other side, Truman's action in Youngstown affected only property rights, while the indefinite detentions violate core due process values.

84. As Hamdi illustrates, a citizen has the right to pursue habeas relief in the domestic courts even when detained abroad. But given the scope of the President's war power abroad, a citizen seized abroad as an illegal combatant in a military setting may well be denied substantive relief, as Hamdi also illustrates, at least in the short term when such relief might interfere with an ongoing military campaign.

By this we do not mean to minimize the issues in Hamdi, which also implicates due process concerns. The justification for the incommunicado, long-term interrogation and detention of a foot soldier in the Taliban armed forces, if that is all Hamdi was, seems hard to square with the Third Geneva Convention, or to justify on the basis of any apparent need. As to what Hamdi was, the facts concerning his combatant status may not be as indisputable as the court concluded. See Hamdi v. Rumsfeld, 337 F.3d 335, 357–64 (4th Cir. 2003) (Luttig, J. dissenting from denial of rehearing en banc, arguing that circumstances of Hamdi's seizure were neither conceded in fact nor "susceptible to concession in law, because Hamdi has not been permitted to speak for himself or even through counsel" (id. at 357)).

85. Congress, in the Posse Comitatas Act, 18 U.S.C. § 1385, passed in 1878 in reaction to the use of the armed forces to support reconstruction in the south, precluded the use of the armed forces "to execute the laws," except "in cases and under circumstances expressly authorized by the Constitution or act of Congress...."

In passing the Homeland Security Act in 2002, Congress reaffirmed "the continued importance" of the Posse Comitatas Act, 6 U.S.C. § 466(b). However, it also affirmed that the Act did not bar the President's use of the armed forces when required "to respond promptly in time of war, insurrection or other serious emergency" (6 U.S.C. § 466(a)(4)).

86. According to the Department of Justice's website, as of January 30, 2004, 284 suspected terrorists have been charged in United States courts, with 149 convicted. (www.lifeandliberty.gov/ subs/a_terr.htm).

87. See generally Clinton Rossiter, Constitutional Dictatorship (1948) (arguing that such is necessary in times of great national peril, such as total war).

88. Having exhausted its interrogation of Hamdi, the Department of Defense explains his continued detention as "not criminal in nature but...permitted under the law of war to prevent an enemy combatant from continuing to fight against the United States" (Press Release, Dec. 2, 2003).

89. Here is one forceful expression of this concern:

> The prime source of intelligence [concerning anticipated terrorist attacks] will be captured combatants; and lawyers, alas, will inevitably turn off that flow of time critical information.
>
> * * *
>
> Any lawyer worth his salt will deliver standard form advice to a client: Keep your mouth shut. Don't talk. Not in court and not in military interviews.

Ruth Wedgwood, Lawyers at War, Wall St. J., Feb. 18, 2003.

90. The case also might be held in a state of suspense—with appropriate Speedy Trial Act findings—while intelligence officials pursue their inquiries.

91. Justice Jackson cautions about permitting the President "of his own volition," to "invest himself with undefined emergency powers." "[E]mergency powers are consistent with free government only when their control is lodged elsewhere than the Executive who exercises them." Youngstown, 343 U.S. at 651.

92. Hirabayashi is said to be:

> perhaps the most clear-cut case on record of the Court's tendency to insist that unusual military actions be grounded, whenever possible, on the combined powers of President and Congress, which when merged are called simply the war powers of the United States.

Rossiter at 47.

93. The Second Circuit's opinion relies principally on the Constitution's allocation of certain specific powers to Congress, not the President: Article I, § 8, cl. 10 (power to define offenses against the laws of nations), Article I, § 9, cl. 2 (suspension of habeas corpus), and the Third Amendment (quartering of soldiers in houses in time of war without owner's consent, permitted only as "prescribed by law"). Padilla Cir. at 714–15.

In our view this analysis is somewhat conclusory. Enemy combatant detentions inescapably require the courts to balance the interests of national security with due process rights. The Constitution's allocation of specific powers to Congress may help inform this balancing task, but it does not avoid it. The balancing required should place heavy weight on the due process values at stake. The Second Circuit's opinion does not expressly recognize those constitutional values as having independent force, entitled to protection by the courts (at least presumptively) even in times of war. It makes only passing reference to the "individual liberty rights" implicated by the detentions, in distinguishing the property interests at stake in The Prize Cases (Padilla Cir. at 717–18), and pays an unexplained tribute to the "guarantees of the Fourth and Fifth Amendments to the Constitution." Id. at 724.

We also would not be as absolutist as the Second Circuit's separation of powers analysis. We believe that the President has some war power to act domestically in emergency circumstances. On the other hand, congressional action authorizing indefinite detentions would not obviate the need for the courts to address due process concerns, as the Second Circuit's opinion may assume.

94. Compare the op ed comment by Prof. Viet Dinh, a former assistant attorney general: "After two years of unofficial criticism...it is time for Congress to contribute its voice—either to affirm the president's authority or suggest refinements to administration policy." Justice for All, Wall St. J., Dec. 15, 2003, at A14.

95. In this context we are troubled by this Second Circuit's dictum in its Padilla decision, quoting the discredited Hirabayashi:

> To be sure, when Congress and the President act together in the conduct of war, "it is not for any court to sit in review of the wisdom of their action and substitute its judgment for theirs." Hirabayashi v. United States, 320 U.S. 81, 93 (1943).

Padilla Cir. at 713.

Again, we say it depends on what kind of "war" and just what measures are taken in its pursuit. Surely the Second Circuit would not hesitate to "sit in review," during the "war" on terror, of a congressionally authorized curfew directed solely at all Arabs and Muslims, similar to the Japanese curfew upheld in Hirabayashi itself.

96. Other suggested approaches may include the creation of specialized so-called "terrorism courts" that would be empowered to try individuals charged with specified terrorism-related offenses while offering core due-process protections. See, e.g., Powers, Due Process for Terrorists? The Case for a Federal Terrorism Court, The Weekly Standard, Jan. 12, 2004. We take no position on any such proposals, but strongly urge that any dilution of long-accepted due process procedures be rejected without, at a minimum, a clear and considered congressional imprimatur.

97. Compare the reported recent remarks by Judge Michael Chertoff, former head of the Justice Department's Criminal Division, suggesting that "we need to debate a long-term sustainable architecture for the process of determining when, why and for how long someone may be detained as an enemy combatant, and what judicial review should be available." R. Schmitt, Patriot Act Author Has Concerns, L.A. Times, Nov. 3, 2003 (www.informationclearinghouse.info/articles5325.htm).

98. The Joint Resolution would appear to authorize at least Hamdi's initial detention in Afghanistan, which was closely related to the engagement of the Armed Forces pursuant to the Joint Resolution against the Taliban, because of its sheltering of al Qaeda.

99. Such a continuing detention, of course, would require confronting the due process question posed by indefinite detentions, a question the Zadvydas Court avoided by narrowly construing the statute before it.

100. The Second Circuit views 18 U.S.C. § 4001(a) as casting in doubt the continuing "usefulness" of Quirin (Padilla Cir. at 716), and it did unearth a few references in the congressional debates on 18 U.S.C. 4001(a) that focused specifically on the possible impact of the proposed statute in precluding executive detentions of suspected spies and saboteurs in wartime (id. at 719–20).

Since we do not view Quirin as a detention case, we do not view the statute as relevant to Quirin. If, as Quirin held, trial by military commission has been authorized by Congress, it follows that a detention in service of such a trial has congressional sanction.

101. A caveat is in order with respect to the seizure of citizens abroad in a theater of armed military conflict, the facts presented in Hamdi.

102. Military Order Regarding Detention, Treatment, and Trial of Certain Non-Citizens in the War Against Terrorism, 66 Fed. Reg. 57833 (November 13, 2001).

103. Quirin's analysis, predicated on no directly supportive legal authority, has come into considerable question since its issuance, including by some of the participating justices. See, e.g., David J. Danelski, The Saboteurs' Case, 21 J. Sup. Ct. Hist. 61, 72–80 (1996); Michael R. Belknap, The Supreme Court Goes to War: The Meaning and Implications of the Nazi Saboteur Case, 89 Mili. L. Rev. 59, 81–90 (1980); Katyal & Tribe, 111 Yale L.J. at 1282–83, 1290–91.

104. Article of War 15, as now codified as Article 21 at 10 U.S.C. § 821, states:

The provisions of this chapter conferring jurisdiction upon courts-martial do not deprive military commissions, provost courts, or other military tribunals of concurrent jurisdiction with respect to offenders or offenses that by the law of war may be tried by military commissions, provost courts, or other military tribunals.

105. For a tightly reasoned contrary view, see Katyal & Tribe, 111 Yale L.J. at 1286–90.

106. E.g., Articles of War, 15 H.R. Doc. No. 81-491 (1949); S. Rep. No. 81-486 (1949). See generally Loving v. United States, 517 U.S. 748, 752–53 (1996).

107. These reforms were made in response to allegations that courts-martial held during World War II (up to 2 million) were arbitrary and lacked independence. Cox Commission, Report of the Commission on the 50th Anniversary of the Uniform Code of Military Justice 2 (May 2001) ("Cox Commission").

108. Article 36(a), UCMJ, provides that procedures, including "modes of proof," for courts-martial, as well as military commissions

may be prescribed by the President by regulations which shall, so far as he considers practicable, apply the principles of law and the rules of evidence generally recognized in the trial of criminal cases in the United States district courts.

Courts-martial procedure is governed by the detailed and comprehensive Manual for Courts-Martial (2002 ed.)

109. Loving v. United States, 517 U.S. 748, 770 (1996) (the Supreme Court interpreted Article 36 as "indicative of congressional intent to delegate [the authority to proscribe aggravating circumstances in capital cases] to the President...").

110. The courts-martial system has jurisdiction over, *inter alia,* active duty members of the armed forces or those working with the armed forces, persons accompanying an armed force in the field during times of war, certain retired servicemen, certain areas under the control of the armed forces "subject to any treaty or agreement", volunteers and those under reserve duty. UCMJ Art. 2.

111. Courts-martials under the Articles of War also applied "in time of war" to "all persons not citizens of, or owing allegiance to, the United States of America, who shall be found lurking as spies in or about the fortifications or encampments of the armies of the United States...." Articles of War, Spies, Sec. 2. 2 Stat. 359–72 (1806).

112. Formerly the United States Military Court of Appeals. See http://www.armfor.uscourts.gov.

113. See generally Cox Commission. An informative website on this topic is Citizens Against Military Injustice, http://www.militaryinjustice.org.

114. Petitions for certiorari are also possible from the Court of Appeals for the Armed Forces to the Supreme Court. UCMJ Article 67 (a), and 28 U.S.C. § 1259.

115. United States ex rel. Toth v. Quarles. 350 U.S. 11 (1955).

116. McElroy v. United States ex rel. Guagliardo, 361 U.S. 281 (1960).

117. Reid v. Covert, 354 U.S. 1 (1957); Kinsella v. United States ex rel. Singleton, 361 U.S. 234 (1960) (wife of soldier charged with his murder).

118. In O'Callahan v. Parker, 396 U.S. 258 (1969), the Court had ruled that the rape of a civilian woman in an off-base hotel room by an active duty soldier was outside of the jurisdiction of a court-martial. The Court's opinion rejected, largely on due process grounds, the courts-martial system as an appropriate venue for trying either civilians or military personnel charged with non-military related criminal acts. In 1987 the Court overruled O'Callahan, and a subsequent case, Relford v. Commandant, 401 U.S. 355 (1971), and reinstated the former rule which based jurisdiction solely upon the military or civilian status of the accused. Solario v. United States, 483 U.S. 435, 447 (1987).

119. See also Shadow Enemies at 136–141 (discussing the use of military commissions in the Revolutionary War, the Mexican-American War, the Civil War and other conflicts); Maj. Michael O. Lacey, Military Commissions: A Historical Survey, Army Law. 41, 41–47 (March 2002) ("Lacey"); NIMJ Guide 4–5.

120. Maj. Timothy C. MacDonnell, Military Commissions and Courts-Martial: A Brief Discussion of the Constitutional and Jurisdictional Distinctions Between the Two Courts, Army Law 19 (March 2002) ("MacDonnell").

121. Quirin at 13 n.10; MacDonnell at 28.

122. Quirin at 13 n.10. Military commissions were used during the Civil War to try Confederate soldiers who had shed their uniforms in attempts to take over civilian ships or commit acts of sabotage, as well as to try spies. Id., 317 U.S. at 31–32, n.9, n.10.

123. Like Quirin, Yamashita upheld the right of habeas corpus to test the authority of the military commission to proceed. "[Congress] has not withdrawn, and the Executive branch of the government could not, unless there was a suspension of the writ, withdraw from the courts the duty and power to make such inquiry into the authority of the Commission as may be made by habeas corpus." 327 U.S. at 9.

124. Duncan v. Kahanamoku, 327 U.S. 304 (1946), reaffirmed this limiting principle in construing the legislation that authorized the declaration of "martial law" in Hawaii during World War II. The Court emphatically rejected the argument that Congress had authorized the military to arrest civilians in Hawaii and try them before military commissions, not for violations of the law of war but rather for civilian offenses. The Court's conclusion that the statutory use of the term "martial law" did not permit the military to supplant otherwise available civilian courts in trying civilian offenses was said to rest on the bedrock of constitutional case law and practice since the Revolutionary War. See id. at 319–24 (citing inter alia, Milligan and emphasizing that "[c]ourts and their procedural safeguards are indispensable to our system of government." Id. at 322).

125. Manual for Courts-Martial, Preamble paragraph 2(b) (2); see generally NIMJ Guide 77–80.

126. City Bar Report at 18.

127. Section 2(c) provides that "any individual subject to this order...shall...forthwith be placed under the control of the Secretary of Defense."

128. Section 3 provides that "[a]ny individual subject to this order shall be—(a) detained at an appropriate location designated by the Secretary of Defense outside or within the United States."

129. Section 4(c)(3): permits the "admission of such evidence as would...have probative value to a reasonable person."

130. Section 7(b) provides, with respect to "any individual subject to this order," that

(1) military tribunals shall have exclusive jurisdiction with respect to offenses by the individual; and
(2) the individual shall not be privileged to seek any remedy or maintain any proceeding, directly or indirectly, or to have any such remedy or proceeding sought on the individual's behalf, in (i) any court of the United States, or any State thereof, (ii) any court of any foreign nation, or (iii) any international tribunal.

The Supreme Court has in the past heard habeas petitions and reviewed the jurisdiction and authority of a military commission despite similarly limiting language. See p. 45 n.38 above; Quirin, 317 U.S. at 23–25.

131. The term "state secrets" is not well-defined in the law, even in the privilege context. See NIMJ Guide 87.

132. Another alternative alluded to by commentators is the possibility of referring at least some terrorism detainees to an international tribunal. See, e.g., Harold Hongju Koh, "The Case Against Military Commissions", 96 Am. J. Int'l L. 337, 339 n.30 (2002). Since our government has forcefully opposed the creation of a permanent international criminal court and has offered no indication that it sees a special multi-national court to be an appropriate means of dealing with suspects detained by the United States, we focus on American-controlled methods of handling such detainees.

133. Article III, section 3, of the Constitution provides:

Treason against the United States, shall consist only in levying War against them, or in adhering to their Enemies, giving them Aid and Comfort. No Person shall be convicted of Treason unless on the Testimony of two Witnesses to the same overt Act, or on Confession in open Court.

134. The court in Sattar later held that 18 U.S.C. § 2339B was unconstitutionally vague as applied to the specific allegations of the indictment that defendants had "provided" telecommunications equipment (through use of a telephone) and personnel (by their own conduct) to a terrorist organization. See , 272 F. Supp. 2d 348, 356–61 (S.D.N.Y. 2003). The government has since filed a superseding indictment

charging the defendants with an alternative violation involving the provision of assistance to a terrorist organization.

135. In the 1990s the federal courts heard numerous high profile cases involving international terrorists, including the trial of members of the Provisional IRA, the Abu Nidal Organization, the Nestor Paz Zamora Commission (CPNZ), the Japanese Red Army, and Cuban National Movement, and the prosecutions arising out of the 1993 attack on the World Trade Center and the 1998 bombing of the American embassies in Kenya and Tanzania. For a detailed discussion and statistical analysis of the prosecution of international and domestic terrorists in federal courts during the 1980s and 1990s, see Brent L. Smith et al., The Prosecution and Punishment of International Terrorists in Federal Courts: 1980–1998, Criminology & Public Policy 311–38 (July 2002) (accounting for 427 defendants charged with terrorists crimes from 1980 to 1998) of those tried from 1988 to 1998, the conviction rate exceeded 80%).

Since September 11, 2001, 284 suspected terrorists have been charged in the federal courts and 149 convicted to date.

136. This observation applies to both citizens and non-citizens. Indeed, due process concerns presumptively give even aliens illegally in the country access to the courts to review removal orders. See, e.g., Wang v. Ashcroft, 320 F.3d 130 (2d Cir. 2003) (applying INS v. St. Cyr, 533 U.S. 289); see also Plyler v. Doe, 457 U.S. 202, 210 (1982).

137. In 1949, at a time of much public concern about the threat posed by the Soviet Union, Attorney General J. Howard McGrath, in his annual report to the United States Judicial Conference, addressed this very question of "protecting against the disclosure of information during espionage trials or other trials involving the national security, which in the interest of national security should be kept secret." Report of the Proceedings of the Annual Meeting of the Judicial Conference of the United States, Report of the Attorney General at 34 (Sept. 22, 1949). The Attorney General indicated that, as a general matter, a series of decisions by the Second Circuit had adequately addressed the issue in upholding the practice of trial courts in declining to admit confidential government documents at trial unless the defendant demonstrated that they were "directly material to his defense." United States v. Andolschek, 142 F.2d 503, 506-07 (2d Cir. 1944); United States v. Cohen, 145 F.2d 82, 92 (2d Cir. 1944); United States v. Krulewich, 145 F.2d 76, 78–79 (2d Cir. 1944); United States v. Ebeling, 146 F.2d 254, 256–57 (2d Cir. 1945).

As Mr. McGrath explained these decisions, the court is to exclude and "seal" any confidential document not "directly material" to the defense, and he suggested that even the sensitive evidence admitted at trial would be shown only to the attorneys, the jurors and the judge (and apparently not to the defendant), an arrangement that he appeared to view as satisfactory. As for appeals, he suggested that any such documents would be filed under seal with the appellate court.

Mr. McGrath did note a practical problem involving cases in which the information needed for trial of the charges was so sensitive "that it cannot be disclosed even to the court, the attorneys or the jury." Id. at 35. He advised that because of this problem, "[i]n many cases of this type the Department [of Justice] has been compelled to refrain from prosecuting, and known violators of the law remain at large." Id.

138. The statute also requires the Attorney General to issue guidelines specifying what factors the Department of Justice is to consider in determining whether to pursue a prosecution in which classified information may be disclosed. CIPA, 18 U.S.C. App. 3, §12.

139. Under this provision, the courts have imposed a variety of conditions, including prohibiting public revelation of the information, requiring that the disclosure of sensitive information be limited to defense counsel only and not to the defendant, and compelling the defense attorney to undergo a formal security clearance by the government as a condition for receiving such information. See, e.g., United States v. Pappas, 94 F.3d at 795, 799-800 (2d Cir. 1996); United States v. Moussaoui, No. 01-455-A, 2002 WL 1987964, *1 (E.D. Va. Aug. 29, 2002); United States v. Bin Laden, No. S (7) 98 CR. 1023, 2001 WL 66393, *2 (S.D.N.Y. Jan. 25, 2001); United States v. Bin Laden, 58 F. Supp. 2d 113, 116–17 (S.D.N.Y. 2000).

140. See, e.g., United States v. Klimavicius-Viloria, 144 F.3d 1249, 1261 (9th Cir. 1998).

141. That public interest is embodied in a number of recognized privileges, including the state secret, informant and various law-enforcement privileges, and in applying the CIPA the courts have plainly been sensitive to the policy considerations undergirding them. See generally Shea, 27 Am. Crim. L. Rev. at 693–96 (citing cases).

142. If the court rules against the government on the disclosure question, the prosecutor may obtain interlocutory appellate review. § 7(a). But cf. United States v. Moussaoui, 336 F.3d 279 (4th Cir. 2003) (Wilkens, C.J., concurring in denial of en banc review) (appellate jurisdiction attaches only after district court imposes sanctions on government). The procedures on appeal are expedited, and appropriate security measures must be taken to avoid disclosure of the classified information while the issue is under appeal. §§ 7(a), 9(b).

143. See, e.g., Fernandez, 913 F.2d at 151, 162-65 (affirming dismissal of indictment).

144. The statute mentions, as some alternatives, the dismissal of specific counts of the indictment, entering findings against the government on issues pertaining to which the classified information is relevant, and either striking or precluding pertinent portions of the testimony of specific witnesses. § 6(e) (2). See, e.g., United States v. Moussaoui, 282 F. Supp. 2d 480, 482–87 (E.D. Va. 2003).

145. The rules also authorize the government to investigate the background, or "trustworthiness", of any individuals "associated with the defense", and to provide such information to the court to consider in framing a protective order under section 3 of CIPA. Id. at § 5. The rules also refer to the jurors, stating that security checks of them are not require[d], but advising that the trial judge should honor any government request for a post-trial instruction cautioning the jurors not to reveal the contents of any classified documents shown to them during the trial. § 6. The rules go on to require specific procedures for the storage and transmittal of such documents within the court, establishment of operating routines in handling sensitive materials, coordination with Justice Department security personnel, and procedures for disposal of the materials after the completion of court proceedings. §§ 7, 8, 9, 11 & 13.

146. Strictly speaking, the Moussouai issue does not concern the required disclosure of classified information, but rather the asserted interest of the government in unhampered access to terrorist sources of intelligence.

147. The portrayal of defense counsel as a potential threat to national security presents a minimal risk, at best. As Chief Judge Mukasey observed, in rejecting the government's objection to provision of counsel to an alleged al Qaeda supporter and activist, when counsel are known to the court as reliable officers of the court and there is no reason to suspect that they would violate stringent and specific requirements concerning the non-disclosure of sensitive information, the risks to national security are minimal or non-existent, and a detainee's access to counsel should therefore be accommodated. Padilla, 233 F. Supp. 2d at 599–605.

We recognize that a member of the bar who represented one defendant in United States v. Rahman, 189 F.3d 88 (2d Cir. 1999), stands charged with having assisted her now-convicted client in communicating to his followers a statement encouraging the commission of terrorist acts overseas. See United States v. Sattar, 2002 WL 1836755, *1 (S.D.N.Y. Aug. 12, 2002). Whatever the merits of this charge, it does not suggest that this attorney had access to classified information during the trial, or that she improperly disclosed any such information during or after the trial, or, of course, that any actual wrongdoing by this attorney exemplifies the behavior of the criminal defense bar.

148. It is also worth observing that the danger of some outsider pressuring a former juror to disclose the substance of secret evidence is remote in view of the ability of the court to require an anonymous jury. See, e.g., United States v. Aulicino, 44 F.3d 1102, 1116–17 (2d Cir. 1995); United States v. Thai, 29 F.3d 785, 800–01 (2d Cir. 1994).

149. Prof. Wedgwood's hypothetical example of reliable evidence that would be inadmissible in a civilian court is a statement by Bin Laden's mother to someone else that her son had called her just before September 11, 2001, and warned her that "a major event was imminent". Wedgwood, 96 Am. J. Int'l L. at 331. It is not self-evident that, if confronted with the question, a court would bar the mother's interlocutor from testifying to the statement under the provisions of Rule 807.

CHAPTER 10

Recommendations Related to the Trial of Saddam Hussein

PREFACE BY MARK R. SHULMAN

Following brief but vigorous military operations, the Ba'athist government led by Saddam Hussein fell to the U.S.–led coalition on April 9, 2003. Mr. Hussein, his family, and many other leaders of his regime fled Baghdad. Within a few weeks President George W. Bush announced the end of major combat operations. At the same time, President Bush acknowledged that much work remained to be done in Iraq. Capturing key Ba'athist leaders was a top priority. In addition, the coalition had soon to acknowledge that it faced a guerrilla war. Searching for fugitives while attempting both to quell the insurgency and rebuild Iraq's infrastructure proved to be a considerable challenge. Nonetheless, acting on a tip secured with the assistance of a large bounty, U.S. troops managed to locate and eventually kill Mr. Hussein's widely feared sons in a July 22, 2003, raid.

Over the half year that followed, the search for Mr. Hussein himself focused increasingly on the vicinity of Tikrit, where he had been born and raised. Tikrit was Mr. Hussein's original power base and remained a center for the resistance. Eventually, the United States offered a bounty of $25 million that appears to have enticed one of Mr. Hussein's entourage to furnish the information necessary to capture him. This dramatic chapter closed with a whimper on December 13, 2003 —nearly eight months after the fall of Mr. Hussein's regime. U.S. troops located Mr. Hussein in an underground hideout and took him prisoner without a fight. Talk turned immediately to his trial, in part perhaps to forestall summary execution of a man apparently responsible for significant crimes against humanity.

As did much of the world, the Association's Council on International Affairs took considerable interest in the prospect of Mr. Hussein's trial. A Task Force of the Council looked into such diverse issues as Iraqi criminal law, the state of the Iraqi judicial system, and the various proposals for venue, in addition, of course, to the principal allegations that Mr. Hussein was likely to face.

The following Report reflects the Council's best judgment about how to move forward as of the Spring of 2004. At that point, the Constitutional status of the government of Iraq seemed ambiguous. Also, duties owed by the United States, as an occupying power, were in flux, as Iraq's own government gained competencies. The growing insurgency appeared to be leading to a split between the minority Sunni population that had enjoyed disproportionate benefits under the Ba'athist regime and the majority Shi'ite and Kurdish people who had suffered mightily under Mr. Hussein's rule. Moreover, the ethnic divide had significant implications beyond Iraq's borders, as nearby Shi'ite Iran and Kuwait had considerable claims against the Ba'athists. Failure to provide them with justice only threatened to spread the conflict.

Many of the issues raised in this Report remain unresolved today. Shortly after this Report was issued, the Iraqi Governing Council did establish the Tribunal and the United States remanded Mr. Hussein to its jurisdiction. The Iraqi High Tribunal was composed of Iraqis only. Its first chief judge was quickly removed, probably because he was related to someone closely tied to the intelligence used to support the move to war in the first place. Mr. Hussein's trial was postponed several times. During the Summer of 2004, the investigative tribunal filed a criminal case against Mr. Hussein and three other former senior officials, for a specific atrocity, the 1982 massacre of Shi'ites in Dujail. After numerous delays, the trial of Mr. Hussein and seven co-defendants began inauspiciously in October 2005; within days of its opening, a defense lawyer had been assassinated. A similar attack killed another defense lawyer and seriously injured a third in November. Meanwhile Mr. Hussein launched his own attacks on the Iraqi High Tribunal's legitimacy and its jurisdiction over him. During succeeding months, the trial was punctuated by grisly allegations and occasional admissions, by political grandstanding, and by a variety of irregularities that continued to call into question the Tribunal's ability to provide a fair trial.

In November 2006, Mr. Hussein was found guilty and sentenced to death. After his appeal failed, he was hanged in December 2006. His speedy execution halted his trial on charges of committing genocide against Iraqi Kurds during the 1988 Anfal Campaign. Respected analysts at Human Rights Watch have concluded that the first trial of Mr. Hussein was deeply flawed and that the special purpose Tribunal was incapable of holding a fair trial for several reasons:

These include: 1) An almost complete lack of familiarity with international criminal law on the part of all Iraqi lawyers and judges involved in the trial; 2) Chaotic and inadequate administration which has given rise to major problems in performing basic administrative tasks necessary for a trial of this magnitude to run fairly; and 3) Such extensive use of anonymous witnesses that the defendants did not get right to contest the evidence against them.

These shortcomings have been compounded by the sharp deterioration of the security environment in Iraq which has resulted in the murder of three defense lawyers, the reluctance of numerous witnesses to come forward, and serious limitations on the defense's capacity to investigate and test evidence gathered by the prosecution.[1]

The concerns of Human Rights Watch echo those expressed in the Report that follows and bode ominously for the Anfal Trial, for the rule of law in Iraq, and for the Iraqi nation more generally. The stakes remain high, since the success of the war in Iraq and of the Iraqi state will inevitably be judged in large part by history's verdict of the justice meted out to Saddam Hussein.

INTRODUCTION

In light of the enormity of the crimes with which Saddam Hussein is likely to be charged, the unique circumstances leading up to his disposition and capture and the fact that his trial presents a timely and significant occasion to promote the rule of law and end the cycle of lawlessness abhorrent to the Association and tragic for the people of Iraq and civilized societies, the Association offers the following observations and recommendations concerning the substance and procedures to be used in the anticipated trial of Mr. Hussein.

The Association believes that clearly articulated and universally accepted legal principles continue to provide instruction even where the particular circumstances found in post-Saddam Hussein Iraq may challenge the successful application of traditional legal solutions.

First, the Association recognizes that the current Iraqi judicial system, after years of neglect and misuse by the Ba'athist regime, is ill equipped to conduct or even support a complex trial involving allegations of such crimes as aggression, crimes against humanity, war crimes and genocide without the participation, in some way, of international experts.

Second, the Association recognizes that with respect to the death penalty the people of Iraq retain the right and burden of determining such a fundamental element in the relationship between a state and its citizens. However, consistent with most relevant human rights international treaties and its own longstanding position, the Association urges that the death penalty not be available for use in this case.

Third, while the Association strongly supports the use and improvement of the multilateral instrumentalities of international law, including the International Criminal Court, it recognizes that the principles of complementarity, sovereignty and dignity accord to the Iraqi people the right to try, in a duly constituted court of law, their former leaders, since the people of Iraq were the primary victims of the crimes alleged. However, serious crimes against non-Iraqi citizens, such as Iranians and Kuwaitis, may require that there be an international component in any trial that is conducted.

The Ba'athist regime led by Mr. Hussein stands accused of some of the most grievous crimes mankind has experienced. Its principal victims were the Iraqi people, mainly ethnic and religious groups disfavored by his regime. Under the totalitarian rule of Mr. Hussein, Iraq also conducted vicious wars against its neighbors and their allies. Trial and punishment by an Iraqi government without international participation might not provide sufficient accountability. To promote the process of creating an accurate historical record and to ensure that justice is done for victims as well as for the accused, the Iraqi people must ensure that any trial meets internationally recognized standards of professionalism, independence, openness and thoroughness.

Compilation of the vast amount of evidence necessary to form the basis for a comprehensive indictment and successful prosecution would launch the healing process in Iraq. This process would likely be enhanced by the experience of trials for the senior leaders of the Ba'athist regime that meet the internationally recognized standards and also by some form of national truth and reconciliation process that enables Iraqi society to come to terms with crimes perpetrated by other agents of the regime.

RECOMMENDATIONS

In addition to bringing Mr. Hussein and his principal accomplices to justice before a duly constituted and competent court of law, an indictment and trial under appropriate international standards would further the following objectives: (*i*) developing the rule of law in Iraq; (*ii*) strengthening the perception of the United States and its coalition partners as helping to spread democratic values; and (*iii*) confirming the United States' commitment to international cooperation and standards. Of the possible venues, a modified form of the recently chartered Iraqi Special Tribunal for Crimes Against Humanity may best be able to fulfill these objectives. Should the charter of the Special Tribunal not be modified to meet these objectives, an international or hybrid national-international court or an international tribunal could be established by the Iraqi government to try Mr. Hussein.

Before turning Mr. Hussein and his principal accomplices over to any tribunal for trial on charges of both domestic and international human rights violations, the United States and its coalition partners should be assured that the trial will be conducted in accordance with established legal standards codified in the Geneva Conventions, the International Covenant for Civil and Political Rights and the Universal Declaration of Human Rights. Political expediency should not permit such standards to be ignored or glossed over. To best ensure legal sufficiency and political legitimacy, remand should be premised on the following conditions:

- Strengthening the Special Tribunal to provide for both Iraqi and non-Iraqi judges, prosecutors, defense counsel and investigative and administrative staffs, with qualifications/experience in handling cases involving complex human rights violations to ensure the competence of the tribunal as required under Article 14 of the International Covenant on Civil and Political Rights. At least one non-Iraqi jurist would serve on each Trial Chamber and at least two on the Appeals Chamber. These non-Iraqis would serve in addition to advisors to the Special Tribunal courts and the Prosecutions Department. A training program for Iraqi judges could be instituted if necessary.

- Selection of judges, prosecutors, counsel and support staff would be made jointly by the Iraqi Governing Council (or its successor) and the United Nations Security Council (or some other international or regional authority). Some preference could be given to the empanelling of secular jurists from countries near Iraq.

- Amending or reenacting the provisions of the Statute of the Iraqi Special Tribunal by the new Iraqi government that assumes power after June 2004 to accommodate these provisions and those that follow:

1. The charges to be considered would be those involving international crimes, and, where appropriate, domestic offenses involving serious crimes.

2. The Special Tribunal would adopt rules of evidence and procedure of what are generally regarded by the international community as the highest standards such as those developed for the International Criminal Court, and would require for conviction evidence of guilt beyond a reasonable doubt. The evidence should be compelling, substantial and well documented.

3. The maximum penalty would be life imprisonment. A finite right of appeal would be included in the trial procedures, as would be customary under international law.

4. The trial would take place in Baghdad, be conducted in the Arabic language (with simultaneous interpretation) and be open to the public and the media. Evidence accepted by the judges would be available in its original language to the public and the media, except where necessary to protect the innocent.

5. Robust security must be provided for all participants in the proceedings. Appropriate provisions would also be made to protect witnesses, including, where appropriate, the identity of a witness.

NOTES

1. See http://hrw.org/english/docs/2006/08/14/iraq13982.htm.

CHAPTER 11

Human Rights Standards Applicable to the United States' Interrogation of Detainees

PREFACE BY MARTIN S. FLAHERTY

On April 28, 2004, CBS first broadcast the now infamous photographs of prisoner abuse, mistreatment, and torture at Abu Ghraib prison. That same week, the Association released its Report, which had been long in the making, on international human rights and humanitarian standards applicable to U.S. interrogation of detainees. The timing of these two developments was entirely accidental but sadly appropriate. The Abu Ghraib photographs touched off a firestorm of moral outrage both inside the United States and around the world. Though its authors had no firm evidence of the Abu Ghraib abuses beforehand, the Association's Report set forth bases for outrage on legal grounds. More generally, the Report almost overnight became among the most widely consulted guides as to how U.S. forces should conduct themselves not just in Iraq, but Afghanistan, Guantanamo Bay, and indeed wherever U.S. forces held individuals in custody in the name of the "global war on terror."

As the Report itself makes clear, the Association first undertook the project in response to widely reported allegations that individuals detained by the United States were being subjected to mistreatment in connection with the conflict in Afghanistan. Yet, as the Report also states, most of the standards it discusses "apply broadly and with equal force to the treatment of detainees captured in other situations." Unfortunately, the broader applicability of the Report proved to be grimly prophetic. In the wake of the Abu Ghraib scandal, the Association nonetheless saw a need to address issues arising out of detention in Iraq, as well as additional issues that had come to light out of Afghanistan. These concerns led to the release of a Supplement to the main Report a month later, in May 2004, to analyze these additional legal settings.

The Report represents what became a fruitful collaboration between the Committee on International Human Rights,* initially led by Scott Horton and succeeded by Martin Flaherty, and the Committee on Military Affairs and Justice, chaired by Miles P. Fischer. Although military lawyers and human rights advocates might not initially have appeared as natural allies, a close collaboration developed over the year-long process of generating the two documents. Not only did the two groups supplement one another's knowledge with regard to human rights law on one hand and humanitarian law on the other, they also discovered the ways in which the two bodies of law complemented one another and reinforced a mutual commitment to uphold the United States' position as a traditional champion of the rule of law internationally. Importantly, much the same partnership emerged in the nation at large. Human rights lawyers and nongovernmental organizations (NGOs) took the lead in criticizing the Bush Administration's actions with regard to human rights law. But so too did military lawyers, especially from within the Judge Advocate General's Corps, who in various formal and informal ways expressed dismay at the Administration's apparent unconcern for abiding by laws of war that the United States had in large part fashioned.

The Report describes "the legal principles which should guide our military and intelligence personnel in their conduct." First and foremost of these is the Convention Against Torture and Other Cruel, Inhuman or Degrading Treatment (CAT) to which the United States is a party. More contentious are the Geneva Conventions, since there remain legitimate questions as to whether members of the Taliban or, more controversially, al Qaeda, qualify for prisoner of war (POW) status and the extensive protections it entails. The Report nonetheless concludes that in cases of doubt POW status should be accorded liberally, and that in any instance, Common Article 3 provides important protections for those detainees who do not qualify for POW status. In addition, the Report also considers safeguards afforded by other international standards, including the International Covenant on Civil and Political Rights, the Universal Declaration of Human Rights, and the Inter-American Convention on Human Rights; customary international law; and *jus cogens*. As a final matter, the Report consults the comparative experience of the United Kingdom and Israel in combating terrorist violence while nonetheless observing strictures against torture and other cruel, inhuman, and degrading treatment.

In light of Abu Ghraib, the Supplement provides additional analysis focusing on the legal standards applicable to detainees in Iraq. Here the Association analyzes the Geneva Conventions with regard to several important questions, among them the broad coverage for "protected persons" during occupations, its conclusion that U.S. detainees do not fall into the few narrow exceptions to protected-person status, and the standards that apply once the formal U.S. occupation in Iraq ends. The Supplement also underlines the Association's position that Common Article 3 provides baseline human rights protections and is not subject to exceptions for persons affiliated with non-state organizations such as al Qaeda that have not signed the Geneva Conventions. In this regard, both the Report and the Supplement flatly contradict positions taken in internal Bush Administration memoranda written by Professor John Yoo, as well as the position later adopted by the D.C. Circuit in *Hamdan*.

The Report concludes with a series of recommendations, which the Supplement reiterates and amplifies. These include calls upon the U.S. government (1) to train and educate all relevant officials in the international legal standards that apply to detention and interrogation, (2) to conduct prompt investigations of possible violations, (3) to expand the scope of 18 U.S.C. sec. 2340 to expressly prohibit torture in extraterritorial detention centers under U.S. jurisdiction, (4) to fully apply and utilize the Uniform Code of Military Justice, (5) to conduct independent investigations with regard to the human rights compliance of countries to which the U.S. might "render" detainees, (6) to grant POW status to detainees whose status is in doubt as a matter of policy, and (7) to restore the role of the Judge Advocate Officers in providing legal advice in connection with detention and interrogation.

The legal conclusions set forth become even more important in light of official responses to both the Association and others regarding U.S. policy. Both the inquiries and the responses are set forth in the appendices. Among these exchanges, William J. Haynes responded to Ken Roth of Human Rights Watch asserting that "the United States condemns and prohibits torture," and that "U.S. personnel are required to follow this policy and applicable laws prohibiting torture." Haynes responded even more fully to an inquiry made by Senator Patrick Leahy that U.S. policy consists of undertaking interrogations in a manner consistent with the Convention Against Torture and other Cruel, Inhuman and Degrading Treatment as ratified by the United States, as well as the Federal Torture Statute, 18 U.S.C. sec. 2340–2340A. Haynes further stated that it was U.S. policy not simply to refrain from torture, but to refrain from cruel, inhuman, and degrading treatment not amounting to torture.

The Report and the Supplement made a significant impact when they were released. Among other things, they served as a basis for press reports on detainee mistreatment in such publications as the *Washington Post, The New Yorker,* and the *New York Times.* They have repeatedly served as a resource for Congress, including the questioning of Alberto Gonzales during the hearing held on his appointment as Attorney General. They were also among the few non-government documents reprinted in the book, *The Torture Papers: The Road to Abu Ghraib,* edited by Karen J. Greenberg and Joshua L. Dratel and published by Cambridge University Press. In these and other ways, the work of the two Committees has sought to live up to the Association's highest ideals of providing dispassionate legal analysis on great public questions. The countervailing regret is that this analysis calls into question the actions and policies of our own government in upholding humanitarian law, international human rights law, Federal law, and the rule of law itself.

In *Hamdan v Rumsfeld,*[1] the Supreme Court confirmed and expanded its commitment to the rule of law against the Administration's ongoing claims of unchecked executive authority. Reversing a D.C. Circuit panel that included now Chief Justice John Roberts, the Court held that special military commissions constituted to try Guantanamo detainees violated the Uniform Code of Military Justice (UCMJ) in two respects. The military commissions failed first because their procedures substantially differed from those guaranteed in courts martial, with no government showing justifying the divergence. In addition, the commissions violated Common Article 3 of the 1949 Geneva Conventions, as incorporated by the UCMJ, insofar as they were not regularly constituted courts. The Association may take some credit for this second rationale because its amicus briefs, both before the D.C. Circuit and Supreme Court, first raised the relevance of Common Article 3's requirements.

HUMAN RIGHTS STANDARDS APPLICABLE TO THE UNITED STATES' INTERROGATION OF DETAINEES

EXECUTIVE SUMMARY/INTRODUCTION

This Report is a joint effort of the Association of the Bar of the City of New York's Committees on International Human Rights and Military Affairs and Justice, undertaken to consider allegations—reported in the press and by human rights and humanitarian organizations conducting their own investigations—that individuals detained by the United States at its military and intelligence facilities in connection with the initial War in Afghanistan and the subsequent ongoing conflict in Afghanistan, are being subjected to interrogation techniques that constitute torture or cruel, inhuman or degrading treatment.[2] We note at the outset, however, that although this project was initially motivated by allegations regarding the treatment of detainees from the War in Afghanistan, the international law and human rights standards discussed herein—with the exception of Geneva Convention protections applicable only to situations of international armed conflict—apply broadly and with equal force to the treatment of detainees captured in other situations, including detainees picked up in other countries in connection with the broader "War on Terror."[3] In this Report, we will examine the international legal standards governing United States military and civil authorities in interrogating detainees and propose ways of assuring that those standards are enforced.

The Alleged Interrogation Practices

These allegations first surfaced in December 2002, when the U.S. military announced that it had begun a criminal investigation into the death of a 22 year-old Afghan farmer and part-time taxi driver who had died of "blunt force injuries to lower extremities complicating coronary artery disease" while in U.S. custody at Bagram Air Force Base in Afghanistan.[4] Since then, details about interrogation techniques allegedly employed at U.S. detention facilities—most of which are off-limits to outsiders and some of which are in undisclosed locations—have come from government officials speaking on the condition that they would not be identified and from the few prisoners who have been released. Some examples of "stress and duress" interrogation "techniques" reportedly being practiced by U.S. Department of Defense ("DOD") and Central Intelligence Agency ("CIA") personnel at U.S. detention facilities include: forcing detainees to stand or kneel for hours in black hoods or spray-painted goggles, 24-hour bombardment with lights, "false-flag" operations meant to deceive a captive about his whereabouts, withholding painkillers from wounded detainees, confining detainees in tiny rooms, binding in painful positions, subjecting detainees to loud noises, and sleep deprivation.[5] In addition, the U.S. is reportedly "rendering" suspects to the custody of foreign intelligence services in countries where the practice of torture and cruel, inhuman or degrading treatment during interrogation is well-documented.[6]

The Administration's Responses

The Association and others have written to U.S. government officials to ask whether there is any factual basis for these allegations and whether steps are being taken to ensure that detainees are interrogated in accordance with U.S. law and international standards prohibiting torture and "cruel, inhuman or degrading" treatment falling short of torture ("CID").[7]

In response to inquiries from Human Rights Watch, U.S. Department of Defense General Counsel William J. Haynes has stated that: "United States policy condemns and prohibits torture" and that, when "questioning enemy combatants, U.S. personnel are required to follow this policy and applicable laws prohibiting torture."[8] CIA General Counsel Scott W. Muller, citing to the need to protect intelligence sources and methods, has responded to our inquiries by stating only that "in its various activities around the world the CIA remains subject to the requirements of U.S. law" and that allegations of unlawful behavior are reported by the CIA to the Department of Justice and are subject to investigation.[9]

In response to an inquiry made by U.S. Senator Patrick J. Leahy regarding U.S. policy, Haynes stated that U.S. policy entails "conducting interrogations in a manner that is consistent with the Convention Against Torture and Other Cruel, Inhuman, or Degrading Treatment or Punishment ("CAT"), as ratified by the U.S. in 1994, and with the Federal anti-torture statute, 18 U.S.C. §§ 2340–2340A, which Congress enacted to fulfill U.S. obligations under the CAT."[10] Haynes also stated that U.S. policy is "to treat all detainees and conduct all interrogations, wherever they may occur, in a manner consistent with" the U.S. obligation, pursuant to Article 16 of CAT, namely, "to prevent other acts of cruel, inhuman, or degrading treatment or punishment which do not amount to torture" insofar as such treatment is "prohibited by the Fifth, Eighth, and/or Fourteenth Amendments."[11] Haynes assured Senator Leahy "that credible allegations of illegal conduct by U.S. personnel will be investigated and, as appropriate, reported to proper authorities."[12] Furthermore, Haynes stated that the U.S. does not "expel, return ('*refouler*') or extradite individuals to other countries where the U.S. believes it is 'more likely than not' that they will be tortured," that "United States policy is to obtain specific assurances from the receiving country that it will not torture the individual being transferred to that country," and that "the United States would take steps to investigate credible allegations of torture and take appropriate action if there were reason to believe that those assurances were not being honored."[13]

Both Haynes and Muller have declined, however, to give details concerning the specific interrogation methods used by U.S. personnel at U.S. military and CIA detention facilities.

Legal Standards Prohibiting Torture and Cruel, Inhuman or Degrading Treatment

Although we are not in a position to investigate the factual basis for the allegations of torture and cruel, inhuman or degrading interrogation practices at U.S. detention facilities that have been made, we can describe the legal principles which should guide our military and intelligence personnel in their conduct. Accordingly, in this Report we examine the international and U.S. law standards against which the interrogation practices used on detainees should be assessed. We also address the question of whether there are any circumstances posed by the post-September 11 world in which abrogation of our country's obligations to prevent and punish torture and cruel, inhuman or degrading treatment should be permitted in the interrogation of terrorist suspects.

The Convention Against Torture

First and foremost, the U.S. obligation to prohibit and prevent the torture and cruel, inhuman or degrading treatment of detainees in its custody is set forth in the Convention Against Torture And Other Cruel, Inhuman, or Degrading Treatment ("CAT"), to which the U.S. is a party.[14] When the U.S. ratified CAT in 1994, it did so subject to a reservation providing that the U.S. would prevent "cruel, inhuman or degrading treatment" insofar as such treatment is prohibited under the Fifth, Eighth, and/or Fourteenth Amendments.[15] Thus, the U.S. is obligated to prevent not only torture, but also conduct considered cruel, inhuman or degrading under international law if such conduct is also prohibited by the Fifth, Eighth and Fourteenth Amendments. In interpreting U.S. obligations, we look to the U.N. Committee Against Torture's interpretations of CAT as well as U.S. case law decided in the immigration and asylum law context, under the Alien Tort Claims and Torture Victim Protection Acts and concerning the treatment of detainees and prisoners under the Fifth, Eighth and/or Fourteenth Amendments. We also examine the procedural mechanisms available under U.S. law to punish violations of CAT—including prosecution under federal criminal law (18 U.S.C. §§ 2340—2340A) and the Uniform Code of Military Justice ("UCMJ").

Other International Legal Standards which Bind the United States

While there is a dearth of U.S. case law applying CAT's prohibition against torture and cruel, inhuman or degrading treatment in the interrogation context, there is a wealth of international law sources which offer guidance in interpreting CAT. Some of these international legal standards are, without question, binding on the U.S., such as: the International Covenant on Civil and Political Rights (the "ICCPR"),[16] the law of *jus cogens* and customary international law. Another international legal instrument which has been ratified by the U.S. and is relevant to the interrogation practices being examined by this Report is the Inter-American Declaration on the Rights and Duties of Man.[17] Other sources, such as the European Convention for the Protection of Human Rights and Fundamental Freedoms,[18] also provide guidance.

The applicability of the Geneva Conventions to the detainees from the War in Afghanistan, however, presents a more contentious issue. The Administration's official position is that the Geneva Conventions do not apply to Al Qaeda detainees, and that neither the Taliban nor Al Qaeda detainees are entitled to prisoner of war ("POW") status thereunder. Nevertheless, the Administration has stated that it is treating such individuals "humanely and, to the extent appropriate and consistent with military necessity, in a manner consistent with the principles of the Third Geneva Convention of 1949," and that the detainees "will not be subjected to physical or mental abuse or cruel treatment."[19] The Administration has never explained how it determines what interrogation techniques are "appropriate" or "consistent with military necessity," or how it squares that determination with U.S. obligations under human rights and customary international law. For POW and civilian detainees who meet the relevant criteria of Geneva Convention (III) Relative to the Treatment of Prisoners of War ("Geneva III") and Geneva Convention (IV) Relative to the Protection of Civilian Persons in Time of War ("Geneva IV"), respectively, all coercion is prohibited.[20] Moreover, any detainee whose POW status is in doubt is entitled to a hearing and determination by a competent tribunal and, pending such determination, any such detainee must be treated as a POW. Concern for the safety of U.S. forces weighs in favor of extending POW status liberally. At a minimum, all detainees—regardless of POW or civilian status—are entitled to humane treatment and prompt hearings under human rights and customary international law, including the protections of Article 3 common to all four Geneva Conventions ("Common Article 3") and Article 75 of the Protocol Additional to the Geneva Conventions of 12 August 1949 and Related to the Protection of Victims of International Armed Conflicts ("Additional Protocol I").[21] We urge the U.S. to promptly establish proper screening procedures for all detainees, whether or not they served with forces that met the specific criteria of Geneva III.

Legal Standards which the United States Should Look to for Guidance

Other relevant sources of law, such as the seminal 1999 Israeli Supreme Court decision on interrogation methods employed by the Israeli General Security Service, *Judgment Concerning The Legality Of The General Security Service's Interrogation Methods,*[22] and decisions of the European Court of Human Rights, although not legally binding on the U.S., also offer useful guidance in our interpretation of CAT. These foreign decisions indicate that the "War on Terror" is not unprecedented. As the Israeli and Northern Ireland experiences demonstrate, the U.S. is not the only country to have faced terrorism within its borders, despite the unique tragedy of September 11 and the potential threat of weapons of mass destruction that could expand the loss of life by orders of magnitude. We can and should learn from the experience of other countries whose courts have grappled with the need to permit effective interrogation while at the same time upholding the standards of human rights and the rule of law.

Standards in the Time of Terror

There is an inherent tension between the need to obtain potentially life-saving information through interrogation of terrorist suspects and the legal requirement of upholding the standards set forth in CAT. We grappled with the question of whether there are any circumstances under which torture or cruel, inhuman or degrading treatment would be permissible in a post-September 11 world. While we acknowledge the real danger posed to the United States by Al Qaeda and other terrorist organizations, we concluded that there are no such exceptions to CAT's absolute prohibition of torture.

Condoning torture under any circumstances erodes one of the most basic principles of international law and human rights and contradicts our values as a democratic state. Permitting the abuse of detainees in U.S. custody, perhaps under so-called "torture warrants," not only harms the detainees themselves; it compromises the moral framework of our interrogators and damages our society as a whole. If U.S. personnel are allowed to engage in brutal interrogation methods which denigrate the dignity and humanity of detainees, we sanction conduct which we as a nation (along with the international community) has clearly determined is wrong and immoral. Accordingly, we unanimously condemn the torture of detainees under any circumstances. We note that U.S. constitutional jurisprudence on "cruel, inhuman or degrading" treatment, which has been made relevant to CAT by the U.S. reservation, is an extremely important source of guidance on this subject. On the other hand, much of this jurisprudence evolved in the context of domestic criminal justice administration, and how these precedents would be applied in a case arising out of the interrogation and detention covered by this Report is, in the absence of more definitive authority, a matter of some speculation.

Recommendations

We applaud the statements in William Haynes' June 25, 2003 letter to Senator Leahy affirming the policy of the U.S. regarding its commitment to CAT. To make that policy meaningful, we make the following recommendations:

1. Training and Education. All law enforcement personnel, civilian or military, medical personnel, public officials and other persons who may be involved in the custody, interrogation or treatment of anyone under any form of detention or imprisonment should be informed and educated regarding the prohibition against torture and cruel, inhuman or degrading treatment, as applied in practice. This requires, as provided in Article 11 of CAT, that the U.S. keep under systematic review interrogation rules, instructions, methods and practices as well as arrangements for the custody and treatment of such detainees.[23] Above all, commanders should not condone non-compliance nor permit an environment in which troops are encouraged to provide lip service to compliance but yet think that non-compliance is acceptable.

Given that CIA personnel are not generally subject to the UCMJ, possibly not even when accompanying the armed forces in the field, special procedures should be available to provide reasonable assurance that compliance with CAT is being taught and maintained by intelligence agencies. That assurance might best be provided by the applicable committees of the Congress exercising oversight responsibility in conjunction with the inspectors general of the applicable agencies.

2.   Prompt Investigation of Violations. As required by Article 12 of CAT, the U.S. must ensure that allegations of abusive conduct are taken seriously and are fully and impartially investigated.[24] Thus, any individual who alleges that he or she has been subjected to torture must be provided with a meaningful opportunity to complain to, and to have his/her case promptly and impartially examined by, competent authorities. Steps must be taken to ensure that the complainant and witnesses are protected against all ill-treatment and intimidation.

3.   Expand the Scope and Reach of Section 2340. Consistent with its obligation under Article 4 of CAT to ensure that all acts of torture are offenses under its criminal law[25]—and since 18 U.S.C. § 2340 does not, by its terms, apply to acts constituting torture committed in extraterritorial detention centers under U.S. jurisdiction—the U.S. must expand the geographic reach of Section 2340 so that the prescriptions of CAT are applicable at all U.S. detention centers.

4.   Fully Utilize the UCMJ. The U.S. must more fully utilize the procedures and protections available under the UCMJ to prosecute all violations of CAT by the armed forces or others subject to the UCMJ.

5.   Independent Investigation of Human Rights Compliance in Other Countries. As provided by Article 3 of CAT, the U.S. must not "render" detainees to other countries where there are substantial grounds for belief that the detainees would be in danger of being subjected to torture.[26] In determining whether there are "substantial grounds for belief" that a detainee would be in danger of torture if rendered to another country, U.S. authorities must take into account all the relevant considerations concerning that country, including independently investigating whether there exists a consistent pattern of gross, flagrant or mass violations of human rights in the country.[27]

6.   Grant POW Status to Detainees Whose Status is in Doubt and Possibly as a Matter of Policy. The U.S. should adhere to Geneva III's requirement that any detainee whose POW status is in "doubt" is entitled to POW status—and, therefore, cannot be subjected to coercive treatment—until a "competent tribunal," which must be convened promptly, determines otherwise.[28] We urge the U.S. to consider the policy grounds for extending POW treatment to regular force combatants, whether or not legally required to do so, as it has done in prior conflicts.

7.   Prompt Screening and Hearings for All Detainees. In keeping with the spirit of the Geneva Conventions and human rights law, we urge the U.S. to provide proper screening procedures and hearings to all detainees.[29]

We now turn to a more detailed discussion of the international standards applicable to interrogation procedures.

I.   THE CONVENTION AGAINST TORTURE

The U.N. Convention Against Torture and Other Cruel, Inhuman or Degrading Treatment or Punishment ("CAT") is the primary source of international law relevant to the treatment of detainees.[30] CAT has been ratified by the U.S., and its prohibitions against torture and cruel, inhuman or degrading treatment or punishment have been implemented in our domestic law.

Specifically, U.S. law implements CAT's prohibition against torture in the immigration and asylum contexts, under the Alien Tort Claims and Torture Victim Protection Acts, by criminal statute and under the UCMJ. Under CAT, the U.S. is also obligated to prevent "cruel, inhuman or degrading treatment or punishment" as defined in international law; however, by express reservation, the U.S. interprets this obligation in keeping with standards of treatment required by the Fifth, Eighth and Fourteenth Amendments. Accordingly, under CAT, American military and intelligence personnel involved in the interrogation of detainees may not torture those detainees, nor may they subject them to cruel, inhuman or degrading treatment that is, or would be, forbidden under the Fifth, Eighth and/or Fourteenth Amendments.

A. CAT's Definitions of—and Prohibitions against—Torture and Cruel, Inhuman or Degrading Treatment

CAT defines and prohibits torture, as defined, and cruel, inhuman or degrading treatment or punishment in general terms. In addition, it also sets out steps ratifying countries must take to prevent, investigate, and criminalize acts of torture;[31] prohibits the extradition or other rendering (also known as "*refoulement*") of a person to a country that would likely subject such person to torture;[32] creates a Committee to oversee the implementation of CAT by ratifying countries; and sets forth procedures for inquiries, individual communications, and inter-State complaints.

CAT's preamble acknowledges that torture and other cruel, inhuman or degrading treatment or punishment are already prohibited under Article 5 of the Universal Declaration of Human Rights and Article 7 of the ICCPR. Thus, rather than simply mirroring the prohibitions from these instruments, Article 1 of CAT provides additional guidance to states parties in preventing and punishing torture by setting forth an explicit definition of torture:

...torture means any act by which severe pain or suffering, whether physical or mental, is intentionally inflicted on a person for such purposes as obtaining from him or a third person information or a confession, punishing him for an act he or a third person has committed or is suspected of having committed, or intimidating or coercing him or a third person, or for any reason based on discrimination of any kind, when such pain or suffering is inflicted by or at the instigation of or with the consent or acquiescence of a public official or other person acting in an official capacity. It does not include pain or suffering arising only from, inherent in or incidental to lawful sanctions.

This definition makes it clear that the result of torture need not be physical pain or suffering, but can also be mental. In addition, torture is defined to include such conduct undertaken for the purpose of obtaining information. Finally, the prohibition is not directed at private citizens, acting independently of government; it applies rather to acts committed by government officials and agents, or persons acting with official consent or acquiescence.

CAT's prohibition of torture is absolute. An order from a superior officer or a public authority may not be invoked as a justification of torture. Specifically, Article 2(2) provides: "No exceptional circumstances whatsoever, whether a state of war or a threat or war, internal political instability or any other public emergency, may be invoked as a justification of torture."

Although CAT does not provide a definition of CID punishment or treatment, Article 16 requires ratifying countries to prevent "other acts of cruel, inhuman or degrading treatment or punishment which do not amount to torture...." This language suggests that cruel, inhuman or degrading treatment is on a continuum with torture.

CAT requires each signatory state to prevent the commission of the prohibited acts within any territory under the state's jurisdiction. Specifically, each ratifying country must ensure that any official who may be involved in the interrogation of anyone under any form of detention or imprisonment is informed of and educated about the prohibitions against torture and cruel, inhuman or degrading treatment. CAT also requires each ratifying country to ensure that allegations of torture and CID treatment are fully and impartially investigated. *See* CAT Articles 12 and 16(1).

B.   CAT's Prohibition against Torture and CID Treatment as Interpreted by the U.N. Committee Against Torture

The U.N. Committee Against Torture, created by CAT, is charged with monitoring implementation of the treaty by ratifying countries through the determination of individual complaints, considering country reports submitted under CAT, and resolving inter-State disputes. Given the importance of international standards in interpreting U.S. domestic law[33] as well as the recent *Lawrence v. Texas* decision, in which the U.S. Supreme Court expressly looked to foreign and international law for guidance,[34] U.N. Committee decisions are relevant to the assessment of whether the actions of U.S. personnel involved in the interrogation of detainees constitute torture or cruel, inhuman or degrading treatment.

The U.N. Committee has concluded that the following acts[35] constitute torture under CAT:

- daily beatings and detaining someone in a small, uncomfortable space for two weeks;[36]
- forcing someone to sleep on the floor of a cell while handcuffed following interrogation;[37]
- in severe cases, sleep deprivation;[38] and
- the threat of torture.[39]

Furthermore, the U.N. Committee has recommended that the use of a blindfold during questioning be expressly prohibited.[40] More generally, the U.N. Committee has expressed concern that States have defined torture too narrowly, covering only "systematic blows or other violent acts."[41] The U.N. Committee has also expressed concern whether the penal law of one State was too narrow in defining torture because it failed to prohibit "certain aspects of torture, such as psychological pressure, threats and intimidation."[42]

The U.N. Committee has found that the following acts amount to cruel, inhuman or degrading treatment or punishment under CAT:

- depriving someone of food and/or water;[43]
- in some cases, binding someone in a restraint chair;[44]
- the use by prison authorities of instruments of physical restraint that may cause unnecessary pain and humiliation;[45] and
- long periods of detention (two weeks or more) in detention cells that are sub-standard (this conduct may amount to torture if the period of detention is extremely long).[46]

The U.N. Committee has found that the following acts may amount to torture when used in combination with other forms of CID:

- being restrained in very painful conditions;
- being hooded;
- the sounding of loud music for prolonged periods;
- sleep deprivation for prolonged periods;
- violent shaking; and
- using cold air to chill.[47]

In sum, the U.N. Committee Against Torture has indicated that the classification of treatment as CID or torture is often a matter of severity, intensity, and the totality of the circumstances. Combining several forms of cruel, inhuman or degrading treatment will frequently amount to torture, and ratifying countries are required under CAT to refrain from all such practices, whether they reach the level of severity to be considered torture or not. Thus, according to

U.N. Committee jurisprudence, alleged interrogation practices such as forcing detainees to stand or kneel for hours in black hoods or spray-painted goggles, 24-hour bombardment with lights, binding detainees in painful positions, withholding painkillers from wounded detainees, and subjecting detainees to loud noises and sleep deprivation, at a minimum, constitute cruel, inhuman or degrading treatment and may, depending on the circumstances, rise to the level of torture. U.N. Committee decisions critical of blindfolding, psychological pressure and threats and intimidation strongly suggest that "false-flag" operations meant to deceive detainees about their whereabouts and "stress and duress" interrogation techniques are also prohibited.

C.   U.S. Law Implementing CAT's Prohibitions against Torture and Cruel, Inhuman or Degrading Treatment or Punishment

The Senate adopted a resolution of advice and consent to U.S. ratification of CAT, subject to the declaration that it be deemed non-self-executing, on October 27, 1990.[48] The U.S. ratified CAT in October 1994, and CAT entered into force with respect to the United States on 20 November 1994.[49] The implementation in U.S. immigration, extradition, criminal and civil tort law of CAT's prohibition against torture, as well as the express application of U.S. constitutional standards to CAT's prohibition against CID treatment, indicates that many of the interrogation practices allegedly being used by the U.S. against detainees may be prohibited under international _and_ U.S. law.

1.   U.S. Understandings and Reservations in Ratifying CAT

The United States conditioned its ratification of CAT upon certain understandings related to CAT's definition of torture in Article 1. In one such understanding, the U.S. specified that mental pain or suffering within the meaning of "torture" refers to prolonged mental harm caused by or resulting from: (1) the intentional infliction or threatened infliction of severe physical pain or suffering; (2) the administration or application, or threatened administration or application, of mind-altering substances or other procedures calculated to disrupt profoundly the senses or the personality; (3) the threat of imminent death; or (4) the threat that another person will imminently be subjected to death, severe physical pain or suffering, or the administration or application of mind-altering substances or other procedures calculated to disrupt profoundly the senses or the personality.[50] Another U.S. understanding pertains to defects in criminal procedure: noncompliance with applicable legal procedural standards (such as Miranda warnings) does not per se constitute "torture."[51]

When ratifying CAT, the United States also took the following reservation: "the United States considers itself bound by the obligation under Article 16 to prevent 'cruel, inhuman or degrading treatment or punishment,' only insofar as the term 'cruel, inhuman or degrading treatment or punishment' means the cruel, unusual and inhumane treatment or punishment prohibited by the Fifth, Eighth, and Fourteenth Amendments to the Constitution of the United States."[52]

2.   The Implementation of CAT's Prohibition against Torture in U.S. Legislation, Regulation and Case Law

CAT's prohibition of official acts amounting to torture has been implemented in the United States through legislation, regulations and case law pertaining to, _inter alia,_ (1) immigration, (2) claims of torture in removal and extradition proceedings, (3) criminal sanctions for torture, and (4) tort claims alleging torture. Through the application of these implementing laws and regulations, U.S. courts have interpreted CAT's substantive provisions in a variety of contexts.[53]

(a)   U.S. Immigration Law and Torture

As previously noted, all countries that ratify CAT are obligated to ensure that detainees are not deported or extradited to countries where they are likely to be tortured. In 1998, the United States enacted the Foreign Affairs Reform and Restructuring Act of 1998, § 2242, Pub. L. No. 105-277, Div. G, 112 Stat. 2681, 2681-822 (Oct. 21, 1998) (the "FARR Act"), implementing this obligation. In 1999, the Immigration and Naturalization Service ("INS") promulgated regulations effectuating the FARR Act in the immigration and asylum context, providing aliens in exclusion, deportation or removal proceedings with grounds to seek withholding of removal based on CAT. *See* 8 C.F.R. § 208.18 (2004), *et seq.* These regulations incorporate CAT's definition of torture verbatim, with the following qualification: "Torture is an extreme form of cruel and inhuman treatment and does not include lesser forms of cruel, inhuman or degrading treatment or punishment that do not amount to torture." *See* 8 C.F.R. § 208.18(a)(2) (2004). These regulations further define mental pain or suffering consistently with the U.S. understandings to CAT, and exclude from the definition of torture acts which result in "unanticipated or unintended severity of pain and suffering." *See* 8 C.F.R. § 208.18(a)(5) (2004).

A number of federal court cases and Board of Immigration Appeals ("BIA") decisions address torture claims in the immigration context. The BIA has held that the following abuses of detainees and prisoners, for example, amount to torture: "'suspension for long periods in contorted positions, burning with cigarettes, sleep deprivation, and...severe and repeated beatings with cables or other instruments on the back and on the soles of the feet,'...beatings about the ears, resulting in partial or complete deafness, and punching in the eyes, leading to partial or complete blindness." *Matter of G-A-,* 23 I & N Dec. 366, 370 (BIA 2002) (internal citations omitted).[54] Furthermore, persons seeking asylum or withholding of removal have successfully challenged deportation under Sections 208 and 241(b)(3) of the Immigration & Nationality Act ("INA") when they have a well-founded fear of future persecution. Although "persecution" is not defined in the INA, it is understood to encompass treatment falling short of torture.

(b)   U.S. Extradition of Fugitives Who Face Threat of Torture

In the extradition context, torture claims are governed by regulations enacted by the Department of State under the FARR Act. Under these regulations, individuals sought for extradition may present a claim that they are likely to be tortured if surrendered to the requesting state. These claims are considered by the U.S. Secretary of State, who is responsible for implementing CAT's obligation not to extradite an individual to a State where he or she is in danger of being subject to torture. Specifically, section 95 of 22 C.F.R. (2004) provides, in relevant part, that the Secretary of State must consider whether a person facing extradition from the U.S. "is more likely than not" to be tortured in the State requesting extradition, and that appropriate policy and legal offices must review and analyze the information relevant to the torture allegation. The extradition regulations, and the decisions interpreting them,[55] demonstrate that U.S. administrative bodies and courts view CAT's prohibition against extradition to torture as binding on the U.S. even when the extraditable individual is accused of wrongdoing.

(c)   U.S. Implementation of CAT's Criminal Law Requirements

18 U.S.C. §§ 2340 and 2340A were enacted to fulfill CAT's requirement that each ratifying country criminalize all acts of torture, including attempts to commit torture and complicity in torture.[56] Section 2340 defines torture as:

an act committed by a person acting under the color of law specifically intended to inflict severe physical or mental pain or suffering (other than pain or suffering incidental to lawful sanctions) upon another person within his custody or physical control...

"Severe mental pain or suffering" is also defined, using the same wording as the U.S. understandings concerning Article 1 of CAT set forth in Section I(C)(1) above. *See* 18 U.S.C. § 2340. As discussed further below, however, this statute applies only to U.S. nationals (or others present in the U.S.) who have committed or attempted or conspired to commit acts of torture "outside of the United States."[57]

(d)   U.S. Case Law Interpretations of Torture in Tort Claims

Two U.S. statutes provide for civil suits against those who commit acts of torture abroad. The Alien Tort Claims Act of 1789 ("ATCA"), 28 U.S.C. § 1350, states that "[t]he district courts shall have original jurisdiction of any civil action by an alien for a tort only, committed in violation of the law of nations or a treaty of the United States." The Torture Victim Protection Act of 1991 ("TVPA"), 28 U.S.C. § 1350, provides that:

[a]n individual who, under actual or apparent authority, or color of law, of any foreign nation—(1) subjects an individual to torture shall, in a civil action, be liable for damages to that individual; or (2) subjects an individual to extrajudicial killing shall, in a civil action, be liable for damages to the individual's legal representative, or to any person who may be a claimant in an action for wrongful death.[58]

The TVPA extends a civil remedy to U.S. citizen torture victims, while the ATCA provides a remedy for aliens only.

U.S. courts applying the ATCA and TVPA have found that the following acts constitute torture: subjecting detainees to interrogation sessions lasting 14 hours (*Xuncax v. Gramajo,* 886 F. Supp. 162, 170 (D. Mass 1995)); beating with hands (*Tachiona v. Mugabe,* 234 F. Supp. 2d 401, 420–423 (S.D.N.Y. 2002); *Cabiri v. Assasie-Gyimah,* 921 F. Supp. 1189, 1191, 1196 (S.D.N.Y. 1996); *Abebe-Jira v. Negewo,* 72 F.3d 844, 845 (11th Cir. 1996)); threatening with death (*Abebe-Jira v. Negewo,* 72 F.3d 844, 845 (11th Cir. 1996)); and using techniques to exacerbate pain or injury (*Abebe-Jira v. Negewo,* 72 F.3d 844, 845-6 (11th Cir. 1996)).

(e)   Conclusion: CAT's Prohibition against Torture as Implemented in U.S. Legislation and Regulation

U.S. domestic laws prohibiting, or providing a cause of action to victims of, torture are consistent with the standards of CAT. However, these U.S. statutes and regulations are limited to specific contexts—such as, refugee claims, extradition of foreign fugitives, criminalizing acts of torture committed outside the U.S. by U.S. officials, and providing compensation to victims of torture committed by aliens. Accordingly, the U.S. has yet to fulfill its obligation, under CAT, to enact laws which adequately prevent U.S. officials and individuals acting with their consent from subjecting any detainee to torture and which punish such conduct wherever it occurs.

3.   CAT's Prohibition against "Cruel, Inhuman or Degrading Treatment," as Interpreted by United States Law

As previously noted, the U.S.'s reservation to Article 16 of CAT provides that the United States considers itself bound by Article 16 only insofar as CID treatment is understood to mean "the cruel, unusual and inhumane treatment or punishment prohibited by the Fifth, Eighth and Fourteenth Amendments."

The Senate Foreign Relations Committee report states that this reservation is the outgrowth of concern that "degrading treatment or punishment...has been interpreted as potentially including treatment that would probably not be prohibited by the U.S. Constitution" and cites, as an example of what the United States would not find "degrading" under the U.S. Constitution, a holding by the European Commission of Human Rights that the refusal of authorities to give formal recognition to an individual's change of sex might constitute degrading treatment.[59] This explanation suggests that the reservation was intended to prevent the importation of foreign social values or mores into U.S. law, rather than any view that international norms of CID treatment are out of step with U.S. law.

In assessing interrogation conduct under Article 16 of CAT, the U.S. should look to international standards defining cruel, inhuman or degrading treatment. If such conduct is prohibited under international law, the U.S. is bound to prevent such conduct unless it would not be prohibited under the Fifth, Eighth and Fourteenth Amendments. The Committees take note that much of the case law under the three Amendments arises in the context of domestic criminal justice proceedings. How this jurisprudence would be applied in a case relating to the detention and interrogation of foreign combatants is not completely clear. For instance, on the one hand some of the special protections provided in the American criminal justice system with respect to interrogations would be of doubtful applicability, particularly considering an asserted state interest in national security. On the other, the absence of a legitimate state interest in punishment might mandate a higher standard of treatment of detainees generally.

(a)   Fifth and Fourteenth Amendment Standards

The Constitution's guarantee of due process forbids compulsion to testify, at least for domestic law enforcement purposes, by fear of hurt, torture or exhaustion. See *Adamson v. California,* 332 U.S. 46 (1947) (armed Texas Rangers on several successive nights took defendant from county jail into the woods, whipped him, asked him each time about a confession, interrogated him from approximately 11 p.m. to 3 a.m. and warned him not to speak to anyone about the nightly trips); *Brown v. Mississippi,* 297 U.S. 278 (1936) (confessions obtained by mock executions and whippings); *Ashcraft v. Tennessee,* 322 U.S. 143, 154 (1944) (defendant was taken into custody by police officers and for 36 hours thereafter was held incommunicado, without sleep or rest, and interrogated without respite by relays of officers, experienced investigators, and highly trained lawyers); *see also Ashcraft v. Tennessee,* 327 U.S. 274 (1946). However, the presence of unlawful police coercion motivated by "immediate necessity to find the victim and save his life" to extract a confession has been found by one appeals court to be insufficient to exclude a subsequent confession.[60]

Due process also prohibits actions taken under color of law that are "so brutal and offensive to human dignity" that they "shock the conscience."[61] The Supreme Court has given content to the phrase "shocks the conscience" by reference to the spectrum of fault standards in tort law. Intentional infliction of injury unjustifiable by any government interest is the sort of official action which could rise to the conscience-shocking level.[62] All applicable sources of law are consistent in prohibiting such extreme conduct.

(b)   Eighth Amendment Standards

The Eighth Amendment prohibits "cruel and unusual punishments."[63] In the context of law enforcement, U.S. courts have long held that the norms articulated under the Cruel and Unusual Punishment Clause establish a minimum level of protection, applicable even to pretrial detainees.[64]

While the Supreme Court initially interpreted the Eighth Amendment as prohibiting only barbaric or torturous punishments, this interpretation was early broadened in two respects: (i) to prevent disproportionate punishments (*Weems v. United States,* 217 U.S. 349 (1910)) and (ii) to address non-physical forms of cruel and unusual punishment (*e.g., Trop v. Dulles,* 356 U.S. 86 (1958) (in case involving denationalization as a punishment for desertion from the United States Army, the Court noted that "evolving standards of decency that mark the progress of a maturing society" should inform interpretation of the Eighth Amendment)). In 1947, the Supreme Court recognized that wanton or unnecessary infliction of pain also constitutes cruel and unusual punishment. *Louisiana ex rel. Francis v. Resweber,* 329 U.S. 459, 463 (1947).

In cases brought by prisoners under the Eighth Amendment alleging that excessive force was used against them by government officials, courts consider both the objective component (whether the wrongdoing was "harmful enough" to implicate the Eighth Amendment) and the subjective component (whether the officials acted with a sufficiently culpable state of mind) of the challenged conduct. *Hudson v. McMillian,* 503 U.S. 1, 8 (1992). In order to establish that the objective component of an Eighth Amendment violation is satisfied, a prisoner need not prove he has sustained significant injury. However, the extent of injury suffered is one factor that may suggest "whether the use of force could plausibly have been thought necessary" in a particular situation, "or instead evinced such wantonness with respect to the unjustified infliction of harm as is tantamount to a knowing willingness that it occur."[65] The subjective component involves, in the context of force used by prison officials, "whether force was applied in a good-faith effort to maintain or restore discipline, or maliciously and sadistically for the very purpose of causing harm."[66]

D.   Enforcement of CAT under U.S. Law

1.   *18 U.S.C. §§ 2340–2340B*

As stated above, the United States' attempt to comply with its obligation under CAT to criminalize torture is codified in 18 U.S.C. § 2340A. Section 2340A criminalizes conduct by a U.S. national or a foreign national present in the U.S. who, acting under color of law, commits or attempts to commit torture outside the United States. The statute is exclusively criminal and may not be construed as creating any right enforceable in a civil proceeding. *See* 18 U.S.C. § 2340B. Section 2340A generally applies to acts committed by U.S. nationals overseas (everywhere *except* "all areas under the jurisdiction of the United States, including any of the places described in sections 5 and 7 of this title and Section 46501(2) of Title 49.") When the Section was enacted the reach of the cross-referenced provisions, notably 18 U.S.C. § 7, was uncertain.[67] However, Section 7 was broadened in the USA PATRIOT Act to clarify jurisdiction over crimes committed against U.S. citizens on U.S. property abroad by extending U.S. criminal jurisdiction over certain crimes committed at its foreign diplomatic, military and other facilities, and by cross-reference excluded those places from the reach of Section 2340A. The resulting drastic limitation of jurisdiction under 18 U.S.C. § 2340A appears unintended. We recommend that Congress amend Section 2340A to assure that it applies to U.S. government premises abroad without prejudice to the expansion of U.S. criminal jurisdiction under other statutes.

The U.S. did not enact a specific criminal statute outlawing torture within the United States, out of deference to federal-state relations and because it determined that existing federal and state criminal law was sufficient to cover any domestic act that would qualify as torture under CAT.[68] It is submitted that the inapplicability of state law to U.S. facilities abroad and the lack of other federal criminal law comparable to Section 2340A leaves a serious vacuum in carrying out the obligations of the U.S. under CAT.

Unfortunately the U.S. has never enforced 18 U.S.C. § 2340A, and has thereby fallen far short of its obligations under international law and its professed ideals. The United States has failed to utilize 18 U.S.C. § 2340A to prosecute either U.S. agents suspected of committing torture outside the jurisdiction of the U.S. or foreign torturers living within the United States. Indeed, Amnesty International reported in 2002 that in the eight years following the enactment of 18 U.S.C. § 2340 and § 2340A, not a single case had been brought under that section.[69]

2. Uniform Code of Military Justice

The UCMJ may be used to prosecute in courts-martial certain acts of ill-treatment carried out, whether within the United States or overseas, by American military personnel and possibly certain civilians accompanying such personnel. This federal statute is essentially a complete set of criminal laws that includes both crimes that are normally part of a criminal code as well as uniquely military and wartime offenses.

As a jurisdictional matter, the UCMJ applies worldwide (10 U.S.C. § 805), and persons subject to the UCMJ include any U.S. service member (10 U.S.C. § 802) as well as certain civilians "[i]n time of war...serving with or accompanying an armed force in the field" (10 U.S.C. § 802(a)(10)) and POWs (10 U.S.C. § 802(a)(9)).[70] Because courts-martial have jurisdiction to try "any person who by the law of war is subject to trial by a military tribunal" for any offense against the laws of war (10 U.S.C. § 818), the UCMJ would seem to apply also to "unlawful combatants" deemed by the Administration not to qualify for POW status under Geneva III.

The broad statutory application of the UCMJ to civilians associated in various ways with the armed forces has been judicially limited in deference to the requirements of Article III, Section II, of the Constitution and the Fifth and Sixth Amendments protecting the right to trial by jury. As so limited, the UCMJ does not apply to civilians who have no military status in peacetime, even if they are accompanying United States forces overseas as employees or dependents. Although courts' interpretations of the terms "serving", "accompanying" and "in the field" suggest a broad application, the "time of war" requirement is construed narrowly when applied to civilians.[71] As recently as 1998, the Court of Appeals for the Armed Forces[72] analyzed the propriety of the application of the UCMJ to civilians and stated:

As a matter of constitutional law, the Supreme Court has held that Congress may not extend court-martial jurisdiction to cover civilians who have no military status in peacetime, even if they are accompanying United States forces overseas as employees or dependents.

Willenbring v. Neurauter, 48 M.J. 152, 157, 1998 CAAF LEXIS 43 (C.A.A.F. 1998). The line of cases in this area generally focuses on the application of the UCMJ to civilian contractors and civilian dependents of service members. *See, e.g., Robb v. United States,* 456 F.2d 768 (Ct. Cl. 1972) (civilian engineer employed by U.S. Navy in Vietnam was not subject to UCMJ); *Reid v. Covert,* 354 U.S. 1 (1957) (no jurisdiction over civilian dependents of service members stationed overseas in peacetime for capital offenses). No cases directly address whether CIA operatives conducting para-military operations with the regular armed forces or interrogations within a military base are considered civilians for purposes of UCMJ application. In *Reid v. Covert,* the Supreme Court stated, "[e]ven if it were possible, we need not attempt here to precisely define the boundary between 'civilians' and members of the 'land and naval Forces.' We recognize that there might be circumstances where a person could be 'in' the armed services ...even though he had not formally been inducted into the military or did not wear a uniform." *See* 354 U.S. at 22.[73] In any event, where a CIA operative is a detached service member who has not been formally discharged from military service (as is often the case in practice), the UCMJ would generally apply to such person in time of war or peace.

The UCMJ provides the strongest substantive basis for potential prosecution of torture or CID treatment in federal criminal law, specifically outlawing cruel or unusual punishment, torture under 18 U.S.C. § 2340 and a variety of related offenses. Article 55 of the UCMJ provides that:

Punishment by flogging, or by branding, marking, or tattooing on the body, or any other cruel or unusual punishment, may not be adjudged by any court-martial or inflicted upon any person subject to this chapter. The use of irons, single or double, except for the purpose of safe custody, is prohibited.

10 U.S.C. § 855.[74] Article 55 is unique in its specific definition of "cruel *or* unusual punishment" as an offense.[75] While most military courts have followed the Supreme Court's analytical framework of protections under the Eighth Amendment as they pertain to cruel and unusual punishment,[76] several military courts have found that Article 55 provides greater protections than those given under the Eighth Amendment.[77] It is notable that Article 55 applies at least the equivalent of the protection afforded by the Eighth Amendment even if the victim is not otherwise entitled to constitutional rights (*e.g.,* a non-citizen apprehended and detained outside the U.S. and arguably not entitled to such rights).[78]

Moreover, the UCMJ effectively provides a basis for the prosecution of military personnel in courts-martial for the offense of torture in violation of 18 U.S.C. § 2340. Article 134 of the UCMJ (10 U.S.C. § 934) provides:

Though not specifically mentioned in this chapter, all disorders and neglects to the prejudice of good order and discipline in the armed forces, all conduct of a nature to bring discredit upon the armed forces, and crimes and offenses not capital, of which persons subject to this chapter may be guilty, shall be taken cognizance of by a general, special, or summary court-martial, according to the nature and degree of the offense, and shall be punished at the discretion of that court.

Article 134 makes punishable acts in three categories of offenses not specifically covered in any other article of the UCMJ: Clause 1 offenses involving disorders and neglect to the prejudice of good order and discipline; Clause 2 offenses involving conduct of a nature to bring discredit upon the armed forces; and Clause 3 offenses entailing non-capital crimes or offenses that violate Federal law.

In order to successfully charge an individual under Clauses 1 and 2 of this Article, the government must show: (i) that the accused did or failed to do certain acts; and (ii) that, under the circumstances, the accused's conduct was to the prejudice of good order and discipline in the armed forces or was of a nature to bring discredit upon the armed forces.[79] Under Clause 1, the acts must be directly prejudicial to good order and discipline, rather than remotely so. Under Clause 2, discredit is interpreted to mean "injure the reputation of," and encompasses conduct that brings the service "into disrepute or which tends to lower it in public esteem."[80] With respect to Clause 3 offenses, as a general rule, any offense created by Federal statute may be prosecuted as an Article 134 offense. *United States v. Perkins,* 47 C.M.R. 259 (Ct. of Mil. Rev. 1973).[81]

Thus, a service member whose conduct is alleged to violate 18 U.S.C. § 2340, the federal enactment of CAT, could be prosecuted under Article 134 of the UCMJ, as a Clause 3 violation. Moreover, multiple counts alleging Article 134 violations also could be brought in such a situation, as such conduct could be construed as prejudicial to good order and discipline and/or of a nature to bring discredit upon the armed forces. *Perkins,* 47 C.M.R. at 263–264.

Finally, criminal charges for torture or CID conduct could be brought under a variety of other provisions[82] including "cruelty."[83] The last of these offenses is generally intended to be applied to mistreatment of U.S. service members by their superiors, but by its terms it is not so limited and has been applied to intentional mistreatment of detainees.[84] And in instances where specific orders are in place regarding the treatment of detainees, as is recommended in this Report, failure to obey such orders is punishable under 10 U.S.C. § 892. A number of service members in Iraq are or have been investigated or tried for assaulting detainees, under the assault provision of the UCMJ (Article 128), and in at least one case the alleged assault occurred in the context of an interrogation.[85]

The UCMJ is thus the substantively most extensive body of federal criminal law relating to the interrogation of detainees by U.S. military personnel and, in time of war, its reach could possibly extend to civilians such as CIA agents accompanying such personnel. It prohibits such persons from subjecting detainees to torture and "cruel or unusual punishment" within or without the United States and regardless of the applicability of constitutional rights.

E. Summary

CAT's prohibition against torture is absolute. By ratifying CAT, the United States has accepted that the prohibition of torture is non-derogable. Moreover, by implementing prohibitions against torture in immigration, extradition, criminal and civil tort law contexts, the U.S. has given CAT's prohibition against torture the force of U.S. law. Furthermore, by stipulating that CAT's prohibition on CID treatment or punishment means the cruel and unusual treatment or punishment prohibited by the U.S. Constitution, the U.S. has made relevant the case law providing that detainees cannot be subjected to interrogation techniques: that force them to answer law enforcement questions by "fear of hurt, torture or exhaustion," *Adamson v. California, supra;* that are "brutal and offensive to human dignity," *Rochin v. California, supra;* that fall below the "evolving standards of decency that mark the progress of a maturing society," *Trop v. Dulles, supra;* or which deliberately inflict force or pain (in the context of restoring prison order or safety), *Hudson v. McMillian, supra.* However, U.S. enforcement of CAT in our domestic criminal law—particularly with respect to acts of torture or CID treatment by U.S. civilians or by U.S. officials in extra-territorial areas under U.S. jurisdiction—has been incomplete. We urge the U.S. to fill in the gaps in preventing and punishing torture and CID treatment left by 18 U.S.C. § 2340A and to fully utilize the UCMJ to fulfill its obligations under CAT.

II. THE GENEVA CONVENTIONS

The four Geneva Conventions of 1949 are the core of the international law of armed conflict applicable to the treatment of detainees, albeit not the complete body of applicable law. The applicability of the Geneva Conventions to persons captured by the United States in connection with the War In Afghanistan and the ongoing conflict in Afghanistan, however, is highly controversial. The most hotly contested issue is whether those Al Qaeda and Taliban detainees who were captured before the creation of the Karzai government are entitled to POW status under Geneva Convention III Relative to the Treatment of Prisoners of War ("Geneva III"). This issue is of particular significance because Geneva III flatly prohibits "any form of coercion" of POWs in interrogation—the most protective standard of treatment found in international law. Likewise, Geneva Convention IV Relative to the Protection of Civilian Persons in Time of War ("Geneva IV") protects "civilian" detainees who qualify as "protected persons" from "coercion."[86] We also should note that the issues regarding Geneva III and Geneva IV are affected by whether the person was detained either before or after the Karzai government was established. Before the Karzai government, the U.S. was engaged in an international armed conflict with Afghanistan, which was governed by the Taliban (albeit the U.S. did not recognize that government). After the establishment of the Karzai government, the conflict in Afghanistan became an internal one—as the U.S. and other international organizations were present in Afghanistan with the consent of the Karzai government to assist in maintaining order. Geneva III and Geneva IV apply only in situations of international armed conflict and, therefore, ceased to apply once the Afghan conflict became an internal one. *See* Geneva IV, Art. 6.

In this section, we will examine the Administration's position that Al Qaeda and Taliban detainees are not POWs under Geneva III and some critiques of the Administration's position. We submit that, regardless of whether a detainee enjoys status as a POW or civilian protected person under the Geneva Conventions, the Conventions nevertheless are relevant to the interrogation of detainees in the following respects:

First, the requirements of humane treatment embodied in Common Article 3 of the Geneva Conventions and Article 75 of Additional Protocol I protect all detainees captured in situations of international or internal armed conflict, regardless of "legal" status.[87] Of course, all detainees—including those captured outside of Afghan territory or in connection with the "War on Terror"—are entitled to the protection provided by human rights law, including CAT, the ICCPR and customary international law.

Second, notwithstanding its position on the POW status of Taliban and Al Qaeda detainees, the Administration has undertaken that it will treat all detainees in a manner consistent with the principles of Geneva III. Accordingly, the interrogation techniques reportedly being used on detainees at Bagram and other U.S. detention facilities should be considered in light of the text and spirit of the Geneva Conventions.

Third, if there is doubt as to whether a detainee meets Geneva III criteria for POW status, that detainee is entitled to interim POW status until a "competent tribunal" determines his or her legal status. Because the U.S. government has not convened "competent tribunals" to determine the status of any detainees, all detainees for whom POW status is in doubt are entitled to interim POW status.[88]

Finally, even accepting the interpretation that the Third and Fourth Geneva Conventions contain gaps leaving certain detainees captured in the War in Afghanistan (*i.e.,* citizens of co-belligerents and neutrals) without POW or "protected person" civilian status, the Geneva Conventions are supplemented by human rights law and customary international legal norms which have the force of law in the United States. For example, even where a detainee may not be entitled to a hearing under Geneva III, he is entitled to a hearing to determine the justification for his detention under Article 9 of the ICCPR. Many detainees may not be combatants at all and may be simply innocent bystanders mistakenly detained or wrongfully turned over to the U.S. military by the Northern Alliance.[89] They deserve prompt hearings in which they are given an opportunity to establish their non-combatant status.

A. Application of the Geneva Conventions to the Afghan Conflict Generally

Both the U.S. and Afghanistan are parties to the Geneva Conventions. Article 2 common to all four Conventions provides that the Conventions "apply to all cases of declared war or of any other armed conflict" between two or more parties to the Conventions so long as a state of war is recognized by a party to the conflict. The Conventions also apply to all cases of partial or total occupation of the territory of a signatory, even if the occupation meets with no armed resistance. *See* Geneva Conventions, Art. 2. Signatories to the Conventions are bound by its terms regardless of whether an additional party to the conflict is a signatory. *Id.* The Administration's position is that the Geneva Conventions apply to the War in Afghanistan.[90]

B. Geneva III

1. *Relevant Legal Standards*

Under Geneva III, combatants are entitled to POW status if they are members of the armed forces (other than medical personnel and chaplains). The specific requirements for combatant/ POW status are set forth in Article 4 of Geneva III[91] and Articles 43 and 44 of Additional Protocol I.[92]

If there is any doubt as to whether captured persons meet Article 4's criteria for POW status, such persons are entitled to interim POW status until a "competent tribunal" determines their legal status.[93]

Geneva III mandates that POWs be treated humanely at all times. This includes freedom from physical and mental torture, acts of violence, intimidation and insult, and exposure to public humiliation.[94] Pursuant to Article 14, POWs also "are entitled in all circumstances to respect for their persons and their honour. ...[and] shall retain the full civil capacity which they enjoyed at the time of their capture."

With respect to interrogation, in particular, Article 17 of Geneva III provides: "No physical or mental torture, nor any other form of coercion, may be inflicted on prisoners of war to secure from them information of any kind whatever. Prisoners of war who refuse to answer may not be threatened, insulted, or exposed to any unpleasant or disadvantageous treatment of any letter="default"/>kind." Under Article 17, POWs are only obligated to provide their name, rank, date of birth, and army, personal or serial identification number or equivalent information. Geneva III does not, however, prohibit non-coercive interrogation of POWs. POWs may be interrogated, but they are not obliged to respond to such interrogation, nor may they be threatened, coerced into responding or punished for failing to respond. The Geneva Conventions also do not "preclude classic plea bargaining"—*i.e.,* the offer of leniency or other incentives in return for cooperation.[95]

Thus, to the extent detainees from the War in Afghanistan are considered POWs or to the extent their POW status is in "doubt" pending the determination of status by a competent tribunal, interrogation tactics which rise to the level of "coercion" are prohibited by Geneva III.

2. The United States' Position

In sharp contrast with past conflicts (such as Vietnam and Korea) in which it was U.S. policy to presume that military prisoners were entitled to POW status regardless of the possible non-qualification of their forces under Geneva III, from the very outset of the War in Afghanistan, United States officials labeled captured Al Qaeda and Taliban prisoners "unlawful combatants," and stated that the Geneva Conventions were, therefore, entirely inapplicable to their treatment.[96] The United States reasoned that Al Qaeda was not entitled to the protections of the Geneva Conventions because: (1) Geneva III could not apply to members of a nonstate organization, such as Al Qaeda, (2) the conflict was not an internal conflict such that Al Qaeda members could benefit from the protection of Common Article 3, and (3) in any event, Al Qaeda members failed to meet the requirements set forth in Article 4(A)(2) of Geneva III.[97] The United States argued further that, since Afghanistan was not a functioning state during the conflict and the Taliban was not recognized as a legitimate government, Geneva III could not apply to the Taliban.[98]

After vigorous criticism was leveled against these arguments, Secretary of State Colin Powell requested that the Administration reconsider its position.[99] On February 7, 2002, in response to Powell's comments, the Administration partially reversed its initial position. Although the Administration continues to argue that the Geneva Conventions are inapplicable to Al Qaeda captives, President Bush announced that Geneva III was applicable to the Taliban because both the U.S. and Afghanistan were signatories to the Convention and the parties had been involved in an armed conflict. However, President Bush further argued that because the Taliban had violated the laws of war and associated closely with Al Qaeda, "[u]nder the terms of the Geneva Convention...the Taliban detainees do not qualify as POWs."[100] The decision in *United States v. Lindh,* 212 F. Supp. 2d 541 (E.D. Va. 2002), which specifically addresses the issue of whether the Taliban are entitled to POW status under Geneva III, sheds further light on the U.S. position.[101]

3. Critiques of the United States' Position

International humanitarian and human rights organizations and legal bodies, including the International Committee of the Red Cross ("ICRC"),[102] the Inter-American Court of Human

Rights,[103] Amnesty International,[104] the International Commission of Jurists,[105] the Secretary General of the United Nations,[106] the United Nations High Commissioner for Human Rights,[107] as well as certain U.S. and foreign international law scholars[108] have criticized the U.S. position on several grounds.

(a)   Article 5 Presumes POW Status Until the Determination of Status by a Competent Tribunal

Critics of the Administration position argue that non-civilian detainees from the War in Afghanistan either clearly qualify as POWs or their POW status is in "doubt." Geneva III mandates that a detainee whose status is in "doubt" must be treated as a POW until his status is decided otherwise by a competent tribunal under Article 5. Indeed, Article 5's presumption that captured combatants are entitled to POW status until their status is determined by a competent tribunal is one that has been consistently honored by the U.S. since World War II.[109] Moreover, like Article 5, customary international law also includes the principle that a competent tribunal must resolve any doubt about the status of a captured combatant.[110] We agree with critics of the Administration position that all combatants whose claim to POW status is "in doubt" must be treated as POWs until such doubt has been resolved by a "competent tribunal." Accordingly, since no tribunals have been convened for detainees from the War in Afghanistan, all such detainees must be considered POWs under Geneva III.

(b)   The Taliban Detainees Were "Regular Armed Forces" and, Therefore, Are Encompassed by Article 4(A) of Geneva III

Critics of the Administration's position that Taliban fighters are not entitled to POW status because they do not satisfy the requirements of Article 4(a)(2) of Geneva III[111] assert that Taliban captured in the War in Afghanistan are entitled to POW status either under: Article 4(a)(1) because they are "[m]embers of the armed forces" of Afghanistan; or Article 4(a)(3) as they are "[m]embers of regular armed forces who profess allegiance to a government of an authority not recognized by the Detaining Power."[112]

(c)   Policy Arguments Favoring Broad Grant of POW Status to Non-Civilian Detainees from the War in Afghanistan

Several policy arguments favor granting POW status liberally even assuming that Geneva III does not apply to Taliban or Al Qaeda detainees captured in the War in Afghanistan.

First, depriving Taliban and Al Qaeda of POW status because they do not obey the laws of war sets a dangerous precedent, inviting other state parties to claim that another party is not obeying the rules of war and that they are, therefore, free from the obligations of Geneva III. International humanitarian law applies regardless of whether or not the other party to the conflict respects such laws.[113] Reciprocity arrangements are generally rejected in international humanitarian law as they can so easily be abused at the expense of civilians or persons rendered "hors de combat."[114]

Second, it is in the U.S.'s self-interest to ensure that the Geneva Conventions—a regime of vital importance to the safety of our own armed forces—are interpreted as broadly as possible. Otherwise, an opposing state party could use the argument that the U.S. has violated the laws of war to deny captured U.S. soldiers POW status. In fact, North Korea and Vietnam have already used this argument as a basis to deny captured U.S. prisoners POW protections under the Geneva Conventions.[115] Indeed, it was reportedly these very examples that prompted Colin Powell, out of concern for the safety of U.S. forces, to request that President Bush reconsider the Administration's initial position.[116]

We accordingly urge liberal extension of POW treatment where that would encourage reciprocal treatment of U.S. service personnel and advance more generally foreign policy and national security interests. We further believe that, even to the extent that POW status is denied to detainees, such detainees must be afforded the protections of international criminal law, as well as international human rights and humanitarian law.

C.   Geneva IV

Geneva IV applies in international armed conflicts to the same extent as Geneva III. It covers "protected persons" defined as "those who, at a given moment and in any manner whatsoever, find themselves, in case of a conflict or occupation, in the hands of a Party to the conflict or Occupying Power of which they are not nationals." *See* Geneva IV, Article 4.[117]

The fact that a person may have unlawfully participated in a conflict is not relevant to Geneva IV protections, apart from a significant national security exemption. The term "protected persons" includes persons detained as spies or saboteurs as well as other persons suspected of engaging in activities hostile to the security of the detaining power. Specifically, Article 5 provides:

Where in the territory of a Party to the conflict, the *latter* is satisfied that an individual protected person is definitely suspected of or engaged in activities hostile to the security of the State, such individual person shall not be entitled to claim such rights and privileges under the present Convention as would, if exercised in the favour of such individual person, be prejudicial to the security of such State

. . . .

In each case, such persons shall nevertheless be treated with humanity and, in case of trial, shall not be deprived of the rights of fair and regular trial prescribed by the present Convention. They shall also be granted the full rights and privileges of a protected person under the present Convention at the earliest date consistent with the security of the State or Occupying Power, as the case may be.

As drafted, (*i.e.,* the use of the words "the latter"), it would appear that the national security derogation is available only to the State on whose territory the conflict is occurring (*i.e.,* in the War in Afghanistan, only to the Northern Alliance), and there is no authority whether or not an allied State, such as the United States, can benefit from such exemption.

In an exception of great importance in Afghanistan, given the number of third country participants in the conflict, "protected persons" does not include "[n]ationals of a State which is not bound by the Convention," "[n]ationals of a neutral State who find themselves in the territory of a belligerent State" and "nationals of a co-belligerent State...while the State of which they are nationals has normal diplomatic representation in the State in whose hands they are." *See* Geneva IV, Article 4. For example, a Pakistani picked up on the battlefield in Afghanistan would fall within the exceptions to "protected person" status under Geneva IV.

However, in no event would such provision permit the State to commit "grave breaches" as defined in Article 147, which includes torture or inhuman treatment and willfully causing great suffering or serious injury to body or health, upon a "protected person". *See* Geneva IV, Art. 146. Furthermore, to the extent that any physical or moral coercion (otherwise prohibited by Article 31 of Geneva IV) might fall below the level of "grave breach" and thus be derogable, the ICRC commentary to the national security derogations contained in Article 5 of Geneva IV, involving persons engaged in activities hostile to the security of the state notes that:

widespread application of the Article may eventually lead to the existence of a category of civilian internees who do not receive the normal treatment laid down by the Convention but are detained under conditions which are almost impossible to check. It must be emphasized most strongly, therefore, that Article 5 can only be applied in individual cases of an exceptional nature, when the existence of specific charges makes it almost certain that penal proceedings will follow. This article should never be applied as a result of mere suspicion.

Like POWs under Geneva III, "protected persons" under Geneva IV cannot be subjected to coercive interrogation tactics. Specifically, Article 31 of Geneva IV provides that "[n]o physical or moral coercion shall be exercised against protected persons, in particular to obtain information from them or from third parties." Article 32 further provides that "any measure of such a character as to the cause the physical suffering or extermination of protected persons" is prohibited and that "[t]his prohibition applies not only to murder, torture, corporal punishments, mutilation and medical or scientific experiments not necessitated by the medical treatment of a protected person, but also to any other measures of brutality, whether applied by civilian or military agents."

By its terms, Geneva IV ceases to apply "on the general close of military operations" in the case of an international conflict. *See* Geneva IV, Art. 6. Whether military operations have reached a "general close" after the establishment of the Karzai government in June 2002 and whether the change in character of the conflict from an international one to a multi-national conflict within a single State against non-State opponents terminated application of Geneva IV are issues open to controversy.[118] Thus, the ability of some civilians captured in Afghanistan to claim "protected person" status under Geneva IV today is subject to additional debate. However, regardless of the characterization of the current conflict, torture and inhumane treatment of civilian detainees from the War in Afghanistan or the ongoing conflict in Afghanistan, whether or not they qualify as "protected persons" under Geneva IV, is not permitted. All such persons are still entitled to the protections of international human rights law and to humane treatment under Common Article 3 and Article 75 of Additional Protocol I.

D.   Summary

None of the detainees from the War in Afghanistan or the ongoing conflict in Afghanistan fall outside of international humanitarian law. An individual detained during the armed conflict in Afghanistan—whether considered an international or internal armed conflict—is either protected by Geneva III as a POW, by Geneva IV as a civilian "protected person," or, at the very minimum, by Common Article 3 and Article 75 of Additional Protocol I. Of course, all detainees—regardless of where or when they were captured—are entitled to the protection of human rights law (including CAT and the ICCPR) and customary international law.

Detainees protected as POWs or civilians under Geneva III or Geneva IV cannot be subjected to coercion of any kind. In addition, those detainees whose POW status is in doubt are entitled to interim POW status until a competent tribunal determines otherwise. At least some Afghan detainees are entitled to such tribunals, and the U.S. is long overdue in providing any process whatsoever to detainees, many of whom may simply be innocent non-combatants, wrongfully detained. We, therefore, urge the U.S. to establish proper screening procedures for all detainees.

III.   OTHER INTERNATIONAL LEGAL STANDARDS

The legal standards set forth in the International Covenant on Civil and Political Rights, the American Declaration of the Rights and Duties of Man, and customary international law also apply to the treatment of detainees held by the United States.

A.   The International Covenant on Civil and Political Rights[119]

1.   Relevant Legal Standards

Like CAT, the ICCPR expressly prohibits both torture and CID. Specifically, Article 7 of the ICCPR provides: "No one shall be subjected to torture or to cruel, inhuman or degrading treatment or punishment."[120] However, the ICCPR goes further than CAT in its non-derogability provision, expressly stating that neither torture *nor* CID treatment can be justified by exceptional circumstances such as war, internal political stability or other public emergencies. (*See* ICCPR, Art. 4). Article 10 also provides that: "All persons deprived of their liberty shall be treated with humanity and with respect for the inherent dignity of the human person."

The Human Rights Committee, established under Article 28, adjudicates complaints filed by individuals or states parties alleging violations of the ICCPR. The Committee has found the following conduct to violate Article 7's prohibition against cruel, inhuman or degrading treatment or punishment: threatening a victim with torture, prolonged solitary confinement and incommunicado detention, and repeated beatings.[121] Moreover, the Human Rights Committee has specifically criticized interrogation procedures such as handcuffing, hooding, shaking and sleep deprivation as violations of Article 7 in any circumstances.[122]

Although the ICCPR does not expressly prohibit states parties from "rendering" individuals to countries where they are likely to be mistreated, the Human Rights Committee has explained that, under Article 7, states parties "must not expose individuals to the danger of torture or cruel, inhuman or degrading treatment or punishment upon return to another country by way of their extradition, expulsion or refoulement."[123] Accordingly, the Human Rights Committee has stated that "[i]f a State party extradites a person within its jurisdiction in circumstances such that as a result there is a real risk that his or her rights under the Covenant will be violated in another jurisdiction, the State party itself may be in violation of the Covenant."[124]

2. Enforcement

(a)　U.S. Courts

In ratifying the ICCPR, the U.S. Senate declared that Articles 1 through 27 are not self-executing. Thus, while the Supreme Court has not squarely decided the issue, the majority of federal appeals courts have held that the ICCPR provides no privately enforceable rights and is not binding on federal courts.[125] The Second and Ninth circuit courts, however, have cited the ICCPR as evidence that customary international law prohibits arbitrary arrest, prolonged detention and torture.[126]

(b)　The Human Rights Committee

The Human Rights Committee is empowered to: (i) receive state party reports and comment on those reports (*see* ICCPR, Art. 40(4)); (ii) rule on complaints filed by a state party that another state party is not fulfilling its obligations under the ICCPR (*see* ICCPR, Art. 41);[127] and (iii) rule on complaints filed by individuals "who claim that any of their rights enumerated in the Covenant have been violated and who have exhausted all available domestic remedies."[128]

B.　Organization of American States' Instruments

1.　Relevant Legal Standards

The U.S. is a member of the Organization of American States (the "OAS"). Article XXV of The American Declaration of the Rights and Duties of Man (the "American Declaration"), which was adopted by the Ninth International Conference of the OAS in 1948, provides:

Every individual who has been deprived of his liberty has the right to have the legality of his detention ascertained without delay by a court, and the right to be tried without undue delay or, otherwise, to be released. He also has the right to humane treatment during the time he is in custody.

On June 1, 1997, the U.S. signed, but has not yet ratified, the American Convention On Human Rights (1969) (the "American Convention").[129] Article 5 of the American Convention, which sets forth Rights to Humane Treatment, provides:

1. Every person has the right to have his physical, mental, and moral integrity respected.

2. No one shall be subjected to torture or to cruel, inhuman or degrading punishment or treatment. All persons deprived of their liberty shall be treated with respect for the inherent dignity of the human person.

Moreover, pursuant to Article 27(2) of the American Convention, the Rights to Humane Treatment may not be suspended "[i]n time of war, public danger, or other emergency that threatens the independence or security of a State Party."

With respect to the treatment of detainees, the Inter-American Commission on Human Rights (the "Inter-American Commission")—which represents all member countries of the OAS and was established under Chapter VII of the American Convention—has determined that, "when the State holds a person in detention and under its exclusive control, it becomes the guarantor of that person's safety and rights."[130] In this regard, the Commission has found the following practices to be violations of Article 5 of the American Convention: threats to summon family members and pressure them to "talk"; threats to kill detainees; blindfolding detainees and forcing them to run around; "prolonged isolation and deprivation of communication"; solitary confinement; confining detainees in small cells with other prisoners; keeping detainees in cells that are damp and/or without adequate ventilation; keeping detainees in cells without beds; forcing detainees to sleep on the floor or on newspaper; depriving detainees of necessary hygiene facilities; beatings with rifles; and kicks in various parts of the body, especially in the stomach.[131]

The Inter-American Court of Human Rights (the "Inter-American Court")—established pursuant to Chapter VIII of the American Convention—has held that, "in order to establish if torture has been inflicted and its scope, all the circumstances of the case should be taken into consideration, such as the nature and context of the respective aggressions, how they were inflicted, during what period of time, the physical and mental effects and, in some case, the sex, age and state of health of the victims."[132] "The violation of the right to physical and psychological integrity of persons is a category of violation that has several gradations and embraces treatment ranging from torture to other types of humiliation or cruel, inhuman or degrading treatment with varying degrees of physical and psychological effects caused by endogenous and exogenous factors which must be proven in each specific situation."[133]

The Inter-American Court has found the following practices to violate Article 5 of the American Convention and/or Article 2 of the Inter-American Convention To Prevent and Punish Torture:[134] forcing detainees to stand blindfolded with their hands cuffed behind their backs; forcing detainees to listen to the cries of others being beaten; threatening detainees with physical torture; restriction of visiting rights; incommunicado detention; incarceration in solitary confinement and/or in a small cell with no ventilation or natural light; prohibiting detainees from engaging in physical exercise or intellectual efforts; deprivation of necessary hygiene facilities; deficient medical treatment; and throwing detainees to the ground.[135] "[A]ccording to international standards for protection, torture can be inflicted not only via physical violence, but also through acts that produce severe physical, psychological or moral suffering in the victim."[136] The Inter-American Court also has held that: "Prolonged isolation and being held incommunicado constitute, in themselves, forms of cruel and inhuman treatment, harmful to the mental and moral integrity of the person and to the right of all detainees of respect for the inherent dignity of the human being."[137]

Moreover, the Inter-American Court has warned that the fact that a State is confronted with terrorism does not, in itself, warrant the use of force:

Any use of force that is not strictly necessary, given the behavior of the person detained, constitutes an affront to human dignity...in violation of Article 5 of the American Convention. The need to conduct investigations and the undeniable difficulties inherent to combating terrorism are not grounds for placing restrictions on the protection of the physical integrity of the person.[138]

In a case brought before the Inter-American Commission by detainees alleging violations of the United States' obligations under the American Declaration by U.S. armed forces in Grenada in 1983, *Coard, et al. v. United States,* the Inter-American Commission expressly extended the protections of human rights and humanitarian norms to extraterritorial conduct by U.S. military forces and criticized the U.S. for delay in providing procedure to detainees.[139] Acknowledging the need to balance between public security and individual rights, the Inter-American Commission in *Coard* held that: "What is required when an armed force detains civilians is the establishment of a procedure to ensure that the legality of the detention can be reviewed without delay and is subject to supervisory control.... [C]ontrol over a detention [cannot] rest[] exclusively with the agents charged with carrying it out." *Coard,* at paras. 58–59.

2. *Enforcement*

The Inter-American Commission has competence with respect to matters relating to the fulfillment of the commitments made by the States Parties to the American Convention.[140] "The main function of the Commission" is "to promote respect for and defense of human rights."[141] Any person may lodge a petition with the Commission complaining of violation of the American Convention by a State Party, so long as effective domestic remedies available to the petitioner have been exhausted.[142]

On March 12, 2002, in response to a petition challenging detentions at Guantánamo Bay coordinated by the Center for Constitutional Rights,[143] the Inter-American Commission adopted precautionary measures addressed to the United States concerning the Guantánamo detainees.[144] Specifically, the Commission asked the U.S. "to take the urgent measures necessary to have the legal status of the detainees at Guantánamo Bay determined by a competent tribunal."[145] In so doing, the Inter-American Commission explained:

[W]here persons find themselves within the authority and control of a state and where a circumstance of armed conflict may be involved, their fundamental rights may be determined in part by reference to international humanitarian law as well as international human rights law. Where it may be considered that the protections of international humanitarian law do not apply, however, such persons remain the beneficiaries at least of the non-derogable protections under international human rights law. In short, no person under the authority and control of a state, regardless of his or her circumstances, is devoid of legal protection for his or her fundamental and non-derogable human rights.[146]

With regard to the Guantánamo Bay detainees in particular, the Inter-American Commission observed that: "[T]he information available suggests that the detainees remain entirely at the unfettered discretion of the United States government. Absent clarification of the legal status of the detainees, the Commission considers that the rights and protections to which they may be entitled under international or domestic law cannot be said to be the subject of effective legal protection by the State."[147] The Inter-American Commission further noted that, regardless of the legal status of the Guantánamo Bay detainees, their legal protections "may in no case fall below the minimal standards of non-derogable rights."[148] Thereafter, the Commission issued a renewed request to the U.S. government for precautionary measures, stating that new factual allegations regarding torture or other ill-treatment of detainees "raise questions concerning the extent to which the United States' policies and practices in detaining and interrogating persons in connection with its anti-terrorist initiatives clearly and absolutely prohibit treatment that may amount to torture or may otherwise be cruel, inhuman or degrading as defined under international norms."[149]

C.   Customary International Law and *Jus Cogens*

1.   *Relevant Legal Standards*

Customary international law has long prohibited the state practice of torture, without reservation, in peace or in wartime.[150] On December 9, 1975, the United Nations General Assembly adopted by consensus the Declaration on the Protection of All Persons from Being Subjected to Torture and Other Cruel, Inhuman or Degrading Punishment.[151] The Torture Resolution together with CAT and the ICCPR—ratified by 133 and 151 States, respectively—embody the customary international law obligation to refrain from behavior which constitutes torture.[152] In addition, in 1985 the United Nations Special Rapporteur on Torture, Pieter Koojimans, noted the widespread existing domestic legislation in many countries, including the United States, expressly or by implication prohibiting torture as well as cruel, inhuman and degrading punishment.[153]

The prohibition of torture is, moreover, one of the few norms which has attained peremptory norm or *jus cogens* status, and is recognized as such by United States courts.[154] *Jus cogens* is defined as a peremptory norm "accepted and recognized by the international community of states as a whole as a norm from which no derogation is permitted and which can be modified only by a subsequent norm of general international law having the same character."[155] While many international agreements expressly prohibit *both* torture and cruel, inhuman and degrading treatment,[156] it remains an open question as to whether *jus cogens* status extends to the prohibition against cruel, inhuman or degrading treatment. What is clear, however, is that cruel, inhuman and degrading treatment or punishment is prohibited by customary international law.

U.S. ratification of the ICCPR and CAT are clear pronouncements that we condemn the practice of torture and CID treatment and that we consider ourselves legally bound to prohibit such conduct. Indeed, in 1999, the United States issued a report to the U.N. Committee Against Torture categorically affirming that:

Every act constituting torture under the Convention constitutes a criminal offense under the law of the United States. No official of the Government, federal, state or local, civilian or military, is authorized to commit or to instruct anyone else to commit torture. Nor may any official condone or tolerate torture in any form. No exceptional circumstances may be invoked as justification for torture. United States law contains no provision permitting otherwise prohibited acts of torture or other cruel, inhuman or degrading treatment or punishment to be employed on grounds of exigent circumstance (for example, during a "state of public emergency") or on orders from a superior officer or public authority, and the protective mechanisms of an independent judiciary are not subject to suspension.[157]

Furthermore, the United States has enacted the Torture Victim Protection Act,[158] has imposed civil liability for acts of torture regardless of where such acts take place,[159] and has enacted the Torture Victims Relief Act, providing for monetary assistance for torture victims.[160] As previously discussed, not only does the U.S. Constitution prohibit cruel and unusual punishment or treatment by state officials (including under the military justice system), but almost all of the U.S. State constitutions have similar prohibitions.[161] Finally, a number of federal judicial proceedings have recognized that the right to be free from torture as well as cruel, inhuman or degrading treatment or punishment is a norm of customary international law.[162]

In the State Department Country Reports On Human Rights Practices, for example, the United States has expressly characterized the following types of conduct—some of which are allegedly occurring at U.S. detention centers—as "torture" or "other abuse": tying detainees in painful positions; forcing detainees to stand for long periods of time; incommunicado detention; depriving detainees of sleep; dousing naked detainees with cold water; denial of access to medical attention; interrogation techniques designed to intimidate or disorient; subjecting a detainee to loud music; forcing a detainee to squat or to assume "stressful, uncomfortable or painful" positions for "prolonged periods of time"; long periods of imprisonment in darkened rooms; verbal threats; and instilling detainees with the false belief that they are to be killed.[163] The following types of conduct have been defined as cruel, inhuman or degrading treatment: stripping; confinement in severely overcrowded cells; beating; imprisonment in small containers; and threats against family members of detainees.[164]

2. Enforcement

As the Second Circuit stated in *Filartiga v. Peña-Irala,* 630 F.2d 876 (1980), the United States is bound by customary international law. Thus, in cases where jurisdictional hurdles have been met, the bans on torture, arbitrary detention, and at least some aspects of cruel, inhuman and degrading treatment have been enforced by U.S. courts as violations of customary international law.[165]

IV.   SHOULD EXCEPTIONS BE MADE FOR THE "WAR ON TERROR"?: THE EXPERIENCE OF OTHER JURISDICTIONS

Notwithstanding the clear legal prohibitions against the use of torture and cruel, inhuman or degrading treatment in U.S. and international law, we considered whether, in a post-September 11 world, the threat posed by terrorists to the United States could ever justify the use of prohibited interrogation practices. We sought to answer the question of whether there are any circumstances in which torture and CID treatment in the interrogation of detainees should be permitted.

For additional guidance in answering these questions, we looked to the experiences of Northern Ireland and Israel, other places where the struggle between fighting terrorism and upholding the rule of law has been waged. Both the European Court of Human Rights and the Israeli Supreme Court have confronted the contradictory demands of national security and human rights against the backdrop of terrorism. The legal debate that infuses these courts' seminal decisions on the use of torture and CID treatment in the interrogation of terrorist suspects offers guidance to the United States in interpreting CAT. These courts have ruled that there are no exceptions to the prohibition against torture and CID treatment. Their rulings express the conviction that the torture and CID treatment of detainees—even when those detainees are suspected terrorists—cannot be justified.

A.   Legal Challenges to Interrogation Practices in Northern Ireland and Israel

1.   The Republic of Ireland v. The United Kingdom

The European Convention for the Protection of Human Rights and Fundamental Freedoms (the "European Convention") came into force in 1953.[166] Article 3 of the European Convention provides: "No one shall be subject to torture or to inhuman or degrading treatment or punishment." The judicial body primarily charged with interpreting and enforcing the European Convention is the European Court of Human Rights (the "ECHR"). The ECHR has, in several decisions, applied the European Convention's prohibition against torture and inhuman or degrading treatment to cases involving interrogation of suspected terrorists who pose a threat to national security.

The most important of these decisions is *The Republic of Ireland*.[167] The Republic of Ireland case was decided in a legal and political environment conditioned by several years of terrorism in Northern Ireland perpetrated by members of the Irish Republican Army (IRA) and Loyalist groups. By March 1975, over 1,100 people had been killed, over 11,500 injured and £140 million worth of property destroyed.[168] To combat a campaign of violence being carried out by the IRA, in 1971, the Northern Ireland Government introduced regulations providing authorities with extrajudicial powers, including arrest for interrogation purposes and internment.[169]

The Republic of Ireland Decision is a landmark legal discussion of whether specific interrogation practices committed by British security forces against IRA detainees constituted torture or inhuman or degrading treatment. The impetus for the ECHR's decision was the Republic of Ireland's application before the European Commission of Human Rights alleging, among other things, that various interrogation practices—including specific practices referred to as the "five techniques"—amounted to torture and inhuman or degrading treatment, in contravention of Article 3 of the European Convention.[170] The "five techniques"—described by the ECHR as methods of "disorientation" or "sensory deprivation"—include a number of practices allegedly being used today by U.S. interrogators:

- Wall-standing: Forcing a detainee to remain spread-eagled against a wall with his fingers placed high above his head against the wall, his legs spread apart and his feet positioned such that he must stand on his toes with the weight of his body resting on his fingers;

- Hooding: Keeping a dark bag over a detainee's head at all times, except during interrogation;

- Subjection to noise: Holding a detainee in a room where there is a continuous loud and hissing noise;

- Deprivation of sleep; and

- Deprivation of food and drink.[171]

The European Commission of Human Rights unanimously found that the "five techniques" constituted torture, and that other challenged interrogation practices amounted to inhuman and degrading treatment.[172] Although the British Government subsequently discontinued the "five techniques" and did not contest the underlying allegations of the case or the Commission's findings in connection therewith, the Republic of Ireland nevertheless referred the case to the ECHR.[173] The ECHR took the opportunity to rule upon the legality of the "five techniques," citing to the European Court's responsibility "to elucidate, safeguard and develop the rules instituted by the Convention."[174]

In *The Republic of Ireland* decision, the ECHR explained that ill-treatment "had to attain a minimum level of severity to fall within Article 3, the assessment of which was necessarily relative, depending on all the circumstances, including the duration of the treatment, its physical or mental effects and, sometimes, the sex, age or state of health of the victim."[175] The ECHR pointed out that, while the term "torture" attached "a special stigma to deliberate inhuman treatment causing very serious and cruel suffering," the distinction between torture and inhuman or degrading treatment "derived principally from a difference in the intensity of the suffering inflicted."[176] The ECHR held that since the "five techniques" "were applied in combination, with premeditation and for hours at a time, causing at least intense physical and mental suffering and acute psychiatric disturbances, they amount to inhuman treatment."[177] The ECHR further held that since the "five techniques" aroused "in the victims feelings of fear, anguish and inferiority capable of humiliating and debasing them and possibly breaking their physical or moral resistance, they were also degrading."[178] The ECHR concluded that the "five techniques" violated

Article 3's prohibition against inhuman or degrading treatment, but that they did not amount to torture.[179]

2.   Israeli Supreme Court Judgment Concerning The Legality of the General Security Service's Interrogation Methods

As the Israeli Supreme Court notes at the outset of its *Judgment Concerning The Legality Of The General Security Service's Interrogation Methods*,[180] the State of Israel "has been engaged in an unceasing struggle for both its very existence and security, from the day of its founding":

Terrorist organizations have established as their goal Israel's annihilation. Terrorist acts and the general disruption of order are their means of choice. In employing such methods, these groups do not distinguish between civilian and military targets. They carry out terrorist attacks in which scores are murdered in public areas, public transportation, city squares and centers, theaters and coffee shops. They do not distinguish between men, women and children. They act of cruelty and without mercy.[181]

In 1987, the Landau Commission of Inquiry into the Methods of Investigation of the GSS Regarding Hostile Terrorist Acts (the "Landau Commission") was established to investigate the interrogation practices of the main body responsible for fighting terrorism in Israel, the General Security Service (the "GSS"), and to reach legal conclusions concerning them. The resulting Landau Report,[182] concluded: "The effective interrogation of terrorist suspects is impossible without the use of means of pressure, in order to overcome an obdurate will not to disclose information and to overcome the fear of the person under interrogation that harm will befall him from his own organization, if he does not reveal information."[183] The Landau Report explained that: "The means of pressure should principally take the form of non-violent psychological pressure through a vigorous and extensive interrogation, with the use of stratagems, including acts of deception. However, when these do not attain their purpose, the exertion of a moderate measure of physical pressure cannot be avoided."[184] The Landau Commission recommended, however, that GSS interrogators should be guided by clear rules "to prevent the use of inordinate physical pressure arbitrarily administered," and formulated a code of guidelines (set forth in a secret part of the Landau Report) which defined, "on the basis of past experience, and with as much precision as possible, the boundaries of what is permitted to the interrogator and mainly what is prohibited to him."[185] The Landau Commission asserted that the latitude it afforded GSS interrogators to use "a moderate measure of physical pressure" did not conflict with the standards set forth in international human rights conventions—such as the UDHR, the ICCPR and the European Convention—which prohibited torture and cruel, inhuman or degrading treatment or punishment.[186]

In 1999, in the *GSS Interrogation Methods Decision,* the Israeli Supreme Court took up the legality of certain interrogation practices employed by the GSS. The Israeli Supreme Court acknowledged that the Landau Commission had approved the use of "a moderate degree of physical pressure," and that the Landau Commission's recommendations had been accepted by the Israeli Government.[187] The interrogation methods considered by the Israeli Supreme Court in the *GSS Interrogation Methods Decision* were:

- Shaking: Forcefully shaking a detainee's upper torso back and forth, repeatedly, and in a manner which causes the neck and head to dangle and vacillate rapidly.

- The "shabach" position: Forcing a detainee who has his hands tied behind his back to sit on a small and low chair whose seat is tilted forward and towards the ground, where one hand is placed inside the gap between the chair's seat and back support, the detainee's head is covered by an opaque sack falling down to his shoulders, and powerfully loud music is played in the room.

- The "frog crouch": Forcing a detainee to crouch on the tips of his/her toes for five minute intervals.

- Excessive tightening of handcuffs: Using particularly small cuffs, ill-fitted in relation to the suspect's arm or leg size.
- Sleep deprivation: A detainee is deprived of sleep as a result of being tied in the "shabach" position, being subjected to powerfully loud music or intense non-stop interrogations.[188]

In examining the legality of these GSS interrogation methods, the Israeli Supreme Court acknowledged that, taken individually, some of the components of the "shabach" position have "legitimate" goals: for example, hooding prevents communication between suspects, the playing of powerfully loud music prevents the passing of information between suspects, the tying of the suspect's hands to a chair protects investigators, and the deprivation of sleep can be necessitated by an interrogation.[189] According to the Israeli Supreme Court, however, there is a necessary balancing process between a government's duty to ensure that human rights are protected and its duty to fight terrorism. The results of that balance, the Israeli Supreme Court stated, are the rules for a "reasonable interrogation"—defined as an interrogation which is: (1) "necessarily one free of torture, free of cruel, inhuman treatment of the subject and free of any degrading handling whatsoever"; and (2) "likely to cause discomfort."[190] "In the end result," the Court noted, "the legality of an investigation is deduced from the propriety of its purpose and from its methods."[191]

Turning to the specific interrogation methods before it, the Court concluded that shaking, the "frog crouch," the "shabach" position, cuffing causing pain, hooding, the consecutive playing of powerfully loud music and the intentional deprivation of sleep for a prolonged period of time are all prohibited interrogation methods.[192] "All these methods do not fall within the sphere of a 'fair' interrogation. They are not reasonable. They impinge upon the suspect's dignity, his bodily integrity and his basic rights in an excessive manner (or beyond what is necessary). They are not to be deemed as included within the general power to conduct interrogations."[193] The Israeli Supreme Court explained that restrictions applicable to police investigations are equally applicable to GSS investigations, and that there are no grounds to permit GSS interrogators to engage in conduct which would be prohibited in a regular police interrogation.[194]

In so ruling, the Israeli Supreme Court considered the "ticking time bomb" scenario often confronted by GSS interrogators:

A given suspect is arrested by the GSS. He holds information respecting the location of a bomb that was set and will imminently explode. There is no way to defuse the bomb without this information. If the information is obtained, however, the bomb may be defused. If the bomb is not defused, scores will be killed and maimed. Is a GSS investigator authorized to employ physical means in order to elicit information regarding the location of the bomb in such instances?[195]

The Israeli Supreme Court stated that it was prepared to presume that if a GSS investigator—who applied physical interrogation methods for the purpose of saving human life—is criminally indicted, the "necessity" defense recognized under Israeli Penal Law would be open to him in the appropriate circumstances.[196] The Israeli Supreme Court also acknowledged that the legislature could enact laws permitting the interrogation methods that its decision struck down.[197] However, the Israeli Supreme Court refused to imply from the existence of the "necessity" defense, as the State argued for it to do, "an advance legal authorization endowing the investigator with the capacity to use physical interrogation methods."[198]

B. The Legal and Moral Implications of the "Ticking Bomb" Scenario

As the *Republic of Ireland* and *GSS Interrogation Methods Decision* demonstrate, in the face of a terrorist threat there is an inherent tension between obtaining potentially life-saving intelligence information through abusive interrogation of detainees and upholding human rights:

> In crystallizing the interrogation rules, two values or interests clash. On the one hand, lies the desire to uncover the truth, thereby fulfilling the public interest in exposing crime and preventing it. On the other hand, is the wish to protect the dignity and liberty of the individual being interrogated.[199]

International and human rights law is clear: torture and cruel, inhuman or degrading treatment of detainees is prohibited. Those who would, nevertheless, support the use of moderate physical force, sensory deprivation or disorientation techniques in the interrogation of terrorist suspects argue that resort to such methods is, at times, the only way to prevent the death of innocent persons and is, therefore, justified in such cases as the "lesser of two evils." Proponents of this view would argue that the legitimacy of an act can be measured by whether its utility exceeds its harm. On this point, the Landau Commission took the following position:

> To put it bluntly, the alternative is: are we to accept the offense of assault entailed in slapping a suspect's face, or threatening him, in order to induce him to talk and reveal a cache of explosive materials meant for use in carrying out an act of mass terror against a civilian population, and thereby prevent the greater evil which is about to occur? The answer is self-evident.
> Everything depends on weighing the two evils against each other.[200]

In the case of detainees being held by the U.S. in connection with the "War on Terror," however, the "ticking bomb" scenario is further complicated. Any utilitarian justification for subjecting these detainees to interrogation practices prohibited by CAT must necessarily be premised on the certainty (or, at least, the substantiated suspicion) that these individuals do, in fact, possess vital intelligence information. But, here, there is no such certainty. Instead, hundreds of detainees at Guantánamo Bay, Bagram Air Force Base and other U.S. detention facilities have been detained for months without any type of hearing or legal challenge permitted to their detention.

Our answer to the question of whether torture of detainees should ever be permitted in a post-September 11 world is that there are no such circumstances. We condemn the use of torture in interrogation of detainees, without exception. By its terms, CAT permits no derogation of the prohibition against torture—stating that "[n]o exceptional circumstances whatsoever, whether a state of war or a threat of war, internal political stability or any other public emergency, may be invoked as a justification of torture."[201] As the Israeli Supreme Court has explained, "A democratic, freedom-loving society does not accept that investigators use any means for the purpose of uncovering the truth. 'The interrogations practices of the police in a given regime are indicative of a regime's very character.'"[202]

We recognize that some legal scholars and ethicists may well argue that circumstances exist (as in the "ticking bomb" scenario) in which torture and CID treatment in the interrogation of detainees should be permitted. However, we stress that torture of detainees—which is prohibited under international and U.S. law—is never permissible, and should be fully investigated and prosecuted in all cases.

*   *   *

In summary, the Association makes the following recommendations:

First, we urge the United States to amend 18 U.S.C. § 2340 to encompass the actions of military and intelligence personnel at U.S. facilities overseas, to fully utilize the UCMJ to protect all detainees from abuse and to independently investigate human rights compliance in countries to which we are "rendering" detainees.

Second, U.S. military and intelligence personnel involved in interrogation of terrorist suspects should be educated regarding the prohibition against torture and CID, and should receive training to comply with those rules.

Third, the U.S. should adhere to its commitments under the Geneva Conventions, extend POW treatment to regular force combatants as a matter of policy, and promptly establish proper screening procedures and hearings for all detainees.

Finally, the Association notes that particularly in these times of terrorism and violence, it is important to protect the rule of law and the standards of decency to which our nation and the community of nations are committed. As the Israeli Supreme Court has stated:

This is the destiny of democracy, as not all means are acceptable to it, and not all practices employed by its enemies are open before it. Although a democracy must often fight with one hand tied behind its back, it nonetheless has the upper hand.[203]

NOTES

* **The Committee on International Human Rights:** Martin S. Flaherty (chair; member of the subcommittee who prepared the Report), Scott Horton (immediate past chair; member of the subcommittee who prepared the Report), Jeanmarie Fenrich (secretary), Charles Adler, Patricia C. Armstrong, Hon. Deborah A. Batts, Nicole Barrett, Aarthi Belani (student member; member of the subcommittee who prepared the Report), Seymour H. Chalif, Amy Christina Cococcia, Catherine Daly, Eric O. Darko, Jane M. Desnoyers, Mark K. Dietrich, Fiona M. Doherty, Barbara Fortson (former member; member of the subcommittee who prepared the Report), Aya Fujimura-Fanselow (student member), Douglas C. Gray, William M. Heinzen, Alice H. Henkin, Sharon K. Hom, Miranda Johnson (student member), Anil Kalhan, Mamta Kaushal, Christopher Kean, Elise B. Keppler, Katharine Lauer (member of the subcommittee who prepared the Report), Sara Lesch, Yvonne C. Lodico, Marko C. Maglich, Elisabeth Adams Mason, Nina Massen, Sam Scott Miller, Elena Dana Neacsu, Dyanna C. Pepitone, Marny Requa (student member), Sidney S. Rosdeitcher (chair of the subcommittee responsible for preparing the Report), Margaret L. Satterthwaite (member of the subcommittee who prepared the Report), Joseph H. Saunders, Christopher A. Smith (student member), and Katherine B. Wilmore.

The Committee on Military Affairs and Justice: Miles P. Fischer (chair; member of the subcommittee who prepared the Report), Michael Mernin (secretary), Donna Ahlstrand (former member; member of the subcommittee who prepared the Report), Steven Barrett, Myles Bartley, Philip Blum, Kenneth Carroll, Brian Cogan, Joshua Eisenberg, Matthew Hawkins, Peter Jaensch, Peter Kornman, Peter Langrind, Gerald Lee, Patricia Murphy, Rose Murphy, Harold Nathan, Timothy Pastore, Stanley Paylago (member of the subcommittee who prepared the Report), Visuvanathan Rudrakumaran, and Lawrence Sloan.

The views expressed herein are solely those of the Association and the participating Committees.

The Committee on International Human Rights and Military Affairs and Justice would like to thank the following persons for their assistance in the preparation of the Report: John Cerone (Executive Director, War Crimes Research Office, Washington College of Law, American University); Ken Hurwitz (Human Rights First); Professor Marco Sassòli (University of Geneva, professor of international law); Brigitte Oederlin and Gabor Rona (International Committee of the Red Cross); Paul, Weiss, Rifkind, Wharton & Garrison LLP ("Paul Weiss") associates Katarina Lawergren and Marc Miller and former Paul Weiss associate Matias Milet; and New York University School of Law students Ari Bassin, Amber A. Baylor, Angelina Fisher, Tzung-lin Fu, David R. Hoffman, Jane Stratton and Stephanie S. Welch; and New York Law School student Holly Higgins. This Report could not have been completed without the indefatigable efforts of Paul Weiss associate Liza Velazquez in helping edit the many drafts of the Report and consolidating the many views and comments of the Committees and Subcommittee into a coherent whole.

1. 548 U.S. __ (2006).

2. For purposes of this Report, the term "War in Afghanistan" refers to the period of international armed conflict in Afghanistan—from October 2001 to June 2002, when the Taliban was the governing force in Afghanistan, and the phrase "ongoing conflict in Afghanistan" refers to the period after June 18,

2002 when Hamid Karzai was elected as Afghanistan's transitional head of state, and the U.S. and other international parties were operating in Afghanistan at the invitation of this new Afghanistan government. This distinction becomes important in discussing the protections afforded to detainees by the Geneva Conventions. *See* Section II of this Report.

3. An assessment of the parameters and legal implications of the "War on Terror," a term coined by the Administration, is beyond the scope of this Report.

4. Carlotta Gall, *U.S. Military Investigating Death of Afghan In Custody,* N.Y. TIMES, Mar. 4, 2003, at A14. According to the *New York Times,* another Afghan man died of a pulmonary embolism or a blood clot in the lung while in U.S. custody at Bagram on December 3, 2002. Both men died within days of arriving at Bagram. Human Rights Watch has criticized the U.S. government for failing, one year after the first two deaths at Bagram—which were classified as homicides, to release the results of its investigation. *See* Press Releases & Documents, Voice of America, Rights Group Criticizes U.S. Military for Treatment of Afghan Detainees (Dec. 1, 2003) (printed at 2003 WL 66801402).

5. *See, e.g.,* Dana Priest & Barton Gellman, *U.S. Decries Abuse but Defends Interrogations; "Stress and Duress" Tactics used on Terrorism Suspects Held in Secret Overseas Facilities,* WASH. POST, Dec. 26, 2002, at A01; Eric Lichtblau & Adam Liptak, *Questioning to Be Legal, Humane and Aggressive, The White House Says Now,* N.Y. TIMES, Mar. 4, 2003, at A13; Jess Bravin & Gary Fields, *How do U.S. Interrogators Make A Captured Terrorist Talk,* WALL ST. J., Mar 4, 2003, at B1; Tania Branigan, *Ex-Prisoners Allege Rights Abuses By U.S. Military,* WASH. POST, Aug. 19, 2003, at A02. While standards and conditions of confinement—addressed by many of the international legal instruments examined in this Report—would be included in any exhaustive inquiry into the treatment of detainees at U.S. detention centers, in this Report we are focusing more narrowly on the legality of interrogation methods.

6. Captives have reportedly been "rendered" by the U.S. to Jordan, Egypt, Morocco, Saudi Arabia and Syria, in secret and without resort to legal process. *See, e.g.,* Peter Finn, *Al Qaeda Recruiter Reportedly Tortured; Ex-Inmate in Syria Cites Others' Accounts,* WASH. POST, Jan. 31, 2003, at A14; Dana Priest and Barton Gellman, *U.S. Decries Abuse but Defends Interrogations; "Stress and Duress" Tactics used on Terrorism Suspects Held in Secret Overseas Facilities,* WASH. POST, Dec. 26, 2002, at A01; Rajiv Chandrasekaran & Peter Finn, *U.S. Behind Secret Transfer of Terror Suspects,* WASH. POST, Mar. 11, 2002, at A01.

7. *See, e.g.,* Letter from Kenneth Roth, Executive Director, Human Rights Watch to President George W. Bush (Dec. 26, 2002) (*available at* http://www.hrw.org/press/2002/12/us1227.htm); Letter from Human Rights Groups to President George W. Bush (Jan. 31, 2003); Letter from Ernest Duff, The National Consortium of Torture Treatment Programs to President George W. Bush (Feb. 5, 2003); Letter from Sen. Patrick Leahy to Condoleezza Rice (June 2, 2002); Letter from ABCNY Committees on Military Affairs and Justice and International Human Rights to Scott W. Muller, General Counsel, CIA (June 4, 2003); Letter from Sen. Patrick J. Leahy to William J. Haynes, II, General Counsel, DOD (Sept. 9, 2003).

8. *See* Letter from William J. Haynes II, General Counsel, DOD, to Kenneth Roth, Executive Director, Human Rights Watch (Apr. 2, 2003). The Administration's use of the terms "enemy combatants" and "unlawful combatants" to detain persons indefinitely without administrative or judicial proceedings is novel.

9. *See* Letter from Scott W. Muller, General Counsel, CIA to Miles P. Fischer and Scott Horton, chair of the Committee on Military Affairs and Justice and then-chair of the Committee on International Human Rights, respectively (June 23, 2003). A CIA senior official has informally indicated that the agency complies with applicable law in reliance on the advice of its legal staff. However, we have been unable to confirm what legal advice has been given by CIA counsel or what means have been used to assure compliance with that advice.

10. *See* Letter from William J. Haynes II, General Counsel, DOD, to Sen. Patrick J. Leahy (June 25, 2003). At the November 20–21, 2003, Annual Review of the Field of National Security Law conference of the American Bar Association's Standing Committee on National Security Law, Muller stated publicly in response to a question by a member of the Committee on Military Affairs and Justice that Haynes' June 25, 2003 letter to Sen. Leahy articulates the policy position of "the entire U.S. government."

11. *Id.*

12. *Id.*

13. *Id.*

14. Convention Against Torture and Other Cruel, Inhuman or Degrading Treatment or Punishment, *opened for signature* Feb. 4, 1985, G.A. Res. 46, U.N. GAOR 39th Sess., Supp. No. 51, at 197, U.N. Doc. A/RES/39/708 (1984), *reprinted in* 23 I.L.M. 1027 (1984) ("CAT").

15. 136 Cong. Rec. S17486-01, 1990 WL 168442.

16. G.A. Res. 2200A (XXI), U.N. GAOR, 21st Sess., Supp. No. 16, at 52, U.N. Doc. A/6316.

17. O.A.S. RES. XXX, OEA/Ser. L.V./II. 82 Doc. Rev. 1, at 17.

18. 213 U.N.T.S. 221.

19. *See White House Fact Sheet: Status of Detainees at Guantánamo* (Feb. 7, 2002) (*available at* http://www.whitehouse.gov/news/releases/2002/02/print/20020207-13.html).

20. Geneva Convention (III) Relative to the Treatment of Prisoners of War, 6 U.S.T. 3316, 1949 U.S.T. LEXIS 483 ("Geneva III"); Geneva Convention (IV) Relative to the Protection of Civilian Persons in Time of War, 6 U.S.T. 3516, 1949 U.S.T. LEXIS 434 ("Geneva IV").

21. Additional Protocol I, *reprinted in* 16 I.L.M. 1391. While neither the United States nor Afghanistan is a signatory to Additional Protocol I, it is generally acknowledged that certain provisions are binding as a matter of customary international law. And although the terms of Common Article 3 specifically limit its scope to internal conflicts, it is considered by customary international law to have broader scope.

22. 38 I.L.M. 1471 (Sept. 6, 1999).

23. CAT, Art. 11.

24. *Id.,* Art. 12.

25. *Id.,* Art. 4.

26. *Id.,* Art. 3.

27. For example, a lawsuit was recently filed by the Center for Constitutional Rights on behalf of Maher Arar, a Syrian-born Canadian citizen alleging that U.S. authorities deported him to Jordan in September 2002, where he was driven across the border and handed over to Syrian authorities. The Arar Complaint alleges that, although the U.S. Department of State's 2003 Country Reports designated Syria as a government that practices systemic torture, U.S. officials allegedly relied on assurances from the Syrian government that Arar would not be tortured. Arar has alleged that he was tortured repeatedly in a Syrian prison for 10 months, often with cables and electrical cords. *See* Complaint in *Maher Arar v. John Ashcroft, et al.* (*available at* http://www.ccr-ny.org/v2/legal/September_11th/docs/ArarComplaint.pdf).

28. Geneva III, Art. 5.

29. We note that the Department of Defense has recently circulated for comment administrative review procedures for enemy combatants at Guantánamo Bay Naval Base. *See* http://www.defenselink.mil/news/Mar2004/d20040303ar.pdf. While welcoming such a review process, we do not consider it to meet the requirement for status determination under the Geneva Conventions.

30. *Supra* note 13.

31. *Id.* Article 4.1 states: "Each State Party shall ensure that all acts of torture are offences under its criminal law. The same shall apply to an attempt to commit torture and to an act by any person which constitutes complicity or participation in torture."

32. *Id.* Article 3.1 states: "No State Party shall expel, return ('*refouler*') or extradite a person to another State where there are substantial grounds for believing that he would be in danger of being subjected to torture."

33. *See Murray v. The Charming Betsy,* 6 U.S. (2 Cranch) 64, 118 (1804) (a statute "ought never to be construed to violate the law of nations, if any other possible construction remains"). *See also United States v. P.L.O.,* 695 F. Supp. 1456, 1468 (S.D.N.Y. 1988) (noting "the lengths to which our courts have sometimes gone in construing domestic statutes so as to avoid conflict with international agreements...").

34. *Lawrence v. Texas,* 539 U.S. 558 (2003).

35. This list is by no means comprehensive. Practices were selected for inclusion here because of their similarity to the practices allegedly used by U.S. agents with respect to detainees held in connection with the War in Afghanistan and the ongoing conflict in Afghanistan. The findings and concluding observations of the Committee Against Torture are available at http://www.unhchr.ch/tbs/doc.nsf.

36. *Case of A. (name withheld) v. The Netherlands,* Committee Against Torture, Comm. No. 91/1997 (1998), U.N. Doc. No. CAT/C/21/D/91/1997.

37. *See* Inquiry under Article 20: Committee Against Torture, Findings concerning Peru (2001), U.N. Doc. No. A/56/44, at para. 35.

38. Concluding Observations concerning Republic of Korea (1996), U.N. Doc. No. A/52/44, at para. 56.

39. Concluding Observations concerning New Zealand (1993), U.N. Doc. No. A/48/44, at para. 148.

40. *See* Inquiry Under Article 20: Committee Against Torture, Findings concerning Turkey (1993), U.N. Doc. No. A/48/44/Add.1, at para. 48.

41. Concluding Observations concerning Azerbaijan (2003), U.N. Doc. No. CAT/C/CR/30/1, at para. 5(b).

42. Concluding Observations concerning Germany (1993), U.N. Doc. No. A/48/44, at para. 167.

43. *Id.; see also* Concluding Observations concerning New Zealand (1998), U.N. Doc. No. A/53/44, at para. 175.

44. Concluding Observations concerning the United States (2000), U.N. Doc. No. A/55/44, at para. 179(e).

45. Concluding Observations concerning Australia (2000), U.N. Doc. No. A/56/44, at para. 52(b).

46. *Supra* note 36.

47. These techniques were found by the Committee to constitute "breaches of article 16 and also constitute torture as defined in article 1 of the Convention. This conclusion is particularly evident where such methods of interrogation are used in combination, which appears to be the standard case." Concluding Observations concerning Israel (1997), U.N. Doc. No. A/52/44, at para. 257.

48. *See* 136 Cong. Rec. 36,198 (daily ed. Oct. 27, 1990). The instrument of ratification included the declaration that "the provisions of Articles 1 through 16 of [CAT] are not self-executing." *See* United Nations Treaty Collection: Declarations and Reservations, (*available at* http://www.unhchr.ch/html/menu3/b/treaty12_asp.htm).

In the case of a self-executing treaty, "no domestic legislation is required to give [it] the force of law in the United States." *Trans World Airlines, Inc. v. Franklin Mint Corp.,* 466 U.S. 243, 252 (1984). By contrast, a non-self-executing treaty is one that "must be implemented by legislation before it gives rise to a private cause of action." *Mannington Mills, Inc. v. Congoleum Corp.,* 595 F.2d 1287, 1298 (3d Cir. 1979).

49. *See* Ratification Status for CAT, United States of America (*available at* www.unhchr.ch). The U.S. has not opted out of the inquiry procedure under Article 20. It has entered a declaration accepting the interstate complaint procedure set up by Article 21. The U.S. has not, however, accepted the competence of the Committee under Article 22 to receive and consider complaints on behalf of individuals subject to its jurisdiction who claim to be victims of a violation of CAT.

50. *See* 136 Cong. Rec. S17486-01 (daily ed. Oct. 27, 1990).

51. *See* 136 Cong. Rec. 36192, 36198 (daily ed. Oct. 27, 1990).

52. Under international law, reservations are invalid if they violate the "object and purpose" of the treaty. *See* Vienna Convention on the Law of Treaties, *opened for signature* May 23, 1969, 1155 U.N.T.S. 331, at Art. 19(c). This Report assumes that the U.S. reservation with respect to Article 16 of CAT is valid.

53. Because the focus of this Report is on what laws apply to agents of the United States government in detention centers located outside of United States territory, this discussion does not examine state or federal penal or civil rights statutes that would also apply to interrogation occurring on American soil.

54. This had also been the position of the Ninth Circuit. *See Al-Saher v. INS,* 268 F.3d 1143 (9th Cir. 2001) (holding that severe beatings and cigarette burns sustained over periods of days, weeks and months constitutes torture). More recently, however, the Ninth Circuit has held that neither serious persecution (*e.g.,* threats, unjust charges, fines, illegal searches and seizures) nor verbal abuse alone amount to torture. *See Gui v. INS,* 280 F.3d 1217 (9th Cir. 2002); *Quant v. Ashcroft,* 2003 U.S. App. LEXIS 6616 (9th Cir. 2003).

55. *See, e.g., Cornejo-Barreto v. Seifert,* 218 F.3d 1004, 1016-17 (9th Cir. 2000) (individuals certified as extraditable by the Secretary of State who fear torture may petition for judicial review of the Secretary's decision using CAT standards protecting against *non-refoulement*); *Mu-Xing Wang v. Ashcroft,* 320 F.3d 130 (2d Cir. 2003) (following *Cornejo-Barreto*'s holding that habeas review is available for CAT claims, but in the context of removal); *Ogbudimkpa v. Ashcroft,* 342 F.3d 207 (3d Cir. 2003) (same).

56. The Senate Committee on the Judiciary acknowledged the relationship of 18 U.S.C. § 2340 to CAT and the Torture Victim Protection Act in a 2002 report. *See* S. Rep. No. 107-44 (2002), at 10–11.

57. A restrictive interpretation of the scope of the statute is found in the U.S. Dept. of Justice, Criminal Resource Manual 20 (Oct. 1997), which provides: "Section 2340A of Title 18, United States Code, prohibits torture committed by public officials under color of law against persons within the public official's custody or control. . . . The statute applies only to acts of torture committed outside the United States. There is Federal extraterritorial jurisdiction over such acts whenever the perpetrator is a national of the United States or the alleged offender is found within the United States, irrespective of the nationality of the victim or the alleged offender."

58. *See* S. Rep. No. 102-249 (1991) (stating that the TVPA would "carry out the intent of the Convention Against Torture and Other Cruel, Inhuman or Degrading Treatment or Punishment, which was ratified by the U.S. Senate on October 27, 1990").

59. *See* Report of the Committee on Foreign Relations, Convention Against Torture and Other Cruel, Inhuman, or Degrading Treatment or Punishment, S. Exec. Rep. No. 30, 101st Cong., 2d Sess. 25 (1990) (statement of Mr. Pell) (citing *Case of X. v. Federal Republic of Germany* (No. 6694/74)).

60. *Leon v. Wainwright,* 734 F.2d 770 n.5 (11th Cir. 1984) (kidnapping conviction confirmed based on a confession obtained following a prior coerced confession).

61. *Rochin v. California,* 342 U.S. 165, 172 (1952).

62. *County of Sacramento v. Lewis,* 523 U.S. 833, 848-49 (1998).

63. The UCMJ, discussed below, provides that no "cruel or unusual punishment" may be adjudged by any court-martial or inflicted upon any person subject to the UCMJ (10 U.S.C.S. § 855). In general, military courts have applied the Supreme Court's interpretation of the Eighth Amendment to claims raised under this provision. *See, e.g., United States v. Avila,* 53 M.J. 99, 2000 CAAF LEXIS 569 (C.A.A.F. 2000). Thus, under the UCMJ, POWs and persons who under the law of war are subject to trial for military offences by a military tribunal are not to be punished in a cruel or unusual manner, within the meaning of the Eighth Amendment.

64. *City of Revere v. Massachusetts Gen. Hosp.,* 463 U.S. 239, 244 (1983). *See also County of Sacramento v. Lewis,* 523 U.S. 833, 849–50 (1998) (citation omitted) ("We held in *City of Revere v. Massachusetts Gen. Hospital* that 'the due process rights of a [pretrial detainee] are at least as great as the Eighth Amendment protections available to a convicted prisoner'").

65. *Hudson v. McMillian,* 503 U.S. 1, 7 (1992) (quoting *Whitley v. Albers,* 475 U.S. 312, 321 (1986)).

66. *Whitley v. Albers,* 475 U.S. 312, 320-21 (1986) (quoting *Johnson v. Glick,* 481 F.2d 1028, 1033 (2d Cir. 1973)).

67. *Compare U.S. v. Gatlin,* 216 F.3d 207 (2d Cir 2000) *with U.S. v. Corey,* 232 F.3d 1166 (9th Cir 2000). However, the question was substantially mooted for most purposes by the passage of the Military Extraterritorial Jurisdiction Act of 2000, Pub. L. 106-503, 112 Stat. 2488, which subjects persons accompanying the armed forces abroad to U.S. civilian criminal jurisdiction, even if outside the "special maritime and territorial jurisdiction."

68. *See* U.S. Dept. of State, Initial Report of the United States of America to the U.N. Committee against Torture, U.N. Doc. CAT/C/28/Add.5 (1999), at para. 178.

69. *Amnesty International Report Charges U.S. is "Safe Haven" for Torturers Fleeing Justice; Eight Years On, U.S. Has Failed to Prosecute Single Individual for Torture,* Amnesty International Press Release (2002) (*available at* http://www.amnestyusa.org/news/2002/usa04102002.html). *See also* William J. Aceves United States of America: A Safe Haven For Torturers (Amnesty International USA Publications 2002), at 50.

70. The UCMJ does not define the term POW. Thus it is uncertain whether POW in the UCMJ has the same meaning as in Geneva III.

71. *United States v. Averette,* 19 U.S.C.M.A. 363, 365–66, 41 C.M.R. 363, 365–66 (1970) (the phrase "in time of war" is limited to "a war formally declared by Congress"; even though the Vietnam conflict "qualified as a war as that word is generally used and understood[,] . . . such a recognition should not serve as a shortcut for a formal declaration of war, at least in the sensitive area of subjecting civilians to military jurisdiction"). *Cf. United States v. Anderson,* 17 U.S.C.M.A. 588, 589, 38 C.M.R. 386, 387 (1968) (United States' involvement in Vietnam conflict "constitutes a 'time of war' . . . within the meaning of" Article 43

(a) of the UCMJ, which provides that there is no statute of limitations over certain offenses committed "in time of war").

72. The Court of Appeals for the Armed Forces (formerly the Court of Military Appeals) is a civilian Article I court hearing appeals from the intermediate appellate courts for each of the Army, Navy (and Marines) and Air Force, subject to possible appeal to the United States Supreme Court.

73. As previously noted, the Military Extraterritorial Jurisdiction Act of 2000, *see supra* note 67, eliminated any gap in jurisdiction resulting from *Reid v. Covert* by conferring jurisdiction on federal courts over civilians accompanying the armed forces abroad.

74. The protections of Article 55 apply to "any person subject to" the UCMJ. And as stated previously, the UCMJ would seem to apply to unlawful combatants under 10 U.S.C. § 818.

75. The Articles of War preceding the UCMJ prohibited "cruel and unusual punishment," but the phrase was changed to "cruel *or* unusual punishment" in Article 55 (emphasis added). *See* Articles of War 41, Manual for Courts-Martial, U.S. Army, 1929 at 212, and 1949 at 284. The legislative history of Article 55 provides no rationale why the word "and" was changed to "or." *United States v. White,* 54 M.J. 469, 2001 CAAF LEXIS 497 (C.A.A.F. 2001).

76. *See United States v. Kinsch,* 54 M.J. 641, 2000 CCA LEXIS 237 (A.C.C.A. 2000). *See also* Section I(C)(3)(b) of this Report for a fuller discussion of the Eighth Amendment prohibition of cruel and unusual treatment and punishment.

77. *See United States v. Wappler,* 2 C.M.A. 393, 9 C.M.R. 23, 1953 CMA LEXIS 897 (C.M.A. 1953); *White,* 54 M.J. at 473; *United States v. Avila,* 53 M.J. 99, 2000 CAAF LEXIS 569 (C.A.A.F. 2000).

78. Compare the federal criminal civil rights statutes, 18 U.S.C. §§ 241 and 242, and the civil statute 42 U.S.C. § 1983, all of which apply only where the victim is entitled to constitutional rights.

79. Manual for Courts-Martial, United States (1995 edition) (the "Manual"), Paragraph 60.b (1–2). The Manual is issued by the President as a regulation under the authority granted by Congress under Article 3 of the UCMJ.

80. Manual, Paragraph 60.c (3).

81. According to the Manual, however, the doctrine of preemption "prohibits application of Article 134 to conduct covered by Articles 80 through 132. For example, larceny is covered in Article 121, and if an element of that offense is lacking—for example, intent—there can be no larceny or larceny type offense, either under Article 121 or, because of preemption, under Article 134." Manual, Paragraph 60.c (5)(a). In effect, Article 134 may not be employed to salvage a charge where the charge could not be sustained under the substantive offense provisions of the UCMJ or Federal statute. Accordingly, conduct which violated Article 55 discussed above or any other substantive provision of the UCMJ could not be charged under Article 134. These remain alternative, not cumulative provisions.

82. For example, murder (10 U.S.C. § 918), manslaughter (10 U.S.C. § 919), dereliction of duty (10 U.S.C. § 892).

For purposes of this Report, we assume that U.S. military interrogations of detainees are conducted for intelligence gathering purposes and not with an investigatory intent to elicit incriminating responses in anticipation of criminal prosecution. However, should the focus of the interrogation shift from an intelligence to a law enforcement nature, Miranda warnings under Article 31 of the UCMJ (10 U.S.C. § 831) would be required. The failure to give such warnings is a criminal offense under Article 98 of the UCMJ (10 U.S.C. § 898).

83. *See* Article 93 of the UCMJ (10 U.S.C. § 893). Two Marines face charges for assault, cruelty and dereliction of duty involving the treatment and death of an Iraqi prisoner. *See* Associated Press Newswires, *Two Marines Face Trial After Iraqi Dies,* Apr. 14, 2004; Tony Perry, *Iraqi Prisoner Died After Marine Grabbed His Throat, Officials Say,* L.A. TIMES, Oct. 22, 2003, at B06. It is not believed that the incident involved interrogation, but it is notable that such alleged offenses involved Marine infantry reservists who had not been trained in the treatment of prisoners (apart from one with relevant peacetime background) and are reported to have been given only a brief orientation before being assigned to this duty. As advocated elsewhere in this Report, proper training of U.S. military and intelligence personnel is essential to achieve compliance with the U.S.'s obligations under CAT.

84. Article 93 prohibits a person subject to the jurisdiction of the UCMJ from committing acts of "cruelty toward, or oppression or maltreatment of, any person subject to his orders." The phrase "any person

subject to his orders" in Article 93 is defined as: "not only those persons under the direct or immediate command of the accused but extends to all persons, subject to the...[UCMJ] or not, who by reason of some duty are required to obey the lawful orders of the accused, regardless whether the accused is in the direct chain of command over the person." Manual for Courts-Martial, United States, (1995 edition), Part IV, P 17c(1).

85. An officer in Iraq was charged under Article 28 (10 U.S.C. § 928) for firing his pistol near an Iraqi detainee's head in the course of an interrogation in order to elicit details about a planned ambush or assassination. Thomas E. Ricks, *Army Accuses Officer In Iraq Of Firing Pistol Near Prisoner,* Wash. Post, Oct. 30, 2003, at A14. The officer faced a possible court-martial and up to eight years imprisonment. Following a UCMJ Article 32 hearing (which is akin to a grand jury or preliminary hearing), the division's commanding general ordered that the officer be fined and allowed to retire. *See U.S. Officer Fined for Harsh Interrogation Tactics* (Dec. 13, 2003) (*available at* http://www.cnn.com/2003/US/12/12/sprj.nirq .west.ruling).

86. *See* Section II(C) for a discussion of who qualifies as a "protected person" under Geneva IV.

87. "Common Article 3" provides that detainees "shall in all circumstances be treated humanely" and prohibits the following acts "at any time and in any place whatsoever": "violence to life and person, in particular murder of all kinds, mutilation, cruel treatment and torture;" and "outrages upon personal dignity, in particular humiliating or degrading treatment." Common Article 3 also provides that the "wounded and sick shall be collected and cared for."

Although neither the United States nor Afghanistan is a party to Additional Protocol I, it is generally acknowledged that relevant sections of Protocol I constitute either binding customary international law or good practice, in particular the minimum safeguards guaranteed by Article 75(2). *See* Michael J. Matheson, *Remarks on the United States Position on the Relation of Customary International Law to the 1977 Protocols Additional to the 1949 Geneva Conventions, reprinted in The Sixth Annual American Red Cross-Washington College of Law Conference on International Humanitarian Law: A Workshop on Customary International Law and the 1977 Protocols Additional to the 1949 Geneva Conventions,* 2 AM. U. J. INT'L L. & POL'Y 415, 425–6 (1987).

Article 75 provides that "persons who are in the power of a Party to the conflict and who do not benefit from more favourable treatment under the Conventions" "shall be treated humanely in all circumstances" and that each state Party "shall respect the person, honour, convictions and religious practices of all such persons." Paragraph 2 of Article 75 prohibits, "at any time and in any place whatsoever, whether committed by civilian or military agents": "violence to the life, health, or physical or mental well-being of persons, in particular...torture of all kinds, whether physical or mental," "corporal punishment," and "mutilation"; "outrages upon personal dignity, in particular humiliating and degrading treatment ...and any form of indecent assault"; and "threats to commit any of the foregoing acts."

The U.S. rejection of Additional Protocol I was explained in a presidential note to the Senate in the following terms: "Protocol I....would grant combatant status to irregular forces even if they do not satisfy the traditional requirements to distinguish themselves from the civilian population and otherwise comply with the laws of war. This would endanger civilians among whom terrorists and other irregulars attempt to conceal themselves. These problems are so fundamental in character that they cannot be remedied through reservations...." *See* 1977 U.S.T. LEXIS 465.

88. *See* Geneva III, Art. 5; *see also* U.S. Dept. of Army, Field Manual 27-10, "Law of Land Warfare", Art. 71 (1956); U.S. Dept. of Army, Regulation 190-8 Military Police, "Enemy Prisoners of War, Retained Personnel, Civilian Internees and Other Detainees," § 1-5 (a)(2) (1997).

89. *See, e.g.,* Dep't of Defense, Secretary Rumsfeld Media Availability en route to Camp X-Ray (Jan. 27, 2002) (*available at*http://www.defenselink.mil/news/Jan2002/t01282002_t0127sd2.html) ("Sometimes when you capture a big, large group there will be someone who just happened to be in there that didn't belong in there.") (remarks of Respondent, Secretary of Defense Donald H. Rumsfeld); Carlotta Gall, *Freed Afghan, 15, Recalls a Year at Guantánamo,* N.Y. TIMES, Feb. 11, 2004, at A03 (quoting released teenager claiming to have been captured by non-U.S. forces and handed over to the Americans while looking for a job); Jan McGirk, *Pakistani Writes of His U.S. Ordeal,* BOSTON GLOBE, Nov. 17, 2002, at A30 ("Pakistan intelligence sources said Northern Alliance commanders could receive $5000 for each Taliban

prisoner and $20,000 for a[n] [al] Qaeda fighter. As a result, bounty hunters rounded up any men who came near the battlegrounds and forced them to confess.").

90. *See, e.g.,* Sean D. Murphy, *Contemporary Practice of the United States Relating to International Law,* 96 Am. J. Int'l L. 461, 476–77 (2002).

91. Article 4-A of Geneva III provides, in part:

> Prisoners of war, in the sense of the present Convention, are persons belonging to one of the following categories, who have fallen into the power of the enemy:
>
> Members of the armed forces of a Party to the conflict as well as members of militias or volunteer corps forming part of such armed forces.
>
> Members of other militias and members of other volunteer corps, including those of organized resistance movements, belonging to a Party to the conflict and operating in or outside their own territory, even if this territory is occupied, provided that such militias or volunteer corps, including such organized resistance movements, fulfill the following conditions:
>
> (a) of being commanded by a person responsible for his subordinates;
>
> (b) that of having a fixed distinctive sign recognizable at a distance;
>
> (c) that of carrying arms openly;
>
> (d) that of conducting their operations in accordance with the laws and customs of war.
>
> Members of regular armed forces who profess allegiance to a government or an authority not recognized by the Detaining Power. . . .

92. Article 43 of Additional Protocol I provides: "The armed forces of a Party to a conflict consist of all organized armed forces, groups and units which are under a command responsible to that Party for the conduct or its subordinates, even if that Party is represented by a government or an authority not recognized by an adverse Party. Such armed forces shall be subject to an internal disciplinary system which, inter alia, shall enforce compliance with the rules of international law applicable in armed conflict."

93. *See* Geneva III, Art. 5; *see also,* U.S. Dept. of Army, Field Manual 27-10, "Law of Land Warfare", Art. 71 (1956); U.S. Dept. of Army, Regulation 190-8 Military Police, "Enemy Prisoners of War, Retained Personnel, Civilian Internees and Other Detainees," § 1-5 (a)(2) (1997). Under U.S. military regulations, a "competent tribunal" pursuant to Article 5 of Geneva III consists of three commissioned officers. The regulations also require that persons whose status is to be determined be advised of their rights; be permitted to attend all open sessions, call witnesses and question witnesses called by the tribunal; be permitted (but not compelled) to testify or otherwise address the tribunal; and be provided with an interpreter. The regulations provide for the tribunal's determination of a detainee's status in closed session by a majority vote and require a preponderance of the evidence to support the tribunal's finding. *See* Erin Chlopak, *Dealing with the Detainees at Guantánamo Bay: Humanitarian and Human Rights Obligations Under the Geneva Conventions,* Hum Rts. Br. (Spring 2002), at 6, 8.

It should be noted that the "competent tribunal" outlined in ARMY REG. 190-8, § 1-6 is a quick, administrative process that is highly dependent upon the availability of witnesses during ongoing combat and support operations. Unsworn statements may be presented as evidence, and a record of the proceedings is developed. Although the tribunal may or may not include military lawyers such as members of the Staff Judge Advocate General ("JAG"), JAG lawyers will subsequently review the record. The record may also be the basis for any further proceedings for war crimes or for any other penalty.

Fundamentally, the tribunal determines only status and does not adjudicate liability. Tribunals are required under Geneva III only when status of the detainee is in doubt. When, for example, ten thousand uniformed members of a regular enemy infantry division surrender as a body, there is no need for a tribunal. When, however, non-uniformed, but possibly military, personnel mix with refugees, that is a classic situation for such tribunals.

94. Specifically, Article 13 of Geneva III provides:

> Prisoners of war must at all times be humanely treated. Any unlawful act or omission by the Detaining Power causing death or seriously endangering the health of a prisoner of war in its custody is prohibited, and will be regarded as a serious breach of the present Convention. In particular, no prisoner of war may be subjected to physical mutilation or to medical or scientific experiments of any

kind which are not justified by the medical, dental or hospital treatment of the prisoner concerned and carried out in his interest.

Likewise, prisoners of war must at all times be protected, particularly against acts of violence or intimidation and against insults and public curiosity.

95. Manooher Mofidi and Amy E. Eckert, *"Unlawful Combatants" or "Prisoners of War": The Law and Politics of Labels,* 36 CORNELL INT'L L.J. 59, 89 (2003).

96. Murphy, *supra* note 90, at 476–77.

97. *Id.*

98. *Id.*

99. Powell asked that the Administration recognize that the Geneva Conventions apply to the conflict between the U.S. and Taliban regime and that the Administration convene a "competent tribunal" to determine the status of the prisoners pursuant to Article 5 of Geneva III. *See* Katharine Q. Seelye, *A Nation Challenged: The Prisoners; Powell Asks Bush to Review Stand on War Captives,* N.Y. TIMES, Jan. 27, 2002, at A01; William Safire, Editorial, *Colin Powell Dissents,* N.Y. TIMES, Jan. 28, 2002, at A15.

100. *See supra* note 19.

U.S. Secretary of Defense Donald Rumsfeld, responding to a request for clarification, referred to Article 4(a)(2) of Geneva III to explain why the Taliban could not qualify for POW status: "The Taliban [like Al Qaeda] also did not wear uniforms, they did not have insignia, they did not carry their weapons openly, and they were tied tightly at the waist to Al Qaeda. They behaved like them, they worked with them, they functioned with them, they cooperated with respect to communications, they cooperated with respect to supplies and ammunition." Secretary of Defense Donald H. Rumsfeld, Remarks on Ferry from Air Terminal to Main Base, Guantánamo Bay, Cuba (Jan. 27, 2002) (transcript *available at* http://www.defenselink .mil/transcripts/2002/t01282002_t0127sd2.html).

101. Applying the four-part test from Article 4(a)(2) of Geneva III to the determination, the *Lindh* court found that the Taliban had an insufficient internal system of military command or discipline, that the "Taliban typically wore no distinctive sign that could be recognized by opposing combatants," and that the "Taliban regularly targeted civilian populations in clear contravention of the laws and customs of war." *Lindh,* 212 F. Supp. 2d at 558. Implicitly the *Lindh* Court held that the four conditions listed in Geneva III, Article 4(a)(2) also apply to "regular armed forces." *Id.* at 557. In concluding that the Taliban were not regular armed forces, the *Lindh* court stated "[i]t would indeed be absurd for members of a so-called 'regular armed force' to enjoy lawful combatant immunity even though the force had no established command structure and its members wore no recognizable symbol or insignia, concealed their weapons, and did not abide by the customary laws of war. Simply put, the label 'regular armed force' cannot be used to mask unlawful combatant status." *Id.,* at n.35.

See also Int'l Comm. of the Red Cross, *Commentaries to Article 4(a)(1) Convention (III) relative to the Treatment of Prisoners of War, Geneva, 12 August 1949,* ICRC Database on Int'l Humanitarian Law (*available at* http://www.icrc.org/ihl.nsf/b466ed681ddfcfd241256739003e6368/ 3ca76fa4dae5b32ec12563ed00425040?Open Document) ("It is the duty of each State to take steps so that members of its armed forces can be immediately recognized as such and to see to it that they are easily distinguishable from members of the enemy armed forces or from civilians."). *See also, generally,* INGRID DETTER, THE LAW OF WAR (Cambridge Univ. Press, 2nd ed., 2000), at 136; Christopher Greenwood, *International Law and the War Against Terrorism,* 78 INTERNATIONAL AFFAIRS 301, 316 (2002); Ruth Wedgwood, *Al Qaeda, Terrorism, and Military Commissions,* 96 AM. J. INT'L L. 328, 335 (2002).

102. ICRC, *Geneva Convention on Prisoners of War* (Feb. 9, 2002) (*available at* http://www.icrc.org/ Web/Eng/siteeng().nsf/iwpList454/26D99836025EA80Dc1256B6600610C90) ("International Humanitarian Law foresees that the members of armed forces as well as militias associated to them which are captured by the adversary in an international armed conflict are protected by the Third Geneva Convention. There are divergent views between the United States and the ICRC on the procedures which apply on how to determine that the persons detained are not entitled to prisoner of war status.")

103. IACHR, DECISION ON REQUEST FOR PRECAUTIONARY MEASURES (DETAINEES AT GUANTÁNAMO BAY, CUBA), 41 I.L.M. 532, 533 (2002) ("It is...well-known that doubt exists as to the legal status of the detainees.")

104. Amnesty International, *Memorandum to the U.S. Government on the rights of people in U.S. custody in Afghanistan and Guantánamo Bay* (*available at* http://web.amnesty.org/aidoc/aidoc_pdf.nsf/Index/AMR510532002ENGLISH/$File/AMR510532.pdf) (The United States' "selective approach to the Geneva Conventions threatens to undermine the effectiveness of international humanitarian law protections for any U.S. or other combatants captured in the future.")

105. ICJ, *Rule of Law Must be Respected in Relation to Detainees in Guantánamo Bay* (Jan. 17, 2002) (*available at* http://www.icj.org./ews.php?id_article=2612&lang=eng) ("The United States has refused [POW] status to Taliban fighters even though, as members of the armed forces, they are entitled to it.")

106. Kofi Annan, Press Encounter outside No. 10 Downing Street, London, (Feb. 25, 2002) (unofficial transcript *available at* http://www.un.org/aps/sg/offthecuff.asp?nid=103) ("The Red Cross has indicated that anyone who was arrested in the battlefield, or picked up in the battlefield, is a prisoner of war and they do not make a difference between the Al Qaeda and the Taliban. And under the convention, where there is a disagreement, normally you have an independent tribunal to resolve this.").

107. Mary Robinson, Statement of the High Commissioner for Human Rights on Detention of Taliban and Al Qaeda Prisoners at U.S. Base in Guantánamo Bay, Cuba (Jan. 16, 2002) (*available at* http://www.unhchr.ch/hurricane/hurricane.nsf/0/C537C6D4657C7928C1256B43003E7D0B?opendocument) ("All persons detained in this context are entitled to the protection of international human rights law and humanitarian law, in particular the relevant provisions of the International Covenant on Civil and Political Rights (ICCPR) and the Geneva Conventions of 1949.")

108. *See, generally,* George H. Aldrich, *The Taliban, Al Qaeda, and the Determination of Illegal Combatants,* 96 Am. J. Int'l L. 891 (2002); Harold Hongju Koh, *Agora: Military Commissions—The Case Against Military Commissions,* 96 Am. J. Int'l L. 337 (2002); Neil McDonald & Scott Sullivan, *Rational Interpretation in Irrational Times: The Third Geneva Convention and the War on Terror,* 44 Harv. Int'l L.J. 301 (2003); Manooher Mofidi and Amy E. Eckert, *"Unlawful Combatants" or "Prisoners of War": The Law and Politics of Labels,* 36 Cornell Int'l L.J. 59 (2003); Michael Ratner, *Moving Away from the Rule of Law: Military Tribunals, Executive Detentions and Torture,* 24 Cardozo L. Rev. 1513 (2003).

109. *See* Jennifer Elsea, Treatment of "Battlefield Detainees" in the War on Terrorism, Cong. Research Serv., RL31367, at 30 (2002) (*available at* http://fpc.state.gov/documents/organization/9655.pdf) (stating that the United States "has in the past interpreted [Article 5] as requiring an individualized assessment of status before privileges can be denied"). *See also* The Judge Advocate General's School, Operational Law Handbook 22 (William O'Brien ed., 2003) (instructing judge advocates to "advise commanders that, regardless of the nature of the conflict, all enemy personnel should initially be accorded the protections of [Geneva III], at least until their status may be determined").

110. Michael J. Matheson, while serving as Deputy Legal Advisor of the U.S. State Department, stated:

> We [the United States] do support the principle that, should any doubt arise as to whether a person is entitled to combatant status, he be so treated until his status has been determined by a competent tribunal, as well as the principle that if a person who has fallen into the power of an adversary is not held as a prisoner of war and is to be tried for an offense arising out of the hostilities, he should have the right to assert his entitlement before a judicial tribunal and to have that question adjudicated.

Matheson, *supra* note 86.

111. Some have argued that the Taliban did comply with the requirements for Article 4(a)(2). *See, e.g.,* Robert Goldman and Brian Tittemore, Unprivileged Combatants and the Hostilities in Afghanistan: Their Status and Rights under International Humanitarian Rights Law (The Am. Soc. of Int'l Law Task Force on Terrorism, Task Force Paper) (*available at* http://asil.org/taskforce/goldman.pdf.)

112. Not only did the Taliban profess such an allegiance, but they were the strongest military partner in the Alliance, effectively controlling Afghanistan. *See* "Taliban Reach Zenith?," 85 National Defense 10 (Oct. 1, 2000).

113. Article 1 of Geneva III states "The High Contracting Parties undertake to respect and to ensure respect for the present Convention in all circumstances." *See also* Military and Paramilitary Activities (*Nicar. v. U.S.*), 1986 I.C.J. REP. 14, 14 (June 27) (holding that Geneva III applies in all circumstances regardless of the actions of the other party to the conflict). *See also, generally,* Theodor Meron, *The Humanization of Humanitarian Law,* 94 Am. J. Int'l L. 239, 248–249 (2000).

114. As the ICRC Commentaries on Article 1 state: "it is not merely an engagement concluded on a basis of reciprocity, binding each party to the contract only in so far as the other party observes its obligations. It is rather a series of unilateral engagements solemnly contracted before the world as represented by the other Contracting Parties. Each State contracts obligations 'vis-à-vis' itself and at the same time 'vis-à-vis' the others. The motive of the Convention is so essential for the maintenance of civilization that the need is felt for its assertion, as much out of respect for it on the part of the signatory State itself as in the expectation of such respect from all parties." ICRC *Commentaries to Article 1, Convention (III) relative to the Treatment of Prisoners of War, Geneva, 12 August 1949,* ICRC Database on Int'l Humanitarian Law (*available at* http://www.icrc.org./ihl.nsf/b466ed681ddfcfd241256739003e6368/ 49cfe5505d5912dlc12563ed00424cdd?Open Document). *See also* Geneva III, Art. 13.

115. George H. Aldrich, *The Taliban, Al Qaeda, and the Determination of Illegal Combatants,* 96 AM. J. INT'L L. 891, 895–96 (2002) (noting that North Korea and North Vietnam denied POW status to all American prisoners on the basis of the allegation that they were all war criminals).

116. Colin Powell apparently made remarks to this effect in a memo leaked to the press on January 27, 2002. *See* Editorial, *Bush's Call on Captives,* THE BOSTON GLOBE, Jan. 29, 2002, at A10.

117. Legal commentators have argued that persons who have directly participated in the War in Afghanistan and who do not qualify as POWs under Geneva III (*i.e.,* detainees considered to be "unlawful combatants" by the U.S.) should automatically be considered "protected persons" under Geneva IV, unless other exceptions apply. *See, e.g.,* Michael Ratner, *Moving Away from the Rule of Law: Military Tribunals, Executive Detentions and Torture,* 24 CARDOZO L. REV. 1513, 1518–19 (2003) ("There is no gap between the two conventions"). Recent decisions of the International Criminal Tribunal for the Former Yugoslavia (ICTFY) have held that, "if an individual is not entitled to the protections of the Third Convention as a prisoner of war (or of the First or Second Conventions) he or she necessarily falls within the ambit of [Geneva IV]." *See The Prosecutor v. Delalic,* IT-96-21-T, at para. 271 (1998); *see also Prosecutor v. Tadic,* IT-94-I-A, 38 I.L.M. 158 (1999).

118. Such determination does not negate application of Common Article 3 to an "armed conflict not of an international character" or certain other provisions of international humanitarian law and the law of armed conflict.

119. The ICCPR, G.A. Res. 2200A (XXI), U.N. GAOR, 21st Sess., Supp. No. 16, at 52, U.N. Doc. A/ 6316, 999 U.N.T.S. 171 was adopted in 1966 and came into force in 1976. It was ratified by the United States in 1992, subject to a number of reservations, understandings and declarations. *See* 138 CONG. REC. S4781-01 (1992).

120. Congressional ratification of the ICCPR with respect to the prohibition against cruel, inhuman or degrading treatment is subject to a reservation mirroring that taken by the U.S. under CAT: "The United States considers itself bound by Article 7 to the extent that 'cruel, inhuman, or degrading treatment or punishment' means the cruel and unusual treatment or punishment prohibited by the Fifth, Eighth and/or Fourteenth Amendments...." *Id.*

121. *See Floyd Howell v. Jamaica,* Communication No. 798/1998 (20 January 1998), CCPR/C/79/D/ 798/1998; *Victor Alfredo Polay Campos,* Communication No. 577/1994 (6 November 1997), CCPR/C/ 61/D/577/1994; *Dave Marais, Jr. v. Madagascar,* Communication No. 49/1979 (19 April 1979), U.N. Doc. Supp. No. 40 (A/38/40) at 141 (1983); *Raul Sendic Antonaccio v. Uruguay,* Communication No. R.14/63 (28 November 1979), U.N. Doc. Supp. No. 40 (A/37/40) at 114 (1982).

122. *See* Concluding Observations of the Human Rights Committee (Israel), CCPR/C/79/Add.93 (1998).

123. *See* General Comment 20, U.N. GAOR Hum. Rts. Comm., 47th Sess., Supp. No. 40, para. 9, U.N. Doc. A/47/40 (1992).

124. *Kindler v. Canada,* Communication No. 470/1991, Human Rights Committee, U.N. Doc. CCPR/ C/48/D/470/1990 (1993).

125. *See, e.g., Poindexter v. Nash,* 333 F.3d 372, 379 (2d Cir. 2003); *Bannerman v. Snyder,* 325 F.3d 722, 724 (6th Cir. 2003); *Wesson v. U.S. Penitentiary Beaumont, TX,* 305 F.3d 343, 348 (5th Cir. 2002); *United States v. Duarte-Acero,* 296 F.3d 1277, 1283 (11th Cir. 2002); *Hain v. Gibson,* 287 F.3d 1224, 1243 (10th Cir. 2002); *United States v. Warden, FMC Rochester,* 286 F.3d 1059, 1063 (8th Cir. 2002);

Dutton v. Warden, FCI Estill, 2002 WL 255520, at *1 (4th Cir. 2002); *Lal v. Roe,* 2002 WL 31356505, at *1 (9th Cir. 2002); *Beazley v. Johnson,* 242 F.3d 248, 267 (5th Cir. 2001); *Kenan v. U.S.P. Lompac,* 2001 WL 1003213, at *1 n.1 (9th Cir. 2001); *Igartua De La Rosa v. United States,* 32 F.3d 8, 10 n.1 (1st Cir. 1994); *see also Beshli v. Dept. of Homeland Security,* 2003 WL 21693668, at *10 (E.D. Pa. July 22, 2003); *Macharia v. United States,* 238 F. Supp. 2d 13, 29-30 (D.D.C. July 30, 2002); *Reaves v. Warden, U.S.P.,* 2002 WL 535398, at *9 (M.D. Pa. Mar. 22, 2002); *Jama v. United States Immigration and Naturalization Service,* 22 F. Supp. 2d 353, 364–65 (D.N.J. 1998).

126. *See Kim Ho Ma v. Ashcroft,* 257 F.3d 1095, 1114 (9th Cir. 2001) (recognizing that an international prohibition exists against "prolonged and arbitrary detention" and citing, among other sources to ICCPR, Art. 9); *Martinez v. City of Los Angeles,* 141 F.3d 1373, 1383–84 (9th Cir. 1998) (same); *United States v. Romano,* 706 F.2d 370, 375 n.1 (2d Cir. 1983) (citing to ICCPR for articulation of rights of a person charged with a criminal offense); *Filartiga v. Peña-Irala,* 630 F.2d 876, 883–84 (2d Cir. 1980) (citing ICCPR as one example that international law universally rejects torture).

127. In ratifying the ICCPR, the U.S. Senate declared that "The United States…accepts the competence of the Human Rights Committee to receive and consider communications under Article 41 in which a State Party claims that another State Party is not fulfilling its obligations under the Covenant." *See supra* note 119.

128. *See* Optional Protocol to the International Covenant on Civil and Political Rights, 21 U.N. GAOR Supp. (No. 16) at 59, U.N. Doc. A/6316 (1966), 999 U.N.T.S. 302.

129. 1144 U.N.T.S. 123, *reprinted in* 9 I.L.M. 101 (1969).

130. *See Manrique v. Peru,* Report No. 56/98, Inter-Am. C.H.R., OEA/Ser.L/V/II.95 Doc. 7 rev. at 983 (1998).

131. *See, e.g., Request for Advisory Opinion OC-16, by the State of Mexico, of December 10, 1997,* OEA/Ser.L/V/III.39, Doc. 5, at para. 23(d) (1998); *Manrique v. Peru,* Report No. 56/98, Inter-Am. C.H.R., OEA/Ser.L/V/II.95 Doc. 7 rev. at 983, at paras. 87–88 (1998); *Congo v. Ecuador,* Report No. 63/99, Inter-Am. C.H.R., OEQ/Ser.L/V/II.95 Doc. 7 rev. at 475, at paras. 55–59 (1998); *Lucio Parada Cea, et al. v. El Salvador,* Report No. 1/99, Inter-Am. C.H.R., OEA/Ser.L/V/II.95 Doc. 7 rev. at 531, at para. 70 (1998).

132. *Villagran Morales et al. Case (the "Street Children" Case), Judgment of November 19, 1999,* Inter-Am. Ct. H.R. (Ser. C) No. 63, at para. 74 (1999).

133. *Loayza-Tamayo Case, Judgment of September 17, 1997,* Inter-Am. Ct. H.R. (Ser. C) No. 33, at para. 57 (1997).

134. The U.S. is not a signatory to the Inter-American Convention To Prevent and Punish Torture, O.A.S. Treaty Series No. 67. Article 2 of this Convention defines torture as "any act intentionally performed whereby physical or mental pain or suffering is inflicted on a person for purposes of criminal investigation, as a means of intimidation, as personal punishment, as a preventive measure, as a penalty, or for any other purpose. Torture shall also be understood to be the use of methods upon a person intended to obliterate the personality of the victim or to diminish his physical or mental capacities, even if they do not cause physical pain or mental anguish."

135. *See, e.g., Cantoral Benavides Case, Judgment of August 18, 2000,* Inter-Am. Ct. H.R. (Ser. C) No. 69, at paras. 43(a), 63(e)–(k), 104, 106 (2000); *Loayza-Tamayo Case, Judgment of September 17, 1997,* Inter-Am. Ct. H.R. (Ser. C) No. 33, at para. 58 (1997); *Castillo-Paez Case, Judgment of November 3, 1997,* Inter-Am. Ct. H.R. (Ser. C) No. 34, at para. 66 (1997); *Suarez-Rosero Case, Judgment of November 12, 1997,* Inter-Am. Ct. H.R. (Ser. C) No. 35, at para. 91 (1997).

136. *Cantoral Benavides Case, Judgment of August 18, 2000,* Inter-Am. Ct. H.R. (Ser. C) No. 69, at para. 100.

137. *See Fairen-Garbi and Solis Corrales Case, Judgment of March 15, 1989,* Inter-Am. Ct. H.R. (Ser. C) No. 6, at para 149 (1989); *Godinez-Cruz Case, Judgment of January 20, 1989,* Inter-Am. Ct. H.R. (Ser. C) No. 5, at para. 164 (1989); *Velazquez-Rodriguez Case, Judgment of July 29, 1988,* Inter-Am. Ct. H.R. (Ser. C) No. 4, at para. 156 (1988). In the *Suarez-Rosero* case, the Inter-American Court explained that incommunicado detention is "an exceptional measure" which can cause the detainee to suffer extreme psychological and moral injury. "[I]solation from the outside world produces moral and

psychological suffering in any person, places him in a particularly vulnerable position, and increases the risk of aggression and arbitrary acts in prisons." *Suarez-Rosero Case, Judgment of November 12, 1997,* Inter-Am. Ct. H.R. (Ser. C) No. 35, at para. 90 (1997).

138. *See Castillo-Petruzzi Case, Judgment of May 30, 1999,* Inter-Am. Ct. H.R. (Ser. C) No. 52, at para. 197 (1999).

139. *Coard, et al. v. United States,* Inter-Am. C.H.R. Report No. 109/99 (Sept. 29, 1999) ("*Coard*"). The *Coard* petitioners alleged that U.S. forces arrested them during the period in which it consolidated control over Grenada; that they were held incommunicado for many days; and that months passed before they were taken to a magistrate, or allowed to consult with counsel. "During this period petitioners were threatened, interrogated, beaten, deprived of sleep and food and constantly harassed." *Coard,* at para. 17. The petitioners alleged that their whereabouts were kept secret, and that requests by lawyers and others to meet with them were rejected. They also alleged that U.S. forces subjected them to threats and physical abuse—including threatening to hand the detainees over to Caribbean authorities and allowing Caribbean authorities to "soften" the detainees. *Coard,* at paras. 18–19.

140. *See supra* note 129, Art. 33.

141. *Id.,* Art. 41. The Commission has also been willing to apply other relevant legal standards, including the Geneva Conventions.

142. *Id.,* Arts. 44 and 46. The Inter-American Court also has competence with respect to matters relating to the fulfillment of the commitments made by the States Parties to the American Convention. *Id.,* Art. 33. Only States Parties and the Commission have the right to submit a case to the Inter-American Court, however, and only after the case has been considered by the Inter-American Commission. *Id.,* Art. 61.

143. A federal habeas corpus petition on behalf of named detainees at Guantánamo which was filed in parallel was dismissed for lack of jurisdiction because "the military base at Guantánamo Bay, Cuba is outside the sovereign territory of the United States." *Rasul v. Bush,* 215 F. Supp. 2d 55, 72 (D.D.C. 2002), *cert. granted,* 2003 WL 22070599 (U.S. Nov. 10, 2003).

144. *See* Rules of Procedure of the Inter-American Commission on Human Rights, Art. 25(1): "In serious and urgent cases, and whenever necessary according to the information available, the Commission may, on its own initiative or at the request of a party, request that the State concerned adopt precautionary measures to prevent irreparable harm to persons.").

145. *Ref. Detainees in Guantánamo Bay, Cuba Request for Precautionary Measures,* Inter-Am. C.H. R., Mar. 13, 2002, *reprinted in* 41 I.L.M. 532, 532. The Commission has ruled that OAS member states are subject to an international legal obligation to comply with a request for precautionary measures. *See Fifth Report on the Situation of Human Rights in Guatemala,* Inter-Am. C.H.R. OEA/Ser.L/V/II.111, Doc. 21 rev. (2001), at paras. 71–72 (2001); *Case 12.243,* Inter-Am. C.H.R. OEA/Ser.L/V/II.111, Doc. 21 rev. 1255 (2000), at para.–117.

146. 41 I.L.M. at 533.

147. *Id.*

148. *Id.,* at 534. The Inter-American Commission invited the U.S. to provide information concerning compliance with these precautionary measures. In response, the United States argued that: (i) the Commission did not have jurisdiction to apply international humanitarian law, particularly the Geneva Conventions, as well as customary international humanitarian law; (ii) the Commission lacks authority to request precautionary measures with respect to States which are not party to the American Convention; and (iii) in any event, precautionary measures are neither necessary nor appropriate because the detainees are not entitled to prisoner of war status, do not meet Geneva Convention criteria for lawful combatants and are, instead, enemy combatants. *See Response of the United States To Request For Precautionary Measures—Detainees in Guantánamo Bay, Cuba, reprinted in* 41 I.L.M. 1015, 1028–1030 (2002). The U.S. stated, however, that it "is providing the detainees with protections consistent with international humanitarian law." *Id.* at 1031. The U.S. also asserted that it had no obligation to convene a tribunal to determine the detainees' status, and that the detainees had no right to counsel or to have access to courts. *Id.* at 1034. The U.S. Response did not address interrogation techniques. However, on December 2, 2003, the Pentagon announced that U.S. citizen and Taliban soldier Yaser Esam Hamdi would be given access to a lawyer, "as a matter of discretion and military policy," but that the decision "should not be

treated as a precedent" and was "subject to appropriate security restrictions." *See* Associated Press News-wires, *Pentagon OKs Lawyer For Terror Suspect,* Dec. 3, 2003; Jerry Markon and Dan Eggen, *U.S. Allows Lawyer For Citizen Held as "Enemy Combatant",* WASH. POST, Dec. 3, 2003, at A01.

149. *Ref. Detainees in Guantánamo Bay, Cuba Request for Precautionary Measures,* Inter-Am C.H.R., July 23, 2003, at 5.

150. In order for a state's practice to be recognized as customary international law, it must fulfill two conditions:

> Not only must the acts concerned amount to a settled practice, but they must also be such, or be car-ried out in such a way, as to be evidence of a belief that this practice is rendered obligatory by the existence of a rule of law requiring it. The need for such a belief, *i.e.,* the existence of a subjective element, is implicit in the very notion of the *opinion juris sive necessitas.* The States concerned must therefore feel that they are conforming to what amounts to a legal obligation.

North Sea Continental Shelf (*F.R.G. v. Den.*), 1969 I.C.J. 3, 44. *See also* Military and Paramilitary Activities (*Nicar v. U.S.*), 1986 I.C.J. 14, 14; R. JENNINGS & A. WATTS, OPPENHEIM'S INTERNATIONAL LAW, (9th ed. 1996); The Paquete Habana, 175 U.S. 677, 700 (1900) (cited with approval in *First Nat'l City Bank v. Banco Para El Comercio Exterior de Cuba,* 462 U.S. 611, 623 (1983)); *U.S. v. Yousef,* 327 F.3d 56, 92 (2d Cir. 2002).

151. GA Res. 3452 (XXX), U.N. GAOR, Supp. No. 34 at 91 (hereinafter the "Torture Resolution").

152. *See Report by the Special Rapporteur,* U.N. Economic and Social Council, E/CN.4/1986/15, at para. 3. The report details state practice and *opinio juris* with respect to national legislation prohibiting tor-ture. *See also* HERMAN J. BURGERS & HANS SANELIUS, THE UNITED NATIONS CONVENTION AGAINST TORTURE AND OTHER CRUEL, INHUMAN or DEGRADING TREATMENT OR PUNISHMENT (Martinus Nijhoff Publishers/Kluwer Aca-demic Publishers 1988), at 1–12. The widespread ratification of regional human rights instruments such as the European Convention for the Protection of Human Rights and Fundamental Freedoms, the American Convention on Human Rights and the African Charter on Human and Peoples' Rights further reinforce the argument that torture is prohibited by customary international law.

153. *Report by the Special Rapporteur, id.,* at paras. 72, 82.

154. *See* RESTATEMENT (THIRD) OF FOREIGN RELATIONS LAW § 702 (1986). *See also Abebe-Jira v. Negewo,* 72 F.3d 844, 847 (11th Cir. 1996); *In re Estate of Ferdinand Marcos, Human Rights Litigation,* 25 F.3d 1467, 1475 (9th Cir. 1994); *Siderman de Blake v. Republic of Argentina,* 965 F.2d 699, 716 (9th Cir. 1992); *Cornejo-Barreto v. Seifert,* 218 F.3d 1004, 1006 (9th Cir. 2000); *Presbyterian Church of Sudan v. Talisman Energy, Inc.,* 244 F. Supp. 2d 289 (S.D.N.Y. 2003); *Mehinovic v. Vuckovic,* 198 Supp. 2d 1322 (N.D. Ga. 2002); *Doe v. Islamic Salvation Front,* 993 F. Supp. 3, 7 (D.D.C. 1998); *Doe v. Unocal,* 963 F. Supp. 880, 890 (C.D. Cal. 1997).

155. Vienna Convention on the Law of Treaties, 1969, Art. 53, 1155 U.N.T.S. 331.

156. *See, e.g.,* Universal Declaration of Human Rights, G.A. Res. 217, U.N. GAOR, 3d Sess., Art. 5, U.N. Doc. A/810 (1948) ("no one shall be subjected to torture or to cruel, inhuman or degrading treatment or punishment"); Declaration on the Protection of All Persons from Being Subjected to Torture and Other Cruel, Inhuman or Degrading Treatment or Punishment, G.A. Res. 3452, 30 U.N. GAOR, Supp. No. 34, U.N. Doc. A/10034 (1976), at Art. 3 ("Exceptional circumstances such as a state of war or a threat of war, internal political stability or any other public emergency may not be invoked as a justification of tor-ture or other cruel, inhuman or degrading treatment or punishment."); ICCPR, *supra* note 119, at Art. 7 ("no one shall be subjected to torture or to cruel, inhuman or degrading treatment or punishment"); Addi-tional Protocol I, *supra* note 21, at Art. 75; Protocol Additional to the Geneva Conventions of 12 August 1949, and Relating to the Protection of Victims of Non-International Armed Conflicts ("Additional Protocol II"), *reprinted in* 16 I.L.M. 1442 (1977), at Art. 4; European Convention for the Protection of Human Rights and Fundamental Freedoms, 213 U.N.T.S. 221 (1950), at Art. 3 (declaring that torture and inhuman or degrading treatment or punishment is prohibited); American Convention, *supra* note 129, at Art. 5 (providing that every person retain the right to be free from torture and ill-treatment); African Charter on Human and Peoples' Rights, *reprinted in* 21 I.L.M. 58 (1981), at Art. 5 (prohibiting torture and ill-treatment).

157. Committee Against Torture, *Consideration of Reports Submitted by States Parties Under Article 19 of the Convention,* United States of America, U.N. Doc. CAT/C/28/Add.5 (2000) ("U.S. Report Under CAT"), at para. 6.

158. 28 U.S.C. § 1350.

159. *Id.*

160. 22 U.S.C. § 2152.

161. *See* Part I of this Report; U.S. Report Under CAT, at paras. 50, 301–348.

162. *See Abebe-Jira v. Negero,* 72 F.3d 844 (11th Cir. 1996), *cert. denied,* 519 U.S. 830 (1996); *Najarro de Sanchez v. Banco Central de Nicaragua,* 770 F.2d 1385 (5th Cir. 1985); *Xuncax v. Gramajo,* 886 F. Supp. 162 (D. Mass. 1995); *Paul v. Avril,* 901 F. Supp. 330 (S.D. Fla 1994).

163. *See* U.S. Dept. of State, Bureau of Democracy, Human Rights and Labor, *Country Reports on Human Rights Practices—2002* (for Brazil, Burma, China, Egypt, Israel and the occupied territories, Jordan, Kenya, Democratic People's Republic of Korea, Laos, Pakistan, Saudi Arabia, Togo, Turkey and Zimbabwe) (Mar. 31, 2003).

164. *Id.* (for Cameroon, Mongolia, Nigeria and Rwanda).

165. *See, e.g., Filartiga v. Peña-Irala,* 639 F.2d 876 (2d Cir. 1980) (allowing a torture claim to be prosecuted under the Alien Tort Claims Act, 28 U.S.C. § 1350); *see also Forti v. Suarez-Mason,* 672 F. Supp. 1531, 1541-43 (N.D. Cal. 1987) (recognizing torture and arbitrary detention as violations of customary international law, but finding that universal consensus regarding right to be free from cruel, inhuman and degrading treatment had not yet been established).

166. 213 U.N.T.S. 221.

167. *The Republic of Ireland v. The United Kingdom,* (1979–80) 2 E.H.R.R. 25.

168. *Id.,* at 30–31.

169. *Id.,* at 36.

170. *Id.,* at 25.

171. *Id.,* at 59.

172. *Id.,* at 25.

173. *Id.,* at 25.

174. *Id.,* at 75–76.

175. *Id.,* at 26.

176. *Id.,* at 26.

177. *Id.,* at 26.

178. *Id.*

179. *Id.,,* at 79–80. In separate annexed opinions, Judges Zekia, O'Donoghue and Evrigenis disagreed with the majority's ruling that the five practices did not amount to torture.

In the years since the *Republic of Ireland* decision, neither time nor the ever-expanding threat of terrorism has diminished the ECHR's commitment to maintaining an absolute prohibition against torture and inhuman or degrading treatment. In *Chahal v. United Kingdom,* Case No. 70/1995/576/662 (Nov. 15, 1996), for example, the ECHR rejected Great Britain's argument that national security considerations justified the deportation of an Indian citizen to India on grounds that he was active in extremist Sikh organizations in England and was suspected of planning terrorist and other violent acts in the country. Chahal argued that, if deported, he would be tortured in India. In ruling that Chahal's deportation by the United Kingdom would constitute a violation of Article 3 of the Convention, the ECHR stated:

> Article 3 enshrines one of the most fundamental values of democratic society.... The Court is well aware of the immense difficulties faced by States in modern times in protecting their communities from terrorist violence. However, even in these circumstances, the Convention prohibits in absolute terms torture or inhuman or degrading treatment or punishment, irrespective of the victim's conduct. Unlike most of the substantive clauses of the Convention and of Protocols Nos. 1 and 4, Article 3 makes no provision for exceptions and no derogation from it is permissible under Article 15 even in the event of a public emergency threatening the life of the nation.

Id., at 79. *See also Aksoy v. Turkey,* Case No. 100/1995/606/694 (Dec. 15, 1996), para. 62 (ruling that Turkish security forces' treatment of a detainee suspected of membership and activity on behalf of the PKK, a Kurdish militant organization operating against the Turkish government, constituted torture).

180. *Judgment Concerning The Legality Of The General Security Service's Interrogation Methods,* 38 I.L.M. 1471 (Sept. 9, 1999) (the "GSS Interrogation Methods Decision").

181. *Id.,* at 1472.

182. Excerpts printed in 23 Isr. L. Rev. 146 (1989).

183. *Id.,* at 184.

184. *Id.*

185. *Id.,* at 185.

186. *Id.,* at 186.

187. *GSS Interrogation Methods Decision,* 38 I.L.M. at 1477.

188. *Id.,* at 1474–76. The Israeli Government argued that such interrogation methods did not need to be outlawed because, before resorting to physical pressure against detainees, GSS interrogators are instructed to "probe the severity of the danger that the interrogation is intending to prevent; consider the urgency of uncovering the information presumably possessed by the suspect in question; and seek an alternative means of preventing the danger." *Id.,* at 1475. The Israeli Government also argued that directives respecting interrogation provide that in cases where shaking—considered the harshest interrogation method of those examined in the *GSS Interrogation Methods Decision*—is to be used, "the investigator must first provide an evaluation of the suspect's health and ensure that no harm comes to him." *Id.,* at 1475.

189. *Id.,* at 1480–81.

190. *Id.,* at 1482.

191. *Id.*

192. *Id.,* at 1482–84.

193. *Id.,* at 1483.

194. *Id.,* at 1485.

195. *Id.*

196. *Id.,* at 1486.

197. *Id.,* at 1487.

198. *Id.,* at 1486.

199. *Id.,* at 1481.

200. *See* 23 Isr. L. Rev., at 174.

201. CAT, Art. 2.

202. *GSS Interrogation Methods Decision,* 38 I.L.M. at 1481 (internal citations omitted).

203. *Id.,* at 1488.